HOW MONEY GOT FREE

'If Brian Patrick Eha can make me, a Luddite dunce, both understand and care about the enigmatic Bitcoin, and if he can also tantalize the novelist in me with a narrative of intellectual daring and primal risk relating to Bitcoin's rise and fall and rise, then he is some kind of journalistic magician. And so he is, because he did all those things and more. Welcome to a new reality and the monetary future. You'll never find a better guide.'

Walter Kirn,
author of *Up in the Air* and *Blood Will Out*

'The nineteenth and early twentieth centuries were ordered by the twin conceptions of mass and energy, and currencies were correspondingly massive – forged from precious metals and wood pulp. The late-twentieth and twenty-first centuries have been ordered by information and computation, and money has become digital, cryptographic, and scattered across a light-speed network of circulating trust. In this fascinating book, Brian Patrick Eha describes the inventor-revolutionary-hackers who made Bitcoin a reality – how they did it, the computing challenges they overcame, the vested interests they overturned, the laws that they broke, and the socio-technological reality that they are creating. This book is like a fiber-optic cable extending into our uncertain economic future.'

David Krakauer,
president and William H. Miller Professor
of Complex Systems, Santa Fe Institute

HOW MONEY GOT FREE

Bitcoin and the Fight for the Future of Finance

BRIAN PATRICK EHA

ONEWORLD

A Oneworld Book

First published by Oneworld Publications Ltd, 2017

ISBN 978-1-78074-658-6
eISBN 978-1-78074-659-3

Typeset by Palimpsest Book Production Ltd, Falkirk, Stirlingshire
Printed and bound in Great Britain by Clays Ltd, St Ives plc

Oneworld Publications Ltd
10 Bloomsbury Street
London WC1B 3SR
England

To the crazy ones

CONTENTS

Prologue

MONEY AND LIBERTY

Anything that is in the world when you're born is normal
and ordinary and is just a natural part of the way the
world works. Anything that's invented between when
you're fifteen and thirty-five is new and exciting and
revolutionary and you can probably get a career in it.
Anything invented after you're thirty-five is against the
natural order of things.

– Douglas Adams

On the third floor of the Time Warner Center in Manhattan, a
glass-fronted mixed-use building that bifurcates as it rises into
gleaming towers of luxury apartments, sat the upscale Italian restaurant A Voce. Like the 750-foot-tall building itself, completed in
2004, the restaurant was a symptom and symbol of post-9/11 New
York City, the New York that three-term mayor Michael Bloomberg
revitalized and sanitized. From the vantage point of someone high
up in one of those extraordinary apartments, the green rectangle
of Central Park – brown now, in late fall – spreads out northward
in its manicured neatness like a welcome mat for money. It seemed
laid out most of all for the new money – real-estate money, private
equity money, technology startup money – that has poured into the
city in recent years and set it gleaming, even as its middle-class
residents have left in droves.

Like other restaurants of its kind, A Voce was routinely used as a stage for client dinners, power lunches, and other indispensable set pieces of business theater. So it has ever been in New York. But the restaurant will enter history as the place where a small group of men have gathered in private to discuss the newest money of all. More than high-frequency trading, more than the Dodd–Frank Act, more than any new regulation, the subject at hand here, on this night, stands a better chance than anything else of unsettling the familiar world of finance. Past the hostess stand and coat check girl and through a door off the main dining room, a dozen or so men are drinking wine and snacking on hors d'oeuvres. It is 10 December 2013 and they are here to discuss Bitcoin, a digital currency and payment system that has grown rapidly from being the plaything of teenage anarchists to the talk of Wall Street.

The magic of Bitcoin is that it enables you to move money almost instantaneously from one side of the planet to the other without needing any bank, corporation, or government. Some of its proponents think it will alleviate poverty in developing nations, plugging everyone into the global economy. Others think it will make banks obsolete. Still others hope it will make governments obsolete.

In March 2013, Bitcoin's market capitalization – the total value of all bitcoins in existence – surpassed $1 billion for the first time. Now, two weeks before Christmas, it is $11.4 billion; units of the digital currency are trading at $948 each. With explosive growth has come intensified media scrutiny as well as greater enthusiasm from investors, hence the need for meetings like this one, to dispel rumors, fight the war of public perception, and spread the gospel. Inevitably, a few members of the press are here, making awkward, predinner small talk over glasses of pinot noir. Most of them are new to the subject, including a *Wall Street Journal* reporter who wrote his first column on Bitcoin less than a week earlier.

Tonight's master of ceremonies is Jeremy Allaire, a big, raw-faced man in a suit and open-collared shirt. He has flown in from Boston, where his new company, Circle Internet Financial, a Bitcoin startup, recently came out of stealth mode announcing that it had raised $9 million of venture capital. Another star of the dinner is Barry Silbert, blond and boyish in his thirties, a brilliant investor and one of the youngest people ever to pass the Stockbroker's Exam. Six weeks ago, he launched a private Bitcoin fund now worth $63 million. Venture capitalist Jim Breyer, who led Facebook's first venture round, can be seen hobnobbing with reporters; so can a lawyer who represents Circle. His cuff links are coins that wink in the light.

Missing from the room, however, are any representatives of the very first wave of Bitcoin adoption, pioneers who risked their money, time, and freedom to build the early infrastructure of a new economy. The lucky ones have gotten rich. More than one, though, will soon find himself on the wrong end of a lawsuit or prison sentence. Two others live as expatriates in Panama. Yet another, a longtime resident of Japan, is preparing to renounce his American citizenship. Before spring, one chief executive will see his company – formerly the largest and most profitable Bitcoin exchange in the world – fall into ruin around him, and file for bankruptcy protection among accusations of incompetence and fraud. Others were disgraced long before.

Tonight, glass of wine in hand, looking out the window of the private dining room onto Columbus Circle where, high above the yellow taxis circling the roundabout, a thirteen-foot statue of Christopher Columbus stands on his pediment, I can't help but think of them, those absent pioneers, while talk of money, the invisible omnipresent animating force, goes on relentlessly around me.

When I first wrote about Bitcoin, in the summer of 2012, my editor at CNNMoney cautioned me not to treat it as anything more than a curiosity, at best a passing fad. By 10 December 2013, however, the computer network undergirding Bitcoin is more than 250 times faster than the combined processing power of the world's five hundred most powerful supercomputers. By the end of the year, the digital currency's value in US dollars will be fifty-six times higher than it was in January – the largest annual price growth, as far as anyone can tell, of any asset in history.

Why, then, one skeptic asks Allaire, shouldn't we dismiss it as a scam or speculative bubble, as yet another Dutch tulip mania? The dramatic rise in value seems absurd, divorced from any fundamentals. 'I have a thesis,' Allaire tells him, 'which is that essentially the rising value of Bitcoin is a large put option, or a bet, that Bitcoin gets adopted as a medium of exchange.'

At bottom, that is, some people are willing to pay an exorbitant amount to own a single bitcoin, just as they would a single bar of gold or a single share in a highly valuable company, because they believe either that its value will increase over time or that it will be a stable store of value.[1] The total supply of bitcoin is finite, so the more that merchants and consumers use the currency, and the more they come to appreciate its benefits, the more desirable – and valuable – it will tend to become. Less than a week before the dinner, Bank of America currency strategists praised Bitcoin's potential for online commerce and estimated its maximum market cap at $15 billion, or about $1,300 per bitcoin.

Some economists and commentators have been scoffing at the idea that a digital currency – a form of commodity money that exists only online, with no central bank or government backing – could ever be widely adopted as a method of payment, much less replace a national currency like the Argentine peso. Worse, to many institutions Bitcoin looks like reputational poison. It may well be the biggest development in finance since the banknote, but it has already weathered more than its fair share of scandal. In late 2013, the biggest headlines it has yet garnered connect it intimately to the online black market Silk Road.

But to others, Bitcoin looks like what money has always aspired to be: a means of exchange that is endlessly divisible and instantly transferable; a store of value that is less like gold than like the essence of gold, the value itself apart from the dead metal, stateless, rootless, weightless, capable of traversing the whole earth as easily as a mile, moving capital to where it is most needed, like a man in Nantucket flinging out a handful of seeds to make flowers bloom in the African desert. Bitcoin looks like money's dream of itself. 'We're talking about a global currency here,' Allaire says at the dinner. 'We're not talking about what's interesting as a speculative investment.'

In fact, Bitcoin is a triple threat to established markets, because it can function as a store of value, like gold; as a method of payment for online commerce, like credit cards or PayPal; and as a global transaction network, like Western Union or MoneyGram. There are about $7 trillion dollars' worth of gold in the world today. E-commerce is a $1.2 trillion industry. And remittances – the practice of workers, usually recent immigrants, sending a portion of their pay back home to their families in another country – are a big source of revenue for many countries, including India and China. According to the World Bank, a total of $542 billion in remittances flowed to nations around the world in 2013. India alone received $70 billion, more than the $65 billion earned from exporting the software services for which the country has become known.

Barry Silbert, who has a knack for spotting investment opportunities at just the right time, knows what it would mean if the digital currency were to claim even a small percentage of any of these markets, never mind all three. Earlier in December, a pair of analysts at Wedbush Securities made an even more dramatic prediction than Bank of America's strategists, estimating that a single bitcoin could one day be worth $98,500. Bitcoin's current price, they thought, reflected only 'a peak penetration of one percent of total potential demand in ten years'. Barry, meanwhile, has been meeting with Wall Street guys – hedge fund executives, forex traders at large financial institutions, portfolio managers, and others – who have already invested personally in Bitcoin, whether through Barry's own fund or by some other means. It appears to be only a matter of time before their firms follow suit. 'We're three to six months away from Wall Street dollars moving into Bitcoin in a big way,' he tells us. In fact, the move is already beginning. But few of the assembled journalists seem to pay much attention to his words. The *New York Times* reporter has already left. As for me, though, I'm hooked. There is nowhere else I would rather be.

AT THE TIME OF THAT dinner, I was a staff editor at *Entrepreneur*, and I became convinced that the remarkable Bitcoin entrepreneurs I had met were at the forefront of something revolutionary. Each of them was a fascinating character in his own right, and each had his own agenda for Bitcoin. Even in the collegial early days, when Bitcoiners gathered on online forums to share news and gossip, to philosophize, announce their startups, and encourage each other in what they often couched as a collective effort to build a new financial paradigm – even then it was obvious that there were differences of opinion, some of them markedly divergent, and it wasn't long before those differences began to express themselves in business ventures.

One leader who emerged, Roger Ver, was already a millionaire by the time he discovered Bitcoin in 2011. He soon became one of its biggest boosters, investing in more than a dozen startups and turning a huge amount of his personal wealth into digital currency. When its value soared, so did his net worth. A hardcore libertarian, he saw Bitcoin as an antidote to government coercion and taxpayer-funded wars.

Charlie Shrem, a middle-class Jewish kid from Brooklyn who dreamed of joining the tech boom, cofounded one of the most successful early Bitcoin startups – the first to receive more than $1 million in venture capital. But he couldn't handle its rapid growth, and later found himself charged with laundering drug money for users of Silk Road. His right-hand man, Erik Voorhees, made a pile of cash by selling a Bitcoin gambling website and went on to operate another digital currency startup down in Panama. But he got in trouble with the US Securities and Exchange Commission (SEC) for selling unregistered securities.

A later pioneer, Nic Cary, one of Erik Voorhees's old college fraternity brothers, was recruited by Roger Ver to be the chief executive of a tiny Bitcoin startup whose main competitor had the backing of one of Silicon Valley's most prestigious venture capital firms. He saw Bitcoin as a tool of financial inclusion – a means of plugging people in developing countries into the global economy. He fought like hell and turned his underdog company into one of the fastest-growing startups in the world, outsmarting regulators along the way.

Barry Silbert, too, had to reckon with unfriendly regulations.

A former investment banker, he could have been a billionaire if his ethics hadn't gotten in the way. For him, Bitcoin looked like a life raft in a world awash in debt. And it offered a chance to save his brokerage firm, in the process making digital currency a mainstream asset class.

The deeper I dug into the subject, the more obvious it became that, just as the digital currency revolution promised to make itself felt around the world, so the story of Bitcoin intersected with some of the largest issues and events of our time: the financial crisis and Great Recession, the reining in of Wall Street, the Silicon Valley startup culture that now informs global capitalism, and the rise of the digital economy which has occurred alongside, in the developing world, a continuing lack of financial inclusion and, in developed nations, a government criminalization of business that hobbles entrepreneurs at every turn.

If Bitcoin's early proponents were united by anything, it was a fierce vision of progress. More than most technologies, Bitcoin starkly illuminates competing ideas of money and liberty, competing visions of – as the title of a book by Ludwig von Mises, a favorite economist of early Bitcoin advocates, would have it – human action. Like the Internet, which also invited mockery in its early years, Bitcoin enlarges the scope of what is possible. With its advent, contrarian theories about privately issued currencies, cross-border trade, and economic justice – theories which were, however, politically impossible to put into practice – could finally be tested.

If Bitcoin is a financial innovation deserving serious consideration, it is also a sign of the deep weirdness of which the Web is capable. The Bitcoin software is open-source, meaning that anyone can inspect the code that makes it function, unlike the software created by most for-profit companies. Satoshi Nakamoto, Bitcoin's pseudonymous creator, designed it that way, and the practice has been continued by the developers who took over from Satoshi when he walked away for good. They are continually alert for bugs that need fixing, improvements that should be made. Consequently, Bitcoin is a living, breathing piece of technology. And it is, in some senses, a grand experiment, still in beta testing.

Consequently, at the dinner in December 2013, it dawned on me that not even the men in that room could say with certainty what Bitcoin would look like in a few years. Indeed, we have now arrived at a point where partisans on all sides are in open conflict over the future of Bitcoin, distributed networks, and money itself. The stakes are high enough that *The Economist* has taken notice, reporting that a 'civil war' has broken out between 'two competing camps of developers and Bitcoin companies . . . One side wants to keep Bitcoin smallish and pure; the other is pushing for it to grow rapidly, even if this means turning it into something more like a conventional payment system.'[2]

This conflict will likely be resolved in time. But larger differences will remain. Some Bitcoiners see digital currency as a business tool, a way to grease the wheels of globalization. Others see it as a way to ensure the financial rights of individuals, or a weapon to wield against the Federal Reserve. Still others treat it merely as electronic cash for buying all kinds of contraband – drugs, guns, and worse.

By 2016, many technologists who were uncomfortable with Bitcoin's checkered reputation were doing their best to change the conversation, speaking more generally of 'cryptocurrency' or 'blockchain', the technology underlying Bitcoin's payment system. To be clear, however, there is only one cryptocurrency that has become a household name. In the late spring of 2016, following a slow rise in value after a sustained period of lower prices, the price of Bitcoin went on a tear, hitting $720 and again boosting the currency's market cap above $11 billion. Few would be arrogant enough to claim that they know what it will do next. But to date, Bitcoin has proved its resiliency many times over.

Critics have pointed to its extreme price volatility, perceived drawbacks in its technology, and its use by criminals as reasons it will eventually fail or be regulated out of existence. Others are more optimistic. 'If Bitcoin has attributes that cause its downfall, for whatever reason, then I guarantee that the next batch of cryptocurrencies will not have that problem,' says Adam Levine, the host of a popular Bitcoin podcast, 'because the prize for creating the thing that becomes the next Bitcoin is unfathomable.' Satoshi Nakamoto, whoever he was, created billions of dollars of value out of thin air.

But how was this possible? And, for that matter, why was an apparent outsider like Satoshi able to achieve this breakthrough when it had eluded the world's biggest technology firms as well as other cryptographers and coders? How did an invention that a few years ago was taken seriously by practically nobody come to be on the lips of people as different as 50 Cent and Bill Gates, the latter of whom, in October 2014, called it 'exciting' and said it was 'better than currency' for moving money around?

For that matter, just how large an effect will Bitcoin have? Already the companies founded upon it are growing by leaps and bounds. After ignoring it for the first few years of its existence, major investors – venture capital firms, Goldman Sachs, the New York Stock Exchange, and billionaires like Richard Branson and Peter Thiel – have decided to risk more than $1 billion of investment capital on digital currency businesses. And the innovations it has inspired are proliferating. The impact of cryptocurrency, it now seems clear, will not be confined to the worlds of finance and commerce but will be felt also in the realms of digital identity, citizenship, taxation, property rights, surveillance, privacy and contract law, and corporate governance. And yet, even as its users reap the benefits, it is making them – and the global economy – vulnerable in new ways, helping cybercriminals to reap hundreds of millions of dollars a year in profits from victims all over the world.

This is the story of how a niche technology gained global attention, and what happened to the pioneers who took it up and used it to advance their own agendas, altruistic or otherwise; a story about a handful of smart people risking everything – their livelihoods, professional reputations, homes, and liberty – to gamble on something they thought would change the world.

This book is also an attempt to reckon with what the future might hold for the rest of us. After all, not only vast sums of money but our ideas about money itself may be at stake. The public Internet has been with us for barely more than one generation, and already there are people who believe that broadband access is tantamount to a human right, so necessary has the Web become as a source of information and economic opportunity. If money is a form of speech, and the US Supreme Court decision in *Citizens United v. Federal Election Commission* holds that it is, then it may be only a matter of time before access to the best form of money – the most effective means of monetary communication – is also considered a fundamental right. Then Bitcoin, or whatever takes its place, will have been fully assimilated into the social contract.

But it was a renegade ideology that got there first, long before any Wall Street banker or Washington regulator had seen the potential (or the potential danger); it was a bunch of outlaws who broke open the frontier on which so many warring parties now want to stake their claims. Bitcoin began not in the unobjectionable light of day but in the shadows, among cryptographers, hackers, Free Staters, ex-cons and drug dealers, teenage futurists and entrepreneurs – heterodox thinkers all, dissenters from consensual reality, holders of grudges against big government and big banks, people committed to stoking the fires of creative destruction. Hephaestus fires: able to melt down and forge anew. It is because of them that any of us have heard the word 'Bitcoin'. For a long time, Bitcoin was their world. We've just moved into it.

Chapter 1

MAKING MONEY

A feeble man can see the farms that are fenced and tilled, the houses that are built. The strong man sees the possible houses and farms. His eye makes estates, as fast as the sun breeds clouds.

— Ralph Waldo Emerson

Bitcoin came into the world fully formed, like Athena from the head of Zeus. It was announced on an Internet mailing list for cryptographers in the fall of 2008 by somebody calling himself Satoshi Nakamoto — an event that some day, if Bitcoin endures, may rank in the annals of invention alongside that moment on 10 March 1876 when a former teacher of deaf children, Alexander Graham Bell, who had already helped his father to disprove the commonly held belief that the deaf could not learn to speak, followed this miracle by forcing electric current to carry the sound of a human voice.

Like Bell, Bitcoin's pseudonymous creator must have spent years on his invention, working long hours against long odds to give people something they didn't even know they wanted. He did it all backwards, writing the code in order to convince himself that it was possible, that it wasn't just a pipe dream, before writing the paper that laid out the concepts realized by the code. When a famous cryptographer, Hal Finney, asked him to provide a detailed explanation of the Bitcoin protocol, complete with algorithms and details of the data structures involved, Satoshi said it would take less time simply to release the first version of the software. Like everyone else, he had seen earlier attempts to create electronic cash go nowhere, or hit a dead end. So enough with theory and spec papers, he figured. He didn't just want to tell them it *could* work. He wanted to show them it would.

'I've been working on a new electronic cash system that's fully peer-to-peer, with no trusted third party,' Satoshi's announcement began. It was 2:16 P.M. Eastern Standard Time on the first day of November and he was telling everyone on the mailing list that he had figured out how to do for money what the Internet had already done for information – set it free as bits and bytes, without gatekeepers, making financial transactions as painless as email. He wanted his peers to know before anyone else.

To explain his invention, Satoshi had prepared a white paper, in which he outlined the features of Bitcoin that were technical advancements on earlier forms of electronic money. It would be decentralized, meaning that a network of people running the Bitcoin software would assume the dual role of a mint, producing the currency, and a central clearinghouse, reconciling and recording transactions. This arrangement was revolutionary. Until the invention of Bitcoin, nobody had managed to overcome without a trusted third party the central stumbling block of electronic cash, which was known as the 'double-spending problem'. With physical cash – US dollars, say – it is easy to prevent someone from spending the same bill twice. If you hand your friend a $10 bill, everyone can plainly see that she, not you, now possesses the ten dollars. You have spent it and can't spend it again. Moreover, cash transactions are irreversible: once you have given your $10 away, you can't get it back without your friend's consent, unless you take it by force. Because cash has a socially agreed-upon value, and because cash transactions are final, it allows two parties who don't trust each other to do business – making it useful for criminals and other untrusting types.

Electronic money, on the other hand, is like any other electronic data; it can be copied and distributed ad infinitum. This is advantageous when you want to send an important file to your boss while retaining the original on your own computer, but it's absolutely ruinous when you want to establish a payment system. Imagine sending $10 of digital money to someone to settle a debt. Because you still have a perfect copy on your computer, what would prevent you from spending the same $10 again and again? It would be like counterfeiting, only worse, because each copy would be identical to the original. Like a man who, much to the chagrin of his genie, has cannily wished for infinite wishes, the bearer of electronic cash would be the richest man alive – if only his digital wealth weren't worthless, since nobody in their right mind would accept payment under these terms.

Before Bitcoin, the solution to the double-spending problem was simple, though with unfortunate side effects: employ a trusted third party. This is the role played today by PayPal, Venmo, and every other online payment processor. The company acts as an authority to verify transactions, debiting a balance from one customer's account and crediting it to another's account, and keeping track in its central ledger of where the money goes. Users trust these services to keep an accurate record of transactions, so that no double payments are possible. In so doing, users give up control over their money. The third party – PayPal, say – can choose to reverse any transaction at any time, and can even freeze customer funds if it finds cause. The final judgment call rests with PayPal, just as credit card chargebacks are at the discretion of the credit card company. Worse yet, the security and integrity of the entire payment network depends on the company operating it. Even as the once-novel idea of 'online shopping' gave way to a booming global e-commerce sector, then, there was still no way to replicate over the Internet the direct, ancient, peer-to-peer experience of money changing hands, finally and irrevocably.

Satoshi Nakamoto devised a way for people to spend digital cash permanently, and for everyone else to be able to check the validity of each transaction. Each bitcoin, as it passes from one person to another, is digitally signed by the person transmitting it. A coin therefore becomes, in Satoshi's phrase, 'a chain of digital signatures' – a record of ownership, like a logbook signed by each person who has ever held the coin. When you wish to transfer to your friend a coin you received from Satoshi, your friend can verify that you truly own the coin by checking that Satoshi's signature on the previous transaction is legitimate.

But this on its own, Satoshi knew, would not be enough to solve the double-spending problem without relying on a bank or other central authority. He went further, requiring that all transactions be publicly broadcast to the entire network running the Bitcoin software, so that anyone with an Internet connection, at any time, might check an enduring record of every transaction that had ever taken place. One could even, at least in theory, trace every single coin back through all its transactions to the moment when it was first created. (This would be difficult for a layman, and actions could be taken to obfuscate the source, but it would be possible.) It was in the rules of Bitcoin creation – a process known as mining – that Satoshi pulled off his most impressive feat, simultaneously establishing a decentralized mint for the cryptocurrency and nailing the lid shut on double payments.

When one person sends bitcoins to another, that transaction is broadcast to every node of the network, spreading worldwide from its point of origin. Each node that receives the transaction broadcasts it still further, amplifying the signal, as it were, so that in a very short time the transaction has been acknowledged by the entire network. If that person were to attempt to spend the same bitcoins twice, the second transaction would likewise be beamed out to the network, but the first would have such a huge head start on the second that it would be all but impossible for the fraudulent transaction ever to catch up, like a runner trying to win the hundred-meter dash after giving his opponent a fifty-meter lead.

But now suppose that a minority of judges are unable to see the first runner, the one who is in the lead. They might think the second-place runner deserves the gold medal. Just so, it is entirely possible that some nodes on the network will receive the second transaction first and broadcast it as being legitimate. By then, however, a majority of nodes will have already accepted the original spend and begun processing it into a batch of transactions known as a block. When that block is completed, it is added to the public ledger – the blockchain – and everyone begins processing the next block. Each block builds on all the blocks that came before. Even if some computers are processing a competing block that contains the fraudulent transaction, the blockchain containing the original spend will end up being longer, because it has a majority of the network's processing power building it. Soon, the entire network will accept the longer blockchain as the true blockchain. As long as honest miners control at least fifty-one percent of the network's processing power, Satoshi wrote, 'the honest chain will grow the fastest and outpace any competing chains.' The judges with imperfect vision can accept the majority decision of the other judges as to the winner of the race.

Processing and verifying transactions requires tremendously difficult computer calculations, analogous to factoring prime numbers. To reward those dedicating computer resources to the difficult process of verifying transactions, Satoshi decided that whoever solved the complex math problems required should be given new bitcoins. It would be a winner-takes-all race by every active node of the Bitcoin network. Every ten minutes, the race would begin anew. Like oil or gold, bitcoins have a limited rate of production and an upper limit on their supply. Every ten minutes, a new block of transactions is added to the blockchain; every ten minutes, a new batch of coins is created mathematically, like gold dug out of the ground. But where gold miners use manual labor and heavy equipment, with Bitcoin miners, wrote Satoshi, 'it is CPU time and electricity that is expended.' The ultimate limit is twenty-one million coins, though each coin is divisible to eight decimal places, or one hundred millionth of a bitcoin. Like an oil well running dry, the supply of bitcoins will one day be depleted. As with other commodities, Satoshi knew, this scarcity would tend to drive up the price over time, assuming people found it worth using. Through cryptography, he had found a way to emulate the properties of a physical commodity. In the words of *The New*

Palgrave Dictionary of Economics, Bitcoin 'allows for the first time the final transfer, not the mere copying, of digital assets in a way that can be verified by users without trusting other parties'. Those who understood it at its inception were astounded. Here at last was the solution to a problem that had bedeviled computer scientists for years.

So far, so elegant. But if all transactions are public, what then becomes of financial privacy? Here Bitcoin is counterintuitive. With a bank, privacy depends not on hiding the fact that you have an account at Wells Fargo or Chase but on keeping to yourself the amount of money stored there. Bitcoin reverses the relationship. Anyone can see how much money is being held at a given address, but nobody knows to whom the money belongs. This works because Bitcoin addresses are strings of random letters and numbers, with no identifying personal information attached. This, too, was revolutionary, allowing people who neither knew nor trusted one another to do business over the Internet without revealing their identities. Anonymous donations to nonprofits would be possible; so would hard-to-trace drug deals. Even if it were necessary to reveal some personal information in the course of a transaction, say in order to take delivery of a physical product ordered online, the customer could simply generate a new Bitcoin address for each new transaction. With no single address revealing their purchase history, and nothing to link their several addresses to each other, they could maintain their privacy.

Cryptographers spend their professional lives studying and creating techniques to keep communications private even when they are being spied on. Their field sits at the intersection of computer science, mathematics, and electrical engineering. The best of them are not easily impressed. Before introducing Bitcoin to his peers, Satoshi was surely braced for criticism. But he may not have expected the chorus of disbelieving voices that rose up to shout him down. 'I've noticed that cryptographic graybeards tend to get cynical,' one member of the mailing list would later relate. 'When Satoshi announced Bitcoin on the cryptography mailing list, he got a skeptical reception at best.'

One of the earliest respondents voiced doubts that Bitcoin could scale up to meet the needs of a large population. But the writer prefaced his critical remarks in a way that made it clear he hoped to be proven wrong. 'We very, very much need such a system,' he told Satoshi.

A resident of the San Francisco Bay Area, who uses the name Ray Dillinger in computer programming circles and has a background in software quality assurance, accused Satoshi of failing to account for the increase in mining power that improved computer hardware would bring over time. A well-known computer science principle, known as Moore's Law, says that computer processing power tends to double approximately every two years. Faster computers would mine more coins than expected, leading to a glut of new money, driving down the value of the existing supply. (It is worth noting that the same thing happens when central banks such as the Federal Reserve increase the money supply, which is why $40,000 in 1975 had the same purchasing power as $176,221 in 2015.) An annual inflation rate of thirty-five percent for Bitcoin 'is almost guaranteed by the technology', Dillinger wrote.

But Satoshi had accounted for that. He explained that his system was designed to keep coin production constant by linking people's efforts to mine new bitcoins to the difficulty of the mining function itself. The more processing power miners brought to bear – in order to crunch the numbers quickly and produce higher yields – the more difficult it would become to solve the math problems that generated the bitcoins. Moreover, the difficulty was designed to increase over time no matter what, keeping pace proportionally with improvements in computer hardware predicted by Moore's Law. That was how Satoshi could be confident not only of the total number of bitcoins that would ever be created – twenty-one million – but of the number of new coins that would be created every year in the future, with the last fraction of a coin being mined in the year 2140.

'The fact that new coins are produced means the money supply increases by a planned amount, but this does not necessarily result in inflation,' he told Dillinger. 'If the supply of money increases at the same rate that the number of people using it increases, prices remain stable. If it does not increase as fast as demand, there will be deflation and early holders of money will see its value increase.' That last statement was particularly important because, almost like a pyramid scheme, it gave people an incentive to buy into the idea as early as possible. And it would prove to be prophetic.

Another objection was more fundamental. Satoshi, whoever he was, appeared to have built a financial weapon against central banking, against the ability of governments to issue money and regulate their economies, and was explaining to his peers, in a calmly confident way, its destructive potential. Who did he think he was, to act as if a mere 31,000 lines of code could cut a Gordian knot that had persisted for decades? And even if Bitcoin *was* a game-changing invention, was it right of him to have invented it? After all, Satoshi didn't put Bitcoin to a vote. Like other creators in the Internet age, he simply wrote the code and released it into the digital scrum of the Web, where it would flourish or not to the extent that people found it worthwhile. 'You will not find a solution to political problems in cryptography,' one correspondent admonished.

It was a charge that would be echoed in various forms and in various forums over the next several years, and one that Satoshi had surely anticipated. Bitcoin, he replied, would at least allow its users to 'win a major battle in the arms race and gain a new territory of freedom for several years'. He had noticed that governments and entrenched corporate interests were quick to demolish any threat to their monopolies, just as the music industry had prosecuted Napster, the early music file-sharing service. But how do you stop a leaderless network whose members are spread across the globe? No one knew who Satoshi was. If there was no central, identifiable figure to serve with a lawsuit, or to arrest and imprison, the government would be at a loss for how to stop Bitcoin.

By the fall of 2008, the folly of launching an alternative currency seemed obvious to most people. Although developed nations were moving steadily toward a cashless future, alternative currencies, much less true digital cash, anonymous and stateless, seemed like science fiction. The field was littered with the bodies of those who had tried and been cut down.

ELECTRONIC MONEY IS ALREADY HERE; in fact, it has been around for decades. Most of the money in the world now exists in electronic form. Although digital currency as conceived by Satoshi Nakamoto and his predecessors is a radical invention, banks were not slow to adopt electronic money. By the mid-1990s, the Clearing House Interbank Payments System, or CHIPS, a clearinghouse for large transactions denominated in US dollars, was moving $1 trillion a day in electronic payments.[1] Owned and used exclusively by big banks, CHIPS makes it easy for American Express, Santander, Deutsche Bank, and other financial institutions to settle their accounts without ever touching cash.

Consumers aren't privy to CHIPS, but they have access to electronic money through debit cards, prepaid phone cards, metro passes – to say nothing of mobile payment options offered by Apple and Samsung. By 1994, the Japanese phone company NTT had already sold 330 million prepaid phone cards.[2] While useful, not to say increasingly ubiquitous, however, these forms of payment have what some consider serious downsides. Electronic money is linked, by law, to a huge amount of identifying information – typically in the United States a person's name, date of birth, Social Security number, geographic location, and transaction history. The government can access this information, and banks sell it to advertisers. Card companies also hold this information on their customers. That means the familiar oligopoly of Visa, MasterCard and, in the US, American Express, present huge targets for cyber theft; hackers stalk them like big-game hunters hoping to bag a lion.

Having millions of people's financial information held by a handful of corporations would be worrying enough. But in fact every retailer that processes card transactions is a possible site of identity theft. The system requires consumers to trust retailers and websites of all kinds, some of which have minimal security, to safeguard their information. Add to that many consumers' habit of using weak, easy-to-remember passwords for their personal accounts, and of repeating these passwords on multiple websites, and you have a disaster waiting to happen.

During the Christmas season in 2013, news of a massive theft of Target customer information sent shockwaves throughout the United States. From 27 November to 15 December, hackers used malware with which they had infected Target's point-of-sale system to steal the credit and debit card data of forty million customers and the personal information of tens of millions more. Despite early warnings that a breach had occurred, Target failed to react in time. As a result, millions of accounts and card numbers were compromised and dozens of lawsuits were filed against the retailer, whose holiday season profit was cut almost in half from the year before.[3]

While unusually massive, the Target hack was not an isolated event. According to the nonprofit Identity Theft Resource Center, US data breaches increased by thirty percent between 2012 and 2013, with more than six hundred major breaches exposing a total of more than ninety-one million customer records. Continuing the trend, the number of data breaches in 2014 surpassed even that figure, hitting a new record high of 783, a 27.5 percent increase in a single year.

And the problem is global. In April 2011, a hacker broke into Sony's PlayStation Network – the online network used to download and play games over the Internet, a $500 million cash cow for the Japanese electronics maker – and stole the personal information of seventy-seven million users, including people's real names, physical and email addresses, passwords, birth dates, and possibly credit card data. The attack prompted Sony to shut down the network for days. In January 2014, it came to light that an employee of a credit rating agency in South Korea had stolen the personal data of at least twenty million customers from three credit card companies while working for them as a consultant. He sold the data to phone marketing companies.[4] Hackers are getting smarter and more numerous, and there are more targets than ever. All of which means consumers in the current system are far more vulnerable than they know.

Merchants, too, have reason to want change. They are required to pay a fee to banks and credit card companies for every card transaction, often approaching three percent of the total purchase amount, hence the surliness of some cab drivers when you pay with a card instead of cash. While the card companies earn billions from these interchange fees, small business owners are squeezed. Incidentally, that is why most small convenience stores require you to meet a minimum purchase amount before you can pay with a card. (Large corporations and chain stores – think Walmart or Pret a Manger – benefit from this system, because they can afford to eat the cost of the transaction fees much more easily than a small business can. Hence they will let you pay even for a single candy bar, if you like, with your debit card.)

These drawbacks to electronic money are among the reasons why, when a team at the US Mint set about studying the payments landscape in 2008, it found that although credit and debit cards had made significant inroads, one-third of all transactions in the US were still conducted in cold hard cash. But cash is hardly ideal money for the Internet age: you can't spend it online or easily send it to someone far away, and in large quantities it's challenging and even dangerous to transport.

That leaves digital currency. Unlike ordinary electronic payments, it was theorized, digital currency would make it possible to spend money online, or even person-to-person, with the speed of the Internet and the privacy of cash. By cutting out the middlemen – banks and credit card companies – it would save business owners money. And with anonymous or pseudonymous accounts – that is, accounts which don't link to any personal identifying information – digital currency wouldn't be subject to the same identity theft concerns as old-style electronic money. It might even prevent the Internal Revenue Service from being able to see your true earnings and assets. On the other hand, because digital currencies act like cash, loss or theft would be final. No chargebacks allowed. Once it was gone, it would generally be gone for good.

Some of the first people to think seriously about digital cash were the Cypherpunks. A group of long-haired computer geeks, math whizzes, and free-market anarchists, they were organized around an electronic mailing list not unlike the one on which Satoshi would later announce his invention of Bitcoin. They were interested in the ways in which encryption technology and peer-to-peer network culture could increase personal liberty and undermine the surveillance state. Not content merely to dream of a better world, they were determined to build it – one piece of software at a time. Their motto: *Cypherpunks write code*. In the fall of 1992, a core group began holding monthly meetings near Palo Alto. At the first meeting, on a Saturday in September, in an office complex housing early stage tech startups, a former Intel employee named Timothy May got up in front of his fellow alpha geeks to read a manifesto introducing the concept of crypto-anarchy. Modeled on the *Communist Manifesto* of 1848, May's brief essay called for a revolution that would 'fundamentally alter the nature of corporations and of government interference in economic transactions'. Crypto-anarchy, he went on, would replace central bureaucracy with decentralized cryptography, government control with individual liberty, the nation-state with the network.

What May wanted was freedom from government coercion of all kinds, the freedom to choose what to think, how to spend his money, and who to associate with. The right to anonymity – including absolute financial privacy – was a starting point. Many of the Cypherpunks shared his goals, which put private e-money high on their wish list. But it would be another six years before two Cypherpunks, Wei Dai and Nick Szabo, published their own ideas about how a digital currency system might work – and even then, their publications were limited to a private mailing list, with no chance of catching on in the wider world.

In the meantime, others were pursuing a similar dream. In 1996, two men in Melbourne, Florida – Douglas Jackson, an oncologist, and his attorney, Barry Downey – began issuing electronic money that could be used anonymously to pay for things online, without the need to exchange one national currency for another. They called it E-gold. Their company, Gold & Silver Reserve, held a store of precious metal to provide an underlying value for the digital currency, allowing people to spend it with confidence. Customers would wire money to Jackson's company and he would buy more gold and add it to his stock, then issue them the equivalent amount of E-gold.

People liked the system, and E-gold gradually became the most popular electronic currency of its time. In the summer of 2001, the company had about 237,000 user accounts.[5] By November 2005, there were more than ten times as many: 2.5 million accounts belonging to people in more than 100 countries. Millions of dollars' worth of E-gold were changing hands every day. It was, by all accounts, a great tool for cross-border payments. Independent E-gold exchanges sprouted up. As backing for its electronic currency, the company held nearly four metric tons of gold, worth more than $85 million, in bank vaults in London and Dubai.[6] Although no large retailers accepted E-gold, it was widely used, prosecutors later claimed, in peer-to-peer exchanges, investment scams, and black market transactions.

The relative anonymity of E-gold over other payment services, along with its ability to move money anywhere in the world, did attract criminals. All you needed to open an account on www.e-gold.com was an email address. You could provide a fake name if you liked, and some users did, signing up with obvious pseudonyms like Donald Duck, Mickey Mouse, and Anonymous Man. As a result, E-gold was a boon to credit card thieves and others who operated in the shadows. Without a system in place to verify user identities or report suspicious transactions, Gold & Silver Reserve ran afoul of new laws which, after 11 September 2001, greatly expanded the definition of a money transmitter, a type of business with extensive reporting and licensing requirements. The company, incorporated in the famously permissive Caribbean nation of St. Kitts and Nevis, became a target for law enforcement.

In December 2005, Secret Service agents raided the company's Melbourne office. They seized more than a hundred boxes of records and, as part of the enforcement action, codenamed Operation Goldwire, froze the company's US bank account. 'They basically raped our computers and also took us offline for thirty-six hours, took all the paper out of our office,' Jackson said.[7] But the foreign currency accounts of Gold & Silver Reserve were held offshore, allowing the company to continue operating.

Now aware of how serious the criminal use of his system was, Jackson began cooperating with the feds. A complete transaction history for every E-gold account, even the pseudonymous ones, was stored in the company database, making it possible to trace users' financial movements. Jackson dug through his customer records to identify active criminals, blocking the accounts – and turning over to authorities the transaction histories – of those he spotted.[8] In December 2006 alone, he blocked about two thousand accounts – evidence both of his earnest desire to clean up the system and of the extent to which that system had been abused by identity thieves, scammers, and other bad actors.

But his efforts weren't enough to satisfy prosecutors. In a 2007 federal indictment, the E-gold operation was charged with, among other crimes, enabling nearly $475,000 to change hands in the sale of child pornography. The following year, after a protracted legal battle, Jackson pled guilty to conspiracy to operate an unlicensed money transmitting service and conspiracy to commit money laundering. He was sentenced to three years of probation and for six months was forced to wear an electronic monitoring anklet that tracked his movements.[9] E-gold's other executives – Jackson's brother, Reid Jackson, and Barry Downey – also pled guilty to operating a money transmitter without a license and were given probation and fines. The companies they had run were fined $300,000; their entire gold reserve was placed into receivership and liquidated to reimburse legitimate customers.

Another failed experiment in alternative currency was the Liberty Dollar. Created in 1998 by a man named Bernard von NotHaus, it was a metal-backed currency that set itself up as an alternative to the US dollar, whose progressive devaluation since the 1913 establishment of the Federal Reserve horrified von NotHaus. With no precious metal to ensure their value, and inflation eating away at their purchasing power year by year, Federal Reserve Notes were gradually turning into Monopoly money, he thought. The Liberty Dollar, which existed not only as metal specie but also as paper money and electronic currency – all of it backstopped by gold and silver – could serve as a replacement. It would never be accepted as legal tender for the purpose of paying taxes or redeeming debts, but it could be used as barter in private transactions.

Von NotHaus, a seventy-two-year-old ex-surfer and fervent pot smoker with a thick head of silver hair that he wears combed back from his forehead, a white beard, big round glasses, and a fondness for Hawaiian shirts, does not conform to the stock image of an entrepreneur. A spiritual epiphany in 1974 led him to produce twenty pages of 'automatic writing' on politics and economics, after which he opened a private mint on the Big Island of Hawaii, where he was living in a cottage with no electricity. The mint, now called the Royal Hawaiian Mint, is still in operation, with a flagship store in Honolulu, turning out collectible coins to commemorate Hawaiian history and culture. Von NotHaus, however, left the mint in 1998 and used his retirement savings to launch the Liberty Dollar.

If this seems an unusual background for a businessman, much less a monetary theorist, neither does von NotHaus fit the prototype of a domestic terrorist, which is what Anne Tompkins, the US Attorney for the Western District of North Carolina, later called him. He did, however, hold strong opinions about US foreign policy. His objection to the dollar was not only that it depreciated over time but that the federal government could harness its inflationary nature to finance military action around the globe. 'There is a moral element to money,' he says. 'There is something morally wrong with a fiat currency that does nothing more than enrich the damn politicians, kills our people, and finances war.'[10]

He was not alone in his beliefs. In its first ten years, von NotHaus's organization distributed as much as $85 million worth of Liberty Dollars to a quarter of a million people. It became, in von NotHaus's words, 'the second most popular currency in the United States'.

It came to an end in the early hours of the morning of 14 November 2007, when a dozen FBI and Secret Service agents stormed the Liberty Dollar headquarters in Evansville, Indiana.[11] They seized everything that wasn't nailed down: more than forty ounces of gold, five hundred pounds of silver, and nearly two tons of freshly minted copper coins bearing the face of Republican presidential candidate Ron Paul, as well as the company files and computers. For the federal agents, it must have been a moment of catharsis following a two-year undercover investigation into the Liberty Dollar. They stayed for six hours, carting everything away. Once they had gotten what they came for, they left the organization's employees to clean up the mess left behind.

Von NotHaus was distraught. In an email following the raid, he told Liberty Dollar customers that the organization's bank accounts had been frozen and all its records confiscated. 'We have no money. We have no products. We have no records to even know what was ordered or what you are owed,' he wrote. 'We have nothing but the will to push forward and overcome this massive assault on our liberty and our right to have real money as defined by the US Constitution. We should not be defrauded by the fake government money.'

But by then the wheels of justice were already in motion. On 6 June 2009, von NotHaus was arrested, and in March 2011, after an eight-day trial, he was convicted under anti-counterfeiting laws of minting and selling an illegal currency. (The case against him rested in part on the resemblance between the medallions he was minting and official US coins.) In all, he says, the government confiscated from his company eleven tons of gold and silver, unwilling to allow a desirable alternative currency to exist alongside 'their piece of shit' fiat money. Prosecutors asked for a prison sentence of at least fourteen years. An old man, he was facing the prospect of spending the rest of his life behind bars. But on 2 December 2014, when he was finally sentenced, he got off easy, receiving only six months of home detention with a concurrent sentence of three years' probation. He was nevertheless marked as a felon for life.

A third major attempt to create a universal alternative currency arose in the hothouse environs of turn-of-the-millennium Silicon

Valley. In the late 1990s, while Douglas Jackson was struggling to get E-gold off the ground, Peter Thiel, a handsome Stanford Law School graduate, was running a competing startup called PayPal. Thiel's original vision for the company was both simple and immense: 'to create a new Internet currency to replace the US dollar'.[12] He had the brains, the drive, and the libertarian convictions to make it happen. PayPal took steps in this direction, introducing direct money transfers from one PalmPilot to another – an early digital analog to the act of handing someone cash – and then, when it became apparent by the fall of 1999 that PalmPilots were a niche product used only by geeks, developing a product with broader appeal that allowed people to send and receive money via email. But two things killed Thiel's vision: the bursting of the dot-com bubble in the spring of 2000 – just before which, fortunately, PayPal had managed to raise $100 million of investment capital that kept it going – and the raft of new financial regulations passed in the wake of 9/11, supposedly to prevent terrorist financing. 'I swore we wouldn't hire any lawyers for the first year,' Thiel once said. 'I knew they would just tell us that we weren't allowed to do what we were doing.' Soon enough, he wasn't. What the PayPal team wanted to do would have gotten them prosecuted under the new laws. And so they settled for building a far less radical company, one that might not change the world but which also wouldn't have to face any federal indictments.

Although Satoshi Nakamoto could not have known the end result of all these cases at the time he released Bitcoin, the US government's zealous prosecution of alternative currencies both in and out of cyberspace would have given most innovators pause. But despite these cautionary tales, Satoshi pushed forward. In time, he knew, government agencies would come sniffing around Bitcoin, too, but he refused to give them any red meat. 'A lot of people automatically dismiss e-currency as a lost cause because of all the companies that failed since the 1990s,' he said a few months after introducing his digital currency. 'I hope it's obvious it was only the centrally controlled nature of those systems that doomed them.' An essential facet of Bitcoin's brilliance is that it is not owned by anyone, so the system can't be held criminally liable. The network, in Satoshi's phrase, 'is robust in its unstructured simplicity'. Individual nodes can leave and rejoin at will, accepting the latest version of the blockchain as an accurate record of all that occurred in their absence. Participants are protected by the network. There is no agent who can be said to have failed to perform due diligence when a transaction is approved, because there is no central agent: everything is verified by everyone. The network has no central point of failure, no leader to prosecute. Satoshi Nakamoto may have been the creator of Bitcoin, but he wasn't about to be the fall guy. Still, there was good reason to be skeptical about Bitcoin's chance of success. Who would be willing to trade their real money for Internet money, especially if it wasn't backed by gold?

HARDLY A WEEK AFTER SATOSHI'S announcement, something fateful happened. A cryptographer of genius in California named Hal Finney, who had been involved with the Cypherpunks and would soon be diagnosed with Lou Gehrig's disease, wrote to Satoshi through the cryptography mailing list. He had a bunch of questions about Bitcoin. Still aflame with intellectual curiosity in middle age, Finney, who in August 2004 had released his own program for a virtual currency – one which failed to catch on – approached Bitcoin with more idealism than most. 'I have always loved crypto, the mystery and the paradox of it,' he later wrote. While others did their best to find fault, Finney called Bitcoin 'a very promising and original idea' and said he looked forward to seeing how the concept would be turned into code.

In its early days, the saga of Bitcoin unfolded across at least two email lists and three online forums. Finney soon became a prominent voice in these virtual spaces. He had good reason to be interested in Bitcoin. He was one of a handful of men who had prepared the way for Satoshi's breakthrough. Although Bitcoin was already Bitcoin from its first day, it was not created in a vacuum. Satoshi's white paper burns with the gathered fuel of years. Generations of cryptographers had a hand in the digital currency; their ideas were stepping stones toward it; the legacy of their successes and failures gives weight to it, even as the global financial crisis shadows it. In the first block of bitcoins ever mined, which has come to be known as the genesis block, Satoshi embedded a headline from the *Sunday Times* of London, so that there could be no mistaking his intentions: 'Chancellor on brink of second bailout for banks'. Surely knowing as he did so that it would become part of Bitcoin's founding myth. The entry was date-stamped in the British style: 03/Jan/2009. Less than three months before, the British government had announced its first rescue package for banks: more than $750 billion in loans and guarantees, plus about $87 billion of direct investment in exchange for pref-erence shares in the lending institutions. In other words, the government was partly nationalizing the British banking sector.

If Satoshi was disgusted with the symbiotic relationship between national governments and big banks, he was hardly alone. By now, the US government had already bailed out AIG to the tune of $85 billion, provided a $29 billion backstop to JP Morgan Chase in its purchase of failed investment bank Bear Stearns, and, finally, rammed its own massive bailout program through Congress – the Troubled Asset Relief Program, or TARP, a $700 billion package to shore up crumbling financial institutions. But even these gargantuan efforts were too late for some. Washington Mutual, the nation's largest savings-and-loan company, with two banking subsidiaries, more than 2,200 retail branch locations, and more than 43,000 employees, failed in September 2008 and was snapped up by J. P. Morgan Chase. Lehman Brothers collapsed and declared bankruptcy with $639 billion in assets, the largest bankruptcy in American history. That fall, Bank of America stepped in to buy a faltering Merrill Lynch for $50 billion, and by early 2009 the entire purchase value of the investment firm had been wiped off Bank of America's market cap. In November 2008, more than half a million people lost their jobs in the United States alone.

All through the credit crunch and the financial crisis that followed, as unemployment skyrocketed and the world slipped into the Great Recession, Satoshi was working on an alternative monetary technology, a counter-logic, a kind of wrench that could be thrown into the infernal engines of global finance. Everything he did, he did with full intention. On the P2P Foundation website where he announced his invention of Bitcoin for the second time, he gave his birthday – among the personal information required to register an account – as 5 April 1975: the day in 1933 when President Roosevelt by executive order made it illegal for average American citizens to own gold – a crime punishable by up to ten years in prison – and the year when FDR's order was finally undone, returning a measure of economic freedom to the masses.

But before Bitcoin could exist, there had to be earlier break-throughs. It was only natural while developing Bitcoin that Satoshi would reach out to some of his predecessors for advice, like Miles Davis looking up Charlie Parker upon arriving in New York. The predecessors to whom Satoshi most often gave credit were Wei Dai and Nick Szabo, each of whom had developed a persuasive concept of how digital currency might work. But there were others even further back who had laid cornerstones of the tower Satoshi was building, and there is evidence that he wasn't even aware of Wei Dai's work until late in the day, that he had arrived of his own accord at many of the same innovations, like Newton and Leibniz independently inventing calculus – two brilliant minds converging on the same idea.

If their denials of being Satoshi Nakamoto can be believed, neither Szabo nor Dai, themselves accomplished and respected in their field, knew at the time who Satoshi was.[13] There was no prior record anywhere on the Internet of a cryptographer or programmer with that name. The loop began to close in September 2008, when Satoshi emailed a man named Adam Back to ask about Back's own cryptographic invention, hashcash, which formed a crucial piece of the Bitcoin mining function. Back recalls pointing Satoshi in the direction of Wei Dai, after suggesting that Dai's 1998 proposal for 'b-money' bore a resemblance to Satoshi's concept for Bitcoin. In this proposal, Dai admitted to being fascin-ated by Timothy May's theory of crypto-anarchy. 'In a crypto-anarchy the government is not temporarily destroyed but permanently forbidden and permanently unnecessary,' Dai wrote. 'It's a community where the threat of violence is impotent because violence is impossible, and violence is impossible because its participants cannot be linked to their true names or physical locations.' What he sought with b-money was a means of enabling people to cooperate, conduct business, and enter into contracts with each other even if they were hiding their real identities behind digital pseudonyms. Satoshi told Back that he had not previously been aware of b-money – though later he would reference it in his white paper.

He now contacted Dai, asking for comments on a draft of the paper. But Dai never responded. Only later would he realize the brilliance of Bitcoin, which, he wrote, 'involved major technical and conceptual/philosophical advances on the existing state of the art'. Its significance was far greater than that of a new smartphone app or website, more even than that of a successful Internet company: 'Its social impact seems larger – if Craigslist or PayPal didn't exist, something essentially identical would have been created very soon anyway, but if Bitcoin didn't exist, another Bitcoin may not have been created for another decade.'

Nick Szabo, a polymath who in later years was often suspected of being Satoshi Nakamoto, is big enough to admit that Bitcoin surpasses his own ideas for a digital currency, which he called 'bit gold' and which never got off the ground. Responding years later to Gwern Branwen, a researcher who claimed that Bitcoin amounted to little more than assembling a given pile of Tinkertoys into a novel structure, Szabo argued the opposite: 'Bitcoin is not a list of cryptographic features, it's a very complex system of interacting mathematics and protocols in pursuit of what was a very unpopular goal.' That goal – to 'replace every use of pocket cash except flipping a coin', in Kevin Kelly's memorable phrase – had been discussed for years. Not until the invention of Bitcoin did it seem within reach. According to Szabo, only he, Wei Dai, and Hal Finney thought such a goal was worth pursuing, and only Finney had gone so far as to write a software program implementing his ideas. And yet, despite his independent development of Bitcoin, in July 2010 Satoshi was generous enough to call it a mere 'implementation' of the b-money and bit gold proposals, crediting Dai and Szabo by name. Small wonder that Finney was so excited by Bitcoin.

Indeed, Satoshi was at pains to situate his invention within the larger history of cryptography. Just as trust was a problem for people dealing with money, he explained, so it had once been a problem for those dealing with electronic information. Passwords were of limited usefulness, as they could always be overriden by system administrators. 'Then strong encryption became available to the masses, and trust was no longer required,' he wrote on the website of the P2P Foundation. 'Data could be secured in a way that was physically impossible for others to access, no matter for what reason, no matter how good the excuse, no matter what. It's time we had the same thing for money.'

And so, in January 2009, in that winter of discontent, when the world's financial systems seemed as untenable as they were irrevocable, Satoshi released the first version of the Bitcoin software, version 0.1. His timing couldn't have been better. Into the breach of trust created by the financial crisis stepped a new form of money, one that identified trust itself as the root problem of conventional currency. Satoshi ticked off one by one the points of failure in the system. 'The central bank must be trusted not to debase the currency, but the history of fiat currencies is full of breaches of that trust. Banks must be trusted to hold our money and transfer it electronically, but they lend it out in waves of credit bubbles with barely a fraction in reserve,' he wrote. 'We have to trust them with our privacy, trust them not to let identity thieves drain our accounts.' Every time we trust another person or company, he knew, we make ourselves vulnerable, exposing ourselves to the possibility of fraud, mismanagement, theft. Properly used, Bitcoin could sidestep these problems by allowing individuals to safeguard their own wealth.

One of the first to run the software, perhaps the very first after Satoshi himself, was Hal Finney. By the following day, he was mulling over the digital currency's value:

As an amusing thought experiment, imagine that Bitcoin is successful and becomes the dominant payment system in use throughout the world. Then the total value of the currency should be equal to the total value of all the wealth in the world. Current estimates of total worldwide household wealth that I have found range from $100 trillion to $300 trillion. With twenty million coins, that gives each coin a value of about $10 million. So the possibility of generating coins today with a few cents of compute time may be quite a good bet, with a payoff of something like 100 million to one! Even if the odds of Bitcoin succeeding to this degree are slim, are they really 100 million to one against? Something to think about.

Betting on a future he would only begin to see, Finney began mining bitcoins. He also received, from Satoshi himself, the first ever transaction using the digital currency, when Satoshi beamed ten bitcoins to him as a test. Finney continued to engage with him over the next several days, reporting software bugs. 'At the time, I thought I was dealing with a young man of Japanese ancestry who was very smart and sincere,' he later wrote. 'I've had the good fortune to know many brilliant people over the course of my life, so I recognize the signs.' Finney mined hundreds of bitcoins in the days that followed, though after a short period he stopped, as he later explained, because constant use of the software 'made my computer run hot, and the fan noise bothered me'. (After his ALS diagnosis, he earmarked the coins he had mined – now stored in an offline wallet for safekeeping – for his children's inheritance.)

In the first weeks after Satoshi's unveiling of Bitcoin, Finney expressed optimism about people's willingness to support the network, provided the Bitcoin system 'turns out to be socially useful and valuable, so that node operators feel that they are making a beneficial contribution to the world'. Satoshi seemed to agree. 'It's very attractive to the libertarian viewpoint if we can explain it properly,' he replied. 'I'm better with code than with words, though.'

True, libertarian goldbugs – people not unlike Bernard von NotHaus – might see Bitcoin as a digital commodity with many of the same properties as precious metal, including its immunity to government inflation. They might also take to it as a tool of individual empowerment. But how could it be legal for Bitcoin to exist alongside the US dollar and other national currencies?

If anyone understands money in its basest, most tangible form, it is Edmund Moy, former director of the US Mint. In his old job, Moy was responsible for overseeing, quite literally, the nickels and dimes of the American economy. 'Bitcoin crosses over several different areas and ignores other areas regarding currency,' he says of Satoshi's hybrid creation. 'Therefore, it's unclear as to how the Constitution would interpret Bitcoin.'

Under Moy, the Mint assisted the FBI and Secret Service with their investigation into the Liberty Dollar, which in his view represented a clear violation of the law. 'The intent of Liberty Dollar,' he says, 'was basically to create an alternative currency in the United States because they didn't trust the US dollar, so they wanted to create something they did trust . . . It would be a direct competitor, an alternative to the US dollar, produced and issued in the United States as a currency.' Bitcoin was different. Satoshi had identified a space of legal uncertainty in which his invention could thrive. In time, this uncertainty would create a quagmire for Bitcoin entrepreneurs. But it was fertile soil for Bitcoin itself.

Moy, the voluble, Michigan-born, Wisconsin-raised son of Chinese immigrants, recalls bringing up digital currency during one meeting of senior Treasury Department staff in late 2008. At weekly meetings like this one, Secretary Hank Paulson would set the agenda and department heads would take turns giving brief reports on their activities. A dramatic decline in the Federal Reserve's orders for quarters, dimes, and other coins earlier that year had prompted Moy to put together a skunkworks group to discover the cause. Were electronic transactions finally beginning to take a big chunk out of cash's market share? (Only later would he realize it was an early warning sign of the impending economic downturn.) 'Figure out what's going on with coin demand and what could possibly impact that in the future,' he told the group. In the course of their research, they discovered Satoshi's white paper.

In any given Treasury meeting, about half of the forty-odd senior staffers – 'all the heads of all the parts that did stuff', as Moy puts it – would say, 'Pass', which meant they had nothing pressing to report on that occasion. This time, when it was Moy's turn to speak, he ran through a preliminary version of his team's report. The other staffers asked questions about some aspects of the report, but when he mentioned digital currency – namely, Bitcoin – he got no reaction. He tried again in a meeting with the cash office of the Fed. 'I basically got no response,' he recalls. 'Everyone kind of looked around the table and said, "We aren't even looking at it. If you find out anything interesting, let us know."' It was the US government's first brush with Bitcoin.

For Satoshi, the time had come to begin promoting Bitcoin as a form of payment. 'It might make sense just to get some in case it catches on,' he mused, days after releasing Bitcoin v0.1. 'If enough people think the same way, that becomes a self-fulfilling prophecy.' In essence, he was asking people to buy into his digital currency as a sort of Pascal's Wager. If it failed, the downside was not very significant; everything would simply return to the *status quo ante*. But if it succeeded, and gained in value, the upside for early adopters – not to mention for the creator himself – would be enormous.

Another way to put it is that Satoshi was offering his peers equity in a promising but risky venture, just as a startup founder will offer early employees a stake in the company in exchange for reduced pay. It is a gamble. If the company takes off, everyone reaps the rewards. Bitcoin could make its early adopters very rich.

But in order for it to take off, a lot of infrastructure would have to be built. Alex Waters, a programmer who joined the small development team that soon formed around Bitcoin, helping Satoshi to spot problems, fix bugs, and make other improvements to the software, says the original Bitcoin client – as the software was known – was intended only as 'a reference for people to go build better shit'. It provided a foundation for future work. 'It's not supposed to be fast, it's not the best user experience; it's not intended to be those things,' Alex says. 'What it's intended to be is secure. And it works. It's a proof of concept.'

Everyone present in those early days understood that in order for Bitcoin to grow and succeed beyond a small hobbyist community, it was essential for businessmen and money people to get involved; for powerful, user-friendly applications to be built; for companies to be founded and markets tapped. All of this would take time. But Bitcoin had time on its side. In comparison with previous attempts at electronic money, Gwern Branwen wrote, Bitcoin's greatest virtue may be 'its viral distributed nature; it can wait for its opportunity'. He quoted a famous proverb: 'If you sit by the bank of the river long enough, you can watch the bodies of your enemies float by.'

The Bitcoin developers worked and waited. In July 2010, the world's first Bitcoin exchange, Mt. Gox, opened in Tokyo. But trading volume, like the digital currency's price, was low, and remained that way for the rest of the year. Mt. Gox had only a few thousand customers. If Bitcoin were to fulfill Satoshi's vision for it, it needed more. It needed champions.

Chapter 2

VIRTUAL CRACK

All ideas rise like music from the physical.
                                        – Guy Davenport

Roger Ver, who was once but is no longer an American citizen, still can't stand the jingle of keys. Even though he has lived for many years now in Tokyo, an insomniac city where you can drink the neon all night without cease or surfeit, a city that even all this time after the boom years of the eighties still beckons like a vision of the future; even though he is a successful entrepreneur and investor, a millionaire in his mid-thirties – not filthy rich, not Zuckerberg rich or Buffett rich or even David Beckham rich, but still the kind of guy who can lose a million dollars and keep on trucking – even though he is trained in Brazilian jiujitsu and among fellow Bitcoiners libertarians is a rock star, the sound of keys jingling takes him right back to a time when he was miserable and scared and alone, the victim of a perceived injustice, unable to strike back or escape.

The sound reminds him of the ten months he spent in Lompoc, a medium-security federal prison in southern California, more than a decade ago, for selling fireworks illegally over the Internet. The guards carried big key rings on their belts, and as they made their rounds, checking cells, the ominous metallic chiming was loud enough for every prisoner to hear; it meant a guard was coming; it meant put away your contraband, straighten up, act nonchalant.

On occasion, though, this pageantry wasn't enough, and the guards would toss a cell. Everything a prisoner owned in the entire world was kept in a small metal locker, about three feet tall and one foot wide, and some of the prisoners, having developed while incarcerated a kind of obsessive-compulsive disorder, were particular about the arrangement of their limited belongings – clothes, toothbrush, toothpaste, notebooks, ballpoint pens – so that it was especially painful for such a prisoner, when his cell was being tossed, to watch the guards ransack his locker, rooting through every item. It was sickening to have no control over your own life, to be forced to surrender at a moment's notice even the last small piece over which you had dominion. 'You didn't really have anything to fear from the other inmates,' Roger says, 'but you did have a lot to fear from the guards.'

Roger was arrested and charged and indicted in 2001, but by the time he was sentenced it was May 2002, and after getting his affairs in order he surrendered himself to Lompoc at 9:00 A.M. on 2 August 2002, a Friday. He showed up thinking he would be placed in the minimum-security camp adjacent to the medium-security penitentiary, a three-story gray stone building with guard towers and fences topped with razor wire. This was what his defense attorney and the US prosecutor both had promised him, he says.

But when Roger arrived, he wasn't placed in the minimum-security camp, which had once housed former White House officials convicted of Watergate offenses. First he was thrown into the medium-security penitentiary's Special Housing Unit, which prisoners call 'the SHU' – pronounced like 'shoe' – or 'the hole', a sort of prison within the prison that often houses the worst offenders, to await classification. Then, on Monday, after three nights in the hole, he was assigned permanently to the penitentiary and given a job in the kitchen. The young man viewed his offense as hardly a crime at all, yet by some process he couldn't fathom he had been classified as a serious criminal.

Thrown back on his inner resources, Roger began to learn Japanese. Before going inside, he'd had a Japanese girlfriend, and he remembered their relationship fondly. By now he was resolved to leave the United States as soon as possible. Japan seemed as good a place as any to relocate once he'd served his time.

For kitchen duty, he got up every day at 5:00 A.M. and started work at half past the hour. Breakfast was over by 8:30, but the kitchen workers had to remain where they were for the next three hours, until the lunch shift started. They weren't allowed anything that would help them pass the time, he recalls, not even a deck of cards. Roger turned these lulls into study breaks. In the prison library, he would photocopy a few pages at a time from his Japanese study book, then sneak them into the kitchen. It was against the rules, but he was desperate to break up the monotony. During these empty hours, he would study over and over the few pages he had brought, memorizing their contents.

One day a guard caught him studying. Furious, he snatched the pages out of Roger's hands. 'What do you think you're doing?' he demanded. The young prisoner reacted with unthinking defiance. 'I'm trying to better myself,' he shot back. The guard looked at the pieces of paper in his hand. Then he tore them up and threw them in the trash.

Undaunted, Roger continued with his covert studies. And when he tired of learning Japanese, when he had exhausted the books on economics and moral philosophy that friends mailed to him – precious parcels arriving, like Noah's dove with the olive twig in its beak, as proof the world was still out there – he brooded on the events of 2 May 2002, the day of his sentencing.

He had signed a plea deal, confessing, in exchange for a reduced sentence, to three felony charges: dealing in explosives without a license, storing explosives illegally, and 'mailing injurious articles' – sending explosives to his customers through the US mail. His lawyer, Cristina Arguedas, had asked that her client's ten-month sentence be split, so that he would serve only the first five months in prison and the remaining five in a halfway house. Roger was running an online business called Memory Dealers, selling computer parts. While the business might survive his absence for five months, with someone else keeping it on life support, Arguedas argued, it could not last ten. 'He's it. He is the business,' she said at the sentencing hearing. 'The question is, do we want to extinguish his business, and I would say the answer should be no.'

But the judge didn't go for it. 'Selling explosives over the Internet doesn't cut it in any society that I can imagine,' he told Roger. 'The conduct here is simply not tolerable conduct.' He paid lip service to Roger's libertarian beliefs, at pains to separate the defendant's crime from his politics. But this was a matter of public safety. 'I don't think one has to be a big-government person or believe in government regulation of every aspect of human life to suggest that people should not be selling explosives over the Internet.'

In truth, Roger says, what he had done was far more innocuous: buying and reselling fireworks on eBay for a small profit. He sold one device in particular, popular due to its impressive bang: the Pest Control Report 2000, an agricultural firecracker used by farmers and ranchers to scare birds away from their fields. Each of these firecrackers contained up to one thousand milligrams of explosive powder, about twenty times the legal limit for consumer fireworks, so they were classified as explosives. Over time, Roger sold hundreds of these devices. In one instance, he bought thirty-six cases of the Pest Control Report 2000 – 2,592 firecrackers in all – for $1,664 from a store called All Purpose Ammo and began reselling them for about a dollar apiece. Meanwhile, the manufacturer, Max 2000, beginning in January 1998, illegally sold more than one million Pest Control Report 2000 firecrackers to retailers and wholesalers around the country: 400,000 to All American Professional Fireworks, of Angola, Indiana; 450,000 to Planet Ammo, of Seneca, South Carolina; 10,000 to Firequest, of El Dorado, Arkansas; 290,000 to Self Defense Supply, of Richardson, Texas; and 33,000 to Astro Spectacular, of Hooksett, New Hampshire. These businesses resold the illegal fireworks to consumers, just as Roger had done, but in far greater quantities. Roger, twenty-two at the time of his arrest, could at least plausibly have claimed ignorance of the firework's illegality. Gun dealers and fireworks retailers should have known better.

But Roger had run afoul of the law at the worst possible time.

In the public imagination, the Twin Towers were still smoldering. Nobody was in the mood to let a kid dealing explosives off lightly. 'This conduct to me would have warranted a much stiffer sentence than ten months,' the judge said. Only the plea bargain that Roger had signed spared him a worse fate; his charges carried a combined maximum sentence of twelve years in prison.

Max 2000, the Missouri company which manufactured the Pest Control Report 2000, was also brought up on federal charges. It finally settled with the government in January 2003 in the US District Court for the Eastern District of Missouri, agreeing not to make or sell the firecracker any longer. In return, neither the company nor its owners faced any penalties.

Roger had his own theory as to why he had been singled out for prosecution, and it boiled down to one thing: his anti-government politics. At the age of twenty, having already converted to libertarianism after teenage encounters with the work of Ludwig von Mises, Adam Smith, Milton Friedman, and other free-market thinkers, he ran for the California State Assembly as a candidate for the Libertarian Party. A debate was held with the Republican and Democratic candidates at San Jose State University, during which Roger told the audience that if elected he would accept no salary, since public officials' salaries were paid with tax dollars and he viewed taxation as tantamount to theft. He declared the war on drugs immoral and called agents of the Bureau of Alcohol, Tobacco, and Firearms 'a bunch of jackbooted thugs and murderers', in the memory – as he would later relate – of 'the people they slaughtered in Waco, Texas' in April 1993. In the audience, Roger says he later learned, were several plainclothes ATF agents, who he believes pursued a vendetta against him from that day forward.

Though Roger remains an idealist, he looks back on his bid for office as a time almost of naiveté. 'I didn't call for an end to all monopolistic government,' he admits. The months he spent in prison, with his life in the hands of the federal government, ended his hopes for any good that could be accomplished by the state. 'That's what pushed me over the borderline,' he says.

When he got out, on 27 May 2003, he set about resuscitating his business. Before going inside, he'd had to lay off all his employees. His mother had been running Memory Dealers on his behalf – though 'running it' wasn't the right term. Even with her help, Roger had managed to do only one deal while in prison, a purchase of computer memory from a Chinese vendor in Beijing, who went by the name John, for $120,000, which he promptly resold for a $40,000 profit.

Now, beginning a three-year probation, he had good reason to throw himself back into work. Probation is not freedom; while on probation a convict is said still to be 'in custody', but with the privilege of moving about more or less freely in the open air. Should a convict's probation be revoked, he must serve out the duration behind bars. For Roger that would have meant another three years in Lompoc. His probation officer, he says, lost no opportunity to remind him of his tenuous position. Once, the older man tracked mud all over the tile floor and pale carpet of Roger's multimillion-dollar house, ignoring pleas for him to remove his shoes. 'That guy was such a jerk,' Roger says. 'He just wanted to exercise his control.'

Three long years he lived in fear of revocation, counting down the days, putting up with his probation officer's petty power games. This too he was determined to outlast. He focused on rebuilding his business, shutting out everything else, a Zen workaholic unwilling to be made an example of. Tokyo was just a dream then, a promise of beautiful women and neon nights, a cultured city where he wouldn't be marked forever as a felon.

By age twenty-five he had made his first million. And as soon as his probation ended, he moved to Japan.

ROGER GREW UP IN SAN Jose, the largest city in Silicon Valley, and from a young age he was interested in economics and computer science. In his early teens he ran a bulletin board system – an early kind of online community, popular in the years before the first web browser was released – out of his bedroom. He paid to have five additional phone lines installed so that more users could dial

it's not worthwhile,"' he says. He put it out of his mind until one morning in February 2011, when he was in the kitchen of his house in San Jose – which he kept as a place to stay when he needed to visit the Memory Dealers office in Santa Clara – eating a bowl of Wheaties and listening to *Free Talk Live*, a libertarian talk radio show he liked. That day, the hosts were discussing Bitcoin. 'I googled Bitcoin again while I was having breakfast,' Roger says. 'I fully intended to go into my office that day selling Cisco equipment. Didn't make it to the office that day, didn't make it the next day, didn't make it for the next couple of weeks, just went on an absolute Bitcoin binge. And literally I didn't leave the house for about ten days, and just ordered food to be delivered to my house and just stayed there and read every single thing I could find about Bitcoin.' On 9 February, for the first time ever, the value of a bitcoin had reached parity with the US dollar – an important milestone it then went on to surpass, closing the day at $1.09 on Mt. Gox. (Roger didn't know it at the time, but a game-changing event had occurred between his first and second encounter with Bitcoin: the opening of an online black market called Silk Road.) At that time, the Bitcoin community's major online discussion board, hosted at bitcointalk.org, was still young enough that 'you could read every single post on the entire forum, and every single new post each day,' Roger says. And he did. The same intensity of focus that had allowed him to learn Japanese in prison now helped him to devour the theoretical underpinnings of this math-based currency. 'It was like virtual crack for me. I couldn't get enough of it.' And like a drug, Bitcoin temporarily compromised his health. For more than a week, caught up in a sort of ecstatic search for knowledge, he slept only one hour a night, like a methamphetamine addict or a religious ascetic undergoing a trial of the flesh. His zeal – or rather, acute sleep deprivation – landed him in the hospital. By the time he was released, he had found his life's calling. It was Bitcoin.

During his February binge, Roger bought his first bitcoins. Memory Dealers now had about thirty employees and annual expected sales of nearly $10 million. The success of that business allowed him to put money into Bitcoin and, later, into Bitcoin startups. He went in hard. By March, he was asking Memory Dealers' vendors if he could pay them in digital currency. (One or two of them even agreed.) He began accepting Bitcoin as a payment option himself, hoping to spread enthusiasm for this new form of money, and he added Memory Dealers to the Bitcoin Wiki, an online encyclopedia that included a directory of Bitcoin-friendly businesses. Says Roger, 'I was the first website that wasn't just selling, like, alpaca socks' – an exaggeration but not far from the truth.

There is a branch of Christian theology known as apophatic, or negative theology, in which God is described only in terms of what he is not, for God is unknowable in his essence. It would be wrong to say that Roger approached Bitcoin in quite that way, but certainly he prized Bitcoin as much for what it was not as for what it was. It was not issued or controlled by any government. It was not under the thumb of any big bank or credit card company. It was not beholden to the whims of any corporate executive. And it was not – at least for now – taxable. Later, he would earn the nickname Bitcoin Jesus for his missionary zeal. He'd had a difficult youth as the son of fundamentalist Christians, and now he was an atheist. But perhaps the proselytizing instinct was nevertheless present in him as an inheritance. Blessed is the man who can make a bitter stalk produce the fruit of his choosing. In May, Roger began paying $2,500 a month to have gee-whiz Bitcoin advertisements broadcast on *Free Talk Live*, which aired on nearly a hundred radio stations in America as well as XM satellite radio. The ads went like this:

Are you tired of watching the value of the dollar plummet? Are you tired of banks charging you fees? Do you want to take back control of your own money? Then take a look at Bitcoin!

Bitcoin is the world's first decentralized, anonymous Internet currency, and it's gaining popularity every day. It's free to use, free to accept, and free from inflation – forever!

You can use bitcoins anywhere in the world, and their value will only grow with time. To learn more, visit weusecoins.org. Again, weusecoins.org.

He also paid $1,200 a month for a billboard along Lawrence Expressway in Santa Clara, which displayed the image of a great golden coin, radiant like the sun, emblazoned with the symbol for Bitcoin – a capital letter B with two parallel vertical lines running through it, as in the US dollar symbol (which is sometimes shown with one intersecting line, sometimes two) – and which advertised Memory Dealers' acceptance of this 'P2P cryptocurrency'. He even convinced some of the Chinese vendors that supplied him with computer parts to accept partial payment in bitcoins. Through it all, he was unremittingly earnest in his evangelism. 'Bitcoin prices will only continue to rise if people begin using bitcoins for their everyday transactions,' he insisted. 'We should be focusing on making it easy for everyone to use bitcoins in everyday life.'

Roger didn't consider himself to be investing dollars in bitcoins but rather cashing out his dollars – antiquated inflationary fiat currency, as he thought of it – for a superior form of money. It was, to be sure, a minority view even in that enclave of radical techno-geeks. But these were heady times. The price of Bitcoin was climbing steadily. On 26 May, Roger announced his intention to buy a large quantity of bitcoins – a thousand or more, worth about $9,000 at the time. By 8 June, that haul was worth as much as $31,900. By the end of spring, Roger had gained a certain prominence in the burgeoning Bitcoin community – the seasoned 'old man' among disaffected millennials – and so it was only natural, perhaps, that when disaster struck he would take it upon himself to stop the bleeding.

On 20 June, at three o'clock in the morning, Tokyo time, a hacker broke into and assumed control of a Mt. Gox account that had vast administrative powers over the exchange, which now controlled ninety percent of the global market for Bitcoin trading. The hacker evidently hoped to raid the piggy bank for all he could get. There was only one thing standing in his way: the daily withdrawal limit. A Mt. Gox user could withdraw only $1,000 a day in digital currency, the equivalent of about fifty-seven bitcoins on the day the hacker broke into the exchange. But if he could drive the Bitcoin price down from $17.50 to a single penny with a massive sell-off and then buy back the cryptocurrency at that depressed price, he could, in theory, make off with 100,000 bitcoins. If and when the price recovered, he'd be a rich man. He began selling like crazy.

On the East Coast it was the middle of the afternoon, and traders watched as – thanks to the hacker's artificial sell-off – the value of Bitcoin plummeted like an elevator with a snapped cable, dropping from $17.50 to $0.01 in a mere half hour. For those who had bet big on the cryptocurrency, it must have been horrifying. But then market forces, of which greed was no small part, kicked in; speculators didn't know why the price had crashed, but they saw an opportunity to buy thousands of bitcoins on the cheap, and their frantic buying began to drive the price back up, unwittingly foiling the hacker in the process. In the end, he escaped with only two thousand bitcoins, about $35,000 at the former exchange price.

Recognizing the threat at last, Mt. Gox's chief executive, a rotund and awkward Frenchman named Mark Karpelès, halted trading while his staff tried to sort out the mess. Karpelès pleaded with his fellow Bitcoiners to help get the exchange up and running again. Roger, who happened to live in Tokyo's Shibuya neighborhood, where Mt. Gox was headquartered, rushed to help the ailing exchange. What he found when he arrived at the Cerulean Tower, the forty-one-story glass-and-steel building where Mt. Gox had its offices, was shocking: Karpelès was running the exchange with only two other men, Mt. Gox's sole employees, who had started just days before. They were overwhelmed. Roger quickly took on a managerial role. And he called an old friend, Jesse Powell, who was also into Bitcoin, for backup.

'I'm at the Mt. Gox office,' he told Powell. 'How soon can you be in Tokyo?' Powell was perplexed. Mt. Gox had tens of thousands of users. *How the hell are you running this exchange with three people?* he wondered.

Powell got on the next plane out of San Francisco. Roger met him at Haneda International Airport, and together – with Powell's luggage still in hand – they set up camp in the Mt. Gox offices, determined to help out.[1] It was up to them to save the most critical piece of the Bitcoin ecosystem. Without Mt. Gox, which handled more than fifty times as many transactions as all the other exchanges put together, it would be impossible for most businesses to accept the digital currency and for traders to turn a profit. It would be like turning off the spigot. People would lose interest; the value of Bitcoin would drop to zero. 'It was pretty important to me that Mt. Gox survive that,' Powell says. So important, in fact, that he dropped $5,000 of his own money on laptops for the exchange's staff and volunteers.

There was a lot of work to do. 'The truth is that Mt. Gox was unprepared for Bitcoin's explosive growth,' Karpelès told users. 'Our dated system was built as a hobby when bitcoins were worth pennies apiece. It was not built to be a Fort Knox capable of securely handling millions of dollars in transactions each day.' That the world's most important Bitcoin company was the digital equivalent of something a hobbyist carpenter would hammer together in his garage was a frightening prospect for those who depended on it and wanted to believe in the potential of crypto-money, but it was unsurprising given the way Bitcoin had come into the world – as the work not of a nation-state or university researchers but of what appeared to be a single brilliant outsider, a kind of one-man Manhattan Project. Moreover, the type of people initially attracted by Bitcoin's open-source, Cypherpunk ethos were almost uniformly young, with more enthusiasm than expertise. 'Bitcoin is coming from a bunch of young computer nerds who saw this thing and thought it was neat,' Roger said later. 'A lot of the early Bitcoiners are nineteen-year-old kids, still living at home with their parents, and they don't have any business experience.'[2] Powell puts it more bluntly: 'It was total amateur hour.' And the amateurs had led their peers off a cliff.

Now reinforcements had arrived, Roger and Jesse set to work alongside Karpelès, his employees, and other volunteers, fielding customer complaints and inquiries about the status of their accounts. As if the flash crash and theft weren't bad enough, Mt. Gox's database of user information, including names and email addresses, had also been stolen and posted online. Identity theft was now a real concern. 'Everybody had to prove they owned the account before they could log back in,' Powell says. 'There were clear cases in which people were trying to claim accounts they didn't own.' To sort it out, he and Roger created a questionnaire with which users could verify their identities. Gradually they worked through the immense backlog of support tickets.

Following the hack, Powell's faith in the viability of any sort of centralized exchange was badly shaken, though he continued trading on Mt. Gox for another year. For Roger, the whole fiasco was an important object lesson. Within the space of a few months, Bitcoin had transformed from 'this joke Internet currency that wasn't worth anything', as Powell puts it, into something of real value, a commodity worth stealing. If it was ever going to succeed on a grand scale, as Roger dearly wanted, serious companies would have to arise, with competent leadership, to build the necessary infrastructure to support this new form of money. Roger wasn't a programmer, so he couldn't build it himself. But he trusted that others could, if they only had the means to do so. And money was something that he had plenty of. He could be an investor. He began looking for Bitcoin startups – anything halfway decent would do – that were in need of seed funding.

On 26 June, nearly a week after Mark Karpelès had pulled the plug, Mt. Gox went back online, rolling out a new and improved website. With it came a rollback of all post-crash transactions. In essence, the company took a snapshot of its records as they had existed before the crash, and reverted all customer accounts to that state, like a golfer taking a mulligan after an unlucky stroke. Everybody had again the balances that had been theirs prior to the crash. Any bitcoins snapped up during the crash and which a quick-thinking user had managed to transfer out of the exchange before the exchange were therefore essentially stolen coins. According to Powell, about two thousand coins were pilfered in this way, through miscellaneous customer actions, along with the haul of two thousand taken by the hacker. Mt. Gox would have to cover those losses.

In the wider Bitcoin community and on tech blogs, which had just begun to take notice of this weird thing called digital currency, some people took the security failure as proof that Bitcoin users were foolish to rely on unregulated exchanges operated by strangers in remote parts of the world. After the hack, the value of Bitcoin slowly deflated, a hot air balloon coming back down to earth. And Mt. Gox paid a price: it lost ten percent of its market share to an upstart exchange in San Francisco called TradeHill.

For the cryptocurrency's early adopters, this series of unfortunate events represented the end of innocence. No one had reckoned with how theft and market manipulation might be handled in an industry without regulation, nor how costly incompetent leadership might be. There were no authorities to whom one could appeal for redress; there was no backstop to the loss of funds. Roger and Jesse's *esprit de corps* was all that saved the troubled exchange – and maybe Bitcoin itself. Crypto-anarchists liked the idea of a financial system not burdened by nanny-state bureaucracy, but its lack of safeguards and oversight also made it appealing to criminals.

EVEN AS MT. GOX WAS suffering, another Bitcoin startup was gaining ground. In Austin, Texas, a twenty-six-year-old former scientist named Ross Ulbricht had launched an unregulated online marketplace called Silk Road. He tucked it away in a hidden part of the Internet, making it accessible only through special software that masked users' identities. Some see the dark web – as this part of the Internet is known – as a nasty swamp of illicit activity, where drug traffickers, money launderers, child pornographers, and even contract killers run rampant. To others, it is a place of unbridled freedom and privacy in a world where both rights are increasingly under threat. Ross's utopian project – 'a website', as he wrote in the journal he kept to document his efforts, 'where people could buy anything anonymously, with no trail whatsoever that could lead back to them' – partook of both conceptions. It became a drug operation run like a tech company, staffed with engineers and administrators, and in time it made Ross a multimillionaire, a crypto pioneer, and a living legend of drug culture.

What made Silk Road possible – and so made it possible for a handsome, big-hearted young Texan, a 'softy' by his own admission, to lead an international narcotics organization – was Bitcoin. To ensure the privacy of buyers and sellers, Bitcoin was the only form of payment accepted on Silk Road. As a result, Ross Ulbricht may be the second-most important figure in Bitcoin's history after Satoshi Nakamoto. Ross created a demand for the fledgling cryptocurrency where before there had been only minimal interest. For two years after their invention, bitcoins were practically worthless, viewed as Internet funny money by all but the most diehard cryptogeeks and anti-establishment types. Bitcoin services were few and far between, and few merchants accepted it as payment, making it a poor competitor to banking services and credit card companies. But in the black market – by definition underserved by traditional finance – Bitcoin could gain a foothold, even thrive.

For most of his life, Ross was nobody's idea of a criminal mastermind. His neighborhood wasn't affluent, and for a long time he didn't even have a computer. He was fourteen years old before he owned his first video game.[3] He grew up in Austin, an idealistic Eagle Scout and bright student who loved drawing, skateboarding, and surfing. Rule-breaking came naturally. But despite heavy drug use in high school, he managed to land multiple merit scholarships as a physics major at the University of Texas at Dallas. He cut an odd figure on campus – a sort of hippie athlete with a bright scientific mind. He had a swimmer's build, strong legs and shoulders, and a fondness for climbing trees. When outside, he went around barefoot; half the time he didn't wear shoes in class, either. Nevertheless, he soon established himself as one of the smartest guys in the program. A few other students had the edge in pure math, a former classmate recalls, but Ross 'could definitely hold his own'. With coauthors, he published papers on solar cell engineering. These papers had titles like 'Multilayer Encapsulation of Flexible Organic Photovoltaic Devices', or 'Temperature and Time Dependence of Heat Treatment of RR-P3HT/PCBM Solar Cell';

they were published in peer-reviewed scientific journals such as *Synthetic Metals*, which bills itself as 'the journal of electronic polymers and electronic molecular metals', and whose purview includes carbon nanotubes. In one instance, he was the lead author on a paper showing a technique to double photocurrent and significantly increase solar cell efficiency. He seemed to have a bright future as a research scientist. Classmates remember his devouring intellect. He was interested in everything.

It was in graduate school that a shift took place in the geometry of his vision. Even while pursuing a master's degree in materials science and engineering at Pennsylvania State University – a program ranked eighth in the nation – under a prestigious research award, he began educating himself in monetary theory, economics, and political philosophy. In these studies he was walking in the footsteps of distinguished, albeit fictional men. A dual education in physics and philosophy is the program Ayn Rand prescribed for her heroes in *Atlas Shrugged*.

Former UT Dallas classmates don't recall Ross as having a strong political bent. But if the seeds of libertarianism had been latent in him before, they now burst into full flower. He wore regularly to class a T-shirt promoting Ron Paul, the Republican representative from Texas who was running for president, whom he considered 'very insightful and wise'. He uploaded a video to YouTube in April 2007 – a response to Mitt Romney's presidential campaign question, 'What do you believe is America's single greatest challenge?' – advocating that the US pull out of the United Nations. He planned to organize in the fall of 2007 a movie and seminar series called 'The Truth About Money', which would serve for Penn State students as a kind of consciousness-raising about government monetary policy. He debated for the College Libertarians, decrying America's 'massively regulated health care system' and pushing for deregulation.

When Paul, a libertarian firebrand, was scheduled to speak at Penn State on 11 April 2008 – after more than a year of requests from the College Libertarians – Ross looked forward eagerly to a packed house. 'There's a lot to learn from him and his message of what it means to be a US citizen and what it means to be a free individual,' he said.[4]

Ross had been a seeker his whole adult life, had been searching – through drugs, through Eastern philosophy – for a unified theory of human action, a guiding principle for his life. 'For years I was frustrated and defeated by what seemed to be insurmountable barriers between the world today and the world I wanted,' he later told Silk Road users. 'I searched long and hard for the truth about what is right and wrong and good for humanity. I argued with, learned from, and read the works of brilliant people in search of the truth. It's a damn hard thing to do, too, with all of the misinformation and distractions in the sea of opinion we live in.'

Only when he encountered the works of Ludwig von Mises, Murray Rothbard, and other giants of the Austrian School of economics – the same authors who had affected Roger Ver so powerfully – did Ross feel as if he had arrived on terra firma. He joined the Austrian Economic Society at Penn State and, with other student members, took a trip to Auburn, Alabama, home of the Ludwig von Mises Institute,[5] whose namesake had done more than anyone else both to pioneer a rigorous school of economic analysis championing free markets and, decades later, to revitalize it when it lay on its death bed, presenting a spirited and systematic defense of laissez-faire capitalism as against the New Deal economics then in vogue in the United States. Government intervention in the free market, even as expressed in the relatively moderate measures taken by Western liberal democracies, Mises argued, hampers economic progress; moreover, such interventionism can never lead to a stable society, for each intervention has unexpected negative consequences which inevitably lead to a public demand for further government intrusion into the economy – and so the bidding and forbidding of economic actors goes on, ad infinitum. In this way, for instance, the housing bubble of the 2000s was inflated in part by the US government providing strong incentives for banks to give loans to subprime lenders who later defaulted on their mortgages. The government's actions were meant to curb supposedly discriminatory lending practices that kept minorities from owning homes.[6] When the new policies collided with greedy lenders, irresponsible borrowers, reckless investors, and other bad actors, the following credit crunch and financial crisis provoked, in turn, a new outcry, louder and more urgent, for more government intervention to save a failing system. So it goes. And then, too, Mises – who had fled Austria for Switzerland at the rise of National Socialism, and then subsequently abandoned Switzerland for the US when his presence there, with German troops practically at his door, became too fraught – remained acutely aware even in his newly adopted country of the state's iron fist, no matter how velvety its glove. 'It is important to remember that government interference always means either violent action or the threat of such action,' he wrote. 'Government is in the last resort the employment of armed men, of policemen, gendarmes, soldiers, prison guards, and hangmen. The essential feature of government is the enforcement of its decrees by beating, killing, and imprisoning. Those who are asking for more government interference are asking ultimately for more compulsion and less freedom.'[7] Far better, he thought, to have free individuals interacting peacefully and voluntarily as they see fit than to have the state compelling people to behave otherwise.

The Austrian School has its fair share of critics, many of whom are concerned less with any errors in its analysis than with the unpopular policies to which its analysis leads. When Mises's magnum opus, *Human Action*, was published in English, one reviewer sneered that the book's author 'sets up Capitalism as a god, which it is sinful to touch'. Nevertheless, the effect upon Ross Ulbricht of exposure to the ideals of classical liberalism – the veneration of private property rights and individual freedom alongside a commitment to limited government, rather than the top-heavy social welfare state now standard in Western countries – was incalculable. The ideas set forth by Mises, his predecessors, and those he inspired, including Rothbard and Friedrich Hayek, who won the Nobel Prize for Economics in 1974, reappeared in the manifestos of Silk Road's webmaster. He later wrote on the Silk Road forums:

From their works, I understood the mechanics of liberty and the effects of tyranny. But such vision was a curse. Everywhere I looked I saw the State, and the horrible withering effects it had on the human spirit . . . But I also saw free spirits trying to break free of their chains, doing everything they could to serve their fellow man and provide for themselves and their loved ones. I saw the magical and powerful wealth-creating effect of the market, the way it fostered cooperation, civility, and tolerance. How it made trading partners out of strangers or even enemies. How it coordinates the actions of every person on the planet in ways too complex for any one mind to fathom to produce an overflowing abundance of wealth, where nothing is wasted and where power and responsibility are directed to those most deserving and able.

Ross had discovered an economic philosophy that hit him with the force of a religious conversion. He began to dream of a world in which every man and woman is a kind of unflagged vessel in international waters, sailing where they please, answering to no external authority. In fact, so preoccupied was he with his independent studies that he flunked his Ph.D candidacy exam. The failure weighed on him, a rare disappointment. Had he only passed the exam, Silk Road might never have existed; an undiscovered country of cybercrime might never have risen up to vex the governments of the world. Everything might have been different.

The summer before, he had spoken confidently to friends and family of his 'passionate pursuit of scientific discovery and exploration', but now he'd come to see that his love for science was being gradually supplanted by a growing attraction to commerce. And he wasn't content to sit on the sidelines. 'Beyond analysis of the markets I also love jumping in and participating,' he wrote in June 2008. 'There are few better feelings than profiting from free exchange with others.' What he wanted now was to make money – and plenty of it.

Back in Austin after earning his master's degree, having abandoned his plan to seek a doctorate, Ross taught himself to code. In a journal later discovered on his laptop, in which he documented his progress creating and running Silk Road, he expressed confidence that his black market would one day 'become a phenomenon, and at least one person will tell me about it, unknowing that I was its creator'. Eventually, to interact with Silk Road users, he would adopt the name Dread Pirate Roberts, taking it from *The Princess Bride*. Eighteenth-century pirates had New Providence in the Bahamas for a home base; Ross Ulbricht would have a rogue nation of his own.

Silk Road opened its doors in January 2011. The first mention of the black market anywhere online, dated 27 January, was made on the discussion forum of Shroomery, a website dedicated to psychoactive mushrooms, by a poster using the screen name 'altoid'. This was Ross Ulbricht, posing as a curious bystander:

> I came across this website called Silk Road. It's a Tor hidden service that claims to allow you to buy and sell anything online anonymously. I'm thinking of buying off it, but wanted to see if anyone here had heard of it and could recommend it.
>
> I found it through silkroad420.wordpress.com, which, if you have a tor browser, directs you to the real site at http://tydgccykixpbu6uz.onion.
>
> Let me know what you think . . .

It was the only post 'altoid' would ever make on Shroomery, though two days later, on 29 January, the same screen name popped up on bitcointalk.org, the very online forum that Roger Ver would begin reading voraciously in early February. (Silk Road's WordPress web domain was registered on 23 January, the 'altoid' Shroomery account four days later, and the 'altoid' Bitcoin forum account two days after that.) On a discussion thread that posed, as a kind of libertarian thought experiment, the idea of a Bitcoin-accepting online heroin store, Ross responded exuberantly, praising the 'great ideas' of his fellow forum members and asking whether any of them had yet seen Silk Road, which functioned, he said, 'kind of like an anonymous Amazon.com' and which, though it lacked heroin, had plenty of other drugs for sale. At the time, these consisted of marijuana, magic mushrooms, and MDMA. To get things started, Ross had cultivated psilocybin mushrooms of his own and sold them to the site's first customers. By the time his ten pounds of shrooms were gone, other vendors had set up shop.

Soon there was a full-fledged community of users, buying and selling heroin, cocaine, methamphetamines, marijuana, and other controlled substances with the casualness and, usually, the confidence of shoppers on eBay and Amazon.

Years later, a Bitcoin forum user with the screen name Timo Y, who had been a member of the forum since June 2010, reflected on the landscape in which such a radical discussion was possible. 'Back then this forum was a more innocent place, full of dreamers discussing what at the time felt like improbable scenarios out of a William Gibson novel. I was really taken by surprise how soon this fantasy became reality, how soon this whole Bitcoin experiment became serious fucking business.'

Silk Road made it serious business. Before the black market launched, opening the floodgates to broad acceptance of digital currency in underground commerce, there was very little on which anyone could spend their bitcoins. On 22 May 2010, a twenty-something software programmer in Florida named Laszlo Hanyecz convinced someone in the United Kingdom to accept ten thousand bitcoins – then worth about 0.003 cents apiece – in exchange for two Papa John's pizzas ordered over the Internet. It was, as far as anyone could tell, the first real-world transaction with bitcoins. Exactly three and a half years later, the bitcoins Hanyecz had mined and sold to satisfy a pizza craving would be worth $7.4 million. 'It wasn't like bitcoins had any value back then, so the idea of trading them for a pizza was incredibly cool,' he says. 'No one knew it was going to get so big.'[8]

Silk Road, by all indications, is what caused Bitcoin to grow big. Ross Ulbricht repurposed what was until then a benign experiment, a utopian invention with scarcely any real-world value, and turned it into the world's first true black market currency. Among early users and experts alike there is a consensus of opinion. Price charts for the Mt. Gox exchange in early 2011 – the only Bitcoin exchange in existence at this time – show a dramatic correlation: on 28 January, the day before Ross announced Silk Road on the Bitcoin forums, the price stood at $0.43; by 31 January it had spiked to more than twice that, and on 9 February it broke $1.00, a sustained and unprecedented rise that lasted for days. After 16 April, the price never again fell below $1.00 during normal market activity.

Then, on 10 May, on the back of what appeared to be some big shot's purchase of a single $50,000 block of bitcoins, the digital currency suddenly shot up to $5.99, sending shockwaves through the tiny community of traders. 'I remember the day we creamed our collective pants about $1 parity,' a Bitcoin forum user wrote.

Roger Ver had a theory: 'Maybe a drug kingpin decided to start using Bitcoin.' The idea didn't trouble him. Although he abhorred the violence of the drug trade, he believed unequivocally in the sovereignty of the individual, and consequently in one's right to put whatever one wanted into one's body, however exotic or potentially harmful, freedom being more important than the desire of others to watch over and enforce one's well-being. The real menaces to society, he thought, as he told multiple media outlets, using the same words each time, were not drug dealers but rather 'the police, judges, and jail guards, who lock people in cages for ingesting substances without the permission of strangers'. More than half the inmates he'd met at Lompoc had been imprisoned for what he saw as victimless crimes.

Even so, there were lines Roger wouldn't cross. Although he later supported Ross Ulbricht, he was no crypto-anarchist; he didn't want to see websites selling child porn and murder for hire – the logical endpoint, it would seem, of Ross's rogue market.[9]

Ross, for his part, was smart enough to see that the underground economy, unlike any regulated industry, offered a chance for Bitcoin to displace other forms of payment – and that from this illicit foundation, or original sin, digital currency could one day prove its value in the wider world. 'There are niche uses for Bitcoin that make it superior to other payment methods, many of which I am sure are undiscovered at this point,' he mused less than four months after Silk Road launched. 'Maybe someday it will become stable, widely accepted . . . but the seed of this economy will come from Bitcoin's edge over other currencies in niche areas.'

Any website that grew to prominence in the niche area he had in mind, however, would be sure to draw unwanted attention from law enforcement. It would be a sitting duck unless it could keep hidden the identities and locations of its administrator, its host server, and its users. No ordinary website would do.

He was in luck. Less than a decade earlier, computer scientists at the US Naval Research Laboratory had released the first version of a piece of software enabling people to surf the Internet anonymously. The three-man team – Roger Dingledine, Nick Mathewson, and Paul Syverson – had been doing work on 'onion routing', a method of disguising the origin of a user's web traffic by diverting it through multiple servers, much as a getaway car will swerve through back streets in order to shake a tail. Their software, TOR, which stood for The Onion Router, was a breakthrough. (The name was later simplified to Tor.) It was originally intended for use by US military and intelligence personnel, who have their reasons for wanting to operate under a cloak of secrecy. But in 2004, perhaps realizing that anonymizing software used only by agents of the US government would be a dead giveaway that anyone using it – a CIA field operative, for example – was, in fact, a US government agent, the Naval Research Laboratory open-sourced the Tor software. 'If you have a system that's only a Navy system, anything popping out of it is obviously from the Navy,' Syverson later explained. 'You need to have a network that carries traffic for other people as well.'[10]

Let's say you want to access Twitter on your computer. Ordinarily, when you punch 'twitter.com' into the address bar of your web browser, your computer will connect through your ISP directly to the website. Tor is different. Tor routes your traffic through three hubs, or relays, in sequential order, before it arrives at the website, leaving your ISP in the dark about where you are going and your destination ignorant of who you are. Your ISP knows only that you are using Tor; the first relay learns your true identity, because your computer is making a direct connection to it, but doesn't know you are going to twitter.com; the second relay, ignorant of both your identity and your goal, knows only that someone is using Tor to do something; the third relay knows only that someone is using Tor to visit twitter.com. None of the relays has the complete picture, thus shielding your activity from prying eyes. This is possible because Tor takes your data, which can be thought of as the message 'I want to visit twitter.com,' and wraps it in three layers of encryption. The outermost layer of encryption can be peeled off by the first node, or relay, the second layer by the second node, and the third layer by the third node, like an onion.

By means of encryption and proxy servers, in other words, Tor enveloped in a cloud of unknowing all web traffic passing over its network, so that it was impossible, observing the traffic going in, to figure out where it was going, and equally impossible, watching the traffic coming out, to know whose it was and where that person was located. Further obfuscating matters – much to the benefit of Tor users – was the diverse range of people who came to rely on the software, from political dissidents enduring repressive regimes to consumers safeguarding their buying habits from marketers, as well as the sheer number who were online at any given time. By November 2007, three years after the Naval Research Laboratory released Tor into the wild, the anonymizing software had 200,000 daily concurrent users; seven years later, its popularity had grown by more than an order of magnitude to 2.3 million – and it had at times been greater still. All of this made it safer to use Tor, for had it been used only by black marketeers then its use alone would be incriminating evidence. But Tor was user-friendly enough to attract a wide range of people across the globe. 'There have always been various solutions to anonymize either your location or what you're doing online or both,' says Runa Sandvik, a former Tor developer. 'But the biggest difference in the past couple of years is how usable these tools are.'

Ross Ulbricht made use of Tor not only to mask his own identity but also to hide his website. From the beginning, Silk Road was accessible only through the Tor network. Its complicated web address – initially http://tydgccykixpbu6uz.onion – took you nowhere if you were browsing the Internet without Tor's anonymizing software. All hidden service web addresses culminate in .onion, which, unlike .com or .org or any ordinary top-level web domain, only exists when you use Tor, much as a corporate intranet is accessible only to people in that organization. Tor provides a service that allows you to run a hidden website, but you have to set up and configure and build that site just like you would any other. Hence Ross Ulbricht's need for web development skills. (It is not accurate to say, as so many news reports have done, that a hidden site like Silk Road is hosted *on* the Tor network or in any way hosted *by* Tor itself. Tor is simply the means of accessing what would otherwise be an inaccessible island.) The combination of Tor and Bitcoin made Silk Road possible.

Once on Silk Road, users confronted a familiar eBay-style interface. Once you found a listing for what you wanted, you would add it to your shopping cart, and initiate the checkout process. There were legal goods and services for sale on Silk Road, but illegal drugs were by far the most popular merchandise. The Drugs category was subdivided into Cannabis (further subdivided into Weed, Hash, and Seeds); Ecstasy; Dissociatives; Psychedelics; Opiates; Stimulants; and the enticingly named Other. Thanks to Silk Road, there was no longer any need for the proverbial back-alley drug deal; buyers and sellers could conduct their business without ever knowing each other's names or meeting face-to-face. Within months of the site opening, weed, Ecstasy, LSD, and heroin were all available. But whoever was running Silk Road obviously had principles; there were some items they refused to allow in their marketplace. Among them were 'anything [whose] purpose is to harm or defraud, such as stolen credit cards, assassinations, and weapons of mass destruction'.[11] Soon enough, most of these rules would be broken; stolen credit card numbers, counterfeit money, hacking tools, and fake IDs all showed up for sale. But purveyors of loose Russian nukes would have to go elsewhere.

Ross Ulbricht had described his marketplace as an anonymous Amazon.com, but that wasn't quite accurate. Silk Road, unlike

Amazon and other web stores, did not sell anything directly. It wasn't an online retailer. It was more like Craigslist or eBay, providing a place for buyers and sellers to meet each other. Nicolas Christin, a researcher at Carnegie Mellon, noted the major difference between Silk Road and its aboveboard brethren: 'Silk Road focuses on ensuring, as much as possible, anonymity of both buyers and sellers.' That in itself isn't illegal. And the owner of a website generally is not liable for what its users do, if the website is merely a space in which they do it rather than a criminal enterprise itself, just as landlords generally are not liable for illegal conduct by their tenants. Later, because of this, Ross's lawyer would claim, in a pretrial motion challenging the indictment of his client, that the government had failed to allege satisfactorily that Ross occupied 'a position of organizer, a supervisory position, or any other position of management' with regard to Silk Road users. Ross may have facilitated criminal activity, in other words, but simply operating Silk Road as a platform for users was not sufficient grounds for prosecuting him under a law aimed at drug kingpins. The lawyer was putting up a good fight on behalf of his client, which in this case meant conveniently ignoring the special nature of Silk Road. On the 'cryptomarket', as this sort of dark web market came to be known, buyers did not pay sellers directly; rather, they paid the marketplace, which took its cut of the proceeds and held the remainder in escrow until the package had arrived safely and the buyer had given the go-ahead to release the funds. This is a very different model from Craigslist, which merely provides a platform for interested parties to make contact about various goods and services, after which they interact directly with each other. Moreover, Craigslist doesn't take a commission on items sold through the site.

And then there are Ross's own words to the Silk Road community when his authority was questioned. 'Whether you like it or not, I am the captain of this ship,' he said. 'You are here voluntarily and if you don't like the rules of the game, or you don't trust your captain, you can get off the boat.' He signed off another message as 'Silk Road admin' – short for 'administrator'. In yet another forum post, he went further, telling the website's users, 'I am Silk Road, the market, the person, the enterprise, everything.'

Nor was he entirely right to say that Silk Road was secure. While it was true that Tor, properly configured, would mask the identity of anyone who visited the site, including its administrator, that didn't mean it was impregnable to law enforcement. For one thing, Ross had coded Silk Road 'on a wing and a prayer', as he himself admitted, using 'patchwork' PHP and MySQL that he had learned on the fly. He found himself frequently updating the code to fix security holes. For another, the site by its very design allowed users to upload data, such as pictures of items for sale. Giving users this permission – especially on a site open to the public, as Silk Road was – runs the risk of someone uploading malicious code, such as a PHP script granting backdoor access to your server, allowing an intruder to take control. Or someone could upload malware that would be downloaded by other users and infect their computers. There are ways to guard against these issues, but a self-taught novice programmer like Ross Ulbricht might not think of them. Because any website set up this way might face security problems, says Runa Sandvik, 'at that point you need to stop looking at it as a Tor hidden service website and start looking at it as a normal website.' More ominously, and unbeknown to Ross, the National Security Agency had already been working for years to crack the anonymity of the Tor network.

Further security challenges cropped up when actually making a purchase on Silk Road. The bitcoins spent had to be sourced from somewhere, and that could leave a trail – on the blockchain if nowhere else – which network analysis techniques could discover and potentially trace back to a particular Bitcoin user. 'It is easier to use Tor to just browse the web than it is to use it for shopping of real-world items,' Sandvik says. And there was, of course, the risk for vendors of shipping a physical package containing illegal goods and, for buyers, the double risk of divulging a physical address and taking delivery of such a package. For this reason, Silk Road's vendor guidelines went into great detail about safety measures designed to thwart inspection. Vacuum sealing would beat drug-sniffing dogs; padded mailer envelopes would prevent the items from being crushed; printed address labels, unlike hand-writing, wouldn't arouse suspicion at a glance. The goal, Ross Ulbricht told sellers, was for their shipments to 'blend in as much as possible with the rest of the mail stream'.

Despite these risks, in the community that grew up around the marketplace a general feeling of invincibility prevailed. In all likelihood, most Silk Road users, whether they came to the site looking for banned books, for porn, or for a fix, had not consid-ered all the possible weak links in the chain. 'They thought that just because they were using Tor and Bitcoin they were anonymous and wouldn't get caught,' Sandvik says. And for a long time it worked, remaining a strictly word-of-mouth phenomenon even as the market grew to hundreds of users.

'Everyone was sophisticated' in the early days, a Silk Road money launderer with the screen name StExo later recalled. 'Everyone was safe, everyone was cautious. There were no [how-to] guides because the only people who could access such things gener-ally were the very security-aware people.'[12]

On the Bitcoin forum, Ross Ulbricht began playing prognos-ticator with the digital currency's price even as his own market influenced its rise. 'My bet is on long-term appreciation of bitcoins, but don't expect the path to be a straight line,' he warned in March. By the end of April, with the price at $2.59, he had concluded, using Elliott Wave Theory – a way of predicting stock market trends – that the price rally which had seen Bitcoin rise above $1.00 again earlier that month would end at $4.54. He planned to sell his entire hoard at $4.25, he said, and would buy back in 'at around parity' – when a single bitcoin was once again worth no more than a single US dollar. On 10 May, the price opened at $3.80 and quickly rose to $4.25, filling Ross's sell order and earning him four times his initial investment, but then, in defiance of his prediction, continued its upward momentum, hitting $5.99 by day's end. Three days later, with the price spiking to $8.45, he remained convinced that a bear market was imminent.

But then something occurred which ruined forever both his price predictions and his underground market's low profile. Gawker, a media website that has made a business model out of straddling the line between gossip rag and legitimate news outlet, published on 1 June 2011 an exposé of Silk Road. Detailing the site's wide selection of drugs and simple e-commerce interface, the Gawker writer managed simultaneously to make the black market sound like 'something from a cyberpunk novel' and a shopping experience as safe and familiar as buying books from Amazon. Crucially, he provided the website's URL and mentioned the need to use Tor in order to access it. The explosive article even quoted from an email exchange with Silk Road's administrator – Ross Ulbricht, in his guise as 'Silk Road', not yet known as Dread Pirate Roberts. Strange as it seems for an unapologetic criminal to consent to an interview, Ross took the opportunity to advocate for what Samuel Edward Konkin- III, a radical left-wing libertarian who sought the total abolition of the state, and whose ideas had a tremendous influence on Ross and other early Bitcoiners, called 'counter-economics' – a strategy of bypassing the state in order to undermine its power, which derives ultimately from tax and tariff revenues. Ross's words in the Gawker interview were right out of Konkin's playbook. 'Stop funding the state with your tax dollars,' he said, 'and direct your productive energies into the black market.'

The Gawker article touched off a firestorm of media attention, culminating on 5 June in a press conference held by Senator Charles Schumer, a Democrat from New York. Schumer condemned Silk Road as 'the most brazen attempt to peddle drugs online that we have ever seen' and called on the US government to shut it down. The DEA, he said, was aware of the site, but he declined to confirm whether or not an investigation was already underway.

For now, Ross trusted in his security protocols, in the privacy afforded by Bitcoin and the Tor network, to keep him out of the hands of law enforcement. Silk Road carried on with business as usual – though now, thanks to an influx of new users brought by the Gawker article, on a much larger scale. Ross had made about $100,000 so far from Silk Road commissions, and his marketplace was now pulling in more than $20,000 a month.

So when Mt. Gox suffered its catastrophic hack, a newly flush Ross was happy to take advantage. The month before, he'd cashed out his bitcoins at $8.50, making a tidy profit. By 6 June the price had jumped even higher, to about $18.50, but he wasn't worried that he'd missed the rocket ship. He planned to buy back in when the price crashed to $1.00 – as he anticipated – 'after Bitcoin has been made illegal and everyone thinks it's doomed'. He set up a $25,000 buy order on Mt. Gox, priced at $1.00 per bitcoin.

He couldn't have known how soon he would get his wish. As the hacker initiated a massive sell-off, driving the price into the floor, Ross's standing order, which he'd since lowered to $22,000, was filled – giving him a digital currency stash worth $371,580 based on the day's opening price. Already, thanks to the speculative frenzy surrounding the fire sale, the price had rebounded from a single penny to about $10. 'Made about $200,000 assuming bitcoins stay where they are around $10', Ross told his fellow Bitcoiners. 'Crazy shit'. He tried to transfer his ill-gotten gains out of Mt. Gox into an electronic wallet, but he ran into the exchange's daily withdrawal limit – the same obstacle the hacker had sought to overcome. He managed to get eighty bitcoins out, essentially stealing money from the exchange. It was ironic that while Roger Ver was working overtime to get Mt. Gox back online, his ostensible brother-in-arms, a man to whose legal defense he would later contribute more than $100,000, was exploiting the hack for his own personal gain. 'Fingers crossed I can get the rest when the site comes back,' Ross wrote. But it was not to be. With Mt. Gox rolling back all the post-crash trades, Ross's windfall disappeared. 'I don't think I'm a millionaire . . . yet,' he concluded. But he would not have long to wait. Silk Road was gaining traction.

As innovative as the cryptomarket was, it was riding the leading edge of a global trend. After the financial crisis of 2008 and the global recession that followed, black market activity spiked around the world. A simple way to think about this shadow economy, or 'informal economy', is that it consists of every transaction that is invisible to government. It is called informal because it is unregulated by the state – and because such trade has been taking place since time immemorial, since long before there were such things as federal tax agencies. Two neighboring farmers who trade a basket of ripe tomatoes for a dozen free-range eggs, without evaluating the dollar value of those goods and declaring it on their taxes, are participating in the informal economy. So is the proverbial little girl selling lemonade in the summer, insofar as neither she nor her parents report the lemonade stand's earnings or pay income tax on the cash she receives from thirsty neighbors. By the fall of 2011, author Robert Neuwirth – using economic data from the year 2003 compiled by Friedrich Schneider, an economist at Johannes Kepler University in Austria – had pegged the value of the global black market at $10 trillion. An article he wrote for *Foreign Policy* dubbed it 'the world's fastest growing economy – and its future'. And no wonder: at $10 trillion, the black market would be larger than the official gross domestic product of every country on the planet except for the United States.[13] (Apart from its literary provenance, Ross's underground moniker, Dread Pirate Roberts, was a fitting identity for a time when enterprising souls in the developing world were lifting themselves out of poverty by selling bootleg DVDs.) But even Schneider's figures may have yielded a lowball estimate. They did not include money earned from babysitting, for instance, nor any other aspect of the 'informal household economy'. Schneider also tried to eliminate from his projections any money resulting from crimes such as robbery and drug dealing. Add in the earnings from these activities, and the global black market – considered as a whole – becomes the largest economy in the world.

Law enforcement agencies had been trying for years, and with limited success, to root out the less savory aspects of Internet culture. As early as 1997, websites dedicated to discussing how to make illegal drugs and where to procure the chemicals and equipment necessary to their manufacture – if not to the outright buying and selling of banned substances – existed in plain sight on the surface Web. And these sites arose from even earlier Usenet groups in the days before the World Wide Web.[14] Despite the inherent difficulty, enough people were interested in such topics, whether driven by idle curiosity or criminal need, to keep the conversation going. Although the FBI eventually busted the Web's most prominent MDMA cookbook author, shut down his chemical company in Texas, which had supplied other cooks with precursors, and broke up various drug rings that had learned from him, websites dedicated to clandestine chemistry remained active.[15]

Silk Road blew digital drug culture wide open. It was different from anything that had come before, not only quantitatively – 'more brazen than anything else by light-years', as Senator Schumer said – but qualitatively. Just as the number of enthusiasts who labor over hand-built cars will always be orders of magnitude smaller than the total number of car owners in the world, so the number of potential drug buyers is exponentially larger than the number of kitchen chemists willing to take the toil and trouble to cook up their own illicit substances. Fervent as the earlier online drug communities had been, Silk Road was unprecedented in its reach and scope – as unprecedented, in its way, as Bitcoin was in the realm of currencies and commodities. When Ross himself addressed this topic, he tended to be thoughtful one moment and jubilant the next. 'How many niches have yet to be filled in the world of anonymous online markets?' he wondered, before exulting, 'The opportunity to prosper and take part in a revolution of epic proportions is at our fingertips!'

By the end of November 2011 there were 220 active sellers with public listings on Silk Road. By early February 2012 there would be 281 sellers, and by late July, 564. Most sellers vanished within three months of joining the site, but that didn't mean they were truly gone. It was a common practice for vendors – once they had established a good reputation and a solid customer base – to go into stealth mode. This meant they vanished from the public marketplace; only people with the exact web address of the seller's page – trusted customers – could then make purchases. Sellers with public pages could also create individual stealth listings for certain customers, for example if they wanted to reward loyalty with discounted merchandise, or if they got their hands on a batch of premium product for a discerning connoisseur. Stealth mode was yet another way for Silk Road users to evade detection by law enforcement. By the fall of 2011 it was clear, as Monica Barrett, a professor at the National Drug Research Institute of Curtin University in Australia, wrote in the academic journal *Addiction*, that Silk Road had 'revolutionized how the Internet can be used to source drugs'.

As customers flocked to the illicit market, their need for bitcoins drove up the price. Like a hot stock, it couldn't stay under the radar for long. Other people began to see how well it worked and took an interest in it – first rebel entrepreneurs, like Roger Ver, and then, in time, serious investors and technologists, people who once would have ignored it or turned up their noses at it, as some early journalists did – those few who were aware of it at all – dismissing it as a plaything for hackers, a kind of Monopoly money for the political fringe. It wouldn't be long before Silicon Valley tried to lay claim to the fledgling technology.

And fledgling it was. Even as it began to gain ground beyond drug peddlers and anarchists, the digital currency remained diffi-cult to obtain; the mechanics of storing and spending it, while appealing to techno-geeks, were offputting to average consumers. Bitcoin needed more than champions now. It needed better infra-structure. It needed somebody who understood its usefulness to make it easier to use.

Chapter 3

THE GRAY HAT

The only way to deal with an unfree world is to become so absolutely free that your very existence is an act of rebellion.

– Albert Camus

Even after he had gone legitimate as an entrepreneur, Charlie Shrem still liked to think of himself as a hacker. He felt he had earned the designation. As a high school freshman he had hacked, so he claimed, into a German airport and taken control of more than a dozen security cameras; later, he'd broken into the computer system of the University of Ghana, a transgression he had followed up with a lengthy email alerting the university to the hole in its security. In the world of computer security, there are 'black hat' hackers, who break into other people's systems for malicious reasons – to steal identities or information or to vandalize them – and there are 'white hat' hackers, who hire themselves out to companies to probe for weaknesses in their security. White hats have a license to hack, in other words, and some of them are paid handsomely to do things that would otherwise be criminal offenses. Charlie, too much of a rebel to be a white hat, and not malevolent enough to be a black hat, lived in the gray zone between these absolutes; if he hacked without permission, he hacked also without malice, and, as with the University of Ghana, he often tipped off his targets to what he had done and how he had done it, making himself a sort of unpaid, *ex post facto* white hat. The victims of his intrusions were generally so grateful for his help, he says, that they didn't pursue legal action.

Online, in the days when he was active in hacker communities, he was known as Yankee, and he ran with a crew led by a young Norwegian named Christer Mustvedt, who went by the handle Casi. Scrawny teenagers both, Christer and Charlie became fast friends. In his Casi persona, Christer presided over a hacker forum with more than ten thousand active members – originally called ZerO-Day, then CasiHacks, and later, as it went through a series of takedowns and relaunches, CyberXtreme, TheUnkn0wn, and XtremeRoot – which, along with the social draw of its discussion boards, offered up to its members stolen credit cards, Trojans and other malware, pornography, hacking tools, tips and tricks of the trade, and pirated movies and television shows. Charlie was drawn in by the excitement, the untrammeled freedom of it all. Like many teenagers, he sought online what he had not found in the real world: a place where he belonged. 'I had been learning how to code, and I was the only one of my friends who knew even what coding was,' he says. 'I wanted a place where I could make friends and talk to people about it.' He couldn't share his intellectual passion – for that is what it was – with his real-world friends. 'What are you talking about, Charlie?' they would say. 'Come play basketball.' But on the hacker forums, and in online chat rooms, 'I was a somebody. I was Yankee.'

What this meant was that Charlie's basement apartment in his parents' 2,500-square-foot house in Sheepshead Bay, a heavily Russian and Jewish neighborhood in deep Brooklyn, opened out, through his computer screen, into a shadow world his parents knew nothing about, a world in which he was both notorious and respected. Like many of his real-world friends, he attended the Yeshivah of Flatbush, an academically demanding private day school for Orthodox Jews. But online, Zionist that he was, he was waging pitched battles with Pakistani hackers; he was fending off incursions from hackers belonging to other forums. In 2009, MakeUseOf, a prominent technology blog, listed CyberXtreme as

No. 1 among the 'top five websites to learn how to hack like a pro'. There was constant competition among online hacker communities, and Charlie, as the administrator Yankee, played a prominent role in CyberXtreme's preeminence.

By the end of his teenage years, that was in the past. But he remained drawn to the underbelly of things, the fringe, where the action was. That was how he first heard about Bitcoin. In one version of the story, he was a member of the cryptography mailing list on which Satoshi Nakamoto announced his invention; in an interview, he recalled seeing Satoshi's email and thinking, 'What the fuck is this guy talking about? This is stupid bullshit, it's not going to do anything.'[1] But then again, he says, he might first have come across the word 'Bitcoin' on a hacker forum he frequented. Memory is an uncertain mount to ride at the best of times, and indeed, the reporter to whom he related the mailing list story gave the year of this incident as 2010, not 2008, the year when Satoshi actually introduced Bitcoin.

But what is undeniable, beyond memory's power to distort, is that by early June 2011 Charlie had become seriously interested in the digital currency. To start accumulating bitcoins, he sent a domestic ING wire transfer to TradeHill, a new Bitcoin exchange that had set itself up as a competitor to Mt. Gox. He began hawking JetBlue vouchers and airline miles in exchange for coins. He was twenty-one years old and already an entrepreneur, cocky, puffed up with confidence from a string of early successes; a hacker emeritus who, in registering a Bitcoin forum account, retained his old handle, Yankee. That June, Silk Road was in the news. 'Damn! These news guys gotta stop writing about Silk Road,' he wrote after one story. 'It's attracting too much attention to it. If it closed, how am I gonna get my cookies??'

Much of his confidence he had gained during high school, both in and out of the classroom. And yet Charlie almost hadn't made the cut for Flatbush. At fourteen years old he was five foot two, lacking in confidence, and with no special computer skills, he says, 'except to turn it on and go onto AOL'. In fact, he had shown no special aptitudes whatsover, and didn't much care for school. 'I was a small kid who was scared to make new friends or try new things,' he said later. Almost in despair, he turned to computers as a pastime. 'I needed an outlet for my energy,' he said, 'so I started to play around with technology and began taking in information like a vacuum cleaner on a dirty rug. I would sit for hours and experiment on the computer, learning new things.' A hitherto unguessed talent unfolded. Four months later, he found himself the watching eye behind those airport security cameras. He became Yankee.

At a rabbi's urging, he joined the school's audiovisual club. He soon became a key figure in student life, using his newfound computer skills to design school publications and create videos. In his free time he ran a computer repair business. 'I had a company called Epiphany Design and Production. I don't even know where I came up with the name,' he told the reporter. 'I just liked the word "epiphany". What it was, was me riding on my bike to fix people's computers.' He charged $50 an hour. People were willing to pay, as it turned out, for the services of a skinny, fast-talking Jewish kid with a knack for computers. 'It was easy money,' he said. 'Easy money.'[2] He went from being a shy, scared kid to a pint-sized dynamo. And the more he achieved, the more he wanted to accomplish.

In early 2009, while attending Brooklyn College, part of the City University of New York system, Charlie started a company called Daily Checkout. In doing so, he joined a fleeting craze for daily deals websites – online marketplaces offering special discounts to customers, often on products and services at local businesses. Groupon, which would become the largest of them, had launched in Chicago in November 2008. Daily Checkout provided deeply discounted electronics, and Charlie took to his duties as marketing director with eccentric flair; once, to promote a two-gigabyte memory card, used for storing digital photos, he wrote a kind of poem:

> Thank you, Daily Checkout,
> For this cheap 2 GB SD card,
> Now my wife won't flip out,
> Because of the pics I had to discard.

He was still leading a double life as Yankee, but his hacking days were almost at an end. As time can ripen, so visibly it can rot; even as CyberXtreme became embroiled in one war after another, Charlie began to lose interest in the cause. 'People started hacking us, and defacing our website, and stealing our domain names, and in retaliation we would have to hack them back,' he says. 'It's a dangerous spiral to go down . . . And it got a little scary, but also it just became a little pointless.' Worse, he recalls, his beloved gray hat forum began to go black: some users got into bed with the hacktivist collective Anonymous. Charlie took a hard look at things. *I can't be involved in this anymore,* he realized, *because I have a startup now. I can't get myself into trouble doing this crap.* Ultimately, he cared more about his business. When he was younger, 'it was just dabbling, it was fun,' but now he had something to lose.

Christer Mustvedt, for his part, doesn't remember the conflicts with other hackers as being so serious, though he does attest to taking down the websites of three other groups who claimed to be at war with CyberXtreme. Nor does he recall any of his site's members helping Anonymous. As for the darkening of the forum, his policy always was to make room for all kinds of hackers, he says, so long as they could walk the walk. 'We were not gray, not white, not black . . . If people would ask about the color of the hat, I'd tell them that we are the friggin' rainbow hat.' Regardless, Charlie Shrem wanted to go legit. He had to make a choice. In the end, he walked away from CyberXtreme.

By early 2011, however, he was growing bored with Daily Checkout. Bitcoin became his new obsession. He started lurking on the Bitcoin forums, reading online posts by Satoshi and others. In June 2011, he came across a post by a twenty-three-year-old Welsh coder named Gareth Nelson, who was looking for people to invest in a proposed web service that would speed up the process of depositing money into Bitcoin exchanges. At the time, there were a small number of methods – bank wire transfers foremost among them – for getting funds into your account at Mt. Gox. But all of them were slow. The rising price of Bitcoin had created a sudden demand for rapid money transfers into and out of the system. With the price soaring, it was beginning to be traded like a real currency; people wanted to buy in before it peaked and cash out before it fell. Having to wait days for wire transfers to clear was maddening.

It was inevitable, under these conditions, that someone would step in to provide financial services. Gareth, who lived in the United Kingdom, published his call to action in the early morning of 13 June. For Charlie, in New York, it was just past midnight. The day before, Mt. Gox had seen its second-highest trading volume ever, and its highest since October 2010, when bitcoins were worth only $0.09 apiece: 151,194.16 bitcoins, or $2.45 million at the prevailing exchange rate. The opportunity for a company like Gareth's seemed ripe. But he was short on capital. To get started he would need at least $1,000, he wrote. 'Would anyone here be interested?'

Charlie was the first to respond. After some back-and-forth, he asked Gareth to provide more details in a private message. 'I could work with you,' he said. The two young men clicked. Gareth was studying computer science and psychology with the goal of some day working on artificial intelligence. He was impressed by Charlie's entrepreneurial background. Charlie told Gareth that he had resources for hosting the web service and could obtain financing. He also offered to kick in $1,000 to jumpstart the project. 'He came across as focused on more than just the money,' Gareth says. 'I originally was only seeking funding, but Charlie had a whole business vision.' Less than eight hours after Charlie's initial overture, they were partners.

'We decided early on that I was going to make all business-related decisions, and he was going to trust me 100 percent on that, and I was going to trust him on all coding decisions,' Charlie says. He and Gareth didn't talk on the phone; they communicated only through email and chat messages. Gareth – who was hampered by two things, a thick Welsh accent and Asperger syndrome – was more comfortable holding conversations from behind a keyboard; Charlie, accustomed to bonding with hackers whom he knew only by their online identities, didn't mind having a partner whom he'd never met. 'I was used to it already,' he says. 'In fact, I prefer it.'

BitInstant, as his and Gareth's startup was now called, launched on 1 September. Demand for its service was immediate.

The first exchange with which BitInstant partnered was TradeHill, which had been gaining market share from Mt. Gox. In July, TradeHill had fallen out with one of its payment processors, Dwolla, over chargebacks. The exchange had partnered with Dwolla for two reasons: its extremely low transaction fee – only twenty-five cents per transaction – which made it a better choice than its much bigger competitor, PayPal; and a stated policy of never reversing transactions. Reversed transactions, or chargebacks, are a safety net for consumers in an age of unsafe electronic money. They are also the bane of merchants everywhere. When a chargeback is issued, the merchant is placed in the unfortunate position of having given away a product or service for which payment has been retracted. What TradeHill emphatically did not want, and was trying to avoid by partnering with Dwolla, was to wind up losing money on fraudulent purchases of bitcoins on its exchange platform.

But that is exactly what happened. It worked like this: A customer would register online for a Dwolla account and link it to her bank account at, say, Wells Fargo. She would buy perhaps ten bitcoins, which on 15 July were valued at an average of $13.90 each, or $139 total. She would select Dwolla as her method of payment, at which point Dwolla would pull $139 out of her Wells Fargo account. So far, so good. But over time, TradeHill noticed that its internal sales figures didn't match the dollar amount of transactions it had received. There was a large and unexplained shortfall. It became clear that Dwolla was initiating chargebacks – sometimes, according to TradeHill, not until days or even weeks after the completed transactions, and always without notice, making it hard to track with any consistency the amount of money flowing into the exchange.

On 25 July, having failed to resolve the issue, TradeHill stopped using Dwolla, which was like cutting off an arm to save the body. Even then, the bleeding didn't stop: in August, TradeHill would claim later, Dwolla reversed multiple transactions dating from the month before. Having lost tens of thousands of dollars, TradeHill was now operating at a significant loss, and its employees were going without pay. In the preceding two months, the exchange had conducted more than $2 million worth of transactions – including the exchange of bitcoins for dollars and dollars for bitcoins, for which it received a small commission – using Dwolla as an intermediary. It could not do without the revenue from users who wanted to pay with Dwolla, but it also could not allow itself to continue using a payment processor apparently so susceptible to fraud.

The beef between TradeHill and Dwolla provided an opening for BitInstant. 'All the pieces fell together perfectly,' Charlie says. BitInstant would hold two balances – one at TradeHill, the other at Dwolla. These companies weren't cooperating any longer, but BitInstant customers could transfer money from their Dwolla accounts to BitInstant's Dwolla account; in return, BitInstant would send money from its TradeHill account to the customers' TradeHill accounts. Charlie and Gareth were bridging the gap.

Customer orders went into a queue and were handled automatically on a first-come, first-served basis. About the service itself Charlie bragged, 'At most it takes five minutes. Our average is eleven seconds from Dwolla to us.' But the company was rapidly becoming a victim of its own success. Once a customer had made a confirmed deposit, BitInstant immediately credited her TradeHill account, but then – since the banks and payment processors were slow – had to wait hours or days to receive the money that the customer had deposited. Consequently, BitInstant needed to hold a substantial amount of cash in reserve. And soon there simply wasn't enough to go around.

Charlie and Gareth had always planned to work with Mt. Gox, the world's first Bitcoin exchange and still the largest – in fact, originally their service was to be named Fast MtGox Pay – but TradeHill offered them a partnership deal. 'Part of the deal was temporary exclusivity,' Gareth says. To help stay afloat, Charlie made a special arrangement with Jered Kenna, a former Marine and the founder of TradeHill. He would send Jered a screenshot of a BitInstant customer transaction and Jered would immediately replace in the company's TradeHill account the money BitInstant had credited to its customer, so that BitInstant would have enough funds to satisfy its next customer order. 'As soon as I gave him a screenshot, he would credit the transaction,' Charlie says. Even so, things looked desperate. BitInstant needed a real investor, and fast.

When Charlie was eighteen, he'd sold his car, a Volkswagen Eos, to a man named Keith Rosenbloom, who evidently took a liking to the cocky Jewish kid. Rosenbloom, who had bushy eyebrows, hair that was thinning on top, and a calm, no-nonsense demeanor, turned out to be the managing member of CARE Capital Group, a New York investment firm. Charlie met him through Swapalease.com, a website that brokers introductions between people with a car to sell and people who want to take over a lease. Rosenbloom offered to help, Charlie recalls, in the event the younger man were ever leading a company that needed to raise capital. In September 2011, short of money, not knowing where else to turn, Charlie gave him a call.

It began well enough. Rosenbloom told Charlie to drop by CARE's offices at 830 Third Avenue, a 141,000-square-foot glass-and-steel aquarium of an office building in East Midtown. Charlie knew nothing about the workings of an investment firm, except that its founder could write him a big check if he was convincing enough. Above him, as he crossed the lobby of limestone and red Spanish marble, the vaulted ceiling soared up twenty feet. It was a far cry from his basement room in domesticated Brooklyn. Once in conversation with Rosenbloom, however, Charlie struggled to make his case. 'I didn't understand Bitcoin even one percent to what I understand it now,' he says with chagrin, 'so I had a very hard time explaining to him what Bitcoin was. I had a hard time explaining to him what we did.' Says Rosenbloom, 'One of the comments I gave him repeatedly was that it seemed there were no safeguards within his exchange to prevent money laundering.'

Nevertheless, he didn't possess the technical know-how to vet the young entrepreneur's claims himself, Charlie recalls, so he introduced him to other investors who did. One of them had made money in Zynga, the mobile video game company; another had invested in hotel reviews website Oyster.com. 'If you can convince one of them to invest, then I will put up $15,000 of my own money,' Charlie remembers Rosenbloom saying. The young founder did his best to woo them, but none went for it. He was just a kid with a laptop. 'It was a joke,' says Charlie, still stung by the memory. 'I was laughed out. Like, super laughed out. No one believed Bitcoin would succeed.'

With that door shut in his face, he didn't know where to turn. Every day brought the possibility of having to shut down. He was begging TradeHill for more credit, he says, and the exchange was crediting funds to him 'out of thin air'. Gradually, Charlie's parents became aware of their son's financial straits. He was no more able to explain Bitcoin to them than he'd been able to explain it to Keith Rosenbloom. But they were willing to bet on him, even if they didn't know precisely what the stakes were. 'I don't understand any of this,' his mother told him. But she handed him a check for $10,000. 'It was a relief at the time,' Charlie says. 'It helped so much. But we knew it wasn't going to last.'

He kept up a brave face in the Bitcoin community. 'I've been flying around the US meeting investors and individuals high in the finance world,' he told everyone. But the hunt for seed money wasn't the only thing on his mind. The month before, BitInstant had endured two attempted hacks and suffered technical problems that took the website offline for hours at a stretch for several days in a row. The hackers had not succeeded in breaking into the company's databases, but their efforts were still cause for concern. Charlie was no longer a hacker himself, happily playing cyber pranks; he was an entrepreneur with something to lose, and he threw himself into saving it. While the site was down, he made himself available around the clock to process manual transfers for customers, fielding inquiries by email, phone, and online chat.

Somehow the business was thriving. By late November, BitInstant had moved a total of nearly $400,000 for customers. Much of that business represented people who were conducting arbitrage between exchanges – that is, exploiting temporary price differences between, say, TradeHill and Mt. Gox, selling on the former for higher than the price they paid on the latter, or vice versa, in the small window of time before the markets reconciled. Bitcoin, being a thinly traded asset for which price discovery was difficult, afforded many opportunities for arbitrage. Given its risk-free profits, arbitrage isn't exactly noble, but it is an easy way to make money if you can move quickly enough. And it can help iron out the very price disparities it exploits. More and more people were beginning to realize that BitInstant was the fastest method of getting money into their exchange accounts. If you wanted to buy cheap on TradeHill, but didn't have enough funds there, you could send money to BitInstant and BitInstant would credit your account on TradeHill. 'Before we had to implement stricter fraud checks, I got it down from hours [or] days to seconds,' Gareth says proudly. 'Everywhere else using Dwolla did bulk processing. My system did real-time.'

And yet, proud as they were of the technical achievements, neither of BitInstant's founders were certain the company would survive. They were hedging their bets. Charlie was still running Daily Checkout. Gareth was still pursuing his studies.

Their luck changed thanks to a man named Bruce Wagner. Wagner, a prominent early Bitcoin advocate, had organized in New York that summer the first major Bitcoin conference. Charlie had missed it, but now he received an invitation from the open-source software nonprofit Mozilla to speak about digital currencies at an upcoming event, the Open Video Conference. Charlie emailed Wagner about the conference, set to take place over three days in September at New York Law School, mentioning that he'd be a speaker and asking if Wagner wanted to come. Wagner said yes.

Two others joined them: Andrew Lee, the CEO of Private Internet Access, a service that allows users to disguise the geographic origin of their Internet traffic, and Yifu Guo, a Bitcoin buddy of Charlie's who, unbeknown to either of them until that year, had grown up in Charlie's neighborhood in Brooklyn. Lee especially was representative of the type of company Charlie liked to keep.

In an interview two years later, Lee said his goal with PIA was 'to bring back the Wild Wild West that we loved so much', an Internet like that of the 1990s, a free space of learning and exploration with limited oversight. 'I know this sounds corny, but an Internet without boundaries or limitations, in which we can achieve our dreams, is our goal.'[3] Charlie may not have been a gray hat any longer, but he still wanted to be seen as fighting the good fight.

After the conference day ended on 10 September, they all trooped up to Koreatown for some barbecue, Wagner being passionately fond of Korean food. Feeling good, he invited Charlie to be a guest on his Internet talk show about Bitcoin. 'Let's talk about BitInstant,' he said. 'Do you have anything you'd want to talk about specifically?' Charlie was honest with him: 'The company is growing. I want to raise some money, but I don't really know how to raise money. I don't know what to do.' Wagner, then a hugely popular figure in Bitcoin circles for his evangelism efforts, understood. 'A lot of people watch my show,' he said. 'Feel free to mention it.' In the ensuing interview, weeks later, the young CEO made a big announcement: BitInstant was partnering with an established money services business to offer instant cash deposits. Soon you would be able to deposit cash into BitInstant's account from your local bank branch, and BitInstant would credit you the equivalent number of bitcoins, minus a small fee. Fast and convenient. Charlie's plan was to debut the service to American customers and then, 'once the kinks are knocked out', roll it out in Europe as well. He teased other cool features, too, like auto-mated bots that would conduct arbitrage on your behalf. But he needed money to make them a reality. 'It's just a funding issue right now,' he explained. 'Any investors out there, give me a call.'

The episode went live on YouTube on 23 November. That night – morning in Tokyo – Roger Ver contacted Charlie. He got right to the point: 'Saw the show. How much do you need?' On a Skype call, they discussed investment terms; Charlie haggled over the equity he was willing to give up. In the end, Roger gave him $120,000 for fifteen percent of BitInstant. And he agreed to join the company in a support role – first as director of marketing, and later as director of business development. 'At the time of BitInstant, I hadn't made as many investments in other businesses yet, so it just made sense to help them,' Roger says. He wired the money on the spot. The deal had been done on a virtual handshake – a sign that BitInstant was still in its infancy but also, in hindsight, perhaps a troubling indication that the company's chief executive sometimes played fast and loose with standard business practices. 'We had no paperwork for weeks after that,' Charlie admits. Even he and Gareth had no formal partnership agreement. 'We just said, "We'll always be fifty-fifty." It wasn't until Roger gave us money that we created the LLC and then we split everything up.'

Roger's money was earmarked even before it arrived: $100,000 for 'float' – that is, the money that was paid out to customers before receiving their deposits, which kept the service running – and the remainder for salaries and operating expenses. Until then, Gareth had been worried that his creation would die in the cradle. The seed investment 'allowed us to breathe', he says. They had their angel investor. There were blue skies ahead.

Chapter 4

BLOOD AND VEIN

When goods do not cross borders, soldiers will.
— Frédéric Bastiat

Roger Ver didn't mind losing money every now and then, but taxes were another matter – to him they were a matter of life and death. There was a YouTube video he watched sometimes to remind himself what the stakes were. It was a 1995 clip from *60 Minutes*, in which a reporter asks Madeleine Albright, then US ambassador to the United Nations, about a recent report by two scientists with the UN Food and Agriculture Organization, who had found that economic sanctions imposed on Iraq by the Security Council – of which the United States is a powerful member – may have led to the deaths of as many as 576,000 Iraqi children since the end of the Gulf War. What, the reporter wanted to know, should we make of this horrifying statistic? Is the price worth it? 'I think this is a very hard choice,' Albright replied, 'but the price . . . We think the price is worth it.' She went on to be confirmed unanimously by the US Senate as Secretary of Defense for the Clinton administration. Roger found this appalling, and he was appalled that tax dollars like his were funding such a government. 'Don't use violence to try to reduce the amount of violence in the world,' he would say, when asked to explain his philosophy. 'Don't use violence *ever*.' (This non-aggression principle, which encompasses more than physical violence, is the bedrock of libertarianism.)

It may sound utopian, given humanity's track record, but there is no need for coercion, Ver believes, when 'voluntary human action leads to the greatest happiness and the greatest material wealth and the best standard of living for everyone on the entire planet.' For him Bitcoin was not an abstract plaything, a digital curio; it was a way to regain control over his own wealth, even if it meant first putting that hard-earned wealth at risk. His peace of mind depended on it.

Roger liked Charlie Shrem, who shared his fervent belief that digital currency was something of real value rather than Monopoly money. But the younger man had a lot to learn about running a business. Now that BitInstant was flush, Roger advised him to hire some people to handle the small stuff. 'You shouldn't be doing customer service,' Charlie recalls him saying angrily. Just as Roger had been shocked to find that Mark Karpelès, following the June 2011 hack, would be spending a full weekend away from the office in spite of the exchange's precarious position, he now seemed surprised by Charlie's rookie mistake. He wanted to grow Bitcoin, but to do so he was being forced to work with people who, whatever passion or skills they might possess, lacked business acumen. If the Mt. Gox disaster had taught him anything, it was that professionalism was in short supply among Bitcoiners. If digital currency were ever to assume the importance he wished for it to have, it would require him and others with real experience to take an active role.

He had seen firsthand how experiments like Bitcoin could end badly. His first foray into digital currency had been E-gold; one of those 2.5 million customer accounts had belonged to him. He had lost money when E-gold was shut down, though not even close to the amount he had now put into Bitcoin. And while Bitcoin's decentralized, open-source design made it resistant to such punitive action, it was entirely possible that it might wither away for lack of support, might share the fate of other fads and speculative manias, might go the way of Dutch tulips and pet rocks. Between Charlie and Gareth, BitInstant was still only a two-man operation, with the Atlantic Ocean in between.

Even so, it was growing rapidly. On 28 November, the company processed $30,000 in transactions, its highest single-day volume ever. It was one of the few Bitcoin startups that seemed worth investing in. Lawrence Lenihan, the managing director of venture firm FirstMark Capital, which later sought investments in Bitcoin startups, doesn't envy Roger his role in those days. 'Roger was there before everybody, so God bless him,' Lenihan says. 'He's a smart motherfucker.'

Gradually, Roger brought Charlie around to his way of thinking. But it would be a long time before the young CEO fully disengaged from customer service. For now, every time a customer sent in a question or complaint it was routed to Charlie's personal email address. He was still thinking like a small business owner rather than the leader of a startup. 'I was doing all the customer support,' he said later. 'And it bit me in the ass.' It would be two years, however, before he had to face the consequences.

For now there were pressing concerns, among them the need to hire someone who could manage BitInstant's communications and branding. Roger remembered meeting in August 2011, at Bruce Wagner's conference in New York, a man who fit the bill. The conference had been a seminal event for the Bitcoin economy. Over the course of three days at the Roosevelt Hotel in midtown Manhattan, some seventy or eighty attendees checked out a vendor expo, participated in a Bitcoin mining workshop, watched presentations by startups, and dined out in restaurants that accepted the cryptocurrency as payment. There was talk of more conferences to come in foreign cities, and even, improbably, a Bitcoin cruise.

And there was gossip. The conference was abuzz with Mt. Gox's acquisition, on 11 August, of Bitomat, a Polish Bitcoin exchange and the world's third-largest after Gox and TradeHill. Bitomat had sold after running aground only a few months after its launch, when it lost seventeen thousand bitcoins – many of them belonging to customers – during a server reboot. There was no thief this time; the coins were simply erased, like any other electronic data. With no backup wallet, the money was gone for good. (This was just the sort of unprofessionalism Roger abhorred.)

Mt. Gox, 'in an effort to restore confidence in the Bitcoin economy', announced that it would be fully refunding lost customer balances. And in order to keep serving Bitomat's users, the exchange would open a Polish-language version of its site and add the złoty to its roster of currencies, allowing transfers from Polish banks.

A Mt. Gox representative even wrote of forming an 'alliance of Bitcoin-related businesses', and expressed hope that the top exchange's show of solidarity with other industry players would spark a recovery in the price of Bitcoin, which had dropped into the single digits for the first time in months. 'Mt. Gox believes that Bitcoin and the community will grow and mature past these extremely unfortunate events, just as Mt. Gox endured the June hack event and has continued to prosper,' he wrote.

But whatever industry drama there was to discuss, it was the Saturday keynote talks – by Gavin Andresen and Jeff Garzik, developers who had once assisted Satoshi in improving the Bitcoin software and who now, ever since he had vanished in April 2011, carried on in his absence – that carried real import for the digital currency's future. Garzik cautioned that Bitcoin was still a 'startup currency', still liable to fail, its net value only about $81 million. But already he foresaw that governments, if it survived, would try to drop a noose around it. 'I predict there will be a Bitcoin-specific law,' he said. 'Hopefully it's not banning.'[1]

It was in this environment that Roger met Erik Voorhees, a tall young man with large intelligent eyes, a high forehead, and sparse blond hair. Erik introduced himself and presented his business card, which, in addition to his name and contact info, read simply, *I'm friends with Satoshi*. There was no company listed. The card struck Roger as a clever marketing technique. The two men hit it off instantly.

They shared, you might say, a common syllabus. Like Roger, Erik had read *Denationalisation of Money*, by the economist Friedrich Hayek, a book that now seemed prophetic regarding Bitcoin. Hayek had advocated for multiple competing currencies rather than a single national currency, claiming that over time the new currencies would tend to displace the existing ones. Essentially,

Hayek saw money as a commodity like any other. He argued that private enterprise in the absence of government intervention 'could and would long ago have provided the public with a choice of currencies'. The ones left standing after a period of intense competition would be more stable than those that came before, he thought. What he could not have foreseen was the way in which his vision, or something like it, might be realized through technology rather than politics.

'New economic thinking', American economist Mark Thoma has written, 'means reading old books'. Years of reading economic theory such as Hayek's had prepared Roger to appreciate the concept of Bitcoin as much as his painful brush with the law had prepared him to embrace its revolutionary potential. Money, he knew, may take various forms; the acceptance of certain forms of money is a social convention, which is why Satoshi said that if enough people ascribed value to Bitcoin, it would become 'a self-fulfilling prophecy'.[2] Roger understood from the first, and on a deep level, that Bitcoin could actually be a *better* form of money than any that had previously existed, because it satisfied more than anything else out there some of the cardinal requirements of money: scarcity, portability, and divisibility. Weightless, Bitcoin could be transferred more easily than cash or coins; unregulated, it could be moved anywhere in the world frictionlessly, while dollars, pounds, and euros were subject to banking fees and delays. Thanks to its fixed and transparent growth rate, it enjoyed artificial scarcity; divisible to eight decimal places, it could be broken into tiny pieces and used for micropayments. Because there was no love lost between Roger and the US government, it would not be long before his understanding hardened into something else: a resolve to use Bitcoin, and to encourage its widespread adoption, as a tool for handicapping the state. 'Bitcoin totally strips away the State's control over money,' he wrote. 'It takes away the vast majority of its power to tax, regulate, or control the economy in any way.' Now, needing someone to take charge of BitInstant's design and communications, he thought of Erik, who relished Bitcoin for similar reasons.

Erik, for his part, had almost not attended the conference. He was short of money, getting by on freelance marketing work; he lived in New Hampshire as part of the Free State Project, a kind of libertarian social experiment designed to produce in the Granite State a critical mass of liberty advocates – as they saw themselves – to influence local government. Making his way to the Big Apple seemed daunting. Ultimately, though, he couldn't pass up the opportunity to meet other people as enthusiastic about Bitcoin as himself. 'From the moment I heard about Bitcoin, I was like, "Wow, this has to be everything I'm doing,"' he says. If he had expected to find a unified front of true believers at the conference, though, he was disappointed. 'It didn't really feel like a community,' he says. 'It wasn't big enough.' But in that disappointment was a kernel of opportunity. One consequence of the scene's immaturity, he says, was that 'absolutely everyone in Bitcoin was a programmer,' the sort of geeks who are always the first to embrace bleeding-edge technology. 'So there just weren't people who could write or do branding.'

Erik could. Already a couple of his freelance clients were Bitcoin startups; he had designed the first logo for BitPay, a payment processor. Attending the conference was for him a networking gambit, and it paid off. In addition to Roger Ver, he met a young computer engineer, cheerful though introverted, named Ira Miller. At the time, Ira was running a Bitcoin wallet service, storing digital currency on behalf of customers. When, some time later, without warning, his partner sold off the server holding these bitcoins – hundreds of them – Ira felt compelled to make the losses up to their bereft users out of his own pocket. After that, says Ira, 'I was pretty disillusioned. Not with Bitcoin but with entrepreneurship.'

At this low point, he found a supporter in Roger Ver. He had been a fan of Ira's now-defunct service, thanks to a unique feature it offered: the ability to send bitcoins to someone's email address, even the address of someone who had never heard of Bitcoin, an ability which had proven useful in Roger's ongoing evangelism. Bitcoin was analogous to email – both offered protocols for remotely sending messages between two parties – but there was no direct connection between them, no point of interaction. Ira, however, had managed to develop what he called 'a simple glue to tie a Bitcoin network message to an email network message'. At Roger's request, Ira resurrected the feature, building a stripped-down website for the purpose. His service would later prove invaluable to BitInstant.

Soon after Erik returned to New Hampshire, Ira contracted him to do freelance design and branding work for his new service. Erik created the website and came up with the name Coinapult, which stuck. He was still hoping to find full-time employment with a Bitcoin startup. BitInstant, though, didn't seem like a natural fit. He and Charlie had butted heads once, on the Bitcoin forums, on the subject of whether capitalism is fair to those living under its sway. Charlie, an opportunistic capitalist if ever there was one, nevertheless argued that the system was unequal. 'Individuals are only free on the condition that the great mass of people taken collectively are not,' he told Erik. 'We could not have capitalism without a working class and they are not free within the capitalist system to cease being wage laborers.' But where labor activists might demand change, Charlie seemed to relish this zero-sum game. 'You cannot have capitalism without someone losing out,' he continued, 'and that's precisely why I'm a capitalist!' His father, a short, powerful-seeming man with a guarded demeanor and strong, blunt features, had been in the jewelry business for more than twenty years, and was the source, so he said, of Charlie's entrepreneurial ambition: 'He gets that from me. His eloquence he gets from his mother.'

But Erik was adamant: 'So long as one is not lying, cheating, stealing, or hurting his neighbors, he is behaving fairly and morally, and a system which enables men to behave fairly in that way becomes a capitalist, or "market-based", system, inevitably.' The issue went unresolved. But when it came time to make a hiring decision, this old disagreement proved to be no obstacle. Erik joined BitInstant as director of marketing on 8 February 2012 – 'a full eleven months', as Charlie joked, 'before the Mayan apocalypse'.

It was an unsettled and unhappy, if no longer – since the end of the financial crisis – a truly apocalyptic time. Early interest in Bitcoin was fueled partly by a loss of trust in national currencies. As the global recession dragged on, investors bought up gold and silver as hedges against inflation. By the fall of 2010, silver had reached $21 a troy ounce, its highest price since 1980. 'The currencies of all the major countries, including ours, are under severe pressure because of massive government deficits,' Joe Foster, portfolio manager of the Van Eck International Investors Gold Fund, a New York-based fund with $1.5 billion in assets, told the *Dallas Morning News*. 'The more money that is pumped into these economies – the printing of money, basically – then the less valuable the currencies become.'[3] With governments around the world proving unable to keep a lid on their sovereign debt, the last thing Bitcoin proponents wanted was for lawmakers and regulators to gain a stranglehold on digital currency. Harmful regulation was an early and persistent concern.

Even in the absence of regulations, banks were getting nervous. To financial institutions cowed by Dodd–Frank, facing harsher scrutiny and higher compliance costs, the legality of Bitcoin – or of the uses to which the digital currency was being put – looked highly questionable. On 11 February, the Canadian company Paxum, one of three payment processors and e-wallet services that BitInstant had used from the beginning to receive customer funds, announced that it was severing ties with its Bitcoin clients – including Mt. Gox, TradeHill, and BitInstant – under threat of losing its relationships with banking partners. Paxum had been working with Mt. Gox since December 2010, with TradeHill since July 2011, and with BitInstant since its inception, but now, thanks to new policy handed down by various banks and MasterCard, continuing these partnerships became impossible. Referring to its banks and auditors, a Paxum representative explained, 'The main fears had to do with the fact that it's a decentralized currency and as such there isn't much control over it.' While Bitcoin was not illegal, it had been designated too hot to handle. 'It is unclear to them how this currency is supported and who pours actual money into it, and more importantly, why.'[4] By the following day, the

Paxum accounts of all Bitcoin companies had been closed. Wire transfer was the only means by which account holders could withdraw their frozen funds.

Not only did this choke off TradeHill's business, but it left the exchange's customers, whose money Jered Kenna intended fully to refund, without a good means to withdraw their dollar balances. Bitcoins they could easily send elsewhere – this being one of the virtues of the digital currency – but dollars were another matter. The very crisis that made it imperative to withdraw money from TradeHill made it difficult to do so. One European customer who had a dollar balance with TradeHill wondered if there might be a way to withdraw his funds to Mt. Gox or another exchange, hoping to avoid the wire transfer and currency conversion fees that would otherwise attend such a maneuver.

Enter BitInstant. Even as Charlie strove to convince Paxum executives to reverse their decision, he was brokering deals with exchanges so that TradeHill customers could move their money swiftly and cheaply to other platforms, where it could once again be put to use in the Bitcoin economy. In addition to Dwolla, with which BitInstant and Mt. Gox still enjoyed working relationships, customers would have the option of moving their money to Mt. Gox (based in Japan), CryptoXchange (based in Australia), VirWox (based in Austria), or Bitcoinica (based in Singapore). Bitcoin was increasingly a global phenomenon, and its users were not above conducting a kind of regulatory arbitrage between countries; if the US didn't want their money, they would just send it elsewhere. From his parents' basement in New York, Charlie dragged together the poles of the world.

It was left to Gareth Nelson, however, to write the code that would allow these foreign systems to talk to each other. In the course of several days, he did just that, making it possible for BitInstant to act as a middleman between the exchanges. 'I have to give super praise to my partner Gareth for figuring out how to build a custom withdrawal method in a matter of days, building upon the systems of four different exchanges,' Charlie told everyone. 'Ain't an easy thing to do.' The withdrawal mechanism became available on 22 February. Ten days after Kenna's announcement that trading would be suspended, the exodus of dollars could finally begin.

Having settled all customer accounts and gone out of business, TradeHill then did something desperate. It sued Dwolla for allegedly violating its own policies on chargebacks. It claimed that Dwolla was withholding nearly $165,000 owed to the exchange – and that the true loss was still greater. In the course of pleading its case, TradeHill revealed that it had given up ten percent of the company in exchange for three valuable web domains – bitcoin.com, bitcoin. co, and bitcoin.co.nz – at a time when the company was valued at $10 million. Shutting down TradeHill meant that control of the domains reverted to their previous owner. Jered Kenna had watched not only his company but a million dollars in digital property – which he had planned to make a hub for a Bitcoin wallet service, merchant tools and various apps – slip through his fingers.[5] That same month, Dwolla raised $5 million of venture capital. It didn't seem fair. By the end of May, however, a California judge had dismissed the case, sending it to arbitration.

The whole affair threw into a harsh light the paradox of the nascent Bitcoin industry. However appealing Satoshi's original vision had been – everyone acting as their own bank, keeping track of their own money – practical considerations made it implausible. It was difficult for average people to master the computer skills necessary to secure their cryptocurrency; merchants and speculators, meanwhile, needed to be able to turn bitcoins back into dollars (or euros, or yen) in order to 'lock in' digital currency profits in their customary unit of account. Bitcoin had undeniable utility as a means of transferring value, being 'both *blood* and *vein*', to use Charlie's phrase, 'not only the payment system of transfer [but] also the unit of value being transferred across the system'.[6] But the whole circulatory system depended, for those who weren't Bitcoin miners, on transfusions from national currencies. Getting those transfusions, for Bitcoin startups, meant doing deals with third parties – wallet services, payment processors, banks – just as an anemic patient would go to a hospital to receive blood. And yet relying on these companies reintroduced what is known as counterparty risk, the kind of risk that comes with depending on someone else to have your best interests at heart – the very risk Bitcoin was designed to eliminate. The dilemma seemed insoluble.

Clearly, however, Bitcoin was becoming big business. The value of TradeHill's domain names proved that if nothing else. Charlie Shrem and his compatriots were like prospectors striking out for California during the gold rush. So certain were they of the fortune to be won in the promised land, they would not be dissuaded even by the ruin of fellow travelers along the way.

But it would not be easy. With TradeHill gone, BitInstant had lost the partner on whose back its business had launched. It had lost Paxum, too. 'Paxum wants to have us back more than we want them back,' Charlie claimed at one point, in the midst of negotiations, telling his peers about scheduled conference calls and a planned flight to Montreal, where the payment service's headquarters was located. But as it became evident that his efforts would fail, he took the opportunity to buck up his fellow Bitcoiners with a reminder of what was at stake. 'The fact of the matter is, the larger Bitcoin gets the more of a threat it becomes. The people and institutions that share the most to lose will do everything in their power to stop it.' As far as he was concerned, Paxum was throwing in the towel, kowtowing to enemy forces. 'This is war, boys,' he continued, 'stop whining, strap in, and get to work.'

That winter and the following spring, Charlie, though in his final semester at Brooklyn College, where he was pursuing a degree in economics, took his own advice. He sold Daily Checkout and redoubled his focus on Bitcoin. At first Erik remained in New Hampshire, working part-time for BitInstant. The team was spread all over the globe. Charlie's office, and therefore BitInstant's nerve center, was the basement of his parents' house in Brooklyn. Gareth remained in Wales. Roger, who was still running Memory Dealers as well as a new e-commerce site, the Bitcoin Store, remained in Tokyo. They were living evidence of a shift, among startups and even some established companies, toward a distributed work force, of the vast collaborative powers afforded by digital communications technology. One expert who has spoken positively of this trend is Adam Kingl, the executive director of learning solutions at London Business School. According to Kingl, the practice of teams widely separated by geography meeting and collaborating virtually can eliminate office politics and foster a 'meritocracy of ideas'. For BitInstant, the setup appeared to be working. In April, despite losing Paxum and TradeHill, the company exceeded $1.1 million in monthly transfers, hitting seven figures for the first time. (By comparison, it had processed only about $500,000 in February.) And it was heading still higher. Charlie and Gareth both felt themselves to be sitting on top of a rocket. 'Seeing sales figures exceed expectations,' says Gareth, 'I could realistically see making a million dollars.'

Charlie's work for BitInstant cross-pollinated fruitfully with his college education. 'I was living economics every day,' he says. In one class he was allowed, instead of taking a final exam, to give a presentation on Bitcoin. He had expected a sort of oral exam, a question-and-answer session between him and the professor. Instead the professor simply yielded the floor and told him to address the class. There was an excruciatingly long pause while Charlie collected his thoughts. Then he began speaking – and continued without interruption for some time, perhaps as long as forty-five minutes, he says. 'I was stoned out of my mind,' he would recall later. 'Thank God I can wing it so well.'

BY NOW, BITINSTANT OFFERED A wide array of services, each with its own attendant fees. (Dollar transfers into exchange accounts using Dwolla, for instance, incurred a fee of roughly three percent, cash deposits a fee of 3.99 percent.) There were two services for which BitInstant relied on its partnership with Erik and Ira's company, Coinapult: delivering bitcoins to a designated wallet and delivering bitcoins to an email address. BitInstant, technically speaking, did not handle bitcoins directly; it helped to fund customer accounts on Bitcoin exchanges with US dollars and moved dollars between them. For orders in which customers wanted to spend dollars and receive bitcoins immediately, without going through an exchange, BitInstant contracted with Coinapult, which would deposit the bitcoins into their wallet of choice.

And Coinapult offered a great way to introduce people to digital currency. If a friend with whom you wanted to share bitcoins didn't have a wallet already set up, you could simply email her the bitcoins; Coinapult would alert her to the fact that bitcoins had been sent to her and were waiting to be claimed. In the meantime, her funds would be stored for safekeeping in a wallet created for her by Coinapult. This bitcoin-to-email tool, combining as it did the ability to transmit and store bitcoins with a means of inducting into the Bitcoin economy those who had never heard of it before, was an advancement on Satoshi's original software, which, as Alex Waters notes, had been intended merely as a provocation 'for people to go build better shit'.

So central was the Coinapult technology to BitInstant's services, and so great was BitInstant's need, as it grew, for additional technical talent to assist Gareth Nelson, that in July Charlie hired Ira Miller and made him director of engineering. The new hire arranged, just as his partner Erik had, to work for BitInstant not as a full employee but as an independent contractor, part-time – though his 'part-time' schedule was to include plenty of long nights as the months went by. BitInstant's system was, for lack of a better word, buggy. The website's customer interface would break down and people's money would get stuck in transit, ruining their opportunity to conduct arbitrage or even to buy coins at a good price. Gareth's infrastructure had not been designed for such a large customer base as the company was now acquiring, and the integration with Coinapult only complicated things further. Ira, whom a coworker describes as 'super competent', naturally specialized in troubleshooting issues that originated with his own system. 'Everything related to Coinapult, Ira was able to fix,' the coworker says. Gareth could be at times protective of his brainchild, the original BitInstant codebase, which often left Ira to work exclusively on Coinapult.

Customers persevered despite the bugs. BitInstant had a monopoly on the kind of services it provided, a fact which helped its bottom line. As BitInstant grew, Erik was keen to make the point – perhaps as a means of defusing jealousy over its success – that it could serve as a sort of barometer for the size and health of the Bitcoin economy as a whole. 'BitInstant is not an endpoint for Bitcoin funds, but merely a bridge to other endpoints,' he noted. 'What this means is that whatever size BitInstant achieves, the real Bitcoin economy must necessarily be some factor larger.'

Although Erik wanted to see BitInstant succeed, his first allegiance was to cryptocurrency itself. He would later explain: 'We're all working for Bitcoin, the meta-organization of Bitcoin. It's the first decentralized, open-source company. Each bitcoin is a share of that company. There's no one leading Bitcoin, but it ties us all together, and as Bitcoin benefits, we all do.' He never lost sight of the big picture, and it was partly for this reason that he became Charlie's right-hand man, gradually assuming the role of de facto chief operations officer. The exaggerated terms in which one former employee describes his role are illuminating: 'When I started, I kind of figured Erik was behind everything, which was true.'

They were starting to look like a real company. Although Erik didn't relocate from New Hampshire to New York until that summer, on 19 April he and Charlie set up a booth at New York Tech Day, a huge startup showcase held at the 69th Regiment Armory, a storied Beaux-Arts building in Manhattan that over the years has hosted such disparate events as the 1913 International Exhibition of Modern Art – which introduced American audiences to radical Modernist works like Marcel Duchamp's *Nude Descending a Staircase, No. 2* – and, far more contemporary in its powers of titillation, the Victoria's Secret Fashion Show. Charlie and Erik hung up Bitcoin banners at their booth and installed a forty-two-inch TV to display educational videos and the current Bitcoin exchange price. The promotion paid off. They made the acquaintance of Richard Beyda and Morris Levy, Syrian Jews like Charlie and owners of The Yard, a coworking space nestled between Williamsburg and Greenpoint, Brooklyn neighborhoods once known for manufacturing and shipbuilding but latterly hubs for young professionals and creative types. The three-story converted red-brick warehouse offered conference rooms, private offices, high-speed wireless Internet, a full kitchen, and shared workspaces designed to encourage collaboration among tenants. It was home to dozens of startups, including Uber. Charlie and Erik took one look and were sold.

In May, having moved into The Yard – the company's first real office space – BitInstant announced its biggest initiative yet, an expansion of its cash deposit service beyond banks to more than 700,000 retail locations, convenience stores, drugstores, and other outlets across the United States, Russia, and Brazil. One of the chief obstacles to Bitcoin adoption by the masses, Charlie admitted in a press release, was the difficulty of acquiring the digital currency – for most people 'a lengthy and confusing process'. By partnering with a cash payments company called ZipZap, BitInstant sought to make Bitcoin acquisition easier than ever, so that customers in three of the world's largest economies could anonymously exchange their local currency for digital money. In Russia, Qiwi and Cyberplat – networks of cash kiosks – provided the local interface for accessing the BitInstant system. In Brazil, it was Boleto Bancário, enabling cash deposits at bank branches, ATMs, post offices, and even some supermarkets and drugstores. It was Americans, however, who were truly spoiled for choice; where previously cash deposits to BitInstant had been possible only at the branch offices of four banks – JPMorgan Chase, CitiBank, Wells Fargo, and Bank of America – people could now trade cash for bitcoins, often without providing any personal identifying information, at Walmart, CVS, 7-Eleven, and thousands of local independent stores and money service providers. The new deposit network 'was just like a different version of the same thing, a better version', says Alex Waters, who eventually became BitInstant's chief information officer.

Better, that is, owing to the ubiquity of MoneyGram. In a press release, the BitInstant team explained their motivation:

This cash deposit network was built for the tens of millions of US residents who don't have a bank account, or don't feel comfortable divulging personal information online . . . By using cash deposits, all these consumers can still obtain and spend credit with online merchants. As Bitcoin is a frictionless online currency that also doesn't require any bank account, bridging the two was a natural fit.

Deposit times varied. Customers might receive their bitcoins almost instantly, though Charlie was not willing to promise anything faster than thirty minutes. (On one occasion, he said cash deposits in Russia and the United States would be credited within an hour, Brazilian deposits within twenty-four hours.) In directing where their funds would go, customers had two options: either to receive their local currency – dollars, rubles, or reals – in a fiat-denominated exchange account, such as Mt. Gox, or to receive bitcoins at a Bitcoin address. In other words, you could receive either electronic fiat currency to spend on bitcoins or bitcoins to spend on just about anything else – up to and including black tar heroin from Silk Road.

If the coins were being sent directly to a Bitcoin address, the transfer was facilitated through Coinapult. The whole system, though cumbersome and prone to malfunctioning, was effective; it gave a growing number of Bitcoin users a way to acquire digital currency that was more or less anonymous and difficult to trace. It was an initiative worthy of the ambitious role that Charlie, under Erik's influence, now envisioned for BitInstant; the company described itself as leading 'the financial integration of the international, open-source Bitcoin payment network' – of linking up a stateless rogue currency to the vast global banking and payments sector. They drew inspiration from prior revolutions; announcing the new cash deposit network, Charlie declared, 'Bitcoin is to money what email is to the Postal Service.'

His enthusiasm was infectious. By now, Gareth was beginning to sound like him, glorying in BitInstant's success and the fruits thereof. That summer, he threw himself what he describes as an 'awesome birthday'. He had every reason to believe the business would keep getting bigger.

Even as Gareth showed signs of mimicking Charlie, however, Charlie was being influenced by Erik, and, later, by Ira, both of them staunch libertarians. The three men were becoming fast friends. For Erik and Ira, who had no prior connections in New York, it was easy to lose themselves in their work – and in the world of digital currency. They found themselves talking about it morning, noon, and night. 'Bitcoin really consumed our lives,' Ira says. 'We were going through something together that very few people in the world could understand.' He even managed to form a bond with Gareth, admittedly a difficult personality. 'It was a pretty good working relationship for two introverted nerds on opposite sides of the world,' is how Ira puts it.

His and Erik's philosophical brand of anti-government politics informed the business. Erik, whose eloquence outmatched even Charlie's, and who unofficially had a great deal of input on business strategy, could be especially harsh and uncompromising in his views. Batting away questions of inequality, he identified the ownership of wealth with the production of value, such that one's net worth is 'a rough proxy measurement of what [one] produced, as valued by the person who previously owned that money and traded it in return. So, properly read,' he went on, 'a stat like "the top one percent own fifty percent of the wealth" should be understood as "the top one percent produced fifty percent of the wealth" . . . and then with that understanding it quite quickly shows the folly of policies which punish, tax, and otherwise hinder such people. It also illustrates the sheer productive uselessness of vast swaths of the population.'

Though college-educated in business and economics, Erik was at bottom an autodidact; his second school had been the work of monetary theorists such as Murray Rothbard, a disciple of Ludwig von Mises who favored a hard-money standard and opposed government intervention in the economy. The inflation that inevitably resulted from such intervention, Rothbard thought, would benefit some only at the expense of others. 'Just as half the economy are taxpayers and half tax-consumers,' he wrote in his landmark tome *Man, Economy, and State*, 'so half the economy are inflation-payers and the rest inflation-consumers.' To many of Bitcoin's early adopters, like Erik, digital currency offered a new kind of hard money impervious to government meddling. Small wonder that Dread Pirate Roberts called Rothbard one of the 'main inspirations' for creating Silk Road.

One venue for airing these views, to which Erik now introduced Charlie, was the Porcupine Freedom Festival, an annual week-long camping event in the White Mountains of northern New Hampshire. PorcFest, as it is known, is the banner event of the Free State Project, a pledge-based effort to persuade twenty thousand libertarians to move to New Hampshire – a state already known for individualism – where they hope to influence local politics, reducing government at every level to a size that will not encroach on anyone's basic rights. Every June since 2004, hundreds of self-styled liberty advo- cates have been converging on New Hampshire for several days of hiking, barbecues, panel discussions, and general merriment. With hot showers and bathroom facilities readily accessible, PorcFest is, Erik admitted, 'camping lite', but nevertheless it makes 'a perfect environment for over a thousand liberty lovers to converge, drink, smoke, talk, laugh, argue, and show off their new semiauto pistol accessories'. The 2012 event was his third PorcFest, and this time he had a new agenda: promoting Bitcoin.

He was helped in this by Roger Ver. Determined to spread the gospel of Bitcoin while supporting anti-government causes, Roger donated a large sum in bitcoins to the Free State Project, on the condition that PorcFest attendees be allowed to pay for their regis- tration in digital currency. The festival organizers agreed, paving the way for Erik to take PorcFest by storm with his very own vendor booth, where he bought and sold bitcoins with a three- percent spread and helped Bitcoin novices install on their phones a wallet app created by a startup called Blockchain. Charlie and Ira manned the booth with him, as did Roger, who flew in from Japan with his fiancée in tow. On this booth – jokingly named Bernanke's Bitcoin Exchange at the expense of Federal Reserve chairman Ben Bernanke – they spared no effort: three laptops and a tablet were connected to a mobile hotspot, giving them Internet access, and screens showed a scrolling list of live transactions happening around the world. Occasionally, and much to Charlie's delight, Erik would blast the BitInstant 'theme song' – whose refrain Roger had suggested months earlier as the company slogan – from his car stereo:

> It's your money, why wait?
> Instant transfers, no delays
> It's your money, why wait?
> Time is money, don't be late!
> It's your money, why wait?
> BitInstant's got lowest rates.
> It's your money, why wait?
> Get bitcoins the fastest way!

Encircled by the scenic mountains, they educated their peers, they drank, they turned a profit. Tuneful woodland birds put Erik in mind of the songbirds found in Disney cartoons. His entire adult life he had been an advocate of a strong and open market, and here was that market – *agora*, in Greek, a place of public assembly that is also a zone of commerce – in miniature, much of it now powered by Bitcoin. Other vendors had taken Roger's well-publicized donation as a catalyst; while Bitcoin was not ubiquitous at the festival, at least half of the vendors were accepting it as payment, Erik recalls. At one point he found himself relaxing in a chair, working on his third beer of the day, and reflecting on the scale of his and his friends' ambitions, on what they had accomplished in comparison with the cruder expressions of freedom so abundant at the festival. *Butterfly knives and unlicensed hair stylists are cool,* he thought, *but we're actually reconstructing an entire financial system from right here on our laptop with a $50 Verizon Mifi.* It was a capitalist's idyll.

Erik wasn't the only one who felt rejuvenated by the experience. For Charlie, whose enthusiasm for libertarian practice at times exceeded his grasp of libertarian theory, it was the best weekend of his life.

EVEN AS BITINSTANT RACED AHEAD with new services, its compliance with state and federal law lagged behind. In the United States, money services businesses are required to register with the Financial Crimes Enforcement Network, or FinCEN, the branch of the Treasury Department tasked with fighting money laundering, and to comply with various regulations designed to thwart criminal abuse of their systems. These anti-money laundering and Know Your Customer regulations, as they are collectively known, obligated BitInstant to report any large transactions or suspicious activity to FinCEN and, at the very least, to record the identity of any customer sending or receiving a sum of \$3,000 or more. BitInstant had launched without any legal protections whatsoever, but on 26 March 2012 the startup belatedly registered with FinCEN as a money services business. On its website, BitInstant announced plainly that it opposed 'money laundering, financing terrorism, and all other illegal uses of the Bitcoin network'. On the surface, Charlie seemed to be doing his best to play it straight.

But internal operations didn't always match the veneer of legality. Rachel Yankelevitz, who was hired in the late summer of that year, recalls the slipshod way in which AML and KYC policies were implemented. 'At first it was kind of a free-for-all,' she says. 'There really was no cross-checking [of identities]. People would put in hilarious names' – John Doe and even more obvious fakes. Customers were supposed to be at least eighteen years old to use the site, but BitInstant had no way of confirming their ages. Some ZipZap locations, when customers were making cash deposits, would ask to see identification, but others wouldn't. 'I'm sure plenty of people found that one 7-Eleven where they just didn't give a shit and would take your money and not care,' is how Rachel puts it. Indeed, anecdotal evidence suggests that the ZipZap cash deposit was Silk Road users' preferred method of acquiring coins, a method even more convenient and anonymous than depositing cash at banks.

BitInstant did place limits on cash deposits; customers were permitted no more than $1,000 per person per day. (One employee later recalled it as no more than $500 per deposit and no more than $2,000 per day.) But if a friend made the deposit on the user's behalf, or the user accessed BitInstant's website using a new email address and alias, he or she could easily circumvent those restrictions. Charlie Shrem and his team must have known that anyone tech-savvy enough to be using Bitcoin would be able to exploit these loopholes.

Other services, such as inter-exchange transfers, were even more permissive, with no monetary limits at all – except for when BitInstant 'didn't have the funds to accommodate the transfer, so it got stuck', Rachel says.

In February, Charlie had paid lip service to AML and KYC policies, saying that even though TradeHill had lifted its daily withdrawal limits – allowing customers to move their entire balance in one go – anyone transferring through BitInstant the equivalent of $10,000 or more in either dollars or bitcoins in a single thirty-day period would be required to verify their identities.[7]

The problem was that US money transmitters – a designation that goes beyond merely being a money services business – are required to obtain a license for just about every state in which they have customers. Forty-seven states, plus the District of Columbia, have such licensing requirements. For BitInstant that would mean complying with forty-eight sets of requirements, enduring forty-eight lengthy bureaucratic processes, paying forty-eight filing fees, and obtaining forty-eight surety bonds.[8] The costs might vary by state, but the approximate total is normally about $200,000, or higher if the company is a bigger risk. And that is far from all. A company seeking a money transmitter license in, for example, New York, must also provide audited financial statements; an extensive breakdown of the company's operations; fingerprints of all owners, officers, stockholders, and directors; a two-year projection of business in the state; and much more, while also submitting to a background investigation of its executives. The process was expensive and time-consuming enough to shut down the world's second-largest Bitcoin exchange, TradeHill.

BitInstant was now in the same position, and Charlie appeared to have learned from TradeHill's fate. But in many respects he and his team played fast and loose with the regulations. Charlie was listed as BitInstant's compliance officer, responsible for ensuring that the company, in addition to registering with FinCEN, abided by all the money transmitter requirements of every state in which it served customers. But there he fell short. New York state, for instance, mandates that a compliance officer must have at least three years of experience performing compliance for a money transmitter or bank, a requirement that Charlie, then twenty-two, didn't meet. But the young CEO chose to keep his startup running rather than close up shop, as TradeHill had, to raise money from investors.

Charlie, Erik, and Ira – to say nothing of Roger – were young guns of the 'move fast and break things' school popularized by Facebook founder Mark Zuckerberg, and they made no more than a passing gesture toward compliance. Neither FinCEN nor the Internal Revenue Service nor any other agency of the US government, whether state or federal, had yet ruled that Bitcoin was money, and although the BitInstant leadership believed that it was – in the truest sense – they nevertheless relied on official silence and inattention as air cover for their actions. The status of this new asset class, about which most of the world remained in the dark, was uncertain. 'It could be information, could be speech, could be a commodity,' Ira says of the lack of consensus in those days.

But even those AML and KYC policies followed within the company were being subverted by its CEO. Charlie, as he fielded customer complaints in the last days of 2011, encountered a fifty-two-year-old BitInstant customer named Robert Faiella, who, on Silk Road, went by the moniker BTCKing. There he was turning a handsome profit reselling bitcoins to other Silk Road users, who wanted to buy drugs but didn't want to go through the hassle – or the exposure – of acquiring bitcoins through normal means. When a Silk Road user came to Faiella for, say, $500 in bitcoins, Faiella would place an equivalent order on BitInstant, using the bank cash deposit method, and once the customer had paid up, he would zap the bitcoins to the relevant Silk Road account, minus his own commission. In fact the whole process was fairly convoluted. But it was easy money.

Faiella's operation would later be described by federal prosecutors as an unlicensed money transmitting business. For the time being, he was simply frustrated that his orders were being stalled in BitInstant's system. The third-party payment processor on which BitInstant relied had flagged Faiella for attempting multiple orders each day, exceeding the $1,000 limit. Within days, Charlie had worked out the nature of Faiella's operation and confronted him in an email, of which a copy was sent both to Gareth Nelson and to the CEO of the cash processing company, TrustCash. He made it clear that Faiella's activity would not be tolerated: 'We have warned you in the past you CANNOT deposit more than $1,000 per person per day according to our limits. You have violated our Terms of Service and we know you are reselling your services on the Silk Road. *This is illegal.*' Charlie told Faiella that he was banned from using BitInstant's services.

He told Faiella that BitInstant was 'a licensed MSB', when in fact the company wouldn't be registered with FinCEN for another two months. 'Your information', he said, 'is already being given to [FinCEN].' But according to Gary Alford, a special agent in the Criminal Investigations division of the Internal Revenue Service, Charlie filed no such report. In a private email to Faiella, he contradicted his earlier statements, telling the older man that he was free to continue using BitInstant so long as he stayed within the $1,000 deposit limit and used a new email address to mask his identity.

When Gareth pegged this new customer as BTCKing, and suggested 'stick[ing] to bans we impose rather than letting it slip after threatening criminal prosecution', Charlie talked him down. Gareth, though he supports drug legalization, is a teetotaler who abstains from drugs himself. 'I never liked Silk Road,' he says. 'I firmly believe in working with the government when you need to. Open rebellion can only slow adoption [of Bitcoin].' As January dragged on and Faiella's customer support inquiries mounted,

Gareth got fed up. He wanted BTCKing banned – for real this time. Once again, Charlie persuaded him otherwise. 'He brings us a lot of business and we won't be able to ban him anyways, he can change all his details.' They had no way of stopping Faiella from coming back again and again, each time with a new email address – no way to link his true identity to all of his aliases. And besides, why would they want to? 'We make good profit from him,' Charlie told his cofounder.

Soon, Charlie was helping Faiella to evade detection by the cash processing company – warning him when one of his email accounts had been flagged, for instance – and advising him on how to exceed BitInstant's daily transaction limits in violation of federal law. 'I just want to let you know, I take care of you, bro,' he told the older man in February. At every turn, according to federal prosecutors, he circumvented his own AML policies to ensure that Faiella's orders were filled, even offering him discounts based on his high volume of transactions. Ultimately, Charlie helped Faiella to pass close to $1 million through BitInstant. The company reaped nearly $15,000 from these transactions – an amount significant enough to the tiny startup that it seemed, for the time being, worth breaking the law.

Faiella was hardly the only Silk Road user obtaining bitcoins through BitInstant. Before Bitcoin ever existed, Gareth had searched the dark web for something like it, but had found nothing he could trust, nothing in which he could take refuge from the default reality around him. 'I had the romantic image of hiding in a digital haven of libertarianism,' he says. His company became such a haven, even as it kept up a law-abiding front. Of the customers, says Rachel, 'No one really used their real names. I had people call on the phone and say, "How do I get this [money] into my Silk Road Bitcoin wallet?" The default response was, "We don't work with Silk Road, we're not affiliated with Silk Road, but we can send [your money] to a Bitcoin address."' (Any address, that is, including the address of a Silk Road wallet.) 'That's not really on us,' Rachel continues. 'If you take money out of the bank and go spend it on drugs, is that the bank's fault?'

The use of BitInstant to fund Silk Road accounts was common enough that it had real-world effects on Gareth, a musician in his spare time. 'A fair few of my friends do weed,' he says. 'One guy I met at a jam literally could not believe he had just played with the cofounder of BitInstant, because he had used the service to fund Silk Road. I told him not to let me know his username. The policy was, it's none of our business what people spend their funds on.' But if he had known the customer's username, he would have been obliged to take action, aware that the bitcoins were, in this case, drug money. In the growth of Bitcoin, to say nothing of BitInstant's own success, says Gareth, 'Silk Road almost certainly played a big role.'

The one man who might have been able to force the issue of meaningful compliance with regulations was Roger Ver, but, as one BitInstant employee recalls, he did nothing of the kind. He didn't encourage Charlie to operate in the shadows, but neither was he eager to see the government meddle in BitInstant's affairs. When, in April 2011, lead Bitcoin developer Gavin Andresen announced that he had accepted an invitation to give a presentation on Bitcoin at Langley, the CIA's headquarters, Roger had been appalled. In the words of one former BitInstant staffer, 'Any opportunity he has to say "Fuck you" to the government, he's going to take.'

Many Bitcoin advocates genuinely believed that cryptocurrency represented a paradigm shift in the history of money, a math-based model resistant to government control; a square peg that couldn't be forced into the round hole of financial regulation. Email had freed people from reliance on government-issued stamps and from the pesky oversight of mail inspectors; why should Bitcoin be subject to the same reporting practices and AML concerns as banks and old-fashioned money transmitters?

And yet there were times – most often when speaking publicly – that Charlie seemed sincerely to want to do everything by the book. Conscious of the fact that Bitcoin was engaged in a war of public perception, he thought it would be pragmatically sound, if not ethically necessary, for Bitcoin businesses to adopt 'some sort of compliance and procedures' to deter money laundering and terrorism financing. 'Doesn't have to be as strict or pain-in-the-ass as the banking institutions, but we still need to come off as [though] we are trying,' he said.

For these views he was openly mocked on an online Bitcoin forum. 'You sound like the kind of person who is willing to give up his freedoms for the fight against "terrorism",' one critic wrote, 'the kind of person who wouldn't mind being anally probed at checkpoints.'

'You're right, it does sound like that,' Charlie shot back. 'However, in this case I'm the one going to jail if I don't allow the probing.'

Finance is one of the most heavily regulated industries on the planet. In the view of Jesse Powell, who runs the Bitcoin exchange Kraken, headquartered in California, regulations are guaranteed to breed outlaws. 'If you're just starting up, you're almost forced to break the law and hope that you can get away with it long enough to produce some traction' so that you can raise money from investors, he says. After that, you can play catch-up on regulatory compliance – in effect asking forgiveness, not permission – 'but every day that you're not legal, you're breaking criminal law.'

Ira agrees. 'That's the state generally in the US today. We're all forced to break the law until someone calls us out.' Entrepreneurs suffer the burden of regulation the most, he says. It is because of the expense and bureaucratic complexity surrounding money-transmitter licensing that in the summer of 2014, one full year after launching, Kraken, despite serving customers throughout Europe, was able to provide Bitcoin exchange services in only five US states.

Finance isn't the only industry in which government involvement can do more harm than good. In the winter of 2014, with the unmistakable stench of corruption hanging over the vast public works of the Sochi Olympics – a 'financial boondoggle' which, with a price tag of more than $50 billion, was more than seven times as expensive as the previous Winter Olympics – the *New Yorker*'s James Surowiecki took the opportunity to write about 'the link between corruption and construction', not uniquely a Russian problem but 'a problem across the globe'.

What makes construction so prone to shady dealings? One reason is simply that governments are such huge players in the industry. Not only are they the biggest spenders on infrastructure; even private projects require government approvals, permits, worksite inspections, and the like. The more rules you have, and the more people enforcing them, the more opportunities there are for corruption.[9]

Surowiecki, presumably, was able to write this without cognitive dissonance. And yet it is precisely the opposite of the received wisdom about finance, to say nothing of health care. While new regulation is usually promoted for reasons of fair play, it often works against younger players who might have the ideas and will-power to improve a sclerotic industry. Ira recalls the negative attention and mounting pressure from banks and regulatory agencies as a 'huge distraction', the biggest obstacle to BitInstant's success. It was this sort of scrutiny that had driven Paxum from the field and which forced BitInstant to employ Patrick Murck, a Seattle lawyer, to try to stay on the right side of the law – at a time when laws concerning Bitcoin were nonexistent.

'For a small company with eight or nine employees, a few of whom are part-time, and you're just struggling with keeping your customers happy, having to pay lawyers $60,000 or $100,000 is very problematic,' Ira says. 'Charlie started BitInstant with ten grand. Could you do that today? No fucking way.'

Two years later, Charlie would reflect on this 'free-for-all' time in the Bitcoin economy. 'There was this mentality that if it was gray, you could try to make it white, you could try to make it legal,' he says. 'If something was in the gray area, if you have good enough lawyers . . . you [could] make it white. I think we're at a point now that if I do all of this all over again, even if it's mildly gray, you have to assume it's black, it's illegal. Because even if it's not, they will figure out a way to pin on you the fact that it's illegal.'

In late 2012, BitInstant stopped allowing cash deposits at banks, because its third-party service, TrustCash, refused to go on serving Bitcoin companies. (BitInstant customers could still make cash deposits at Walmart, CVS, 7-Eleven, and other retail locations, however.) At the same time, Charlie stopped processing orders for Faiella.

The former gray hat may have wanted to be seen as a rebel, may have wanted to circumvent unhelpful laws and win the respect of his libertarian friends, may even have been willing to make a cornerstone of his company the illicit economic activity of an underground drug market. 'I knew that much of the business conducted on Silk Road involved the unlawful buying and selling of narcotics,' he said later. 'I knew that what I did here was wrong.' But in the final analysis what he wanted most was to keep his competitive edge in the high-stakes startup world, to keep posting impressive growth numbers and keep BitInstant moving forward, like a bullet train that can't afford to slow down. If, from now on, that meant playing nice with the feds, 'making it white', or at least appearing to do so, then so be it.

Chapter 5

A MEETING IN IBIZA

The investor's chief problem – and even his worst enemy
– is likely to be himself.

– Benjamin Graham

Charlie Shrem was losing sleep. It was February 2013 and his investors had given him an ultimatum: either convince Erik and Ira to sign over the Coinapult code to BitInstant, gratis, or fire them. Erik and Ira have to be team players, the investors insisted. As far as Charlie was concerned his directors of marketing and engineering were exemplary team players, but they were also, legally speaking, contractors, not full-time employees, and their contracts specifically granted them the right to work on side projects, including Coinapult. As a result, Coinapult was their intellectual property, not BitInstant's; he had no right to take it from them, nor to make them give it up without compensation. Yet that was what the investors wanted him to do.

Though not all of the investors. Roger was against the ultimatum, against firing Erik and Ira, his brothers-in-arms. But he was no longer the only man Charlie had to please. In a Faustian bargain to keep BitInstant alive and growing, the young CEO had made himself answerable to people who understood little about the special needs of a Bitcoin startup and cared even less for the bonds of friendship between the three men at the heart of it.

It had begun the previous spring, when Charlie was introduced to David Azar, a private investor who owned a few check-cashing businesses. He had heard that Azar and his uncle, Victor Azrak, fellow Syrian Jews, might be interested in what Charlie was working on. When Charlie arranged to meet Azar, he was hoping only that he might convince the other man to join BitInstant in some advisory role. He wasn't looking for Azar to invest. But Azar had other ideas. 'Soon as I walked in,' Charlie recalls, 'he said, "We want to invest a million dollars."' The problem, he told Azar, was that BitInstant already had a term sheet with other potential investors, its landlords at The Yard, Richard Beyda and Morris Levy. Ever since moving into their office space, the BitInstant team had been in agreement that Beyda and Levy would lead a round of investment in their startup.

But David Azar was adamant, and now he was threatening to ruin the arrangement. A meeting between the three would-be investors, Charlie recalls, resulted in Azar making it plain to the other men that he intended to make BitInstant an offer of his own. Charlie didn't know what to do. 'My morals are telling me, "Go with Richard and Morris. They're nice guys, they're not sharks,"' he says. But Azar talked a good game, he was insistent, and Charlie believed his experience with financial services could be a boon to the startup. Erik wasn't so sure. Neither was Roger, who had his own reservations about Azar. A debate raged between the principals of BitInstant. Emails went back and forth arguing the merits of various options.

In June 2012, while Charlie was mulling over the future of his company, he and Erik took a trip to Vienna to try out working prototypes of a smart card designed to be a secure, self-contained Bitcoin wallet and payment mechanism. They were joined in Austria by Roger Ver and Gavin Andresen, the middle-aged coder who, ever since Satoshi's disappearance, had shouldered the responsibility of leading the development of the core Bitcoin software. While there, the four men began brainstorming ideas for a digital currency trade association. Their ideas would bear fruit in the fall with the launch of the nonprofit Bitcoin Foundation, of which Charlie, Roger, and Gavin would all be founding members. Vienna, they found, had its charms. They ate schnitzel and goulash and palled around with other Bitcoiners – Amir Taaki, a young half-Iranian crypto-anarchist and skilled C++ programmer, and Nejc Kodrič, the CEO of Bitstamp, a Slovenia-based Bitcoin exchange, both of whom had come to see what all the fuss over the card was about.

Then, unexpectedly, David Azar showed up. He had known Charlie was going to Vienna but had not been invited, a fact which stopped him not at all from launching a full-court press to woo the young entrepreneur. When paying for dinners didn't cut it, he sweetened the pot, promising to give Charlie and his cofounder, Gareth Nelson, signing bonuses for assenting to a term sheet with a ninety-day no-shop agreement, which would prevent them from speaking with any other investors for three months. A no-shop is the engagement ring of the venture capital world; it is supposed to signal that your search is over – you have found The One – and that both parties will work in good faith toward closing the deal. Though hard to enforce legally – much as divorce law doesn't cover breaking off an engagement – a no-shop is an important commitment. And David Azar was offering Charlie and Gareth $15,000 each to sign their names on the dotted line. '*Personal money*', Charlie was to emphasize later, marveling in the way an orphaned child might marvel at finally having been chosen by a foster family. Personal money, that is, not capital for the business. 'Sold me,' Charlie says. 'Sold me.' He had been on the fence, but now he believed David Azar was the right investor for BitInstant. 'I convinced Roger and Erik that David was the better move. There was a lot of debate, but ultimately it was my decision, and they complied.'

And Azar, as it turned out, had partners. That summer he had met Cameron and Tyler Winklevoss, lantern-jawed twins and Olympic rowers most famous for a series of legal actions against Facebook founder Mark Zuckerberg, with whom they had attended Harvard and who, they argued, had stolen from them the idea for his social networking site. In the years since, Zuckerberg had dropped out, founded Facebook, and become the world's youngest billionaire; the Winklevosses had graduated, placed sixth in the men's coxless pair event at the 2008 Olympics in Beijing, settled with Facebook for $65 million in cash and stock, and, in 2010, earned twin MBAs at Oxford University, after which they had founded a venture firm for startups, Winklevoss Capital. They thought of themselves as 'angel accelerators', providing money and guidance to promising companies.[1] It is perhaps significant for the role they would play as investors in BitInstant, and emblematic of the way new money was moving into the Bitcoin world, that the twins learned about the digital currency not through professional channels, as a computer scientist might have, nor through online discussion forums, as many early enthusiasts had done, but from a fellow money man on a beach in Ibiza.

Giving up his lounger for the Winklevosses, whom he recognized – and it would have been difficult not to recognize the six-five, 220-pound brothers, both of whom had been portrayed by Armie Hammer in *The Social Network* – David Azar began telling them about Bitcoin. They had given little thought to digital currency before, but now began considering whether it might not represent a sea change in e-commerce and financial services. 'I got really fascinated by the implications for the financial world,' Cameron says.[2]

David Azar introduced the Winklevosses to the BitInstant team. 'They came to us and didn't know a lot but were really excited,' says Ira, who set up the twins with their first cold storage wallet for, as he puts it, 'the war chest that they were accumulating'. Much of that war chest – tens of thousands of bitcoins – was acquired through BitInstant. After Charlie, Erik, and Ira had given them a crash course in digital currency, 'they just dove right in,' Ira says. At the same time, David Azar had another reason for putting the Winklevosses in a room with Charlie and his team. He was presenting them with an investment opportunity.

Meanwhile, the no-shop agreement with Azar had torpedoed Charlie's relationship with Morris Levy and Richard Beyda. In June, upon returning from Vienna, BitInstant left The Yard and began looking for a new home. In the meantime, Charlie and Erik worked out of Erik's Brooklyn apartment. In August, with Ira having joined the team, they moved into an office at 20 West 23rd Street in the Flatiron District. It was a prestigious location for a tech startup, the heart of what is called Silicon Alley – New York's answer to Silicon Valley – and it was to this office that Azar brought the Winklevosses.

Behind the scenes, however, the relationship with David Azar was deteriorating, and the ninety-day clock on the no-shop agreement had almost run out. There were a few clauses of the proposed deal on which he refused to budge, including a provision that the investment capital would be drip-fed to BitInstant as needed rather than provided as a lump sum. Roger and Erik no longer wanted to make a deal with him. Once again Azar applied pressure, Charlie recalls, 'giving me the Syrian Jewish guilt trip: "I'll banish your name in the community. I'm not a person you want to [mess] with."' There was nothing professional about it. For Charlie, who had been steeped in his family's history, the threats had real weight. His grandparents, as he had once put it, 'tell me stories of what it was like growing up in wealthy Syria and then being kicked out, all their belongings and money taken from them when they moved here and had to restart from scratch. Insane stuff.' BitInstant employees who witnessed the arguments between Charlie and David Azar were put in mind of the spats of a married couple, or of a father berating his son.

Salvation arrived for BitInstant in an unexpected form: an investment banker turned entrepreneur named Barry Silbert, who was beginning to make a name for himself as an angel investor in Bitcoin startups. Peter Vessenes, a founding member with Charlie and Roger of the Bitcoin Foundation, in whose cryptocurrency startup, CoinLab, Barry Silbert had invested, introduced Erik to Barry, and the two men – both finance and economics geeks – hit it off immediately. Two years later, Barry would be perhaps the most prominent angel in the world of Bitcoin, having put seed money into some thirty startups. But in the summer of 2012, when he first began looking for prospects, the pickings were slim. 'The only ones I could find that were outside-looking-in investable were

CoinLab, BitPay, and BitInstant,' he says. At their second meeting Barry told Erik that he was looking for Bitcoin companies to finance. 'I'd be happy to take a look at what you guys are doing,' he said.

So began a capital-raising dance the full choreography of which was obscured even to many of the participants. Until Barry entered the picture, Charlie had been on the verge of taking David Azar's money, unhappy as that course of action seemed. Now he was eager to switch partners. 'Don't take his money yet,' Charlie recalls Barry saying. 'Just hold off.' Because the startup needed cash imminently in order to grow, Barry offered to invest $100,000 in the form of a convertible note – a type of short-term loan often used in seed financing which converts into shares of preferred stock for the investor once the startup has raised a Series A round of venture capital. Where the issuance of shares of preferred stock is a lengthy and expensive process, often requiring the startup to pay legal fees of $10,000 to $30,000 or even more, a convertible note deal can be closed in as little as a single day with a simple prom-issory note, costing no more than $1,500 to $2,000.[3] In short, Barry was offering Charlie a loan in exchange for equity in BitInstant, which he would receive alongside the Series A investors. And for the purpose of raising this Series A round he had a venture capital firm already waiting in the wings.

Barry introduced Charlie, Erik, and Ira to Lawrence Lenihan, the handsome, silver-haired, Wharton-educated managing director of FirstMark Capital, a New York venture capital firm with $225 million at its disposal. While the firm focused broadly on early stage technology startups – of which BitInstant certainly was one – Lenihan himself had a professed interest in 'the future of finan-cial services' and for this reason had already invested in Barry's own company, SecondMarket, an innovative brokerage for exotic assets. Assembled in a room together, the BitInstant team resembled three crayons drawn at random from a box. Erik and Ira were tall and lean and fair, one blond – though balding – and the other red-haired, while Charlie was much shorter and swarthier, with a thick head of black curls, an insistent beard, and eyebrows like two woolly caterpillars. In more than one way, BitInstant's CEO was the odd man out. 'Charlie was kind of the class clown,' says Lenihan, who found himself as impressed by Erik and Ira as he was bemused by their leader. 'I bought into their vision of their company—' he says, before correcting himself: 'Erik's vision of the company. I couldn't understand what the hell they were doing with Charlie, but I just assumed that Charlie must be some kind of genius, because these two guys were with him.'

As Erik saw it, BitInstant would become the primary on-ramp and off-ramp for the Bitcoin network, the access point by which fiat currency became digital currency and, in turn, by which bitcoins were converted into dollars, rubles, and reals. Once having established this kingly position within the realm of cryptocurrency, BitInstant could sally forth into a wide territory of products and services: wallet software, payment processing, remittance solutions. FirstMark wanted to gain exposure to the Bitcoin industry, but on one condition – that any startup in which it invested was already generating revenue. On this score Lenihan believed BitInstant was better positioned for growth than any of its competitors: at the time, it was raking in $100,000 a month, not bad for a one-year-old startup providing services for a virtual currency.

Where he diverged from Erik was in his political stance toward Bitcoin, or rather his vehement lack of one. He cared only about Bitcoin's utility. 'I don't give a shit about the big political view,' he says. 'This is not a political statement to me. It's not a protest against authoritarian fiat currency regimes. It's about how money should work. If you were an alien and you came down and you created a currency system for people to exchange goods and have a place to store value, you'd create something that looks damn near like Bitcoin. And that's why I'm interested in it.' He was interested enough to invite Charlie and his team to the FirstMark offices to deliver a formal pitch to his partners.

Charlie came away from the meeting believing that Lenihan had fallen in love with him and his colleagues. What happened next did nothing to disabuse him of the notion. Following the presentation to the partners at FirstMark Capital, Lenihan told

Charlie that his firm wanted to invest in BitInstant. He presented the young CEO with a new term sheet, the consequence of which would be that he would have to stop all negotiations with David Azar, whom Lenihan openly believed had conflicting ideas of where to take BitInstant and whom he privately despised. 'David just wanted to build a business that was generating cash,' he says. In short, he lacked vision.

But informing Azar that he was being cut loose would not be easy. Charlie was anxious about making the call. Finally he summoned up the courage and, with Erik Voorhees joining him in his office for moral support, he picked up the phone. The conversation quickly devolved into a shouting match, with the spurned investor yelling down the phone lines about the time and effort he had already spent on BitInstant, and how can you do this, leveling accusations of betrayal – 'all this total bullshit', as Erik calls it. Finally the call ended; more than likely, one of them hung up on the other.

And then the phone rang. It was the uncle, Victor Azrak. Having been informed of what was going on, he proceeded to pack Charlie's bags and whisk him away on the selfsame guilt trip that David Azar had booked for him, only now the load was heavier, Azrak being a more senior member of New York's Syrian Jewish community and one who therefore wielded more influence. Erik, listening in, was disgusted by the manipulative tactics and felt terrible for his friend: 'The business side of it was hard enough – trying to figure out what was a smarter business move – but then for them to levy on thousands of years of ethnic blame was crazy.'

Azar would not be denied. He presented a new, more attractive deal, one that gave him less equity and BitInstant more money, with the result that Charlie would retain control of his company. More importantly, he finally caved on the clauses of the contract which had been the source of so much discord – including the idea to drip-feed money to BitInstant – and about which he had been so stubborn before. 'I really want to do this deal,' he told Charlie in apparent earnestness.

Among the BitInstant staff the debate over outside investment now flared up again with new ferocity. Charlie sums up the dilemma as follows: 'So now here I have in front of me either a term sheet from Larry or a done deal with David. Erik and I couldn't deal with David at this point. We hated David. He was meddling, he was intense, he was ridiculous, he's annoying, he's loud. He's just the worst. But we needed the money. And we couldn't take the risk of having to wait for Larry.'

Lawrence Lenihan had no inkling of this internal debate. Neither did Barry Silbert. Yet this would be the excuse Charlie proffered in the months to come for why he threw over a worthy suitor – FirstMark Capital – in favor of David Azar, Victor Azrak, and Cameron and Tyler Winklevoss. He had wanted to make a deal with Lenihan but 'it just took too long,' he says. BitInstant needed the capital urgently – for hiring, for legal expenses, for float – and so there was nothing for it but to traipse out to the home of David Azar's lawyer, a man with whom he could still converse amicably, bringing Erik along for backup and with Roger riding shotgun, as it were, on a long-distance phone connection from Tokyo, to sign the papers. But before signing, Charlie recalls, he insisted that Erik be given two percent of the company and Ira three percent in recognition of all they had contributed. 'I pulled Erik to the side, I said, "Erik, in the contract right now, before I sign, I'm giving you two percent." And that's how I convinced him to be okay with the deal.' Ultimately, David Azar and Victor Azrak together invested about $500,000 in BitInstant and the Winklevosses invested $1 million alongside them.

All that remained was to break the news to Lawrence Lenihan. Charlie had breakfast with him at Coffee Shop, a generically named but trendy downtown diner and bar whose large windows look east onto Union Square Park. Sunlight filled the diner as Charlie looked at his would-be investor and explained that he had taken the deal with David Azar.

Lenihan did the younger man the courtesy of not hiding his disappointment. 'Charlie, you're a nice guy,' he said, 'but you're naive, and it's going to bite you in the ass some day.' The way Charlie had handled himself – juggling multiple deals, planning to do a deal and then going back on it – was for Lenihan a sign of inexperience, even foolishness. Worse, it showed a lack of decisiveness. He didn't think Charlie had what it took to lead the company. 'You're not assertive,' he said, and went on listing the younger man's faults. Charlie dismissed what he was hearing, not rudely but in a way that left no doubt in Lenihan's mind that he would take none of the older man's words to heart. Lenihan would say, months later, that he believed Charlie was simply enamored of the 'Winklevii' – as the brothers are sometimes impishly called – and that this led him foolishly to choose these investors over FirstMark Capital.

Well, it couldn't be helped. The deal was done. Now Charlie would have to live with it.

PERHAPS TO WATCH OVER THEIR investment, the Winklevosses in January moved into a 5,000-square-foot office in the Flatiron district, the same neighborhood where BitInstant was located.[4] One night the previous fall, not long before they settled on terms, they had asked Erik and Charlie to meet them at the BitInstant offices. They were still wrapping their heads around Bitcoin and there were some things they wanted to discuss. When the Winklevosses arrived, Charlie and Erik offered them a drink. It was, after all, half past nine. What they had lying around the office were a few bottles of NEFT, a brand of Russian vodka whose website features the Bitcoin logo along with the declaration – written in the sort of article-dropped English employed when mimicking a Russian accent – 'We support Bitcoin economy.' It was booze you could buy with bitcoins. *Neft* is Russian for 'oil', and so the libation they glugged that night out of the black bottle shaped like a miniature oil barrel must have seemed especially appropriate, for they were all men with discriminating taste in commodities. 'We drank, between the four of us, a whole bottle of vodka – just chugging it out of the bottle, passing it around like a joint,' Charlie says. 'We got completely wasted.' He and the Winklevosses adjourned to a loft party, where, he says, a 'crazy time' was had. (Erik had excused himself on this occasion, though on another night he did go out with Charlie and one of the Winklevoss twins – he can't remember which.)

They made the rounds of various bars and speakeasies. They began to meet women, magically, effortlessly. The women would approach the Winklevosses, who towered over Charlie. The twins tried to wingman for him. 'They gave me two different opportunities to get laid with girls, and I screwed them both up,' he recalls. The first time, he threw up all over the girl's shoes. The second girl he brought back to the Winklevosses' place. The twins each had a girl. Charlie had stuck around, playing catch-as-catch-can lothario to the Winklevosses' 'leftovers', he says. Now he found himself on the couch with his new lady friend, his hosts having retreated to their bedrooms. 'We were hooking up on the couch, and going to second base,' Charlie recalls, 'and then she's like, "Well, I'm conservative . . . I don't want to do this any more." And I was like, "Stop being a fucking pussy. Don't be a bitch." She took it the wrong way and she just fucking got up and left.' It was, he would later say, 'a crazy fucking night'. And it demonstrated just how far the Winklevosses were willing to go to seal the deal with BitInstant. Their Flatiron office made perfect sense. Now that they were sinking seven figures into the startup, they weren't about to give Charlie and his team any breathing room.

Their involvement, however, which former BitInstant employees say became increasingly overbearing with time, did not prevent other youthful shenanigans. In BitInstant's Flatiron space were two large offices. Charlie took one for himself; the other he repurposed as a meeting room and hangout space, not wanting to play Solomon in the matter of who else among his employees deserved an office with dimensions equal to his own. Like many startups, BitInstant was a pressure cooker in those days, and work often continued well past five o'clock. Many nights found Charlie, Erik, and Ira hanging out in this second office after hours, smoking pot – a bonding ritual so common that they dubbed the room the Bakery. For Charlie it was something of a necessity. 'I won't hire you unless I drink with you or smoke weed with you – that's a 100 percent fact,' he said later.[5]

It was a blurring of the line between work and social life that most millennials would recognize – more extreme than most, perhaps, but as a matter of degree, not of kind. 'Charlie's main qualification for coworkers was if they could smoke weed or drink with him and chill together,' says Rachel Yankelevitz, who had reservations about this hiring criteria. 'I don't necessarily think that makes you qualified for the job, just because you can hang with Charlie and bro down.' The fortunate fact, she hastens to add, was that Erik and Ira, in addition to their merits in this regard, were indeed qualified.

As early as January they were gearing up for a complete over-haul of the website and its services, an improved version they described among themselves as BitInstant 2.0. Having broken ground with their initial service, Charlie and his team now aspired to build a new kind of company altogether, one that would sell bitcoins directly to customers and buy bitcoins directly from them, operating in the cryptocurrency ecosystem much like a dealer in securities, which buys and sells for its own account rather than on behalf of clients as a brokerage firm does. Still further develop-ments lay on the horizon, the very ones Lenihan had anticipated – customer wallets, merchant processing, remittance tools. They would leave the old site running as it was to serve existing customers, while, in a separate sandbox, they wiped it all away to start from scratch. Once the new version was finished they would release it onto the web, like swapping out an old tenement for a condominium tower overnight. Ira was doing the heavy lifting of developing its back end, but he needed help. The previous fall, BitInstant had hired Alex Waters, a soft-spoken, intense college dropout who for a time had performed quality assurance on the core Bitcoin software code. Initially, Alex worked on Bitcoin Wireless, a BitInstant project aimed at the South American market that allowed people to top up their prepaid phone minutes by paying with bitcoins. But the project was later scrapped, and Alex began working side-by-side with Ira on BitInstant 2.0.

At least in theory, the revamp would allow BitInstant to continue growing at a rapid clip while staying on the right side of the law. 'After hundreds of thousands of dollars, the lawyers came up with a list' of laws with which they believed BitInstant should be in compliance, says Ira, 'but at the end of the day, all you've done is make a best guess.' After all, he adds, this new asset class, cryptocurrency, was a question mark – 'could be information, could be speech, could be a commodity'. But everyone knew the odds were better than fair that the regulators – starting, no doubt, with the Internal Revenue Service and including soon enough the New York Department of Financial Services – would seek to define it in such a way as to get their hands firmly around its throat. As yet they didn't seem to be casting a jaundiced eye on BitInstant. But the company's transaction volume was growing month by month. It was only a matter of time before the hyenas noticed the fattening of the gazelle.

By upgrading to version 2.0, BitInstant hoped to forestall regulatory action. 'Our lawyers told us that if you're a direct buyer and seller of bitcoins and have your own inventory, it's not money transmission,' Charlie says. Even so, BitInstant had registered with FinCEN as a money services business, and as such it had a responsibility to know who its customers were. The company at last implemented background checks. It was a tiered system; the amount of information collected on any given customer depended on the size and volume of a customer's transactions. BitInstant now seemed in a better position than ever before. 'It was a great team – me, Gareth, Rachel, Erik, Ira,' Charlie says. 'The company was growing, we had a great dynamic. Gareth and Ira were working so well together. We were all best friends.'

But a sticking point remained. As independent contractors for BitInstant, Erik and Ira were in a unique position, caught between Charlie's company and their own startup, Coinapult, and what had once seemed like an enviable measure of freedom had come increasingly to look like a conflict of interest. Coinapult initially was not a true company but merely a bundle of software Ira had written; because of this fact, along with their shared allegiance to 'the meta-organization of Bitcoin', Erik and Ira charged BitInstant no commission on customer orders fulfilled using

Coinapult's technology. As the businesses grew together, however, tensions arose as a result of their competing commitments. It became hard to see where one startup ended and the other began. The interests of both were already aligned; it was time to strike a deal that would make them not merely simpatico but united. It was time for a merger.

A plan swiftly took shape. BitInstant would buy Coinapult's technology and make Erik and Ira full employees in a single stroke. It would be historic, the first ever merger or acquisition between two Bitcoin companies. It would also seemingly solve the regulatory issues: Coinapult's technology would allow BitInstant to hold its own inventory of bitcoins rather than passing digital currency along from a third party.

Satisfied, Charlie and his team took the plan to David Azar. He was against it. Coinapult had been all this time giving free milk to BitInstant; buying the cow was not in the cards. When they turned to the Winklevosses for a second opinion, the brothers exploded. 'They were so pissed about it that they made David start to look reasonable,' Erik says. Evidently the twins had not understood that Coinapult was a separate company. Nor had they known that two of BitInstant's best employees were independent contractors. As far as they were concerned, the Coinapult code already belonged to BitInstant; any request by Ira Miller and Erik Voorhees for compensation could only be an attempt to defraud the company, and any payout would be tantamount to highway robbery. 'They seemed pretty upset that they couldn't steal Coinapult from us,' Ira was later to say, drily summarizing the dispute. Roger Ver did his best to mediate between BitInstant and the other investors, but his efforts were in vain.

For the next week or two, Charlie found himself on the receiving end of a torrent of verbal abuse. The yelling matches on the telephone began anew, with BitInstant's CEO insisting that he couldn't run the company without Erik and Ira. But the Winklevosses wouldn't let up. 'Erik and Ira are trying to take advantage of you!' he recalls the investors telling him. 'They're your friends, so you're not thinking clearly. *We're* the good guys.' Charlie, to his credit, continued to fight for his people. 'January was the month of hell,' Erik says.

One day in February, at a meeting with the Winklevosses, things came to a head. Charlie was there, as were Erik and Ira, who had already decided before entering the room that they would resign on the spot if the investors couldn't be made to see reason. In the meeting, Cameron and Tyler took the opportunity to lay down the law. They were not about to be extorted by a couple of twenty-something libertarians. Erik and Ira were replaceable, they insisted. BitInstant could build its own version of their technology. Finally they delivered an ultimatum: either Erik and Ira would sign over to BitInstant the sum total of Coinapult's intellectual property, or they would be fired. 'And if you don't fire them, Charlie,' the investors said, 'then we're going to block every business decision you ever try to make, and your company is just going to be fucked.' Any large purchases, additional fundraising, 'or doing anything momentous for the company', as Charlie puts it, required the shareholders to be unanimous. The Winklevosses were threatening to cripple BitInstant. They evidently possessed not only the power but the will. 'Basically they were just total dickheads,' Erik says of their behavior in the meeting. Finally, after another round of insults from the hulking twins, Erik and Ira stood up from the table and walked out. There was nothing more to discuss.

They knew what their next step would be. Coinapult would become their full-time job, soon to be headquartered in Panama, away from the prying eyes and subpoenas of US regulators. It was not a spur-of-the-moment decision. Erik and Ira had previously suggested to Charlie that Panama – where the US dollar is accepted as legal tender and which, lacking a central bank, is unable to print money at will or manipulate exchange rates – might be an ideal home for BitInstant, and they now took up this thread again, doing their best to persuade Charlie to relocate with them. For Coinapult it was a no-brainer. 'They were never going to bother with getting the licensing or abiding by the regulations they would have needed to operate in the US,' says Rachel Yankelevitz. But for Charlie, a native son of Brooklyn, leaving New York was too much of an unknown.

And he knew the investors would balk at any attempt to relocate. He decided to stay. His friends, on the verge of trading an icy New York for the sun-kissed tropics, warned him of the likely outcome. 'After we left, there wasn't a lot to hold it together,' Ira says. 'We thought the direction things were going was pretty untenable.'

Barry Silbert agreed. The capital provided by David Azar, Victor Azrak, and the Winklevosses had not triggered the conversion of his note into equity as a larger investment round from FirstMark Capital would have done, leaving him in a position no angel investor could enjoy: holding a pumpkin which, without the expected fairy godmother, may not transform any time soon. He saw Erik and Ira's departure as putting his money at unacceptable risk. So he asked for it back. Charlie would later interpret his request as an indication of antipathy for the Winklevosses, that he couldn't stand to be an investor alongside them, though Barry says he learned only months later whose money Charlie had taken. When he speaks about the decision now, Barry is diplomatic, saying little but implying much: 'There was a . . . I won't say a *long* list, but there was a list of flashing danger signs, and so I decided that I would take my money out.' Charlie wired him the money – his original $100,000 plus interest.

Barry reinvested it in Coinapult. (Erik and Ira's unceremonious departure from BitInstant had done nothing to cool their ardor for Bitcoin.) Later in the spring of 2013, Larry Lenihan's firm made a six-figure investment of its own in Coinapult, in reality an investment in the raw intellect and can-do engineering spirit of its founders. 'These are the best of the technologists and tinkerers in the Bitcoin world,' he was to say, 'so it was a no-brainer to be able to take a stake in them.'[6]

Meanwhile, Charlie seemed reluctant to look outside the company for new blood, believing, perhaps rightly, that it would be easier to promote from within someone who already understood Bitcoin. And so into the great sucking vacuum left behind by Erik and Ira stepped Alex Waters. He was the obvious choice. Not counting Gareth Nelson, BitInstant had only two full-time developers, including Alex, and the other one worked remotely.

Bitter feelings about the breakup lingered. Rachel Yankelevitz recalls Ira's girlfriend telling her something that put the whole affair into perspective – that whereas some people see an opportunity and seize it, while others don't see it and miss it, 'the Winklevosses see an opportunity and they fuck it up.' The following month, wanting to break free of their influence, Roger offered the twins a deal: either he would buy them out at 115 percent of the value of their stake, or they could buy him out at half the value of his stake according to the valuation they had just given the company. (Roger owned fifteen percent of BitInstant.) No way, they said. Fifteen percent apparently wasn't a big enough return on their investment, and besides, Charlie says, 'These guys, they don't care about money. If someone had come along and offered them twenty million, they wouldn't have taken it. It's ego. It's power. BitInstant was the biggest Bitcoin company at the time, and would have been still today *the* biggest Bitcoin company.' Months later, Roger still couldn't believe it. 'They could have made fifteen percent on their investment in like two weeks. You tell any businessman that story and he'll say the Winklevosses were crazy.'

To avoid losing customers, BitInstant had no choice but to continue making Coinapult's services available to them – services for which it now began paying a commission. The 'significant technological synergies' between the two companies, to use Ira's words, were now kept in place only by a contract, as if time were leasing itself to space to keep the continuum going. And yet Charlie nevertheless found himself on 15 March, after what he described as a rough couple of weeks, apologizing to his customers for delays in processing their orders. Coinapult had been 'upgrading core components' of its system, he explained. As a result, Coinapult's ability to send bitcoins directly to customers' Bitcoin addresses had been down for days and had only now been turned back on. To placate disgruntled users, Charlie offered to honor any unsuccessful orders at the exchange rate that had been current when they were originally placed – a boon to customers and a significant cost to BitInstant, since the Bitcoin price had risen from $30.90 on 28 February to more than $47 by the ides of March – and to waive all processing fees for those orders. 'Growing pains are inevitable,' he wrote, 'but it's still not acceptable for our customers to be affected by them.'

But these were more than growing pains; they were cracks in the facade. With the benefit of hindsight, he now sees the departure of Erik and Ira, his friends and confidants – respectively the start-up's eloquent visionary and its withdrawn master coder – as the beginning of the end for BitInstant. 'That's when the company fell apart,' he says, 'February 2013.'

Chapter 6

REGULATION BLUES

Every spirit makes its house; but afterwards the house confines the spirit.

— Ralph Waldo Emerson

The task that Ira Miller had left unfinished at BitInstant was enormous: rewriting the source code underlying all of BitInstant's services. This codebase, Gareth's creation, had not been designed to function with a large number of users. A cowboy coder, a lone wolf and an autodidact, Gareth wrote code in his own idiosyncratic way, and, like a rickety bridge that becomes more precarious the more people pile onto it, his faulty system now began to show its flaws. What were once minor bugs – the sort of thing that might cause orders to get stuck one percent of the time, say – became major problems; one percent of hundreds or thousands of trans-actions, after all, was a headache-inducing number for the company's customer support staff. All this the new lead programmer, Alex Waters, understood completely and summarized simply: 'There were a shitload of problems.'

Alex was only twenty-six years old but was, in the way of ambitious college dropouts, already well along in his career. He had previously held project management positions at Arc90, a product design agency, and at Grossman Interactive, a small New York web design firm. He had also been in business for himself as a web developer. Officially he now became BitInstant's chief information officer, though increasingly, as time went on, he would be expected to assume the responsibilities of both Erik and Ira – hiring new people, spearheading development of BitInstant 2.0, doing his best to translate the requirements given to him by the CEO and the investors into workable solutions.

His tenure was to be in more than one sense a changing of the guard. He was not on the side of the elites, but neither was he entirely simpatico with the angry young men who saw every regulation as a hurdle to overleap, who wanted entirely to divorce global commerce from government oversight. 'I get the libertarian arguments and "Fuck the state" and all that,' he says, 'but you don't go changing geopolitics by giving a middle finger to those sitting in power.' At a deep level, he was a pragmatist, or rather his idealism expressed itself through practical action. 'I care about what's effective. We have constraints, and we can do things within those constraints that push the boundaries of those constraints.'

He was not, in other words, Erik Voorhees, given to saying things like 'Bitcoin is absolutely the Wild West of finance, and thank goodness.'[1] Instead what he found most compelling about Bitcoin was its potential to alleviate global inequality, redistributing power from the wealthy few to the impoverished masses. He had little patience for those industry insiders who wanted to co-opt the digital currency for their own political ends, 'like saying the banks are bad and Bitcoin is a tool to bring about their demise . . . Bitcoin is a much bigger thing than that.' Bitcoin the ideological weapon had become the enemy, he felt, of Bitcoin the technology. This was his position, and it was not an ignoble one. It must be regarded, then, as one of life's little ironies that the first major test of BitInstant's system under his watch occurred because of an economic crisis triggered by a government intent on picking its citizens' pockets.

Cyprus, a Mediterranean island nation with a population of scarcely more than one million, had hit the skids. It shouldn't have mattered except to Cypriots, because the island's gross national product accounts for just 0.2% of total eurozone GDP. But its bloated banking system was sheltering $31 billion for Russian banks and companies, much of it perhaps of illicit origin.[2] The Cypriot banks had plowed these depositor funds into Greek loans and bonds as well as into Cyprus's own sovereign debt – a good move only as long as the economies of both nations stayed strong. When Greece stumbled, it threatened to take Cyprus down with it.[3] The rest of Europe organized a $13 billion bailout to avert a national bankruptcy, but only on the condition that the Cypriot parliament agree to a radical proposal: a tax of no less than 6.75 percent levied against all deposits in Cypriot banks – that is, against not only the wealth of Russian oligarchs but the savings of every native citizen, all 1.1 million of them, even the poorest.

An attempt to force Cyprus to foot part of the bill for its own rescue, it was an unprecedented move. David Zervos, the chief market strategist at Jefferies, described it in a note to clients as 'a nuclear war on savings and wealth'.[4] Economists lined up to warn of dire consequences. Joachim Fels of Morgan Stanley pulled no punches, telling clients the plan was 'a worrying precedent with potentially systemic consequences'.[5] Peter Bofinger, a longtime member of the German Council of Economic Experts and a professor of monetary policy and international economics at the University of Würzburg, warned that it would 'shake the trust of depositors across the Continent. Europe's citizens now have to fear for their money.'[6]

And they did. When the markets reopened on 18 March, a Monday, stocks fell around the world, as did the prices of government bonds issued by other unsound European countries – Italy, Spain, Portugal, and Ireland. The value of the euro dropped and Cypriots lined up at ATMs to withdraw their money, leading the nation's central bank to impose a daily withdrawal limit of 100 euros in order to prevent massive bank runs.[7] The ominous news was felt as far away as Japan.

But there were two assets that climbed in value while nearly everything else seemed to be falling. One was gold, which rose for the first time in weeks above $1,600 a troy ounce, an increase of 0.8 percent.[8] The other was Bitcoin. To all appearances, Cyprus offered an unignorable vindication of the views espoused by libertarian Bitcoiners – that banks and governments deserve neither your money nor your trust. Suddenly the experimental currency looked like an experiment worth trying. In Spain, Bitcoin apps for the iPhone began rocketing up the download charts. As people started buying, the price of Bitcoin, which had started the year at only $13, shot up from $20 in early February to more than $90 by the end of March. For the first time ever, the total market value of all bitcoins in existence – which, at that moment, was 10,958,700 – passed $1 billion. It was an important symbolic threshold. Crossing it meant that the digital currency was a greater body of wealth than the official money supply of twenty-three countries, including the Central African Republic and Liberia, and within shouting distance of a dozen more. And Bitcoin continued to climb even after the Cypriot parliament redesigned the deal on 25 March to preserve insured deposits of 100,000 euros or less – though Cyprus Popular, the nation's second-largest bank, was to be shut down, with a heavy tax of around thirty percent imposed on deposits of more than 100,000 euros there and in the Bank of Cyprus, the island's largest. By early April the price hit $150. Charlie, together with other early adopters, was suddenly a millionaire.

But he had little time to revel in his wealth. In the markets of America, Europe, and Asia a kind of gold fever now took hold, and the twenty-four-hour, seven-days-a-week online exchanges run out of Slovenia and Bulgaria and Japan bore witness to a massive surge in trading activity, which, along with a simultaneous and unprecedented appreciation in the value of Bitcoin, pushed the daily trading volume on top exchanges by the middle of April to forty-three times what it had been, measured in dollars, at the beginning of March – from $895,000 to more than $38 million. On Mt. Gox alone, 75,000 new accounts were opened in the first ten days of April, 10,000 more than the number of sign-ups for the whole of the preceding month. As new enthusiasts and speculators piled into the cryptocurrency, many availed themselves of BitInstant's fast deposits and inter-exchange transfers. The company's transaction volume jumped by an order of magnitude – from perhaps three hundred transactions a day to as many as three thousand. Suddenly the BitInstant staffers, some of whom were already on extended startup hours, were working overtime. 'Things have been insane,' Charlie told a documentary filmmaker who visited him at the BitInstant offices. 'I haven't slept in days.'

Every time a customer order didn't go through, for any reason, a support ticket was created, leaving Rachel Yankelevitz and other staffers to retry the orders by manually reentering all the information. Always a slow and painstaking process, it was now wholly inadequate for the volume of orders BitInstant was receiving. Worse, with some of the exchanges also suffering unprecedented traffic, their APIs – the set of rules by which other software could communicate with them – were continually going down. With the lines of communication cut, BitInstant customer orders weren't getting through. So not only had the number of orders increased by ten times but the percentage of orders that were unsuccessful was also rising.

To relieve some of the pressure, Alex hacked together a solution that he called the 'requeue'. It sorted failed orders into a smart queueing system that would retry them at more opportune times. This piece of engineering reduced by a factor of a hundred the number of orders that had to be retried manually, Alex says. And it soon became apparent that what had been a spur-of-the-moment solution to BitInstant's backlog could also help the business in calmer weather to serve a larger customer base.

But for now, there was a popping price bubble to contend with. On 10 April, trading activity on Mt. Gox tripled overnight, and Bitcoin peaked at $266, an all-time high that had seemed unimaginable just weeks earlier. But then the rollercoaster crested the rise and began to plummet down, shedding fortunes as it went – the price fell to $105 before returning to $130, less than half of what it had been only hours before. Within days, as skeptics sounded death knells, the price would sink to a low of $50 (though it soon rebounded into triple digits). For the time being, the frenzy was over. BitInstant survived the bubble, but it had just barely passed the Cyprus test. If Alex Waters took one lesson from the ordeal, it was this: he needed more developers.

In early May, with the blessing of Charlie and the investors, Alex went on an aggressive hiring spree, scooping up engineering talent wherever he could find it. Some of the new hires were so young that Rachel, much to Alex's chagrin, began calling the room where they worked the Puppy Pen. He was under orders from the Winklevosses to fire any employees who didn't prove themselves within a month or two. 'It's a trivial expense in the long run if things work,' Cameron told him. 'If things don't work, we have much bigger problems. Just GO, and don't look back.'

Having now outgrown the Flatiron office, the company relocated to a furnished space at 256 West 36th Street, where they occupied the entire third floor, some 3,400 square feet, in the process upping their monthly rent from $4,500 to $16,000. The Winklevosses approved of the expense, counting on the posh new digs to be a recruiting and promotional tool. But they had mounting doubts about Charlie's leadership. They wanted to make a change.

Later that month, Cameron and Tyler Winklevoss pulled Alex aside and broached the subject of BitInstant's top job. They were hoping he would step up and run the company, they told him.

Alex was receptive to the idea. It was not uncommon for tech startups to reach a point at which their initial founders could take them no further, so this would not be a coup, not exactly, though it was clear to everyone involved that Charlie – who so loved the spotlight – might not be keen to give up the top job in the company he had built. They didn't plan to give him any choice. That month, the investors demanded to see a new website, complete with an upgraded service, within thirty days. Miss that deadline and they would pull their money, ruining BitInstant. 'They were just kind of being dicks,' Rachel says. 'But to be fair, we had kept pushing back the launch date.'

There remained the matter of the new CEO's compensation. Alex wanted a raise and he wanted an ownership stake in the company. As it stood, he says, he had no equity and was drawing a salary of about $90,000 – not bad for a junior developer in Manhattan, but not at all commensurate with the responsibilities he'd already taken on, and certainly not with what was now being asked of him. He considered aiming high, asking for six percent of the company and allowing himself to be negotiated down to five percent. Charlie had even mentioned six percent, had assured him more than once that he would be given something that reflected the value he provided to the company. But Alex wasn't the type to use hardball tactics. He figured he could be happy with five percent. With five percent he would have the confidence he needed to devote himself fully to BitInstant. Having grown up in a family of modest means in Long Beach, he still felt an obligation to justify to friends and family the way he spent his time, and mostly these days his time was spent working for BitInstant. It was not that he minded the all-nighters – 'What I like to do is work,' he remarked recently – but he wanted to be sure that he would have something to show for them.

The investors were confident a deal could be reached. But ten days later, when Cameron Winklevoss checked in, there was nothing to report. Charlie was stalling. Alex explained his terms. 'Okay, let me talk to the guys and circle back,' Cameron said.

Alex continued to run operations and development as best as he could, doing alone the jobs once done by Erik and Ira, and for a company now two or three times larger. The challenges were numerous. Angry customers heaped abuse on Rachel and the other customer service reps. Awkward flirting from the 'basement-dwelling nerds' who had been BitInstant's early user base she could handle, but things got scary when one guy told Rachel that he had a gun and would come find her. More than once, a customer with a grievance did show up at the office, putting everyone on edge. A lot of money was at stake: earlier that spring BitInstant had been processing $6 million a month in transactions, of which it was capturing about $300,000 a month in fees. But in April, the month of the price bubble, it had processed a whopping $9.1 million. Charlie was the only signatory for the company bank accounts, which, employees say, he continued to treat like his personal accounts. He seemed to be running a sideline selling bitcoins to the company from his own stash. He claimed it was necessary for float, but these claims were difficult to verify, especially because

Charlie for so long insisted on maintaining exclusive control of the finances. There would be a wire transfer to his account for, say, $50,000, but scant documentation on what the money was for. To an outside party, Rachel says, it might have appeared to be embezzlement, even money laundering. 'It would have looked bad if we'd been audited, that's all I can say.'

He had other things than audits on his mind. That spring he had met and swiftly fallen for a blonde, blue-eyed *shiksa* of whom his strictly religious parents disapproved, an aspiring film actress in her early thirties named Courtney Warner. As the romance consumed more of Charlie's time, the demands of running BitInstant receded in importance. But it was a startup facing regulatory challenges and rising competition, founded on a technology barely older than toddler age. It was not something you could put on cruise control.

Meanwhile the ground was shifting under his feet. In March, the Financial Crimes Enforcement Network released guidance forecasting how it would apply existing law to digital currencies – or, as it called them, virtual currencies.[9] It was the first time a US government agency had spoken openly about decentralized digital currencies such as Bitcoin. According to FinCEN, any business exchanging bitcoins for fiat currency or vice versa, or even one virtual currency for another, could be considered a money transmitter.

'FinCEN is clearly trying, in its somewhat bumbling way, to squeeze a square technological peg into its round regulatory hole,' noted one observer.[10] Until now, nobody had been able to say for certain under what regulatory regime Bitcoin businesses might fall. A great deal of uncertainty remained, as state laws said nothing about digital currencies, but FinCEN, though not a lawmaking body, had now planted the standard of government oversight some furlongs further forward into the chaos of digital currency. 'Even without having the force of law, it was an absolute game-changer,' says Marco Santori, a lawyer who has advised several Bitcoin startups. 'It completely terraformed the regulatory landscape.'

The guidance was a mixed bag. On the one hand, it represented official recognition by an agency of the US government that Bitcoin was money, that it had value and should be treated for some intents and purposes just as dollars were treated. Indeed, Erik had thought the rising Bitcoin price in March and April had less to do with events in Cyprus than with the FinCEN guidance, which, though it sought to maintain a distinction between virtual currency and 'real currency', signaled that Bitcoin itself was not illegal and that it would not seek to regulate the core Bitcoin network. Consumer use of Bitcoin to pay for goods and services had not been criminalized, nor were individuals required to register as money transmitters. Mainstream investors could now make deals with Bitcoin startups, confident that federal regulators weren't going to scorch the earth. By mid-May, a handful of companies had raised a total of more than $14 million in new funding. One of them was the payment processor BitPay, in which Roger Ver had previously invested. Among those providing BitPay with $2 million in seed money was Founders Fund, Peter Thiel's venture capital firm. While the Silicon Valley billionaire had been unable to realize his own dream of an electronic currency outside of government control, he could now get a piece of Bitcoin.

On the other hand, it was clear that the guidance would have deleterious effects both on major Bitcoin companies like BitInstant and on smaller, less well-capitalized players, who would be shut out of the US market entirely. For BitInstant, the regulation, according to Santori, would immediately wipe out 'a big swathe of [the] customer base, who at this stage are those crypto-anarchists who embrace Bitcoin because it does not embrace the government. You immediately have to stop doing business with them, if they aren't willing to give up their information.'

One option for companies was to go offshore, as Coinapult had done, though even there they could run afoul of US laws. According to most state regulators, overseas financial companies need licenses to serve customers in their states, even if the companies have no physical presence there. As late as July 2014, Jesse Powell, the CEO of Kraken, could say, 'Fortunately most of the world right now isn't regulating Bitcoin at all,' and a company like Coinapult could serve customers in Europe, Asia, and other parts of the world. But it was forced to shut its doors to Americans.

All through that hot New York summer, Marco Santori, in his office at Nesenoff & Miltenberg – a law firm which that July began allowing clients to pay their bills in bitcoins – fielded phone calls from people who wanted to pick his brain about cryptocurrency regulations. But when he obliged the callers, most of them entrepreneurs hoping to set up shop in America, with a primer on the legal outlook for Bitcoin companies, they would lose all hope.

It wasn't long before FinCEN's talk turned to action. Anyone who had thought it could not label an entire industry of cutting-edge startups as potential criminal enterprises got a wake-up call in May 2013, when agents from the Baltimore office of Homeland Security Investigations – the very office running the Marco Polo task force whose mission was to take down Silk Road – seized funds in a Dwolla account belonging to a US subsidiary of Mt. Gox. The subsidiary company, Mutum Sigillum, was operating without federal registration and without any state licenses. It also wasn't identifying customers and monitoring their transactions in accordance with AML and KYC standards. Indeed, Mutum Sigillum had been hiding from its own bank. In 2011, according to the seizure warrant, Mark Karpelès had opened a Wells Fargo business account for the company, of which he was the single authorized signatory. In doing so, he had filled out a document that asked whether Mutum Sigillum dealt in or exchanged currency for customers, and whether it transmitted customer funds. To both of these questions, Karpelès had answered no. (In his defense, the US government would almost certainly have been loath to describe Bitcoin as money in 2011.) Now viewing the company as an unregistered money transmitter, Homeland Security proceeded between May and July to seize more than $5 million from Mutum Sigillum. Stung, Mt. Gox belatedly registered with FinCEN and began verifying its customers' identities, requiring them to provide a scanned image of their passport or driver's license, along with other information.

And the hits kept on coming. In July, the SEC filed charges against a thirty-year-old Texan named Trendon Shavers, whom the agency accused of running a Bitcoin Ponzi scheme. On the Bitcoin Forum, where he went by the screen name pirateat40, Shavers had started soliciting investments in early November 2011 for a kind of unincorporated hedge fund he called Bitcoin Savings & Trust. The fund – initially called First Pirate Savings & Trust – promised lenders a daily return of one percent, an absurd enough offering that the first reply to his solicitation was, 'Smells like a classical [high-yield investment program] scam.' But dozens of people did entrust him with their money; over the next nine months, he received more than 700,000 bitcoins, or $4.6 million in terms of the average exchange rate over the period. He also paid out just over 507,000 BTC, keeping the rest for himself, which he sold or used for day trading on a Bitcoin exchange. Shavers made entry to the fund increasingly exclusive, but eventually people began to catch on, and his fund wound up heading a high-profile Bitcoin Forum watchlist of Ponzi schemes to avoid. All of them would go bust by the end of 2012, including Bitcoin Savings & Trust. 'Bitcoin has grown a lot since I started this,' Shavers told his lenders when he shut down the fund in August 2012, 'and [I] want you to know that you were a vital part in helping it grow.'

Less than a year later, the SEC charged him with running a Ponzi scheme. Unusually, the agency followed up its enforcement action with a press release; more unusually still, it also issued an investor alert, telling people to beware of fraudulent Bitcoin investments. Federal regulators clearly wanted maximum exposure. 'The message was very clear,' says Marco Santori. 'The SEC will regulate investments whether they are denominated in dollars, puka shells, bitcoins, potatoes – they don't care.' A new technology had appeared, and the SEC wanted a piece of it. It was a regulatory land grab. And it was a huge blow to Bitcoin as a vehicle for raising capital. There was a segment of the industry composed of unlicensed, unregistered exchanges selling what were essentially illegal securities. People were buying shares in companies directly from the companies themselves, in blatant violation of securities laws. Erik Voorhees, who was running a Bitcoin gambling website called SatoshiDice alongside his work for Coinapult, used one of these exchanges, MPEx, to sell thirteen million shares of SatoshiDice. He later had to settle an SEC case of his own related to this offering of unregistered securities.

There had been early warning signs of the government's response, but they had gone unheeded. In December 2012, Cody Wilson, an avowed crypto-anarchist who later became infamous for making the world's first 3D-printed handgun, ran into Bart Chilton, the head of the Commodity Futures Trading Commission (CFTC), while queueing for security at the airport in Little Rock, Arkansas. He introduced himself and said he was involved in Bitcoin. 'Oh?' Chilton asked. 'And how's that going for you?'

'I have to admit it's going pretty good,' Wilson said.

Chilton looked back over his shoulder at the young anarchist as he shuffled ahead in the security line. 'For now,' he said.[11]

Where Bitcoiners had once reveled in their under-the-radar monetary system, now – at every convention, on every message board, in every corner of the industry – there was a growing obsession with regulation.

BitInstant had three options. It could get licensed, avoid the license requirements (which would have meant radically altering its business model), or ride the coattails of an existing money transmitter. Following the March 2013 guidance from FinCEN, BitInstant had pursued the third option, negotiating a deal to be the agent of a mobile-payments company called Obopay. In addition to holding money-transfer licenses in most states, Obopay, a company with revenue of $8 million, was tied into debit networks like Visa's Interlink, meaning that for the first time BitInstant might be able to offer its customers the ability to send money straight from a bank account to BitInstant and receive bitcoins in return – no cash deposits, wire transfers, or third-party payment processors necessary, and no need to deal with an overseas, unlicensed Bitcoin exchange. But the negotiations dragged on. 'Every week they would come up with a new requirement for us; they were really jerking us around,' Rachel says. (For one thing, Obopay refused to sign an agreement until Charlie sent over a copy of BitInstant's AML policy.) When the deal was finally done, it gave

BitInstant the ability to transact with customers in dozens of states. But the bank transfers remained a pipe dream. 'Long story short, they didn't have their shit together,' says Rachel Yankelevitz. 'They weren't really equipped to integrate with us the way we needed to integrate with a company to do [it]. I don't think their tech was that good, I don't think they had the banking relationships that we would have needed . . . It was kind of a mess.'

Amid all the drama, the clock was running down on BitInstant 2.0. Charlie, feeling pressure from the investors, put pressure on his number two, Alex Waters. On 10 June, with customers' ability to make cash deposits temporarily disabled, he asked Alex for a status report on the new website. It was only hours away from being functional, though for the time being the new site would operate as a closed beta, by invitation only – a way to limit the pool of customers temporarily and give the development team a chance to catch and repair any bugs before allowing a flood of traffic into the system.

But Charlie wasn't satisfied. 'I think we should launch fully,' he told Alex over Skype chat. 'We need to make sure that we allow ALL transactions. Even [transactions] that don't require an account.' He also wanted to make sure that the new website's home page and How It Works page were ready. The latter was fine, BitInstant's CIO told him, but the home page still needed some work. 'As far as allowing all transactions, that's an easy flip of a switch,' Alex went on.

'OK, amazing,' Charlie replied.

Alex worked through the night, telling Charlie at 7:00 A.M. that he was going to grab a few hours of sleep but that he and David Iserovich, a junior developer, should be back in the office by 2:00 P.M. 'to start fixing shit'. By the late afternoon, Charlie was in a panic. The ability to do transactions without creating an account was still disabled, and customer support tickets were piling up. 'Tix are nonstop,' an employee told him. 'It's more of a question of what is working rather than not.' Charlie figured that enabling 'guest transactions' would solve a lot of the complaints. Customers, he said, 'should be able to do 1,000 per day' without registering on the site. In other words, Charlie wanted to make it possible for someone to move $1,000 a day through BitInstant without even creating an account, which would have forced the company to collect the customer's personal information, verify his identity, check it against terrorist watch lists, and then monitor his transactions, in accordance with the AML and KYC policies mandated by FinCEN. But a guest transaction could ghost through the system, going more or less unmonitored.

Alex patiently explained that he still had some back-end work to do before he could enable guest transactions, but that the feature would be ready soon. 'All these angry customers are angry because they can't create an account, not because we're holding their money,' he told the CEO. 'By tomorrow they can create an account and chill the f out, or do a guest transaction.'

'I agree,' Charlie conceded. 'Do you know why they can't create an account?'

There was still work to be done on a crucial database, Alex told him. 'We're hustling, the [development] team is shooting miracles out of our programming wands and not sleeping.'

In mid-June, BitInstant 2.0 finally launched. It was loaded with features the old version didn't have, including a greater number of partnering Bitcoin exchanges, an improved support request ticket system, and a cleaner user interface. The new version also provided live bitcoin-to-dollar exchange rates with a better explanation of BitInstant's fee schedules. It wasn't a mere facelift; Alex Waters and his developer team had rewritten the website's entire back-end from scratch. They had pulled it off – and within the Winklevosses' thirty-day deadline.

But the technical achievement did not guarantee stable finances. On 19 June, the developers' paychecks bounced. BitInstant's bank account had been closed, possibly due to suspicious activity, and Charlie – who was, according to Rachel, 'notorious for forgetting to pay people' – hadn't bothered to inform anyone. When Alex went on behalf of the development team to find out what was the matter, Charlie told him, 'We'll get it sorted out in a couple of days.' At times, Charlie was so cagey about the finances that the investors, losing patience, would contact Alex directly for a status report, even though he didn't know the finances firsthand; he could only tell them what he had heard from Brandon, the recently hired comptroller. In the investors' eyes, that was another problem: one internal accountant wasn't enough, not even if he was working on the company books – as, by now, he was – with outside counsel. 'We need an accounting firm. And we need transparency,' David Azar insisted in June, at which point the company had yet to file its 2012 tax return. 'We need transparency if we are going to raise more money. If anyone wants to look under the hood.' But then Charlie, who had entered the room, broke in – grabbing Alex's phone to text Azar: 'Please don't bother Alex. He's busy working on tech. You have my number and Skype.' In no uncertain terms, Charlie was attempting to cut off the investors from talking to anyone but him. Azar was dumbfounded. 'Free country,' he responded. 'No respect. Grow up.'

By now, Charlie was as frustrated with the investors as they were with him. He couldn't meet their demands. He was an entrepreneur but he wasn't CEO material, not for a company that had grown as BitInstant had, and the investors seemed unwilling to provide the mentorship necessary for him to grow into the role. 'I needed to be groomed,' he says. 'David wanted to be hands-off, he wanted to be able to leave me for two weeks, not say anything, come back two weeks later and find that things were amazing, things were better. It's like, "No, I either needed you to be on top of me – teach me how to be CEO, teach me how to run a company – or don't bother me at all. You can't have both."' The Winklevosses were harsh taskmasters, too, Charlie recalls. 'Sending me emails calling me a child, yelling at me and everything, and just making me feel like shit. It was really bad. I didn't know how to be CEO; I was trying to learn.'

Something had gone out of him with the resignation of Erik and Ira, a kind of innocence that comes of running a startup with your best friends, with whom you share a shining future: a heady cocktail that is equal parts camaraderie, youthful ambition, and naiveté. They were going to change the world and get high while doing it. That certainty – 'It was very much a feeling of, "We're gonna be millionaires and retire at thirty,"' Gareth says – was now gone, and Charlie could no longer see the way forward. And then, too, he was in a serious relationship for the first time in his life. 'He was kind of in party mode,' says Rachel. 'He was just acting like a twenty-three-year-old. He didn't really want to work; he wanted to sleep in and hang out with his girlfriend.'

When he did show up at the office, he had less direction than ever. For the most part, after the blowup over Coinapult, says Charlie, 'We stopped speaking, me and the Winklevosses. They left me to my own devices. They said, "Fix the company." And I tried. I promoted Alex, I hired more people; I thought what I was doing was for the best, but I wasn't a good CEO. I didn't know how to run a company of more than five people, and we were growing quickly. I didn't know how to fix any of these issues.' During a dispute with Mt. Gox at the height of the April price bubble, Charlie threw up his hands. 'Guys, this is extremely stressful,' he wrote in an email to Mark Karpelès and others. 'I'm not getting involved in this anymore. Alex, please take over.'

At times, when the investors deigned to speak to Charlie, they made absurd demands, which he relayed faithfully to Alex. 'The investors were awful,' Rachel says. 'I don't think they're evil people, I just think they were very clueless about Bitcoin.' As late as June, they were still asking basic questions: Where can we learn about the price fluctuations of Bitcoin since its inception? (Answer: On the website Blockchain.info.) Where can we find a chart showing global Bitcoin supply and demand from day one, in January 2009, to the present? (Answer: There is no single chart that captures this data.) Not wanting to miss out on another revolutionary technology, these men who believed themselves to be the inventors of Facebook had parachuted into the world of Bitcoin carrying a briefcase full of cash, but in their eagerness had scarcely bothered to learn the native language of the territory they were entering, to study its terrain or appreciate the special intricacies of its culture. As a consequence, though they were now embarking on a remedial course in Bitcoin 101, they were unable fully to convey their expectations for the business, or even to measure accurately whether those expectations were reasonable. They vacillated between micro-managing and being aloof. 'We couldn't win,' a former employee says. 'Whatever we did was a problem for them.'

For months now, Charlie had been thinking of quitting while he was ahead. He had already made his mark – and his fortune. 'After Erik and Ira left, I pretty much fucking checked out,' he says. Alex Waters was 'effectively CEO, we just didn't do paper-work. It was nothing. He was pretty much the CEO.' And yet Charlie resisted the loss of his title, which gave him so much clout among his peers and on which handsome speaking fees depended. The absence of paperwork was no mere formality; without it, Alex had no equity stake in the company he was now expected to lead. Later, Charlie would argue strenuously that he'd gladly have abdi-cated in full if only a viable replacement had been found. But Alex, he says, wasn't it. 'He didn't have the experience necessary. I thought he could [do the job]; if I didn't think he could, then I wouldn't have given him the opportunity. But I should have listened to Gavin [Andresen]. When I asked Gavin about hiring Alex in the beginning, Gavin was like, "You know, Alex is a good developer, but he should never be a team leader." And I didn't listen to his advice.'

This was at best an oversimplification of what Gavin had told him, and at worst an attempt to cloak his own sentiments in someone else's words. Gavin Andresen had been working as the lead developer of the Bitcoin software during the period in which Alex Waters was doing quality assurance testing of the core code – a job he was great at, according to Andresen. In a 2012 email, the developer told Charlie Shrem that Alex was 'smart and easy to work with'. While admitting that he was 'maybe a little inex-perienced' to be a team leader, Andresen noted that Alex 'could grow into that position', provided he had 'somebody to mentor/manage him to help him set priorities'. By the time Alex began to assume more responsibility, he had already worked under Ira Miller for months – and of course Charlie was there, or should have been there, to help him grow into the CEO position if indeed Charlie truly wanted to vacate it. 'If you're hiring him to be a QA team member' – the job for which Alex was first hired by BitInstant – 'I can recommend him without any reservations,' Andresen concluded.

And yet Charlie refused to see Alex as a worthy and capable successor. Charlie continued to be the face of the company, impelled in part by a sense of obligation to his investors and customers. Although it may not come across in his public persona, says Ira Miller, 'he has a large sense of responsibility and duty. Whenever he makes commitments to people, it weighs on him a lot.' It weighed on him because he had gotten used to thinking of BitInstant as *his* company. How could it continue to exist without him? Who else would see to the needs of its customers? But he couldn't find it in himself to be the leader his company needed. The dynamic that thus obtained, with a largely absent CEO delegating much of his responsibility but none of his authority or privilege, was untenable. It was, to use one former employee's pungent term, 'a clusterfuck'.

To make matters worse, BitInstant's legal team at the high-powered Perkins Coie – the thirty-third largest law firm in the US, whose clients have included Google, Amazon, and Boeing – had grown concerned about the nature of the company it was advising. Charlie had been ducking the lawyers, Rachel Yankelevitz says. If it had not already been clear that under existing law BitInstant was a money transmitter, the FinCEN guidance should have left little doubt. But Charlie had essentially misrepresented how his business worked. Even though BitInstant had improved its AML and KYC procedures – at least for those customers who bothered to create accounts – they weren't sufficient, because the company wasn't licensed to serve customers in all fifty states, and its safeguards weren't strong enough to keep out customers from proscribed jurisdictions.

One day in June, not long after the launch of BitInstant 2.0, Rachel got a call from one of the lawyers at Perkins Coie. He asked her to walk him through BitInstant as if he were a customer, to lay out its nuts and bolts for him as best as she could. The lawyer listened attentively as she explained. When she had finished, his response was blunt: 'You need to take the site offline immediately. We cannot represent you if you keep this site online.'

Now came more sleepless nights, as they pulled the site offline and the developers went through the codebase to 'rip out a whole bunch of parts', as Alex puts it. BitInstant's developers were told that they would have to figure out how to trace every customer's IP address to determine whether it was located in a state where BitInstant could operate. They would have to put these new checks in place before the site could go back online. They came up with a solution and put the site back up, only for the lawyers to raise further objections, occasioning a second takedown. By now Alex was furious. His expected CEO title and improved employee agreement had still not come through, and he found himself wasting time on 'triage and Band-Aid shit again', which by now must have felt like trying to stop the bleeding of a hemophiliac. 'This is no way to do engineering,' Alex says. 'You can't build a bridge and every ten minutes change the foundation. It's not possible.'

It was never entirely clear where the company stood in its licensing. Initially, Charlie and the others had thought they could save thousands if not millions of dollars by piggybacking on Obopay's licenses. But some of the licenses were expired or irrelevant, recalls Rachel Yankelevitz. Worse, they had wasted a lot of money on the negotiations – enough, according to the legal team at Perkins Coie, to have obtained four or five licenses of their own. 'If we had really done our due diligence on [Obopay], we would have realized they were not worth it,' Rachel says.

Charlie, for his part, seemed unable fully to accept the new restrictions on his business. After the Mutum Sigillum seizure, says Alex, 'we had received several legal notices telling us, "Do not transact with Mt. Gox."' He and Gareth agreed to shut off BitInstant's pipeline to the embattled exchange. But Charlie told them to turn it back on. Alex said he would do it only if Charlie provided written instructions to the effect that he was ordering Alex to do so. Charlie gave it to him, Alex recalls, and Alex did what was necessary so that money could once again flow from BitInstant customers to Mt. Gox. But he remained unhappy about it. 'It was like, "Dude, you're fucking killing this company. You're putting us in legal hot water by doing this,"' he says. 'And the reason he wanted Mt. Gox turned on is that he was making a shitload of money from it.'

At one point, Charlie and Gareth instructed Alex to set up the old website again so that customers could use that. It took considerable time to relaunch, since Alex had to spin up all of the old databases. But the lawyers soon told the founders of BitInstant that they couldn't do that; the new rules applied not only to BitInstant 2.0 but to all versions of the company's website and services.

Caught in the middle and without sufficient power to effect change, Alex found his enthusiasm ebbing away. 'There were no incentives for Alex,' Rachel says. 'He wasn't being paid that much. None of us were being paid that much. But Alex became very aware of his value.' Other companies were trying to poach him. In late June, another Bitcoin company approached him with an extraordinary offer: a signing bonus of more than $500,000, plus a salary and share of the company profits. The head of the company was someone Charlie had angered, and he wanted to get revenge by taking Charlie's best employee. But nobody, no matter how vengeful, throws half a million dollars at a new hire unless the guy is worth it. Alex had undeniable skills, and skills were all that mattered in the high-stakes world of tech startups, to say nothing of Bitcoin. By the end of June, he was fed up. BitInstant had waited too long to make him a solid counteroffer. And an even better opportunity had come up – a substantial grant to conduct research into possible applications of blockchain technology to things other than currency, such as voting. It was a new challenge to sink his teeth into. It was a way out.

On 1 July, he tendered his resignation. He sent an apologetic message to Cameron Winklevoss, offering to spill his guts, in a fair-minded but critical fashion, about the health of the company. But Cameron never took him up on it, perhaps because the offer had one caveat: Alex had already shared his thoughts with Charlie and said he felt he would need the CEO's permission before spreading them further. There was little chance that Charlie would sign off on a soon-to-be-former employee making him look bad to the investors. Despite everything, and in marked contrast to some of the other employees, Alex still believed that Cameron and his brother had the necessary experience to guide the company. And he did want to see BitInstant succeed. He even offered to assume an advisory role after stepping down as an executive. 'I'm not asking for compensation,' he explained to Cameron on 11 July, 'I just want to continue to help.' But the advisory role never materialized. Four days later he was gone, stepping neatly off the deck of a sinking ship into the lifeboat that was waiting for him. Before he left, the whole office threw him a send-off party – perhaps much in the spirit of prisoners celebrating a fellow inmate's successful escape.

Two days after Alex's departure, the BitInstant website went offline for the final time. By then, some customers had already given up hope that the company would get its act together. 'Screw Bitinstant now as I will never use them again,' a user named hojo wrote on an official BitInstant customer support discussion thread on a Bitcoin forum. He had found other, more expensive ways to fund his exchange accounts and buy bitcoins. 'Those processes will take longer but that's fine . . . Middle finger to Bitinstant and the Winklefuck twins.'

Others were not content merely to hurl angry words. On 8 July, one week after Alex Waters gave notice that he was quitting, a lawsuit was filed against BitInstant in a federal court. The three plaintiffs who brought the suit – making it a putative class action, though ultimately the class was never certified by the judge who heard the case – accused the company of false representations about the speed with which it could satisfy customer orders and about its refund policy, which claimed to reimburse the fees of customers who experienced 'undue delays' in their transactions. The case was to be voluntarily dismissed eleven months later, and dismissed with prejudice – a term of art meaning the plaintiffs could never refile their case. Although it is impossible to say whether a private, off-the-books settlement occurred to make the lawsuit go away, a plaintiff almost never agrees to such a dismissal unless he is getting something in return. Regardless, in July 2013 the lawsuit brought bad press at the worst possible time. In the

BitInstant offices, a siege mentality took hold. 'It was a mixture of everything,' Charlie says. 'Losing the bank account, couldn't fix shit fast enough, too many customer complaints. It was just a big shitshow. Just a big, big shitshow.'

Before they left the company, Erik Voorhees and Ira Miller had told Charlie that his decision to stay would go badly for him. 'It didn't look like there were huge chances of all the different problems that BitInstant had resolving well,' Ira says. 'But he felt that it was his duty as CEO and founder . . . He'd made his promise to investors to give it his best, and so he felt the need to see it through.' Even now, Charlie tried to give the impression that BitInstant was suffering only a temporary setback. The back cover of the August 2013 issue of *Bitcoin Magazine* featured an advertisement trumpeting BitInstant's new website. And he wasn't the only one offering false hope. As late as 19 September, the Winklevosses told *Bloomberg Markets* that 'the BitInstant team is working hard to get its site up and running, and we hope that happens soon.' The truth was that the barriers to a comeback were now insuperable. Watching events unfold from a distance, Ira Miller could only shake his head. 'They frankly didn't understand the business very well,' he says of the investors, Roger Ver excepted. 'On the last day they didn't understand it much better than they had on day one.'

One employee who hung on until the bitter end was Rachel Yankelevitz. 'I held out hope until our bank account was pretty much empty,' she says. Charlie, who relied on her as much for moral support as for anything else, was loath to part with her, but finally, in the fall of 2013, she had no choice but to give her resignation. 'I saw the account balances. There was nothing there. There wasn't enough to cover another payroll.' Oddly enough, however, when she asked Charlie if he had any money of his own that could be used to keep BitInstant running, he said no, he had no real assets, nothing to contribute.

In April 2013, BitInstant had processed $9.1 million in customer transactions. Three months later it was offline, and within half a year – by which time the New York Department of

Financial Services had sent subpoenas to more than a dozen Bitcoin startups, including BitInstant, demanding to see their records as part of a fact-finding mission to learn more about digital currency – it wasn't even on life support. It was gone. Charlie had blown up the gold mine.

Lawrence Lenihan wasn't surprised, having never trusted David Azar's instincts or Charlie Shrem's leadership. Where once BitInstant had held so much potential to dominate the digital currency landscape, he says, 'They just completely flubbed it. They dropped the ball.'

Charlie himself, while acknowledging his faults as CEO, proposed an alternative theory of the collapse. 'I let Alex effectively be CEO, but he couldn't handle it. He fucked up,' Charlie says. 'And then he left.'

One man caught in the fallout was Gareth Nelson. He had never known wealth before BitInstant; the money, when it came, had been a shock to him. He had spent it recklessly, and now no more would be forthcoming. Although he and Charlie had ostensibly been equal partners, Charlie seemed to be in no financial straits, while Gareth was suffering. 'Being broke while others came out ahead has been hard. I could so easily be a millionaire now if I'd made just slightly different decisions with my investing,' he says. 'I had never been in that position and I wanted cool stuff.' In the aftermath, he was forced to pawn many of his new possessions at a loss.

The BitInstant era was over. Better options for obtaining bitcoins were already coming to the fore. Indeed, it was eloquent testimony to Bitcoin's incredible resilience as a technology that the combined weight of the wreckage of BitInstant, the SEC case against Trendon Shavers, the loss of millions by Mt. Gox, the second collapse of TradeHill, the FinCEN guidance, and the subpoenas of more than a dozen Bitcoin startups by the state of New York did not sink Bitcoin straight to the bottom, there to rest for eternity beside such ill-conceived inventions as digital audio tape, 1990s virtual reality gear, and the Apple Newton. On the contrary, instead of suffering this fate, Bitcoin had a 'rosy' future ahead, according to Marco Santori. It was entering the mainstream. 'It's kind of like childbirth – it's a painful entry,' he said, 'but it's entering nonetheless.' Benjamin Lawsky, New York state's super-intendent of financial services, who headed the agency that had sent out the subpoenas, preferred a different metaphor. The Department of Financial Services, he said, wanted to bring crypto-currencies 'out of the darkness and into the light of day'.

Roger Ver, who had no interest in seeing governments around the world get Bitcoin under their thumbs, began looking for another company to carry forward Satoshi Nakamoto's vision of a stateless currency, of decentralized value transfer and the private ownership of wealth. He provided seed money to Coinapult, just as Barry Silbert and Lawrence Lenihan did. But it was on a company called Blockchain that he now pinned his hopes.

Chapter 7

BITCOIN NEVER SLEEPS

Our only method for escaping the future is to move into it and claim it as the present.

— Denis Johnson

The girls were dancing on a neon tank, wearing sequined bikinis lit up by red and green laser light. A strobing fixed-wing aircraft passed overhead like the acid-trip kissing cousin of a Mitsubishi A6M Zero, with more sequined women dangling from it, trapeze-style. Flashing robots had preceded them – wheeling through the room, pumping their fists at the crowd – while the audience, seated on tiers of glittery red plastic swivel chairs, waved glow sticks. As the music throbbed, twin walls of video screens threw up bizarre images. The Technicolor dream machine the women were using as a stage displayed, at the end of its barrel, a rainbow-colored star – just where, on an ordinary tank, the death comes out. But this was no ordinary tank. It was a fixture of the one-hour show that takes place three times a night at Robot Restaurant, a kind of eye-melting Japanese dinner theater, a cabaret show of such migraine-inducing decadence that Las Vegas falls silent before it.

On this hot Tokyo night in July 2013, two Americans, Roger Ver and Nicolas Cary, sat in the crowd. As far as Nic could tell, they were the only *gaijin* in the place. He was drinking a beer, while Roger, as usual, was abstaining. Their unappetizing bento boxes sat untouched: you don't go to Robot Restaurant for the food. In the midst of the cartoonish spectacle – earlier, a woman wielding an oversized mace had ridden in on a stegosaurus to battle two heavily armored robots – they had business to discuss. Roger wanted to see if Nic could become the chief executive of Blockchain, a Bitcoin startup in which Roger was the sole investor and majority stakeholder. Nic had come highly recommended by Erik Voorhees, his old college friend, who in turn had given Nic an earful about Roger Ver. Talking to Roger over Skype, Nic had liked what he'd heard enough to hop on a plane from Seattle the following weekend to continue the conversation in person. But his visit to Japan would be a short one; he was booked on a red-eye that would have him back at his desk on Monday morning.

Roger met him at the airport and offered to carry his bag. They dropped Nic's things in a subway terminal locker and, thus unencumbered, headed straight for Kabukichō, an entertainment and red-light district in the Shinjuku ward. The perfect home for Robot Restaurant. Roger, too, as Nic could not fail to notice, was at home; though an American citizen, he had lived in Tokyo for much of the past seven years and was fluent in Japanese. They paid the six-thousand-yen entrance fee, headed downstairs through the glare of thousands of multicolored light bulbs, and took their seats.

Robot Restaurant is Roger Ver's first choice when it comes to entertaining Western visitors, presenting as it does the spectacle of Japanese eccentricity and excess beyond one's wildest imagination. To experience the show is to partake of a kind of Tokyo overdrive, a cheerful version of the neon-lit cyberpunk dystopia that writers once imagined as the future of Japan. He wanted Nic to have a good time, because he wanted to end his search for a CEO. He had been interviewing candidates for weeks and had no strong contenders. He had been relieved when Erik reached out one day and said, 'I think I know the right guy for you.'

The spectacle was also part of his self-presentation. As a teenager, he had read a lot of science fiction – Arthur C. Clarke, the techno-utopian *Foundation* series of Isaac Asimov, Neal Stephenson's *Cryptonomicon* – and for him the language of sci-fi was bound up with Bitcoin and with the libertarian principles it was founded on. At that first Bitcoin conference in New York in 2011, where he had met Erik, it had felt as if he were entering the most exciting science fiction novel of all. Having read so much about futuristic systems of money and credit, he found himself thinking, *This world-changing invention is finally here.* 'Before Bitcoin,' Roger says, 'I was just waiting around for the Singularity – the hypothetical point at which, some people believe, technological progress will reach a sort of event horizon, past which human civilization will change in radical and unforeseeable ways, becoming 'posthuman'. And now here he was in Tokyo with his digital millions and a Japanese wife, living fifteen minutes into the future. He was living proof, if anyone was, that a new kind of expatriate existence was possible, bankrolled by borderless money.

Nic, then twenty-eight, with a round, approachable face that telegraphed his openness to the world, listened with interest to what the older man had to say. Roger's pitch was simple. He painted a picture of a world with no barriers to financial inclusion, a world where people could transact peacefully without government interference. He explained the role that Blockchain could play in building this world. And then he said three words: 'We need help.'

At stake was the best Bitcoin company remaining from the first wave of startups. Many of the others had gone down in flames, due to mismanagement or fraud, or had been hacked, taking thousands of bitcoins with them. Some – like Bitcoinica and BitInstant – had even generated lawsuits. Blockchain was different. Despite being the most popular Bitcoin wallet service in the world, it had never suffered a major crisis. Its founder, Ben Reeves, was smart and dedicated. He had already built the website, released iPhone and Android apps, and was handling customer support. 'It's amazing that one human being was able to do all of that,' Roger says. But Reeves, a British programmer who for two years had been running Blockchain as a one-man show, was getting overwhelmed. Roger didn't have time to run the company himself. They needed new blood at the top, and Nic Cary seemed like a real go-getter. The other candidates had failed to impress. 'They didn't seem to have a strong enough personality type or they didn't seem to be in a big enough hurry,' Roger explains. 'Bitcoin never sleeps. We need to move quickly and grow quickly and do everything sooner rather than later. I felt that sort of drive and energy and passion from Nic.'

For Nic, the opportunity meant a chance to revitalize himself. After more than six years at his current job, a software company he'd joined only months after graduating from college, he was burned out and looking for an escape hatch. Taking the top job at a Bitcoin startup would hardly lighten his load, he knew, but it would fill him with new purpose. The world Roger had described was one in which Nic himself wanted to live.

Blockchain was perhaps uniquely suited among Bitcoin startups to make that world a reality. Although the Bitcoin protocol had been designed to eliminate counterparty risk – the risk that comes with giving up custody of one's money – services had quickly sprung up offering to take this newfound digital wealth, and the hassles that came with storing and securing it, off people's hands. Some of these were exchanges; others were wallet services. Several ended up being disasters. In September 2012, an exchange called BitFloor was robbed when an unencrypted wallet backup was accessed by hackers during a manual transfer of data. Around 24,000 bitcoins – about $250,000 worth – were stolen, causing the exchange to halt operations briefly. When it reopened, it began slowly recouping users' losses, but shut down for good on 19 April 2013, after its US bank refused to continue providing it with banking services.

Another flameout was PicoStocks. Launched on Christmas Eve, 2012 as an unregulated stock market denominated in bitcoins, and supposedly incorporated in the Marshall Islands, PicoStocks attempted to circumvent federal securities regulations by operating as if PicoStocks itself owned the assets and traders merely purchased dividend streams. According to its founder, the stock market suffered a hack attack in June 2013 in which 1,300 bitcoins were stolen, the result of PicoStocks using duplicate passwords for multiple accounts – a practice the founder himself described as 'just extremely stupid' and 'clearly our fault'. Five months later, PicoStocks announced that it had been robbed again. This time a total of 5,896 bitcoins were missing from both its 'hot' and 'cold' wallets.[1] Because cold wallets can't be accessed in online attacks, the theft may have been an inside job.

Worst of all was Bitcoinica. The brainchild of a seventeen-year-old named Zhou Tong, who lived in Singapore, Bitcoinica launched in September 2011 as a service allowing people to trade digital currency on margin, a high-risk, high-reward strategy that can potentially yield huge profits. The trading platform soon became immensely popular, home to more than $1 million in customer assets. At its peak, Bitcoinica's trading volume was nearly as high as that of Mt. Gox.[2] Its downfall began in March 2012, when its host server was hacked and some 43,000 bitcoins were stolen, an amount then worth about $220,000. Customers' faith was shaken, but Bitcoinica covered the losses out of its own reserves. Then disaster struck. As would later happen with PicoStocks, Bitcoinica was robbed a second time. This time, on 11 May 2012, the hot wallet was hacked, and 18,547 bitcoins – $92,500 worth – were stolen. It was too much. Bitcoinica shut down immediately and started a claims process by which customers could attempt to recover their deposits. But the hacker had deleted the platform's account registry, making it impossible to verify users' account balances without making a painstaking examination of the trading records. It was a sobering lesson in what can go wrong when teenagers get their hands on the levers of finance. At the time, Roger Ver himself had 24,841 bitcoins on deposit with Bitcoinica. He didn't want to see it die. Behind the scenes, he began working on a plan for him, Jesse Powell, and two other men to buy Bitcoinica for enough money to make every customer whole – everyone except themselves.

But the lesson still wasn't over. Only a few weeks before the second hack attack, Zhou Tong had sold Bitcoinica to a group of investors, who in turn had hired a three-man team with prior digital currency experience to build and manage the service. While the claims process crawled along, one of the team members, Charlie Shrem's friend Amir Taaki, decided against all reason to publish Bitcoinica's source code on the Internet. Releasing the code publicly like this – evidently in keeping with the Cypherpunk attitude that software wants to be free – immediately tanked Roger's proposal to buy Bitcoinica, since whatever value its intellectual property had retained was now destroyed. Worse yet, within the code was the password to an account which, like a digital strongbox, held everything necessary to access Bitcoinica's account at Mt. Gox. Realizing this, a thief on 13 July took advantage, withdrawing from the Mt. Gox account the maximum amount possible: forty thousand bitcoins and $40,000, worth a total of $350,000 at the time. Bitcoinica – its finances now in shambles, its leadership team no longer communicating or even attempting to issue refunds – went into receivership so that whatever funds remained could be disbursed to former customers. Nobody, including Roger Ver, had any hope of recovering all of their money.

When Zhou Tong had first announced Bitcoinica to the world, a member of a forum had given him a warning: 'Systems that work with money are attacked hard and often, by intelligent skilled people . . . Spectacular failure is your destiny if you don't work very hard to prevent it. Spectacular failure may be your destiny even if you do work very hard to prevent it. You should plan accordingly.'

Blockchain's founder, Ben Reeves, had planned accordingly. These mistakes, this incompetence, could not have occurred at Blockchain. Unlike other early companies, it had no custody over users' accounts. Not even its creator could access the money stored in their wallets, which were encrypted before being uploaded to the cloud. Without access to customer money – indeed, without even the ability to view account balances – the startup had no need to register as a money services business. This had certain advantages. The anti-money laundering and Know Your Customer requirements that had hamstrung TradeHill and BitInstant were of no concern. When sending or receiving bitcoins, Blockchain users interfaced directly with the Bitcoin network. 'There's no counterparty risk, there's no central authority, there's no merchant processor, there's no bank, there's no one telling somebody what they can and can't do,' Nic says. That meant no government could freeze your Bitcoin assets if they were stored in a Blockchain wallet.

No government could bar you from sending money to whomever you liked – say, a relative in Cuba. And no government could ever force Blockchain to divulge information about customer assets, making it the wallet of choice for Erik Voorhees, Charlie Shrem, and thousands of other privacy-conscious individuals.

The radical notions underlying this business model included taking seriously the power to let users be their own banks, despite the inherent challenges. 'The true promise of Bitcoin is to let money move around the world instantly and basically for free, just like email does for information,' Nic says. 'And in order to do that, you have to trust people with the custody of their own funds.'

When Nic met Roger in Tokyo, there were only about 350,000 Blockchain wallets, while the market cap of Bitcoin itself, depressed since the popping of the April price bubble, hovered at around $1 billion. A drop in the bucket compared to most of the world's national currencies. But the potential was there – the potential for it to be much more than simply the coin of the realm for the digital underground. As Alex Waters puts it, 'Privatizing Bitcoin for one thing – black markets – is really unfair to humanity.' And Nic is the kind of man who thinks about humanity; who considers, in choosing his personal path, what might be best for the world at large. On this basis, Bitcoin attracted him. 'You can let people have universal financial sovereignty. That's the promise,' he says.

And so he allowed himself to be led through Kabukichō, past maid cafés and blaring pachinko parlors, strip clubs and ramen shops, past kanji climbing skyward up the sides of buildings in a canyon of raw commerce, air thrumming with lust and money, streets full of punters alive to the lure of ancient enticements, a carnival amid which stood the strobing portal of Robot Restaurant. It was the gaudiest thing around in maybe the gaudiest district in all of Tokyo. 'Only the Japanese mind could think of this,' Roger says. Even then, on the brink of an epileptic's nightmare, neither man knew all that much about the other. But they would soon learn.

NIC CARY WAS BORN IN Denver, where he grew up loving the cold and the outdoors, a child of three cultures. His mother's family had emigrated to New York from France in 1946, and his mother, with whom he lived after his parents' divorce, imparted to him a fluency in her native tongue. His father settled in Chile, where Nic visited him once or twice a year, picking up Spanish while being inducted into the joys of fly fishing and the Hemingway tradition of literate manhood.

At sixteen, enamored of the Internet despite the cratering of the dot-com sector, Nic started a small web design company with a friend, building online storefronts and custom software tools for businesses. Two years later he enrolled in the business leadership program of the University of Puget Sound, a liberal arts college in Tacoma, Washington. A hive of intellectual curiosity, with many interdisciplinary programs, Puget Sound proved to be fertile ground for his development. Students in the international political economics and business leadership programs were pushed to expand their thinking beyond their own narrow fields; they were encouraged to cross-train in the history department. Another student from Nic's class of 2007 recalls a freshman-level course on the warrior poets of Asia. It was a campus that prized broad-mindedness, intellectual discussion.

It was a fateful choice. There, during his first week of classes, Nic met a fellow transplant from Colorado, a tall blond freshman, likewise majoring in business leadership, named Erik Voorhees. They clicked immediately. It was one of those rare occasions in life when a glancing blow with someone is sufficient to cement a friendship forever. Living across the quad from each other, they developed an incredible rapport. Together they pledged Sigma Chi – a dry fraternity, like all the fraternities on campus – of which Nic eventually became president. Though Erik lacked the natural leader's talent for consensus-building that Nic displayed, he enjoyed playing devil's advocate, and was more precocious in the formation of his philosophy and politics. 'He really challenged my perceptions on politics, on economics,' Nic says. 'We used to discuss all kinds of wild things.'

In turn they challenged their fellow students. A fraternity brother, Nick Vasilius, who also shared classes with them, recalls them sticking to their guns and challenging preconceived notions. 'One thing they did not like was when people would just read a textbook and then regurgitate it back in class without thinking about the context or the implications,' he says. 'You know, the type of person who just read the assigned reading and came to class ready to write it in a test. They really prized people being able to defend their points of view, and they were not shy about doing so.'

One class, 'The Illicit Global Economy', provided more than its fair share of provocative discussions. Students were asked to analyze the international markets for organs, narcotics, exotic animal parts, weapons, antiquities, and even human beings, seeking to understand how they operated, who was involved, and why the trade in such contraband persists. According to its Fall 2015 syllabus, the class also examines ethical questions arising from 'relationships that exist between states, illicit entrepreneurs, criminals, multinational corporations, rebel groups, and consumers'. If any material was going to push Erik's laissez-faire brand of political economics to the breaking point, this was it. Nic, who thought it a good policy to listen more than he talked, found the class enlightening. 'Any time that you create a regime to manage a marketplace, you also increase the incentives to break the rules,' he says, explaining the crux of what he learned. 'The people that can work around the rules make an incredible amount of money.' In other words, illicit economies arise as a result either of governments outlawing certain desirable commodities or of deficits in their supply.

Class discussions were spirited, and produced surprising intellectual bedfellows. Radical feminists found themselves advocating alongside libertarians for the legalization of the sale of organs and other body parts, on the grounds that women have the right to do what they want with their bodies. Nick Vasilius, who took the class with Nic and Erik, remembers the War on Drugs providing fodder for one of the most enjoyable classroom discussions he ever had. He recalls it this way: 'Basically the viewpoint that Nic and Erik and a few other classical [liberal] guys put forward was, "This is something that people want. This is something that has a negligible negative impact, especially given that it's already happening" – here we were speaking specifically about marijuana, not other drugs . . . "The market is going to meet these needs, and it's just going to enrich drug cartels if the government doesn't acquiesce to the global market." And I remember we had another class member who took kind of an absolute moral viewpoint that drugs are bad, period, and drugs lead to moral decay, period; and it's the job of the state not only to facilitate life, liberty, and the pursuit of happiness, but to protect us from ourselves . . . Every time the student who took the absolute moral position would make her case, Erik would counter. She would say, "Anything that changes your body chemistry and your emotional state and your perception of reality shouldn't be allowed, and is bad, and could be abused." And Erik – this is more of an example than what he actually said – he would say, "Well, what about coffee?" and she would pause and say, "What about coffee?" "Well, coffee has caffeine, it's a stimulant; coffee can change your perception of time, it can change your mood, it can make you agitated, it can calm you down, depending on how it influences you." And she paused and he said, "What about cold medicine? Should that be illegal? Should that be tightly controlled? Should that be a Schedule I drug?" . . . Every time she would make a point he would make a little needle of an argument, deflating the thesis she had built. And that's, in my mind, very demonstrative of who Erik was.'

Erik's main takeaway from the class was not the depth of human depravity, as evidenced by the perennial existence of black markets – by, for instance, the poaching of animals and the exploitation of the poor. However much he abhorred violence, what stuck with him was the immense scale of the economic activity taking place in the shadows. And then, too, he found the actual mechanisms of the illicit economy worth thinking about. Black and gray markets rely on cash and can only exist because cash exists. But cash is difficult to transport across borders, keeping much of the shadow economy confined to specific geographical regions. Years later, he was struck by the fact that Bitcoin could function like cash while allowing transnational payments. He foresaw the expansion of the illicit economy into the digital realm. 'Now the gray market can operate beyond the bounds of anyone's community,' he says. Mark Williams, a lecturer in finance at Boston University, agrees: 'A black market that can exist on fiat currency will only multiply on virtual currency if unchecked.' The tide of history was perhaps on Erik's side. In 2014, both Washington and Colorado passed laws legalizing marijuana for recreational use.

Even outside of class requirements, Nic found himself reading deeply in politics and economics, though his classical liberal tendencies never shaded, as Erik's did, into extreme libertarianism. Nevertheless they agreed more than they disagreed, making them brothers-in-arms. 'With UPS being such a liberal bastion,' Nic says, 'we were in battle constantly, debating people on politics, economics, religion, science, everything.' Iron sharpened iron. But there was a key difference between them. If Erik was a crusader, Nic was a pragmatist.

Nic wound up spending most of his twenties working for a software startup called Pipeline Deals, which required him to move – 'with one box and a duffel bag' – from Washington to the East Coast. 'I had run out of money, basically,' Nic explains. 'I moved to Westchester, Pennsylvania, on a handshake. The role was very simple; I got a one-line email about it. My job description was to "grow the company" . . . So, what did that mean? It meant everything. I was the janitor. I was the tax guy. I did our product management; I did our sales; I did our customer service; I did design. Everything.' Nic thrilled to the challenge. He was like a tightrope walker working without a safety net, who knew only that he needed to cross the chasm by whatever means necessary. Armed with this simple mandate – and paired with a developer – he flourished; within six months, the company's founders had made him a partner in the business at the age of twenty-two. 'For me, that was a huge endorsement,' Nic says. 'I didn't really care about the money. I cared about the acknowledgment.'

He had once envisioned working for a big software company like Amazon or Microsoft – he felt called to management – but the interviews he went on after college failed to inspire him. He didn't want a long slow climb up the ladder; he wanted a rapid ascent. That was why he had taken the job at Pipeline Deals. For the next four years he was married to his job – addicted to the nonstop work, the high stakes, the rapid pace. For four years he took not a single vacation day. He saw the company through its adolescence. But by the end of four years he was getting restless. After his 'tour of duty' in Westchester, he moved back to Seattle, but there, too, he was dissatisfied. This dissatisfaction was eternally with him, a 'grass-is-greener-on-the-other-side thing', as he puts it, that made him a perpetual nomad, always hungry for the next horizon. 'It's one of the things that makes me pretty successful,' he says, 'but it's also one of the things that makes me really hard to live with, because I'm just going to constantly want to blow up something and change it and do something new.'

Not long after returning from Tokyo, six and a half years after he'd accepted a position at Pipeline Deals, he sat his bosses down and told them he was tired. At first they didn't know what to make of it. Nic was their star employee. His work ethic was unparalleled. What do you mean, you're tired? 'I'm *really* tired,' he told them.

Granted a three-month sabbatical, Nic headed to Morocco, where his sister, Tatiana, was stationed with the Peace Corps. Though he jokes that his family members get along better when living on separate continents, at this moment he needed his sister's calming influence, needed to absorb, as if by osmosis, her 'even-keeled, *hakuna matata* attitude'. Nic, a born traveler, enters deeply into the places he visits, and Morocco was no exception. (Later, he took with him everywhere a laptop decorated with a yellow sticker bearing the word *Essaouira* – the name of a town on Morocco's Atlantic coast where he'd spent time.) Even so, he couldn't help but think back to Tokyo – and to Roger Ver's offer. There was ample cause for reflection. A mysterious chain of cause and effect seemed to be at work. It was a weekend the previous summer that had prepared him to hear Roger's pitch as the opportunity it was.

After graduating in 2007, Nic and Erik had gone their separate ways – Erik to Dubai, where he hoped in vain to make his fortune, arriving just in time to watch the property boom grind to a halt, and Nic to India, where he spent four months in what he describes as 'an incredibly rural area, where the poorest people on the planet live', teaching English to rural Dalits – the so-called 'untouchables' who fall outside the fourfold Hindu caste system and are discriminated against at every level of Indian society. But the two men remained close; they had stayed in touch since college, had followed one another's budding careers, and once a year they reunited – with a dozen other college friends, mostly fraternity brothers – for a getaway trip they called Mancation, so named for its boys'-own-adventure spirit and exclusion of women. 'We just pick a new spot in the United States somewhere and everyone flies in and we have a crazy weekend,' Nic explains. In the summer of 2012, Erik was moving to New York for BitInstant, and Nic invited his friend to stay with him for a couple of days at a small beach house owned by relatives on Long Island's North Fork. While they fished for flounder in the Long Island Sound, Erik, thrilled with his new position, talked nonstop about Bitcoin.

'For forty-eight hours, we're roasting in the sunshine, I'm plucking out fish from the water, and he's just constantly going on and on and on about it,' Nic says. 'It was like he'd had a religious experience. It was exhausting. We're on this little tiny dinghy with a shit motor – one of those ones that never starts, you know, and it's leaking, and he's talking to me about the future of finance, the Internet for money, how it's going to change everything, digital property rights systems. He's like, "Nic, this is the perfect form of money, and here are the reasons why." I was like, "Whew! Well, all right, maybe I should invest some of my money in Bitcoin."'

Being unable to shut up about Bitcoin 'was my affliction ever since I found out about it', Erik admits. 'I'm not going to talk about the weather or superfluous stuff when there's this world-changing technology that I've discovered.' Impressed by his friend's passion, Nic bought some bitcoins through BitInstant on three occasions, when the price was $7, $9, and $13 respectively. At the time, he was earning an annual salary of about $40,000. The most he will say when asked about the value of his bitcoins is that he spent a four-figure amount to acquire them. He stored them in a Blockchain wallet for safekeeping. But even then, he didn't see his cache of digital currency as a serious investment. It was a vote of confidence in a friend. 'You know when you've got a buddy who's, like, a really big sports fan in Denver, so you buy the Broncos jersey? That's what it felt like to me,' he says.

A year went by: burnout, Tokyo, sabbatical. The more he thought about it, the more Nic found Bitcoin irresistible, the 'perfect confluence' of things he was passionate about: economics, politics, technology. Like Erik two years earlier, Nic decided to throw himself into it with all his heart and mind. 'To have those three things come together in an opportunity to participate in changing the world,' he says, 'for me was like, "Oh my God. I'm going to dedicate everything I can to this."' Roger had found his man. But it wasn't until Nic went to Morocco that the full potential of digital currency was brought home to him.

HIS VISIT TO HIS SISTER soon turned into a family reunion; his father, stepmother, and stepbrother joined them in Morocco. His stepmother, Camila, a born adventurer, decided it would be fun to spend a night camping in the Sahara, so they hired a Berber guide and trekked with him by camel well out into the desert. As night came on, Nic watched a glorious Arabian sunset throw a wash of flame across the face of the western sky. Just then, he heard a jarring sound – a sound that, while familiar, seemed out of place in the empty wasteland. His profound experience of nature was interrupted. His guide's cell phone was ringing.

Objects take meaning from their surroundings. A cell phone is unremarkable in a city, but in the Sahara, surrounded by wind and blood-red sand as far as the eye can see, the mundane occurrence hits Nic with the force of an epiphany. He sees the Berber guide silhouetted against the desert in his blue djellabah, his shoulders fronting the horizon, holding a mobile phone that connects him to half the planet. This nomad has more power to project his presence than did Rockefeller and Carnegie. He is tied into networks of a complexity he can scarcely comprehend. Nic, who has not yet decided to become the CEO of Blockchain, realizes all at once what Bitcoin could mean for the developing world. 'This guy probably doesn't have a bank account, he probably doesn't have identification,' Nic said later. 'Yet he has access to a financial system on his smartphone that gives him access to send and receive wealth anywhere in the world instantly and basically for free. When I saw that, I knew that we could change the world with this kind of technology.'

Consider the developing world's adoption of mobile phones. Many parts of Africa are going straight to wireless technology, leapfrogging over the expensive installation of universal landline phone networks that was undertaken many years ago by industrialized nations. The Berber guide would not have purchased a landline telephone even if the infrastructure existed to make it possible. His mobile phone was more than adequate. Similarly, why would the Third World invest in creating a full-scale reproduction of the Western banking system if the technology already existed to plug every man and woman directly into the global economy? Nic didn't think it would. Having a Bitcoin wallet on your phone is like having a bank in your pocket, and for the two billion people worldwide who lack a bank account, the digital currency could be life-changing.

In United Nations parlance, people without access to banks and credit unions are known as the unbanked. To an entrepreneur with the right vision, they represent a huge untapped market. Even in the United States, nearly one-third of the population lacks sufficient access to mainstream financial services. Ten million households have no bank account, and a further twenty-four million are underbanked, meaning that in the absence of bank loans and other services they often turn to loan sharks, check-cashing services, and other financial predators. About thirty percent of households – more than ninety million people – don't have a savings account. And the numbers have been getting worse. Between 2009, when the FDIC first conducted this survey, and 2011, an additional 821,000 households were added to the total number of unbanked American individuals and families.

But the greatest need – and so, for Bitcoin, the greatest opportunity – lies in the developing world. There were about 1.9 billion
smartphone subscribers worldwide at the end of 2013, but that
number is expected to grow to 5.6 billion by 2019.[3] Bitcoin could
push deep into the developing world, riding a wave of cheap hand-
sets. Bringing financial services to the unbanked 'could boost
economic growth and opportunity for the world's poor', Robert
Zoellick, then president of the World Bank, said in a 2012 report.
'Harnessing the power of financial services can really help people
to pay for schooling, save for a home, or start a small business
that can provide jobs for others.' In short, it would reduce global
inequality. Bitcoin may have a significant role to play in this effort.
'It may take a little time,' Nic says. 'But you can't stop ideas. And
you can't uninvent Bitcoin.'

Another thing Nic soon wrapped his head around was that
Bitcoin is a pay-to-play technology. In order to take advantage of
its low transaction fees and reliable money transfer capabilities,
you have to use the units of digital currency called bitcoins. It is
as if, when email was first invented, you had to buy and spend
'email tokens' in order to send messages electronically. Those tokens
would have had value based on the utility of sending messages
anywhere in the world without relying on the postal service. The
more people came to rely on email, the more valuable the tokens
would tend to become. That was why some investors were excited
about holding bitcoins, because their intrinsic usefulness seemed
to argue for a higher future value.

And yet Bitcoin is not the only new payment system entering
the vacuum left by banks. In Kenya, sixty percent of adults use
M-Pesa, a phone-based payments service backed by Safaricom, a
telecom company. One M-Pesa advertisement employs imagery not
unlike what Nic saw in the Saharan desert, showing a herdsman in
an arid landscape receiving a text message update on his account
balance. Credit card companies are also beginning to bypass banks
in search of innovative solutions. On 28 August 2014, in partnership
with the government of Nigeria's then president, Goodluck Jonathan,
MasterCard rolled out a biometric ID card for Nigerians that also

functions as a prepaid debit card. In a country of 167 million, only thirty percent of whom have bank accounts, the card will allow millions more people to make electronic payments, receive money, and withdraw cash from ATMs. By 2019, it will be mandatory in order to cast a ballot in elections.[4] If all goes according to plan, the card – enrollment for which requires fingerprinting and an eye scan – will eventually cover all Nigerians aged sixteen or older.

The audacity of the solution, however, only amplifies the long-standing privacy and security concerns related to electronic money. The government agency behind the ID card is trying to consolidate all the disparate sets of records on Nigerian citizens, including those pertaining to health insurance, voting, driver's licensing, tax payments, and pensions. Anna Crowe, a legal officer at Privacy International, a human rights organization dedicated to fighting illegal surveillance, recognizes the ID program's Orwellian potential: 'Centralizing and combining government databases makes it easy to link together pieces of information about an individual and build a near-complete picture of someone's life. This type of capability is extremely invasive.'[5] Others are unhappy about MasterCard putting its logo on mandatory ID cards, which at least one Nigerian commentator has compared to branding practices used during the transatlantic slave trade. Rhetoric aside, the card will effectively compel all adult Nigerians to become customers of MasterCard.

Bitcoin falls prey to none of these objections. By the summer of 2013, however, its merits had been obscured by sensational headlines about online drug markets and price bubbles; media commentators were comparing enthusiasm for Bitcoin to the long-ago speculative mania for Dutch tulips. Nic thought it deserved a better public image – one rooted in its open-source bonafides. 'Bitcoin doesn't need to be in the shadows. Bitcoin needs to be out in the open,' he says. 'Its benefits are transparency, decentralization, and openness. I think companies that embrace that are going to be successful.' Only by going legit could Bitcoin grab a piece of two enormous pies – the retail e-commerce market, worth $1.9 trillion, and global remittances, which, according to World Bank estimates, totaled more that $601 billion in 2015. This flow of capital is projected to increase massively in the years to come.

That was the pragmatic business motive. There were other motives as well. From a certain angle, Bitcoin looked like a democratizing technology, one which could take power away from big banks and corrupt politicians and put more money in the hands of the world's poor. Nic wasn't alone in feeling the pull of these noble ideas. As awareness of Bitcoin grew throughout 2013 and into the following year, the world of cryptocurrencies began attracting a certain breed of high-minded, college-educated young person, distinct from the earlier adopters by reason of his politics, which were not crypto-anarchy or libertarianism but a more mainstream technocratic liberalism. This new breed of Bitcoiners wanted to stick it to banks without abolishing government or slashing the social safety net.

One convert in this mold, Jeremy Gardner, went from being skeptical about Bitcoin – seeing it as little more than the currency of Silk Road – to cofounding in early 2014, while enrolled at the University of Michigan, the College Cryptocurrency Network, an association of Bitcoin clubs that soon grew to include campuses around the world. He believed the technology could improve millions of lives. 'All of a sudden, people who have come to America for the American Dream, and are trying to support their family back in Kenya, and they're a taxi driver in New York, and they want to send money back to their family, and they don't want to give nine percent of their hard-earned cash to Western Union – Bitcoin allows them to do that,' Jeremy says. 'That alone is a worthy cause for me to pursue.' (In fact, Western Union and MoneyGram charge money transmission fees as high as *ten* percent for certain amounts and destinations.) Six months after Nic Cary's meeting with Roger Ver at Robot Restaurant, a payments industry insider would confide that legacy money transmitters such as Western Union and MoneyGram were 'very worried' about Bitcoin. Small wonder. 'If they don't adapt, they'll be the Kodak of the next decade,' says Barry Silbert. 'Incumbents like these tend to not innovate. They get disrupted and decimated.'[6]

On a global scale, the amount paid annually in fees to banks and credit card companies and to money transmitters had come to seem a great squandering of wealth, a squandering in some cases by those with little to spare, who had spared it until now out of necessity, lacking any alternative, but who now could retain more of the money they had earned. Makers of fine whiskey, whose product must age for years in oak casks, speak of an 'angel's share' – a portion of liquid lost to evaporation during maturation. It can be as much as two percent a year or even more. For them it is an unavoidable cost of doing business. But how quickly, how gladly, if they could, they would strike a new bargain with the heavenly host in order to retain and bottle more of their valuable spirits. For merchants and consumers alike, though many were slow to realize it, Bitcoin presented the possibility of a new bargain in e-commerce, in remittances, in cross-border payments – one which could be struck without needing the permission of a higher authority. For business owners there was, quite simply, no reason not to accept Bitcoin.

Well, there was one reason: the price volatility. This was a fluctuation not in Bitcoin's intrinsic utility, of course, but in its exchange rate against dollars and other currencies. Merchants with an appetite for risk could accept payment in bitcoins and hold onto them as an investment or spend them at will. But larger companies would be loath to put on their balance sheet a form of money whose spending power might be cut in half overnight. In the six months preceding Nic Cary's visit to Tokyo, the price of Bitcoin had risen from less than $20 to a high of $266 in April on Mt. Gox – though slightly less on other exchanges – followed by a crash later that month to less than $80. More yo-yoing followed; by early July the price was below $70, though it would recover to more than $100 in August. Where it would go next was anyone's guess.

One Bitcoin startup that arose to combat this problem was BitPay. It served as a merchant processor, making it possible for businesses to accept Bitcoin payments from customers without ever handling actual bitcoins. By converting the digital currency on their behalf instantly into dollars, BitPay eliminated the problem of price volatility for merchants. By the end of 2013, BitPay had processed more than $100 million worth of Bitcoin transactions. It was a sign that although the cryptocurrency wasn't yet able to serve most businesses as a unit of account – one of the three principal functions of money – it could nevertheless be a fantastic medium of exchange.

Another startup, Coinbase, with which the founder of Blockchain had a tortured history, offered a similar service. But Blockchain declined to follow suit. Its founder, Ben Reeves, believed in Bitcoin – in the thing itself, not merely the underlying payment system, however brilliant. Roger, too, believed in Bitcoin. So did Nic Cary. After all, why should the money of the future not be simultaneously a commodity and a global payment system and a networked means of determining ownership of assets? Our phones are compasses, computers, stereos, and cameras all at once, all these genies jostling within one bottle and ready at a moment's notice to answer our every whim. As Nic would later tell a roomful of venture capitalists, 'There is no reason to believe we can't create a better form of money.'

After Morocco, Nic never went back to Pipeline Deals. Instead he went to York, in northern England, to meet the reclusive developer who had founded Blockchain. There, in a city of fewer than 200,000 people, Ben Reeves ran the whole operation by himself. Founded in August 2011, his website, rich with market information and charts showing the growth of Bitcoin, had quickly become popular, as had the wallet application he created, first for the web and later for mobile devices. In January 2012, Erik Voorhees felt moved to tell Ben, 'You've been doing an awesome job with [Blockchain], keep it up! I use the site almost every day.' Yet a month later, faced with technical challenges, Ben wrote, 'I'm so tired of this, I'm supposed to be taking a break from Bitcoin development for a bit.' Eighteen months after that, he was drowning. Nic intended to throw him a lifeline. It was an open question, however, whether the developer would accept it.

* * *

KNOWING HIS MEETING WITH BEN might prove difficult, Nic sought to arm himself in advance with an intimate knowledge of the company he'd been asked to helm. He wanted to learn everything there was to know – the good, the bad, and the ugly – so there would be no surprises later. He wanted to sweep its closets for skeletons. He hadn't accepted Roger's job offer immediately, needing first to determine what sort of investor the other man would be. 'Is he someone who's passive? Is he a micromanager? Does he trust decision-making?' Nic wanted to know. He had other reservations, too. 'You do a quick Google search on Roger Ver, and it's like, "Huh. Felon. Interesting history . . ."' While confiding in family and friends, he was aware how bizarre it must sound, the path that was unfolding before him: 'So, my plan is to go work in a cryptocurrency startup that's funded by a felon. And I have to leave the country. Good idea?'

He went looking for answers to his own question. From Agadir, a Moroccan coastal city, he flew to London, and at King's Cross station caught a train on the East Coast Main Line, which delivered him to York in just under two hours. It was eleven o'clock at night when he arrived. His American cell phone was useless, but, granted a few minutes of free Wi-Fi on the train, he had fired off a message to Ben saying he was on his way. Knowing nothing about York, not even knowing Ben's address, he got off the train 'with my gigantic go-around-the-world backpack, and I'm the only person in the train station,' Nic recalls. Seeing no one, he sat down to wait and opened his laptop, the glow of the screen eerie in the empty station. Suddenly the man he'd been waiting for walked through the door. 'I was so glad to see somebody that I gave him a hug,' Nic says. 'I don't think he was quite ready for hugging, but I was totally ready.'

Ben drove him to a house Nic and Roger had rented, which they planned to use as a 'crash pad for whichever one of us was going to be in York at any given time'. Ben had taken the liberty of buying groceries for his American visitor so that he wouldn't go hungry. But as if playing into the stereotype of his profession, he had stocked up on junk food: Cocoa Krispies, gummy worms, potato chips. Nic, an avid runner, was amused. 'It was like a sixteen-year-old had shopped for groceries,' he says. 'Ben has one of the worst diets in the history of humanity.'

Eating habits notwithstanding, Nic needed to forge a partnership with the young engineer – and to overcome serious resistance in doing so. 'The key to this entire project is building cooperation with Ben,' he had told Roger in Tokyo. 'If I can't do that, then you need to find someone else.' He would later describe it as 'mission fucking impossible', for he knew all too well that Ben had been burned before; his first partner, an American named Brian Armstrong, was now the head of Blockchain's chief rival, Coinbase.

Their partnership had begun in the spring of 2012, when Armstrong, a twenty-seven-year-old computer engineer at Airbnb, latched onto Bitcoin as potentially a faster, cheaper means of processing transactions in all 192 countries where Airbnb had customers. If he could make it easier for people to get and spend bitcoins, Armstrong figured, consumers would catch on and merchants would follow the money.[7]

He made Ben's acquaintance on a Bitcoin forum, just as Charlie Shrem had connected with Gareth Nelson, another British coder, the summer before. By then, Ben was already well known among Bitcoiners for building Blockchain.info, a website that tracked the burgeoning cryptocurrency ecosystem. He had also created a wallet service, but it was still small; fewer than ten thousand people had signed up for it. Nevertheless, Armstrong recognized that he was someone who understood the technology, someone who could help him build what he envisioned.[8] Roger Ver, having the same intuition, had given Ben seed money some months earlier, in the process acquiring a majority stake in Blockchain. Now Brian Armstrong began talking to Ben about building a platform that would broker the purchase and sale of digital currency, combined with simple wallet and payment-processing services for businesses. Exchanging dollars for bitcoins or the reverse would incur a small fee – say, 0.5 percent or one percent – but spending money on goods and services would be free.

Excited by the prospect, Ben took roughly ten weeks off from developing Blockchain to write code for the new platform, setting his own venture aside at a crucial time for the Bitcoin economy, when BitInstant was launching its cash deposit service in Russia and Brazil and thousands of new users were looking for a way to store their digital currency. At first, the decision seemed like a good one. So promising was the concept that Coinbase, as the platform came to be called, was accepted into the summer 2012 class at Y Combinator, a prestigious and exacting boot camp for startups. (Incubator programs for fledgling tech companies are now legion, and Y Combinator – located in Mountain View, California, south of Google headquarters – is the *ne plus ultra* of the type. As of October 2016, the 1,300 startups it has nurtured over the years are worth a combined $80 billion.)

Between Coinbase's cofounders, however, a rift was growing. Ben Reeves wanted to remain true to what he saw as Satoshi's vision of financial independence, in which users were solely responsible for their own private keys and weren't forced to entrust their money to someone else for safekeeping. Though beyond help if they forgot their wallet password – since Coinbase, never having known it, would have no way of recovering it – users would never have to worry about an unscrupulous employee stealing their money or hackers gaining access to their funds. Governments, too, would be unable to touch the money in customers' wallets. In other words, as Roger Ver later put it, Ben wanted to position the venture 'as a true software company' – not a custodian of people's funds.

Armstrong took a different view. He wanted Coinbase to operate more like a traditional financial services firm, which would mean having access to users' funds and private keys and would bring down on his company the full weight of regulation pertaining to money services businesses, the same regulatory requirements that had stymied and finally crushed TradeHill and BitInstant. But if Coinbase could bear up under that weight, it would have the advantage of legitimacy in the eyes of the law, which would surely bring comfort to future banking partners. It would also be welcoming to average consumers.

The rift, unbridgeable, provoked Armstrong to drastic action. Practically on the eve of Y Combinator's summer program, he changed the passwords on their shared accounts, locking Ben out. And he sent a kiss-off email that left no doubt about his intention to move forward with Coinbase on his own. 'Cofounding is really like a marriage, and even though I think we have mutual respect for each other, we don't work together extremely well,' Armstrong wrote.[9]

It was a divorce with no prenuptial agreement. Like other idealistic founders, Ben had neglected to obtain any written guarantee of his role in the enterprise he was building. Armstrong was able to seize control of everything. 'He didn't just screw Ben, he *fucked* him,' Nic says. Before the breakup, Armstrong had even suggested transitioning Blockchain's thousands of users to Coinbase's new wallet; had that happened, he would have taken from his former partner everything he needed to make Coinbase an overnight success.

Y Combinator wanted no part of the conflict. Eventually, an arbitration was held – Ben was awarded a small percentage of Coinbase. Knowing his share of the company could be diluted in future investment rounds, however, he was forced to sell immediately for a sum inconsequential in light of what the company would later be worth. He retreated to York while his ex-partner was welcomed into the class of summer 2012.

The experience scarred Ben. It also cured him of the temptation to sell out his ideals. He became determined to build Blockchain into a world-beating company in its own right. 'He went back and put his head down and worked like a dog,' says Nic, who was later made privy to the email correspondence pertaining to Coinbase and who came to understand something of the young programmer's mind as he worked alongside him during the fall of 2013. From across the ocean, Ben had watched as Coinbase became a darling of Silicon Valley, first raising $600,000 in seed money in September 2012 and then, the following April, a further sum of $5 million from Union Square Ventures and Ribbit Capital. Nic was wary of touching a nerve. 'You don't just start doing a software company with a guy who has built an enormous technical footprint by himself,' he explains. He knew Ben might be skeptical of his abilities. 'Keep in mind his relationship with Brian Armstrong went to total shit. So here I am, another white guy with software experience coming in from the United States to *fix it all*.'

Building a rapport wasn't easy, but Nic gradually won over the young engineer. He began doing project work for Blockchain, still trying to learn what he could about its vitals. When X-raying a software company, he figured, the first limb to examine is the users, whose unvarnished opinions will tell you a great deal about the health of the company as a whole. On a freelance basis – a possible prelude to assuming the CEO position – Nic gained access to Blockchain's customer support system and began reading through the backlog of queries. There were 35,000 unanswered messages. At some point, the task of addressing them must have become too much for Ben, and he'd thrown in the towel. But Nic began to answer them.

Soon enough, he was spearheading a redesign of the Blockchain logo and typeface, the visual shorthand by which a company conveys its identity as a brand. The original logo was a Rubik's Cube, which struck Nic as unrelated to Bitcoin. 'The logo didn't make any goddamn sense,' he says, 'and I wanted something that looked more appealing.' He contracted a team of developers in Argentina to do the work. It was an easy way to get his feet wet as a project manager. By the time the new design elements were delivered, it was November; the clock on his three-month sabbatical had run out. He told his former bosses that he was moving on. Then he came out to the world as the CEO of Blockchain.

Chapter 8

THE BILLIONAIRE
WHO WASN'T

Just as one can go on counting upward to any figure,
so money can be devalued to any depth.

— Elias Canetti

Barry Silbert needed to find a new asset class. For a while now
auction-rate securities had been his trading desk's most profitable
asset — in fact the biggest source of revenue his company had
ever seen. But auction-rate securities wouldn't carry his company
forever; no new ones had been issued in years, and the secondary
market for these debt instruments was beginning to dry up. The
traders knew it and he knew it. A former investment banker,
Barry had built a successful company by making it possible for
hapless investors to unload their illiquid assets, including stock
in companies that hadn't gone public yet. Auction-rate securities
were one of several asset classes for which he had almost
single-handedly made a market amid the chaos of the financial
crisis, when investors were panicking and banks were underwater
on their obligations. He had a gift for spotting investment opportunities. On vacations, he liked to read books about the history
of money and debt, about market cycles, about entrepreneurial
success stories like PayPal. He ate information in a way few others
could. But to look at him, blond and boyish, especially in his

earlier days as a young CEO – his unassertive features softened further by a few extra pounds – you wouldn't guess his many talents, nor would you have a hint of the fire inside him. His eyes, watchful and fringed with pale lashes, were the oldest part of him. At the age of thirty-six, he was still letting it ride after a daring roll eight years before, when he'd left his lucrative banking job to start his own brokerage firm.

As an investor, one of his greatest gifts was patience. But it didn't take him long to decide which new asset his company, SecondMarket, should get into. He had been personally invested in Bitcoin since the summer of 2012. Initially he had kept quiet about his stake in the digital currency, worried it would damage his reputation if it came out. Even his wife was in the dark at first. And yet, in the weeks leading up to Bitcoinica's implosion, Barry was buying bitcoins. He had become convinced that its technology could change the world and, consequently, that it was a spectacular long-term investment. But the process of acquiring the digital currency – going through an unlicensed online exchange whose office was located in Japan – had him sweating bullets. 'I would wire like $5,000 to Mt. Gox, be scared shitless that I was never going to see it again,' he says. Once he'd bought his first batch of bitcoins, though, he didn't wait long to buy more. He had caught the bug. Over the next two and a half months, with the price of Bitcoin slowly climbing from $5 to $10, he invested about $200,000 in the digital currency. He reasoned that if Bitcoin were to fulfill its potential, then a significant investment now could bring life-changing returns later on. 'If I'm going to make an investment in a high-risk opportunity like Bitcoin, I'm only going to do it if it's going to move the needle for me,' Barry says. In other words, go big or go home. The value of Bitcoin relative to the dollar, he thought, had the potential to increase by fifty or even 100 times. 'If it does that,' he told himself, 'I will always look back on this time and say, "Why were you such a pussy? You had the money, why didn't you do it?"'

Bitcoin had first captured his attention the summer before. After two years as a practically worthless digital curio, it was steadily climbing in value. On 15 April of that year, the price of a single bitcoin on the Mt. Gox exchange reached $1 for the first time. It was an important symbolic moment: the crypto-currency achieving parity with the US dollar. Two major events had taken place in the months prior. In January, Silk Road had opened for business and had quickly become a thriving market-place. And in March, Jed McCaleb, the original founder of Mt. Gox, had sold the company to Mark Karpelès. Buoyed by new management at the only exchange and undergirded by an Amazon for illicit drugs, the price of Bitcoin began to climb. By the end of May, it stood at $8.88. It was during this time that Barry came across a Bitcoin-themed episode of a YouTube show called This Week in Startups. The guests were Bitcoin's lead developer, Gavin Andresen, and the crypto-anarchist Amir Taaki. As the host, Jason Calacanis, grilled them on cryptocurrency's funda-mental properties and potential, Barry found himself hooked.

When it comes to economics, Barry is a man of no school; as in everything else, a deep vein of pragmatism runs through his thinking. It was because of this that he found Bitcoin interesting. By 2011, with the world still stuck in the doldrums of a global recession, there was a race among countries to make their currency more attractive to foreigners in order to stimulate economic growth. The way to do that was to inflate it – that is, print more of it – so that its value relative to other currencies would decrease. While this encourages spending, boosting tourism and helping some businesses, it hurts those who try to live within their means and set aside money for the future. If you stick $1,000 of an inflationary currency under your mattress, or even in a low-yield savings account, you will find that it has less spending power a year from now than it did when you first socked it away, and less still the year after that. 'When you have a world that is printing money, the concept of a decentralized, non-government-controlled, non-company-controlled currency that has a finite supply had a certain amount of appeal to me,' Barry says. He understood that money, which is a social institution, depends not on physical attributes or even government support but merely on general acceptance. If enough people decide to use shells, or colored beads, or pieces of paper, or mathematical tokens as currency, then those items will *be* currency, with all the economic power that that designation implies. 'I didn't fully appreciate the whole technical aspect [of Bitcoin] at first. But economically it just kind of made sense.'

Then, on 1 June 2011, Gawker published its exposé of Silk Road, and the price went nuts. On 9 June, Bitcoin hit $29.58. Barry watched as the bubble grew and then, on 10 June, began gradually to deflate. By the middle of November, the price had dropped to barely more than $2. Bitcoin looked as if it would sink into oblivion. 'When the price crashed, I pretty much wrote it off,' Barry says. He still liked the idea of a decentralized cryptocurrency, but he figured the market wasn't ready for it.

When he checked back a few months later, he was surprised to see the price and trading volume increasing. 'I know a thing or two about technical analysis, and it was actually a very healthy-looking chart. You saw bubble, crash – volume dries up – and then slowly the price starts going up and the volume starts going up. So that was when I really started digging in on Bitcoin.'

He spent the next several months educating himself while keeping one eye on the market. He showed Satoshi's white paper to his head of strategy, Jeremy Smith, an old fraternity brother from Emory University. Smith was nonplussed. 'I don't know if this thing has legs, but it's really fascinating,' he told his boss. Even Barry, who wanted to dive in, had yet to appreciate the lasting value of blockchain technology. He was still thinking in purely economic terms. Nevertheless, he says, over time it became obvious to him that Bitcoin was going to have a second chance. He began making angel investments in digital currency startups, including BitInstant.

By the spring of 2013, with his personal holdings shooting up in value, Barry was convinced that the time had come for his company to get involved. He went to Jeremy to solicit his thoughts. Still a Bitcoin skeptic, Jeremy expressed doubts, but ultimately threw his support behind the idea. He trusted in Barry's leadership and was willing to see where it took him. 'You need to follow your founder's passion,' he says. 'It was clear, and had been clear for months, that Barry was super-passionate about this, had a vision for it, and for that reason I thought we should be doing this – even if I'm not a big believer in Bitcoin.' At the next all-hands meeting, on 5 June, Barry broke the news: SecondMarket was going to launch a private investment fund for Bitcoin.

The entire staff, more than fifty employees, had gathered in the rec space on the top floor of their building in the Chelsea neighborhood of Manhattan. A kind of loft with hardwood floors, up a staircase from the work area, it was kept stocked with snacks and drinks and served as the event space for twice-monthly 'town halls' – loosely structured meetings at which employees were encouraged to speak up and ask questions. Most of them knew next to nothing about Bitcoin. Their CEO, wearing casual summer clothes, his short blond hair combed forward in a youthful style, gave a PowerPoint presentation using the digital projector that hung from the ceiling. He had briefed his senior leadership team ahead of time, but he knew that what he was about to say would come as a surprise to the rest of his staff. He introduced the concept of Bitcoin, giving an overview of its innovative features – its immunity to counterfeiting and double spending – before taking a stab at evaluating its potential for their business. He compared it to gold, to major fiat currencies. 'Look at the size of those markets,' he said. If Bitcoin could capture just a fraction of that wealth, its value would skyrocket, making it the most lucrative asset in SecondMarket's nearly ten-year history.

But he also gave a few words of caution. There was no guarantee that Bitcoin would survive. It was a highly speculative investment, and that made his new direction for the company a risky one. 'In the end, it's too early to tell,' he told them. Despite the potential, 'there is a real chance that it will go to zero and this was a passing fad.' Even while laying out his strategy, he wanted to present the facts as soberly as possible. Throughout the presentation, however, Silbert made no attempt to hide his enthusiasm. He clearly envisioned Bitcoin as not merely a new asset but a new corporate focus.

And he had a surprise for them. In order to familiarize his staff with the digital currency on which their CEO was placing such a large bet, he was going to give each of them, out of his personal hoard, two bitcoins – one to save and one to spend. At that point, most of them had heard Barry talk about Bitcoin, but very few understood what it was. 'I've always thought that until you actually receive it or spend it or buy something with it, you don't fully appreciate how powerful the concept of Bitcoin is,' Barry says. 'So what I figured was, one, I want my employees to understand why I've been excited about it firsthand, and two, I want them to have some skin in the game.' By spending one of their coins, they would experience the Bitcoin technology, and by holding one they would enjoy the potential upside of Bitcoin as a speculative investment. For storing their bitcoins, Barry recommended Blockchain's web wallet, the same one that he had used when he first started buying the digital currency.

For staffers, the big takeaway from the meeting – besides their free money – was the enormous opportunity in front of them. Bitcoin was unprecedented. Its market cap had recently passed $1 billion – and that might be only the beginning. As Michael Moro, director of the SecondMarket trading desk, recalls: 'Barry called Bitcoin "the biggest opportunity of my career".'

BARRY SILBERT BEGAN TRAINING FOR his career not long after leaving the cradle. No one in his middle-income family in Gaithersburg, Maryland, had any background in finance, and so his aptitude can't be easily explained. His father, who passed away when Barry was ten years old, held a government job; his mother was a physician's assistant. His older brother, Alan, had no interest in finance. But from a young age Barry was watching the stock market. Most acorns go into the ground and come up oak trees. Barry Silbert went into the ground and came up a violin.

At age thirteen he was selling baseball cards – learning then that some things have monetary value simply because enough people agree they do. He invested his bar mitzvah money in stocks. As a high school junior, after brief stints as a stock boy in a liquor store and a sales clerk in a shoe store, he landed a part-time job at a Washington brokerage firm. Sensing his interest in the markets, the portfolio managers and traders there encouraged him to take the six-hour, 250-question General Securities Representative Exam, which would qualify him to be a stockbroker. If he passed, he would be granted a Series 7, or General Securities license, allowing him to buy and sell stocks, options, and all other types of securities. Barry took the test at the age of seventeen, becoming one of the youngest people ever to pass. 'A nice, mild-mannered guy,' one of his college friends would later say, 'who had a burning fire inside driving him'.

In August 1998, having earned a finance degree from Emory University in Atlanta, he moved to New York and began working as an analyst at Houlihan Lokey Howard & Zukin, a boutique investment bank. Like other analysts, he routinely worked eighty hours a week. In his second year he was adopted into the financial restructuring group, run by a managing director in the New York office named Michael Kramer. The restructuring boys were like a cleanup crew. When a company got too deeply into debt and went bankrupt, or was in danger of doing so, Houlihan Lokey might come in to cut costs, sell off its assets, or consolidate its debt. It was interesting but unglamorous work. Then the dot-com bubble burst, and suddenly companies were failing left and right. The restructuring group at Houlihan Lokey, formed in 1987, now became one of the firm's most influential and profitable divisions.

Jeff Werbalowsky, who cofounded the restructuring group, worked alongside Barry on the liquidation of Lernout & Hauspie, a Belgian speech and language technology company. Although Barry was by far the most junior member of the team, Werbalowsky remembers him as being integral to the process, 'a smart kid with a lot of energy'. After two years and eight months, he was promoted from analyst to associate, unusual for someone without an MBA degree. He was a rising star.

The years 2000 to 2003 were 'the boom years of the bust', Barry says, fat years for the restructuring division of Houlihan Lokey. He worked personally on some of the decade's headlining bankruptcies, including Enron and WorldCom. But then the pool of clients began to dry up, even as competition for their business grew fiercer – not only between but within firms. Houlihan Lokey had always prided itself on being less tribalistic than the larger banks, less dysfunctional, but now it was like ten dogs fighting over one bone. And Barry had become bored with the work. He wanted a change. He spent the second half of 2003 brainstorming business ideas.

There was a great opportunity, he realized, in making a market for restricted stock in public companies. This type of security usually results from a private investment in public equity, in which a publicly traded company raises capital by issuing shares of stock to select investors at a discount to the market price. Shareholders are barred from trading these restricted shares on a public exchange – the New York Stock Exchange or Nasdaq, say – for a year from the date they are issued. This cooldown period hamstrings investors who find themselves suddenly in changed circumstances, needing to turn their stock holdings into quick cash. But it applies only to selling on public exchanges. Private transactions are allowed. So if you met a guy on the golf course, you could make a deal with him. A buyer who wanted quickly to unload stock might be left flipping through his Rolodex, hoping someone he knew would take it off his hands. Or he could go through a broker, who would quote him a take-it-or-leave-it price.

Barry thought he could do better, creating a competitive trading platform that would expose each seller to multiple potential buyers, while keeping transactions private in accordance with SEC regulations. It was a huge opportunity. In 2004, the market in restricted securities was worth more than $1.2 trillion – greater than the GDP of Australia or Mexico.[1] Restricted stock in public companies was, in a sense, low-hanging fruit: unlike more exotic asset classes, it was easy to price because the companies involved, by definition, had publicly traded stock which could serve as a benchmark. For the restricted stock, Jeremy Smith says, 'really all you got to do is come up with a discount to the public price, and *boom* – you've got your price.' But the market had a liquidity problem. No one else had yet done what Barry was proposing to do. He thought the time was right. He had identified a growing category of buyers for restricted stock: hedge funds, whose positions depended on buying large blocks of stock in private transactions – so-called 'over-the-counter' purchases – as opposed to snapping up a few shares here and there on Nasdaq or the NYSE. Acquiring a large position through public purchases alone can take a long time. Restricted stock was attractive to hedge funds because it traded not only in large blocks but at a discount, allowing them to gain more equity in companies they liked. Once the cooldown period was over, they could sell the stock for a profit on the public market. It was because of the 'proliferation of hedge funds' that, despite skepticism on Wall Street about the need for his trading network, Barry thought it just possible 'that restricted securities will become another widely accepted investment strategy like bank debt and high-yield bonds.'[2]

When he told his twenty-five-year-old girlfriend, Lori, that he was planning to give up his high-paying Wall Street job to start a business, she hesitated to congratulate him. 'That's great,' she said, 'but do you know how much *I* make?' Her salary as a talent agent, about $27,000 a year, would hardly be sufficient to build a life together. Without her parents' help she wouldn't even have been able to afford to live in Manhattan. But Barry thought he might have just enough money in the bank to pull it off. In 2003, his last year at Houlihan Lokey, he made more than $300,000 in salary and bonus. He was twenty-six years old. If he was ever going to take this leap, now was the time.

The following January he took his bonus and left the firm, and, after a sojourn in Hawaii to clear his head, he promptly set to work. His business plan – 'an investment banker's version of a business plan', as he ruefully said later, remembering the labor it had cost him, was a real work of art. Dozens of pages long, with charts and graphs, it laid out a vision for a whiz-bang technology platform for trading restricted securities, like an eBay for illiquid assets. To start it up would require raising about $2 million from investors right off the bat, Barry figured.

He approached Jeff Werbalowsky, who had become co-CEO of Houlihan Lokey, to ask if the firm would like to invest in the company he was planning to launch. If Barry has the ability to see five miles down the road, Werbalowsky has a talent for spotting obstacles on that road. He expressed concern about the legal ramifications of selling restricted securities to a broader group of investors. He also wondered openly how much the company would be able to charge its clients and how its platform would function.

Ultimately, as an investment bank, Houlihan Lokey was too risk-averse to invest, but what struck Werbalowsky most about the young former associate was his entrepreneurial zeal. 'He decided to go out and do what I thought was a risky business plan, but he was absolutely committed. He didn't take no for an answer. He took all of my thoughts and suggestions and critiques in stride, and answered them or said, "We'll surmount them,"' Werbalowsky says. 'There are some people who are created to be entrepreneurs and there are some people who are not, and he was.'

SOME OF THE STARTUP CAPITAL Barry used to launch Restricted Stock Partners – later to be renamed SecondMarket – came from his personal savings; the rest came from successful investments, including a few unorthodox stock bets. He bought shares of New Frontier Media, a 'smut peddler' – provider of adult video content to cable TV companies – at a time when the demand for pay-per-view skin flicks had not yet been gutted by Internet porn. So-called vice stocks tend to perform well during tough times, dependent as they are on the human need for solace, and in the late spring of 2003, with the military occupation of Iraq beginning, New Frontier stock – after remaining relatively flat for the previous six months – shot up from $0.80 a share on 9 May to $3.20 a share on 11 July, reaching an eventual peak of $11.38 a share on 16 January 2004. The timing coincided perfectly with Barry's need to raise money. He sold the stock at a handsome profit and washed his hands of the porn industry. Getting out proved to be a judicious move: New Frontier's stock subsequently plummeted, bottoming out at $1.07 a share by 11 November 2011.

Another savvy investment – and one of which Barry is prouder than his foray into vice stocks – was buying stock in Force Protection, a South Carolina company that pioneered the development of military vehicles capable of withstanding a blast from an improvised explosive device. During the occupation of Iraq, IEDs became a leading cause of death for American soldiers. Even armored Humvees – originally the Pentagon's troop transport of choice – provided inadequate protection at best, and thousands of them had no underside armor, leaving passengers vulnerable to IEDs detonating from below. Force Protection sought to change the equation, introducing heavily armored vehicles with V-shaped hulls designed to deflect IED blasts away from occupants. At the time, the company was building its armored trucks in an old General Electric engine plant near Charleston, with only a dozen workers on its production line.[3] Thanks to a defense industry website, Barry says, 'I was able to discover that this company was getting a bunch of these [vehicle] contracts and was not announcing them publicly.' Its monopoly on what would become a tremendously sought-after type of vehicle – each of which carried a $500,000 price tag – wasn't yet being reflected in its stock price. He bought in when the stock was selling for between $1 and $2 a share. The fundamentals looked solid, and moreover, he says, 'It just felt *good* to invest in a company like this.' From March 2003 through January 2008, Force Protection vehicles endured 3,200 attacks with explosives. Only five soldiers were killed.[4] In 2007, the stock price briefly broke $30, though Barry had already sold long before, at some multiple of his original investment.

To those who know him, Barry's market foresight is legendary. 'Barry is a very good entrepreneur,' Jeremy Smith says, 'very good. But he is a *world-class* investor. He is in the top one percent of investors maybe in the world, in my opinion. It's not necessarily because he knows stocks and bonds better than other people. That's not where he excels. He is able to identify whole investment classes years before anybody else does. He has this vision where he can put together the whole long-term picture of how certain things will play out.' He had been early on tech stocks before the dot-com boom. He had started buying shares of Chinese companies before they reached public awareness. With SecondMarket, he was building a company in his own image. 'The entrepreneurial manifestation of his investment strategy', is how Smith puts it. SecondMarket operated as a brokerage, bringing buyers and sellers together and charging clients a straightforward commission, between three and five percent, on the value of what was being traded.

In true startup fashion, Barry took no salary for all of 2004. The company hadn't even opened its doors yet; he was still working from home, which meant the living room couch in his Union Square apartment.[5] But he had socked away enough money to give himself a year, maybe a year and a half, to get his business off the ground while not drawing a paycheck. Having dropped the idea of launching a fancy eBay-esque online platform in favor of a simple phone brokerage, he and his business partner, a Vanderbilt-educated lawyer named Brad Monks, drew up a revised business plan and began seeking investors, as well as trying to sign up members – hedge funds, banks, high-net-worth individuals – for their trading network. In early 2005, having raised $350,000 from angel investors at a $1.7 million valuation – meaning that Barry had to give up more than twenty percent of his company in exchange for the seed money – they opened a little shop near Wall Street. 'It was five of us, five telephones, and an Excel spreadsheet,' Barry said later. 'That was it. That was our marketplace.' The no-frills office lacked conference space, so client meetings took place at a nearby Starbucks.[6] That year, as CEO, he drew a salary of $60,000. Lori struggled to understand why Barry couldn't reward himself more when he was working so hard. But ultimately, she says, 'I only have good memories of that period. All good things were happening.' On 4 June 2005, she and Barry were wed.

In the pages of the *New York Times*, however, Wall Street executives were predicting failure for Restricted Stock Partners. 'It's not an innovation that needed to be done,' one of them said. 'Demand is being met by the marketplace.'[7] And failure was not cool, not at that time, not in the world of finance. Today the Silicon Valley startup ethos has spread widely enough that having an abortive venture or two on your résumé is considered practically a badge of honor, but in those days there was little glory in jumping off a cliff and trying to build your wings on the way down, especially not if you'd given up a six-figure banking job to do it. But Barry's company wasn't failing. By September, it had signed up 125 members who had at their disposal a combined $50 billion of assets.[8] In 2006, the company turned a profit for the first time.

The following year, Brad Monks died of cancer. Dealing with the loss, Barry was more emotional than his wife had ever seen him. His father's death had in some way fanned his entrepreneurial spark into flame; now the death of his friend and business partner fanned the flames hotter. Whereas 'a lot of people would wallow' in their grief, says Lori, it made Barry all the more determined to succeed. It was the resilience of a man who had entered middle school and high school and college without a father; who had earned a college diploma with no father to congratulate him; who had proved himself on Wall Street with no father to be proud of him. As devastated as he was, she says, 'there was no moment like, "Oh my God, my partner is gone. What am I going to do?"'

In late 2007, the Restricted Stock Partners trading desk got a call. On the line was a former Facebook employee. He had been hired early on and was holding a number of shares of company stock that he now wanted to cash out. For whatever reason, he couldn't wait for Facebook to go public – which wouldn't happen for another four and a half years. He said, 'Hey, I know you guys don't do private company stock, but could you help me sell my shares?'

Barry took him on. Throughout 2008, SecondMarket was quietly, unofficially trading Facebook stock – nearly $50 million of it. That was how the company got into buying and selling stock in private companies, making a market for early investors and employee shareholders who wanted to liquidate their stake in hot startups. Facebook was a popular one, as was video game maker Zynga. In the world of startups, early employees often accept low pay in exchange for a stake in the company. There had never been an organized market for turning these shares into cash, but now, suddenly, there was.

It was another instance of Barry identifying an asset class that was about to heat up. He could have bought up some of the Facebook shares with his own money, earning a huge windfall in the IPO, but he was now thinking like an entrepreneur, not an investor. 'All that value is now in his company, because he redirected the river, as it were, toward the company for all these opportunities,' says Jeremy Smith. 'So what could have been personal wealth is now the enterprise value of SecondMarket.'

The company didn't officially open its marketplace to private company stock until April 2009. By then, Barry had added a whole raft of new asset classes as a result of the financial crisis. First, in February 2008, came auction-rate securities. These were debt obligations that investment banks had marketed to investors as being as good as cash but which, when the market froze up that month, had become what one reporter called 'Wall Street's version of the Hotel California . . . an investment they can never leave.'[9] Brokerages wouldn't let their customers cash out, and investment banks were loath to advise issuers to redeem their notes at a discount, knowing that if they sold at a loss it might force the banks to mark their own holdings of these distressed securities down to the new market price. The prevailing stasis actually allowed them to avoid taking this hit. 'The firms hold a lot of this themselves,' Barry Silbert explained, 'and they are trying to minimize the damage to their balance sheets.'[10]

Barry stepped in to provide a way out. If he could create a secondary market for auction-rate notes, allowing investors to offload their bad paper on people who were willing to assume the risk, he could put money back in people's pockets and get millions of dollars' worth of frozen assets moving again.

Hearing what her husband intended to do for auction-rate securities, Lori had just one question: 'Do you even know what they are?'

'Nope,' Barry said. 'But I'm going to figure it out.'

By early May 2008, about $3.5 million of auction-rate securities were being traded over his company's platform every day.[11]

Barry now had premium gas in his engine – $3.8 million of it, thanks to a 2007 Series A investment by Lawrence Lenihan's FirstMark Capital, then called Pequot Ventures. It valued Barry's company at about $16 million. For Barry, as a first-time entrepreneur, it was an offer he couldn't refuse. 'I never wanted to look back and say, "If we'd only raised that money from this venture capital firm we'd be still around today,"' he said later. With Pequot's money he started hiring aggressively and accelerating progress on the electronic trading platform that his company had recently launched. And then, in the fall of 2008, 'the wheels really fell off the economy,' he says. 'And we were incredibly well positioned to expand our marketplace.'

The following year, with further chaos roiling the financial sector, was perhaps SecondMarket's most frenzied ever. In February, Barry's company added a marketplace for limited partnership interests, drawing $540 million worth of listings by opening day.[12] April, as ever, bred lilacs out of the dead land, as SecondMarket opened its doors to all manner of exotic financial instruments: mortgage-backed securities, collateralized debt obligations – 'the really toxic stuff', as Barry puts it. It was a brutal time for the Wall Street establishment, but for SecondMarket it was a bonanza. 'Trillions of dollars of assets that were once liquid have turned illiquid during the financial meltdown,' he said.[13] Hardly anybody wanted to touch them. Barry was cleaning up the mess made by Wall Street.

As a restructuring guy at Houlihan Lokey, he had become used to making the best of a bad situation, salvaging whatever he could after other people's unwise decisions, but this time it wasn't an isolated company that had shit the bed – it was nearly the entire financial sector. 'The world was falling apart at that time,' says Jeremy Smith. 'All of these assets were freezing up, and we said, "Hey, we're a marketplace for creating liquidity." So every time an asset froze up, we created a marketplace for it.'

In 2008, the company's revenue was $20 million – more than triple the previous year's. In 2009, revenue jumped again, by seventy-five percent, reaching $35 million. Given the company's three-to-five-percent commission fees, the revenue suggests that between $700 million and $1.17 billion of assets were traded through SecondMarket that year. 'If back in 2006 Barry had said, "You know what, I want to manage my own hedge fund and identify and invest in asset classes before anyone else,"' says Smith, 'he'd probably be a billionaire right now.' At every step, careful to grow his business within its means, Barry had resisted the urge to lease expensive office space, but now, with a hundred employees, he moved SecondMarket into its first name-brand digs: the Standard Oil building in lower Manhattan. He had come home to the heart of the Financial District, 26 Broadway, a famous address fronting on Bowling Green, the stomping grounds of a seven-thousand-pound bronze sculpture of a charging bull that has come to symbolize Wall Street in the world's imagination. He had arrived.

And the extraordinary growth continued. One year later, SecondMarket had 23,000 customers – up from 6,500 at the start of 2010 – with $30 billion in assets for sale on its platform. By early 2011, the company had brokered sales of private company stock – including that of tech darlings Twitter, Facebook, Zynga, and LinkedIn – totaling more than $500 million.

That year, Barry was named a Technology Pioneer by the World Economic Forum. In an interview for the occasion, he spoke about bringing 'trust and transparency' to the financial system. Having seen how big banks and other firms profited unfairly from opacity in the market, he was determined to disrupt the status quo. 'We think that by providing this global platform, bringing together the world's buyers and sellers, we can bring some trust back into the system and really revolutionize the financial markets.' His concern for trust and transparency primed him for Bitcoin.

SecondMarket, now valued at $200 million after raising two new rounds of investment capital, became the world's largest centralized exchange for a wide variety of illiquid assets.[14] Li Ka-shing, the richest man in Asia, was an investor, and Chamath Palihapitiya, a former vice president at Facebook, sat on the board.

The naysaying from Wall Street was ancient history. But eventually the company ran into problems. As the financial sector recovered from panic and the economy at large began dragging itself slowly out of recession, secondary trading in many of the exotic financial products that had fueled SecondMarket's success began drying up. And as for brokering sales of private company stock, that suddenly looked like a losing proposition. 'Companies weren't comfortable having their shares liquidated to unknown investors, people who weren't associated with the company,' explains one SecondMarket employee. As a result, some tech firms wrote new rules forbidding employees from selling their shares to just any old buyer – or from selling their shares at all, so long as the companies remained in private hands. And startups with Facebook-level IPO potential were, in any case, few and far between. Worse yet, the SEC began scrutinizing the market in private-company shares, following federal regulations which required private companies with more than five hundred shareholders to be in many ways as transparent as public companies.[15]

It was all too much. At its height in 2011, SecondMarket employed 140 people in New York and had regional offices in San Francisco, Israel, and Hong Kong. That year, says Bill Siegel, then SecondMarket's vice president of operations, 'was the fever pitch of pure, over-the-counter, pre-IPO private company stock trading mania, centered mostly around Facebook'.[16] But by the end of the year, with the market shifting and the regulatory outlook dimming, the Israel office closed, followed by the Hong Kong office. In New York, Barry moved his company out of the Standard Oil building and into an office in Chelsea. More than half of the company's work force was eventually laid off. After Facebook's IPO, some people expected SecondMarket to fold entirely.

But Barry refused to go down. Instead he shifted SecondMarket's focus toward becoming 'a product and technology company', Bill Siegel says, developing a software package to help private companies control the selling of their stock. While companies might not look favorably on someone selling shares behind their back, they might be persuaded to see the benefits of an internal stock sale, Barry figured. Employee shareholders still wanted the chance to turn their equity into cash; private companies wanted to control who held their shares, so as to make sure shareholder interests were aligned with company goals. SecondMarket built a product that let the company control everything, says Siegel: 'the rules, the price, who can sell and how much, not the external broker or some buyer that is scalping around for shares'.[17] Companies would line up investors and use SecondMarket's software to manage the whole offering, saving themselves 'dozens if not hundreds of man-hours', according to Jeremy Smith.

Once again Barry was ahead of the curve. But even as his firm simplified for its clients a once-laborious process – and earned large fees for doing so – the success of its product meant paring down its own staff. No longer was it a traditional phone brokerage, with necessarily large sales and marketing teams. A few traders remained to handle auction-rate securities, but the new software for sales of private company stock required little tending; and software that worked for one company could work for all of them. It was, in other words, scalable, and 2014 would see a return to the 'gargantuan' number of private company transactions that SecondMarket had brokered in its banner years – nearly $1 billion worth in the first six months alone.[18]

Barry had saved his company. But his personal interests soon began to diverge from its mission. From 2012 on, 'disillusioned with the stock market and how it's broken', as he puts it, he invested only in Bitcoin startups. (By 'broken' he meant the increase in short-term trading, the focus on quarterly earnings instead of lasting value, the growth of dark pools, and the rise of high-frequency trading – structural problems which had eroded his faith in the public stock markets and made him less inclined to take his own company public.) By launching the Bitcoin Investment Trust, he hoped to incorporate his newfound passion for Bitcoin into his business.

INITIALLY BITCOIN WAS SIMPLY BARRY Silbert's hedge against what he saw as an over-leveraged world. After spending his early twenties helping to liquidate failed companies, he then built his own startup on the bones of Wall Street's failures, its toxic assets, on other men's bad luck or reckless behavior. By the time he heard about Bitcoin, he felt a little like Noah in his ark, looking out on a world awash in debt.

The way he saw it, this debt was endemic at all levels; it went all the way from individuals living beyond their means on maxed-out credit cards up to cities and states and finally to nations.[19] At one time he had been something of a goldbug, but no longer. Too many governments were stockpiling gold as a backstop to their economies. Gold had history on its side, but eventually Barry came to see Bitcoin as a far more secure investment than precious metals. 'On a probability, risk-adjusted basis, if I'm going to make a bet on what people want to own if the shit hits the fan, I'm going to want to make a bet on something that's not being held by all the central governments whose fan is being hit with the shit,' is how he explains his changed attitude. 'If you are trying to support your currency, if you are trying to stave off the creditors, you're going to sell your gold before you sell off your monuments.'

That was all well and good. But once he launched the Bitcoin Investment Trust, personal security would become professional risk. He wasn't just planning to provide a market for Bitcoin trading, as he had done with other alternative investments; he was creating a private Bitcoin fund. If investors didn't buy in, he would be in trouble. SecondMarket would survive, he knew, because it was doing brisk business in private company stock, but he would have to lay off most of his traders. He'd also have to fire legal and technical staff who were focused on the intricacies of Bitcoin. The failure of the BIT would mean cuts across the board.

He was also putting a lot of company money on the line. In preparation for launching the fund, SecondMarket bought up $3 million worth of bitcoins at between $105 and $110 a coin. His plan was to kick-start the fund with two-thirds of the company stash; the remaining $1 million would be kept on SecondMarket's balance sheet to satisfy client orders for BIT shares, with the trading desk immediately sourcing new bitcoins to replace those sold to clients.

Despite the risks, Barry forged ahead, partly because he didn't have a sound alternative and partly because he was convinced that

Bitcoin was more than a good investment – that it was a good thing for the world. 'I haven't seen Barry so passionate about something since he first started the company,' Lori says. 'He thinks Bitcoin, and even more so digital currency, could be life-changing for our daughter.'

Money was not the most important thing to Barry. He had turned down money before. In 2012, Jeremy Smith, SecondMarket's head of strategy, approached his boss with a proposition: How about opening a market for life insurance settlements? This had huge potential. It isn't something most people think about, isn't very pleasant to consider, but in the event an old man's wife up and dies on him, say, with his children grown and comfortable, wanting for nothing, the old man may decide that he is better off selling his life insurance policy to a third party and burning the resulting cash to brighten his declining years, given that there's nobody left who will be in need of a big payout once he is gone. In that event, he may sell a $1 million policy for $600,000, say, if he can find a willing buyer. If the old man is sixty-five and has fifteen years left on his life insurance policy, and the buyer figures the old man will live another ten years at most, then he stands to reap a $400,000 profit in ten years' time. In the end – and here is the uncomfortable part – the new owner will be happy if the original policy owner dies on schedule. The one thing the buyer absolutely does not want is for the old man to live to eighty-one, because by then the policy will have expired and he will have thrown away $600,000. Best of all, of course, would be if the old man got hit by a bus tomorrow – that would mean an overnight profit of four hundred grand.

Barry thought about it. He had to take seriously any option presented to him by his chief of strategy, and the proposal was an interesting one. No new assets had been added to SecondMarket since 2009. To create a marketplace for trading people's life insurance policies would be highly lucrative, Barry knew. By rights, he should have welcomed a new source of revenue. But he said no. 'I just don't want to be involved in that kind of thing,' Barry told his friend. There was nothing unethical about it per se, but it seemed like a morbid way to make money, facilitating trades for people who got a return on their investment by predicting accurately when the original owner of the life insurance policy was going to die. Jeremy agreed. 'It's just kind of icky,' he told Barry.

Barry also passed up the opportunity to enter the marketplace for intellectual property – patents – because it was dominated by 'patent trolls', people who scoop up intellectual property merely in order to launch extortionate lawsuits against those who may be infringing on it. It was a huge moneymaking opportunity for SecondMarket, but there were other considerations. Says Jeremy Smith, 'If it was a good opportunity then there was always the second question, which was, "Is this good, neutral, or bad for people?" And if it were good or neutral, then we got into it. But if it was bad for people, then we would avoid it despite the business opportunity.' Now, with Bitcoin, Barry felt he had put his finger on an asset with huge business potential that would benefit everyone.

In setting up the Bitcoin Investment Trust, he had at least two advantages. First, he now had years of experience in creating markets for esoteric and illiquid asset classes. In fact, an argument could be made that auction-rate securities, when SecondMarket first started trading them, were even more complex and less transparent than Bitcoin. Comparing him to earlier Bitcoin entrepreneurs, Lawrence Lenihan says, 'Barry forgot more about how markets work today before breakfast than all these other guys have ever known.' And second, as a former Wall Street guy himself, Barry believed that sooner or later the finance industry was going to wake up to digital currencies. Even as Roger Ver and other radical early adopters insisted on a hardline approach, wanting to keep Bitcoin separate from Wall Street, Barry could see the writing on the wall. Whether or not the libertarians welcomed their involvement, financial firms were going to want a piece of the action, first their employees – traders, managing directors, and finance geeks who would be drawn by the technology or simply by the potential to make a killing – and then the companies themselves. Barry began designing the BIT with their interests in mind, targeting institutional investors and the affluent. 'These are guys that are looking for a long-term investment. They're not trying to trade it daily. They want to make a significant purchase in Bitcoin and hold onto it for a couple of years and not have to worry about it,' says a SecondMarket employee. Only accredited investors – people with a net worth greater than $1 million, not including the value of their home, and with an annual income of more than $200,000 (or joint income with a spouse of more than $300,000) – could invest in the BIT, and there was a $25,000 minimum investment. It was also open to institutional investors. Bitcoin's future, it seemed, lay in playing nice with the finance industry.

But there was a problem. For eighty years, private funds like the BIT had been banned from openly soliciting investors. Privately owned companies were also forbidden from advertising publicly to attract investment capital, whether on television or in print or anywhere else. Even approaching a stranger privately about an investment counted as 'general solicitation'. A niche fund for Bitcoin would obviously have a tough time succeeding if it couldn't market openly to a large group – ideally to all seven million accredited investors in the United States.

By June 2013, however, when Barry announced to his staff that SecondMarket would be launching a Bitcoin fund, a piece of legislation called the Jumpstart Our Business Startups Act, or JOBS Act, was set to change all that. The act, which had won bipartisan support and been signed into law by President Barack Obama, would lift the restrictions that had hampered entrepreneurs for decades. Barry himself had lobbied hard for this outcome. On 21 September 2011, he had spoken to the Subcommittee on Capital Markets and Government Sponsored Enterprises of the US House of Representatives Committee on Financial Services, telling its members that in the interest of helping companies grow, the pool of accredited investors who could access an offering – the only people legally allowed to purchase unregistered securities – should be made as wide and deep as possible. 'It should not matter that non-accredited individuals know that unregistered securities are available for sale,' he argued. 'No one prohibits car manufacturers from advertising, even though children under the legal driving age are viewing the advertisements, and pharmaceutical companies are free to advertise to people who do not have (and are not eligible for) prescription medication.' Three months later, he repeated his argument to a subcommittee of the US Senate Committee on Banking, Housing, and Urban Affairs. His efforts paid off. It took a while for the SEC to draft new rules, but on 23 September 2013 – more than a year after the president had signed the law – the agency finally approved general solicitation in private offerings. The change passed unnoticed by most of the world, but it was a watershed moment in the financial history of the United States.

Barry lost no time. He opened the Bitcoin Investment Trust to outside money on 26 September, having first seeded it with $2.25 million worth of bitcoins. It was the first American fund investing solely in digital currency. 'Because this regulation came out where you could now generally solicit investors, it was a great opportunity for us,' says Jack Collins, a BIT account executive. In a statement, Barry noted that Bitcoin's market cap now stood at $1.5 billion, with twenty-four million transactions having been conducted using the digital currency since its creation in 2009. The BIT had been created, he said, 'to alleviate the problems of direct Bitcoin owner-ship, including having to wire money to newly established and potentially unregulated entities around the world'.

The Bitcoin Investment Trust actually operated as a client of SecondMarket. Its traders would hunt for investors and, once it had sold them on the fund, direct them to SecondMarket. When the new investors signed up, the staff of SecondMarket, using its proprietary platform, would verify their accreditation through background checks and other means. If all was in order, the invest-ors would wire money to SecondMarket and be issued shares of the BIT, a legitimate titled security that any finance guy could look up on his Bloomberg terminal. The fund's value was determined entirely by the price of Bitcoin. So if the BIT was holding thirty thousand bitcoins and the value of one bitcoin was $100, then the fund would be worth $3 million.

Although holding shares of the BIT didn't give investors a premium on the open market price of Bitcoin, it was a way of getting direct exposure to Bitcoin as a high-risk, high-reward asset without taking any of the risks of sourcing, storing, and securing the bitcoins for themselves. 'Ultra-high-net-worth people in the world hear about Bitcoin and want to get involved, but they have no idea how to start a wallet, they don't know who to buy it from, and they don't want to wire money to Slovenia,' is how one SecondMarket employee describes the BIT's appeal. (Slovenia is where one of the largest Bitcoin exchanges is based.) The BIT, on the other hand, was backed by a regulated brokerage firm that had existed for nearly a decade – far longer than any Bitcoin exchange. 'So they can just say, "Here's a million dollars, give me a million dollars' worth of exposure to Bitcoin." No headaches.'

But regulators wouldn't be regulators if they didn't introduce new wrinkles into an otherwise straightforward process. The reason the BIT accepted only accredited investors was, quite simply, that the SEC insisted all purchasers of generally advertised securities must be accredited investors. And SecondMarket was responsible, under new SEC rules, for verifying each investor's accreditation and providing documentation to prove it. For most entrepreneurs this would have been a burdensome requirement, but Barry had already built a software platform that could do investor verification; that was part of the service SecondMarket provided to private companies whose employees wanted to sell their stock. Again he found himself ahead of the curve. As soon as the JOBS Act kicked in, he was ready to capitalize on it.

But no one was ready for what happened next. Five days after the Bitcoin Investment Trust opened – a sign of a maturing market for the digital currency – news broke that FBI agents had arrested Ross Ulbricht, the alleged founder of Silk Road, in San Francisco. What was more, the feds had wiped his black market out of existence. Erik Voorhees had boasted in April 2012 that the government was 'pitifully impotent' in its desire to take down Silk Road, but he was wrong: his faith in its invincibility was misplaced, and so was that of the site's nearly one million registered users. Users who attempted to access the drug bazaar now found it replaced by a red-bordered announcement superimposed over the site's distinctive logo of an Arab mounted on a camel: THIS HIDDEN SITE HAS BEEN SEIZED.

It was the culmination of a massive and sustained investigation by an alphabet soup of federal agencies. Not long after the publication of the Gawker article that introduced the world to Silk Road, officials at the Department of Homeland Security had received a tip from an informant in Maryland suggesting they look into the underground market. In what must have been for the authorities an eye-opening conversation, the informant explained how the market worked. Armed with this information, agents of the Immigration and Customs Enforcement's Homeland Security Investigations division launched an investigation into Silk Road in September 2011, eventually forming a Maryland-based task force codenamed Marco Polo, after the famous explorer who traveled the Silk Road and visited the court of Kublai Khan. The task force included members of the FBI, the DEA, the IRS's Criminal Investigation Division, the Secret Service, the US Postal Inspection Service, and the Bureau of Alcohol, Tobacco, and Firearms. The FBI's cybercrimes division in New York launched a parallel investigation. The black market now had formidable adversaries.

In January 2012, the feds got their first big break: they scooped up in Baltimore a twenty-nine-year-old drug dealer named Jacob Theodore George IV, who had been peddling heroin and other drugs on Silk Road. Dead to rights, and with prior convictions on his record, George surrendered to investigators his email account, shipping records, and financial statements. He turned over his laptop and desktop computers, which contained his customer records. He gave up everything. Federal authorities promptly took over George's Silk Road account, giving the Marco Polo task force its first real look behind the curtain of the cryptomarket.

In the ensuing months, investigators arrested more dealers and discovered that Ross Ulbricht had made some crucial missteps by which he could be linked to the Dread Pirate Roberts identity. But the consequences were slow in coming. During the summer of 2012, Ross was raking in $180,000 a month in commissions – even more than Mt. Gox, the world's largest Bitcoin exchange. (After his arrest, the FBI seized 144,336 bitcoins from the personal cache on his computer and 29,656 bitcoins in user funds from the server hosting Silk Road.) He moved to San Francisco at the invitation of an old high school friend who had given up making films – his former obsession – to join the startup boom. It was the twenty-first-century gold rush, and Ross Ulbricht was part of it, running a highly successful, highly illegal e-commerce startup.

But even as large quantities of drugs and digital cash began to flow through the marketplace, its sheer mundanity belied the logic of harsh drug prohibition laws. James Martin of Macquarie University in Sydney, Australia, who has studied Silk Road, notes the 'prosaic blandness' of the way business was done on the crypto-market, complete with holiday sales, refunds for drugs that didn't reach their destination, and users 'complaining about minor delays in shipping'.[20] This prosaic, user-friendly approach seems to have fueled its popularity. In late 2012, a global survey of recent drug buyers found that sixty-five percent of respondents in the United States, fifty-three percent in Australia, and forty percent in the United Kingdom had heard of Silk Road.[21] And fully eighteen percent of respondents in the US, ten percent in the UK, and seven percent in Australia admitted to consuming drugs they had bought on Ross Ulbricht's 'little hidden market'. Long before his trial Ross was already a folk hero to thousands of people, disaffected members of a generation shaped by economic collapse and WikiLeaks, by drone warfare and the surveillance state; a group fired up by the revelations of Edward Snowden and loaded down with student debt. A powder keg of a generation.

Prosecutors were determined to lock up Ross and throw away the key. But it was a gesture akin to locking the gate after the horse has bolted. By now it had become apparent that Silk Road repre-sented, as Martin put it, 'only the tip of a vast and rapidly proliferating body of cryptomarkets'.[22] Indeed, by the fall of 2013, Bitcoin had become the payment method of choice across much of the underground economy. The arrest of Ross Ulbricht, this twentysomething surfer, in a San Francisco library was always, then, in some sense theatrical, a muscular show of police work hiding a very real and deep inability to enforce existing drug laws across a broad swath of the globalized Internet; it was a mask concealing despair, for even as news trickled in over the ensuing weeks about more arrests connected with Silk Road – even as, that is, a few stray cows of the million-strong herd were rounded up and penned in – the majority of users, fleeing the defunct marketplace, in the very act of desertion were already given up for lost. Within a month of Silk Road's shutdown, the number of users on Sheep Marketplace, a Silk Road competitor, increased sixfold; the number on Black Market Reloaded, another cryptomarket, doubled. Dread Pirate Roberts had shown them the Promised Land. There was no going back to Egypt.

And yet, while Silk Road copycats had sprung up, thousands of legitimate businesses were now also accepting digital currency. The crypto-anarchist strain in the Bitcoin community was gradually giving way to a more conventional wisdom. Where once Bitcoin and Silk Road had been thoroughly intertwined, with scams and technical problems on Silk Road causing the digital currency's price to drop, now the 'Napster of meth' was no longer needed.

'A lot of crypto-anarchists are looking at this as a real loss, whether or not they used Silk Road, just on principle,' Marco Santori said at the time. 'Those of us in the mainstream see this as a great development. If there was any question before whether there would still be Bitcoin use outside of Silk Road, the answer is yes, absolutely.'

And so, while the arrest of Ross Ulbricht sent shockwaves throughout the Bitcoin world, SecondMarket's offices remained an oasis of calm. The Bitcoin price recovered quickly from a brief dip. Barry Silbert was sanguine. It was, he later reflected, a positive event: 'It proved that the bad guys can [and] will get caught, even in Bitcoinland.' He was also hopeful that, with Silk Road gone, the press would move on to other things, no longer obsessed with 'the "dark side" of Bitcoin'.

The ranks of BIT investors were, by all accounts, equally unperturbed. 'The earliest investors were already Bitcoin evangelists and therefore really didn't pay too much attention to the noise created by Silk Road, because they knew that it was just that: noise,' says Michael Moro, then a trader at SecondMarket. They were so excited to have an investment vehicle for Bitcoin that the headline news about drugs and murder for hire did little to dampen their enthusiasm. It may have been one of the best investment decisions of their lives. On 1 October 2013, the day of Ross's arrest, the average price of a single bitcoin was $121, according to Coinbase's charts. One month later, it was $208. By the first of December, it had passed $1,000.

It was as if Silk Road, which had once buoyed the Bitcoin economy, had become its anchor. Freed of the weight, the digital currency was riding a flood-tide of enthusiasm like never before. In the ensuing weeks, its price increased so rapidly, even as the BIT accumulated tens of thousands of units of the digital currency, that Barry didn't know whether his fund was responsible for driving the price up or whether the skyrocketing price was driving additional interest in the fund. Whatever the cause, the BIT ballooned faster than anyone had expected.

In truth, Barry had the government partly to thank for his fund's overnight success. In late summer, Senator Tom Carper, head of the Senate Committee on Homeland Security and Governmental Affairs, had sent a letter to Janet Napolitano, the outgoing secretary of Homeland Security, announcing that he had launched an inquiry into virtual currencies. He wanted to know what stance her agency was taking toward them and what resources it was dedicating to their regulation. Identical copies were sent to the heads of the Justice Department, Treasury Department, SEC, CFTC, and Federal Reserve. In the letter, which was cosigned by Senator Tom Coburn of Maryland, Senator Carper expressed concern that while 'virtual currencies' – as US government officials insisted on calling them – held promise, 'their near anonymous and decentralized nature has also attracted criminals who value few things more than being allowed to operate in the shadows.' He brought up the case of Trendon Shavers, the Texas man charged with running a Bitcoin Ponzi scheme, describing it as 'just the most recent incident' in which the digital currency industry had run headlong into existing law. It wasn't likely to be the last.

For one thing, paperwork had been filed with the SEC in July to get the ball rolling on an exchange-traded Bitcoin fund, allowing institutional investors to begin investing in the digital currency. Behind this filing were the Winklevoss twins, who, in trying to launch a Bitcoin fund of their own, automatically became Barry Silbert's rivals.

For another, ICE had felt it necessary only a few months earlier to seize millions of dollars in accounts belonging to Mt. Gox. Senator Carper called for a 'holistic and whole-government approach' to this emerging technology so that a sensible regulatory framework might be implemented. But his overall take on Bitcoin was quite positive. 'As with all emerging technologies, the federal government must make sure that potential threats and risks are dealt with swiftly,' he wrote. 'However, we must also ensure that rash or uninformed actions don't stifle a potentially valuable technology.'

Replies from the various agencies trickled in over the next several months. The senators had asked for replies by the end of August, but the last letter, from Gary Gensler, chairman of the CFTC, didn't arrive until after Christmas. That was government bureaucracy for you. Nevertheless, by mid-November Senator Carper felt he had a pretty good handle on where things stood in Washington. He decided to hold a hearing with his committee on the potential risks and benefits of digital currencies.

But the hearing wouldn't be Washington's first engagement with the Bitcoin community. Two weeks after Senator Carper dispatched his letters, representatives of FinCEN and other state and federal agencies, including the SEC's Division of Trading and Markets, had a sit-down with members of the Bitcoin Foundation, covering the basics of the technology as well as legal and law enforcement issues. And the senator's staff had been looking into Bitcoin ever since the price bubble in April, spending months quietly interviewing entrepreneurs, investors, academics, regulators, and members of law enforcement. The responses that came in from the agencies to which the senator had sent letters were still more enlightening. From the Treasury Department he learned that while digital currencies could be used to launder money and finance terrorists, the practical constraints of low liquidity and price volatility had so far prevented them from becoming 'the predominant mode of large-scale illicit transactions'. Nevertheless, both FinCEN and the Treasury Department's Office of Foreign Assets Control stood ready to identify and impose fines on virtual currency businesses that criminal organizations and terrorists were using to move money. Justice informed him that in early 2012 the FBI had founded an interagency group, the Virtual Currency Emerging Threats Working Group, in which Treasury took part, to tackle head-on the problem of digital currency money laundering. The SEC explained that while a digital currency may not itself be considered a security – it would likely be classified as a commodity – any entity providing a return to investors based on digital currency assets would be seen as issuing securities and would be subject to SEC regulation.

Most comprehensive of all was the letter from Homeland. The lifeblood of international crime organizations, wrote Brian de Vallance, the DHS's acting assistant secretary for legislative affairs, is the ability 'to quickly and quietly move large quantities of money across borders. The anonymity of cyberspace affords a unique opportunity for criminal organizations to launder huge sums of money undetected.' Digital currencies made this relatively simple, and so the DHS had adopted an 'aggressive posture' toward what it saw as a new threat, targeting criminal black markets and virtual currency exchanges alike. De Vallance proceeded to outline for the senators a handful of big investigations, including one run out of the Washington field office which had resulted in the recent takedown of Liberty Reserve, a virtual currency network through which more than $6 billion in criminal profits had been laundered. (Although the feds tended to lump Liberty Reserve in with Bitcoin, it had little in common with decentralized cryptocurrencies. It was a kind of centralized electronic money, not unlike E-gold.) Still, it was a big win for law enforcement. Five people had been arrested and some $29 million had been seized. Another investigation involved the seizure of bank accounts belonging to TrustCash, BitInstant's old payment processor. But even as DHS agents were going about educating the anti-money laundering departments of financial institutions on this kind of criminal activity, de Vallance was forced to admit to Senator Carper that digital currency transactions 'may not meet the definition of a financial transaction' as defined by existing anti-money laundering laws. If a Bitcoin user or company were to be prosecuted for laundering money, he wrote, 'certain legislative remedies may be needed' to make the charges stick. Legally, that is, they were in uncharted waters.

As if this weren't enough for Senator Carper and his aides to digest, there turned out to be on the matter of digital currencies a great deal of what is known as interagency cooperation. There was so much interagency cooperation, in fact, that it was hard to keep it all straight. The Secret Service, for instance, as part of the DHS, coordinated its efforts with the Justice Department's Asset Forfeiture and Money Laundering Section and the Treasury Department's Office of Terrorist Financing and Financial Crimes. The SEC's Division of Enforcement kept lines open to the departments of Justice and Treasury as well as to the New York State Office of the Attorney General and the New York Department of Financial Services. Clearly, the agencies involved wanted to project the image of a well-oiled machine, its various parts working in perfect harmony. In fact, just as different ideological factions were now fighting for the soul of Bitcoin, the federal agencies were engaged in something of a turf war. But there was more to it than that: the mobilization of manpower across multiple agencies mirrored the government's respect for Bitcoin's global reach.

Beyond respect, however, the letters evinced a positive, even an optimistic outlook. Both the Treasury and the Justice Departments were quick to note that digital currencies and other online payment systems did 'provide legitimate financial services'. Ben Bernanke, chairman of the Federal Reserve, went still further. He reminded the senators that in 1995 the House of Representatives Subcommittee on Domestic and International Monetary Policy had held its own hearings on 'the future of money' to discuss early versions of digital currencies and other innovations in payments technology. At that time, Alan Blinder, then vice chairman of the Fed, had testified, as Bernanke put it, that 'while these types of innovations may pose risks related to law enforcement and supervisory matters, there are also areas in which they may hold long-term promise, particularly if the innovations promote a faster, more secure, and more efficient payment system.'

It was a better endorsement of Bitcoin than one could have expected. And it came from the chairman of the Fed himself.

This positivity carried over to the Senate hearing. The witness panels included not only Bitcoin boosters like Jeremy Allaire of Circle Internet Financial and Patrick Murck of the Bitcoin Foundation but also representatives of the Justice Department, the Secret Service, and FinCEN. One might have expected these government types to see cryptocurrencies less as a miracle technology than as a twenty-first-century headache for law enforcement. But Silk Road was gone. The government could afford to be generous. 'Exploitation by malicious actors is a problem faced by all types of financial services, and is not unique to virtual currency systems,' Mythili Raman, the acting assistant attorney general of the Justice Department's criminal division, said in her testimony. With appropriate anti-money laundering and Know Your Customer controls, she added, a digital currency startup 'can safeguard its system from exploitation by criminals and terrorists in the same way any other money-services business could'. Just as in the letters, the Washington suits were surprisingly loath in the hearing to come out swinging against Bitcoin. And this time their magnanimity was a matter of public record.

But there was a darker reason for their understanding attitude, and it could be summed up in one word: China. Even as the Bitcoin price that fall was climbing well above its former April highs, about a third of the world's Bitcoin transactions were flowing through a single exchange, BTC China, which was open only to Chinese users. BTC China had recently unseated Mt. Gox as the world's largest exchange by trading volume. Mere days before the Senate

hearing, Linke Yang, BTC China's vice president, had waxed philosophical for Agence France-Presse about the reason why Bitcoin
had 'become big in China'. It was, he said, speaking from a Bitcoin
conference in Singapore, quite simply because 'Chinese people are
savers, and more people are seeing Bitcoin as a way to store and
invest their money.' He knew what was coming even if the rest of
the world didn't. On Monday, the day of the hearing, news broke
that BTC China had raised $5 million of investment capital. By
1:00 P.M. in Washington, the value of a single bitcoin had hit a
record of nearly 4,300 yuan, or about $700.

Surprisingly, the Chinese government, well known for its
currency controls, had not yet stepped in to regulate it. Possibly
officials had been caught flat-footed by the sudden surge of interest
in this digital gold. And yet the television station CCTV and the
newspaper *People's Daily* – both state-run media outlets – had run
positive reports on Bitcoin over the summer. Now even a fraud
case involving Global Bond Limited, a Bitcoin-trading platform
that shut its doors abruptly in October, allegedly taking more than
$4 million of investor money along with it, had barely dampened
Chinese enthusiasm. Bitcoin, it seemed, would move forward even
without American involvement. After all, none of the top three
exchanges was based in the United States. Along with BTC China
and Mt. Gox in Japan, there was Bitstamp, which was located in
Slovenia. Imagine that! Slovenia!

These grim facts hung over the Senate hearing like a dark
cloud. There was a new Cold War on, went the thinking in some
quarters. The economic rivalry between East and West looked set
to define the century. Cybercrime and cyber-espionage were costing
the world economy as much as $1 trillion annually – a cost the
director of the National Security Agency, General Keith Alexander,
called 'the greatest transfer of wealth in history'. China was by
far the biggest offender. Its state-sanctioned hackers stole technology blueprints, trade secrets, business plans, partnership
agreements, and customer lists – siphoning away from the victims
many billions in lost revenue. American nuclear plants and defense
contractors were top targets. Design specs for more than two dozen

major weapons systems, the most unbelievably sensitive stuff, intellectual property vital to the nation's security, were stolen out from under the Pentagon's nose. In 2013, federal agents notified more than three thousand American companies that they had been hacked.[23]

It was in this context that the issue of digital currencies had to be considered. God forbid America should take second place to China on this new frontier, as it for so long had been forced to accept second in the space race with the Soviets! Although US officials were leery of Bitcoin's potential for criminal use, they seemed even more afraid of quashing innovation among American companies at a time when China was relentlessly gaining ground. Jeremy Allaire shared their concerns. 'We do not think that it is in anyone's best interest for digital currency to become an offshore industry or an industry dominated by China,' he told the assembled senators. And so the hearing became a 'lovefest', as the press would later report. Senator Carper got things started with his very first question, asking whether it didn't make sense to treat Bitcoin like the early Internet – unregulated and for that reason appealing to ne'er-do-wells, but capable of providing tremendous benefits to people around the world, making possible previously unimaginable services. And in reply, Obama administration officials practically fell over themselves to assert their commitment to entrepreneurial spirit and technological progress. 'Innovation is a very important part of our economy. It's something for us to be proud of,' FinCEN director Jennifer Calvery said. Mythili Raman, for her part, reaffirmed the basic legality of digital currencies themselves. Neither Calvery nor Raman nor any other government official testifying that day asked for new regulations to keep Bitcoin in check. Were it not for China, they might well have been less inclined to grant the importance of Bitcoin's legitimate uses.

As news of the Washington 'lovefest' spread, the price of Bitcoin kept rising day by day – beyond $700, beyond $800, beyond $900 . . . It was immensely encouraging. Astonishing, really. But for Barry, it wasn't enough. Even at its 2013 peak of $13.9 billion, he knew, Bitcoin's market cap was too small for the cryptocurrency to make a real dent in the world of international money transfers – dominated by Western Union and MoneyGram – or in e-commerce, still the bailiwick of Visa and MasterCard. Only when its market cap was $50 billion or even $500 billion would Bitcoin be able to fulfill its true potential. And for that to happen, new companies would need to be built, new products and services developed; the IRS and other government agencies (to say nothing of the governments of other countries) would need to issue clear guidelines. A whole new wave of investors, consumers, merchants, and institutions would need to get involved. It would take time, but the signs were already there. The year to come, he felt confident, would be the year of Bitcoin.

Chapter 9

INNOVATION AND ITS DISCONTENTS

Capital controls are difficult in a world where I can cross
a border with a million dollars in my brain.
                                            – Naval Ravikant

Within weeks of taking over as the CEO of Blockchain, Nic Cary
found himself living in airports. CheapAir, a travel-booking site,
had begun accepting Bitcoin as payment for plane tickets, the first
travel agency in the world to do so. For Nic, who received his
salary in bitcoins, the timing was perfect. In his first six months
he would make forty border crossings, traveling, he estimated,
more than half a million miles. It was almost certainly an exag-
geration; Ryan Bingham, the perpetually airborne protagonist of
Up in the Air, manages only 350,000 in twice that time; but then
again, the fictional Bingham is only crisscrossing a continent, not
soaring over oceans. Had Blockchain not worked out for him, had
he not liked what he'd seen and instead turned down the CEO
position, Nic says, he would have lived abroad and undertaken a
'walkabout' – traveling the world with no particular aim except
to 'wander and wonder'. But now his globe-trotting had a purpose.
Although he spent much of the fall of 2013 in York, working
alongside Ben Reeves, he found time to visit Amsterdam and Las
Vegas for Bitcoin conferences and to join Bitcoin meetup groups

in Paris. And these jaunts were merely the warm-up for the marathon to come.

Wherever Nic went, his money was waiting for him. His cell phone was linked to his Blockchain wallet, which lived in the cloud – meaning it was accessible online but not stored on his device or in a central server somewhere – so that as soon as the plane touched down and he could get a signal he had thousands of dollars in bitcoins at his fingertips. Unlike money in a bank account, it was subject to no monthly fees, no waiting periods, no geographic limits on where it could be sent or spent; it came and went at his sole discretion, on his sole authority. And what of the requirement, standard on customs forms, to disclose any amount of money greater than $10,000 which you're bringing into a foreign country? 'I have no comment on that,' he laughed once, on an international flight. Even if there were a law against carrying bitcoins across borders – there wasn't – it would be hard to enforce. And he wasn't *bringing* the bitcoins with him, not really. It would be more accurate to say they already existed everywhere in the world at once. Nic's world, it goes without saying, was so new it hadn't reached most of us yet, was still incipient somewhere on the horizon, along with driverless cars and 3D-printed food and other unambiguous marvels.

Nic wasn't worried about the theft of his phone. In order to get at his money, the thief would have to brute-force his way past the four-digit pincode locking the phone as well as the pincode and secondary password protecting the wallet itself. By that time, Nic would have moved his funds elsewhere, at which point it would be a simple matter to link a new phone to his new wallet and continue on as if nothing had happened.

While Blockchain as a company operated entirely without a bank presence, Nic did maintain a personal bank account at Wells Fargo, and he used that money in airports. Considering the nature of his work, which, if it succeeded to the furthest extent, would make bitcoins ubiquitous in commerce, however, one couldn't help feeling that his attitude toward fiat currency was that of Ralph Waldo Emerson giving alms – though he sometimes succumbed and gave the dollar, it was a wicked dollar which by and by he would have the technology to withhold. He was already beginning to feel like a citizen of the world, a guy with two passports (American and French) and hybrid genes – part Russian, part Ukrainian Jew, part French, part Scots-English – still rendering unto Caesar what is Caesar's come 15 April every year but otherwise untethered from obligations of place or custom. Credit cards, another means of carrying purchasing power across borders, were anathema to him. His philosophy of personal finance was simple and persuasively austere: Don't spend more than you earn. Set aside some savings. Don't go into debt; or, if you must, have a plan for getting out. A credit card is an instrument of debt, a shovel made to dig you into a hole. For one thing only he went into debt, and that was college; when his bitcoins appreciated in value, he paid off his student loans.

December found Nic in Chile, staying at his father's house in Pirque, a semirural area in wine country on the outskirts of Santiago. But it wasn't a vacation. Save for a four-day fishing trip with his father, Philip, down to Patagonia – a legendary region, including parts of both Chile and Argentina, which Charles Darwin visited on the *Beagle* and where some of the best fly fishing in the world can be found – Nic's mind was on his work. Staying by himself in the *casita*, guest quarters that sit a short distance from the main house on his father's property, he had ideal conditions for it. There was a big bed and a desk, a pile of Indian blankets and a map of Paris on the wall. Battered felt hats, family photographs, fishing tackle. And dominating the space, lining the walls, was his father's library, totaling hundreds of books: works of history and politics, foreign novels, Bruce Chatwin's travel essays; a complete Dickinson, Yeats, Frost, Milton; and, even better, just about every line ever published by Nic's favorite writer, Ernest Hemingway – his novels, stories, journalism, poetry, even a collection called *Hemingway on Fishing*. Nic himself had volumes of Hemingway's letters packed away with the rest of his books in a storage locker in Seattle. He felt at home here, in this room of the life of the mind. It was a room built for reflection.

He had a lot to reflect on. The price of Bitcoin had been going wild for weeks, since shortly after the shutdown of Silk Road. It was a watershed moment. Once so crucial to the digital currency's economy, Silk Road had become an obstacle to mainstream investment and a public relations nightmare for aboveboard entrepreneurs such as Nic Cary. Now, with Silk Road gone and its alleged founder in custody, Bitcoin was soaring like a hot air balloon with its tether line cut. By early December, the price was above $1,100. The governor of the Reserve Bank of Australia said publicly that he found Bitcoin 'fascinating' and that there was nothing to stop Australians from using it for transactions. Venture capitalists were rushing in where banks still feared to tread. The fourth quarter of 2013 saw nearly $50 million of venture capital invested in Bitcoin startups across eighteen deals, by far the lion's share of the $74 million total for the year. Among those deals was a $25 million Series B round for Coinbase. For the largest-ever investment in a Bitcoin startup to go to Blockchain's bitter rival must have frustrated Ben Reeves. Coinbase now hosted more than 600,000 consumer Bitcoin wallets, though Blockchain, with more than 800,000 wallets, had a comfortable lead. But Coinbase also provided merchant services to recognizable brands such as OKCupid, a popular online matchmaking service, and the social news site Reddit, both of which, in the digital economy, were practically blue-chip clients. Coinbase made it possible for them to accept Bitcoin payments and then, on their behalf, would exchange the bitcoins for dollars so that the clients never had to touch digital currency directly or expose themselves to its violent price swings. And Coinbase also had gained a new adviser, Gavin Andresen, who was chief scientist of the Bitcoin Foundation and who called Blockchain's competitor 'a critical piece of the Bitcoin infrastructure in the US . . . a trustworthy and easy way to buy, sell, trade and store bitcoins'.[1]

All of this activity was creating information overload. To stay abreast of news and check on the price, Nic had been relying on a mobile app called ZeroBlock, released by a startup of the same name. A college buddy who knew he was involved in Bitcoin had told him about it three or four months earlier. Now he was checking the app obsessively, dozens of times a day. He admired ZeroBlock's clean, innovative design and ease of use. The main screen displayed the current market price per bitcoin, along with the market cap, network transaction volume, total number of bitcoins in circulation, and twenty-four-hour highs and lows across multiple Bitcoin exchanges. Users could swipe up and down, left and right to obtain, respectively, price alerts, a bitcoin-to-dollar conversion calculator, a curated list of breaking news stories, and trading history. Blockchain.info provided an even greater wealth of information, but at the time, says Cary, 'I thought our design was atrocious. I believed that our website was successful *despite* our design.' It was well suited to early adopters, miners, and others who understood the network and were looking for specific information. But it wasn't right for average people. And not only the website – the web wallet, the marketing emails, everything needed to change. He had already redesigned the logo. Now he saw an opportunity to gain real ground.

He offered to buy ZeroBlock outright from its founder, Dan Held, and his cofounder, Kevin Johnson, in the process bringing Held into the fold as a full-time employee of Blockchain. Nic had had only glancing contact with Held before, but there was mutual respect between them. 'We'll cross-market your app to Blockchain's one million users,' he promised. 'We can give it a ton of exposure, and you can help make Blockchain more successful by working on the world's premier Bitcoin site.' Within a week, the deal was done. 'It happened super-fast, because it was a great fit,' Nic says. 'We created a commercial agreement that I think is very cool for both of us.' Soon afterward, Nic discovered that a lot of ZeroBlock's features relied on Blockchain's APIs. From a technical standpoint, the two companies were already aligned.

Most observers hadn't expected to see any mergers or acquisitions in the Bitcoin economy for some time to come. Mt. Gox's deal with Bitomat had been less an acquisition than a bailout. BitInstant and Coinapult had failed to merge. Erik Voorhees had sold SatoshiDice for a tidy profit, but the anonymous buyer was an individual. No Bitcoin company had ever truly bought one of its peers before. Now, all of a sudden, Blockchain became the first to do so. The deal, for an undisclosed sum, was announced on Christmas Eve. It was settled entirely in bitcoins.

With the acquisition, Held became Blockchain's product lead, responsible for the design and delivery of good products, services, and user experiences across the entire company. 'It's a hell of a lot of responsibility,' Nic says. 'But we didn't have anybody who could do what he had done with ZeroBlock, so he was the man for the job.'

For his part, Held was thrilled. He had been holding down a day job at a small investment firm in Dallas called Dunhill Partners and working on ZeroBlock in his spare time, hardly an ideal arrangement. Now ZeroBlock *was* his job. A finance and tech nerd, he saw Bitcoin as 'the Holy Grail'; now he was living in the Bitcoin economy full-time.

And Nic was just getting warmed up. One month later, at a Bitcoin conference in Miami, he announced that Andreas Antonopoulos, a half-Greek, half-British computer scientist widely respected in the world of cryptocurrency, would be joining Blockchain as chief security officer. Bitcoin had come to Antonopoulos's attention in 2010, but he hadn't given it much thought until the following year, when he finally read Satoshi's paper explaining how it worked. He would later describe Bitcoin – and was not alone in doing so – as not merely the money of the Internet but 'the Internet of money'.

With him on board, Blockchain now had twelve employees, all of whom were being paid in bitcoins, and was still operating with no bank account. By May it would have eight more.

THE YEAR 2014 DAWNED BRIGHT for Bitcoin. On 9 January, Overstock, an online retailer with $1.3 billion in annual revenue, announced that it would begin accepting Bitcoin payments for every product on its website, from flatscreen TVs to patio furniture. The news provoked a kind of frenzy. In the first twenty-four hours, Overstock received 840 orders totaling $130,000 worth of bitcoins, nearly all placed by new customers. Within two months, the company had received more than $1 million in Bitcoin sales and its CEO, a libertarian named Patrick Byrne, was projecting $10 million to $20 million by year's end.

On 21 January, the *New York Times* published an editorial on Bitcoin by one of Silicon Valley Kingmaker's, Marc Andreessen. His venture capital firm, Andreessen Horowitz, had already bet nearly $50 million on Bitcoin startups, including, only weeks earlier, Coinbase, in whose $25 million round of funding it had played the role of lead investor. Andreessen compared Bitcoin's position in 2014 to that of personal computers in 1975 and the Internet in 1993 – both revolutionary inventions that had emerged 'seemingly out of nowhere', faced down tremendous skepticism, and changed the world. He ran down a list of possible uses for Bitcoin: remittances, financial services, micropayments. Given that Bitcoin transaction fees were low to nonexistent, adopting it for remittance payments was a no-brainer. 'In fact, it is hard to think of any one thing that would have a faster and more positive effect on so many people in the world's poorest countries,' Andreessen wrote.

With its patient tone and positivity, the op-ed was manifestly an attempt to change the conversation around digital currency, heretofore dominated in the press by fear and doubt over online drug markets, hacks, and scandals. It was also a 3,100-word salvo in an ideological war that was brewing between the anti-government early adopters of Bitcoin and the mainstream investors – good technocratic liberals, most of them – who hoped to make a fortune on it. Where Roger Ver wanted Bitcoin to put an end, in his words, 'to all these central banks printing money and using it to kill people', Andreessen didn't see Bitcoin as a weapon against central banking; he saw it as a 'digital bearer instrument', a way of exchanging assets and confirming their ownership over the Internet. Those assets could be digital currency, or they could be digital contracts, digital pink slips and deeds to physical property, digital stocks and bonds . . . The sky was the limit. 'Far from a mere libertarian fairy tale or a simple Silicon Valley exercise in hype,' he concluded, 'Bitcoin

offers a sweeping vista of opportunity to reimagine how the financial system can and should work in the Internet era.'

Andreessen had seen before how experimental technologies at
their inception attracted idealists, who gradually dropped away or
were marginalized as the technologies matured. But the idealists
weren't going away this time. The day after his editorial was
published, BitAngels, an angel investment network comprising 324
investors across twenty-three countries, announced that it had
raised a total of $7 million for twelve Bitcoin startups since its
founding in May 2013. Leading members included Roger Ver, a
former child actor from the *Mighty Ducks* franchise named Brock
Pierce, and former TradeHill CEO Jered Kenna. At $815, Bitcoin
was down more than $300 from its late November high – though
nearly identical to the market value it had held exactly two months
before – but its value was still more than high enough to give early
hoarders sizable war chests. And they were willing to use them to
turn their vision for Bitcoin into reality. 'We take more risks than
the VCs do,' says Michael Terpin, one of the founding members
of BitAngels. 'We put money into companies that are still in the
concept stage, that have no revenue, that are maybe two guys in
a garage. As an angel group should.'

There was one man, more than any other, who exemplified
these internal divisions, who had first profited by them and then
suffered from them. In New York, Charlie Shrem, now twenty-four,
was living the high life. Having finally moved out of his parents'
house, he had a spacious apartment in Midtown one flight above
EVR, a bar of which he was a part owner and which accepted
Bitcoin as payment for rounds of Stella Artois. He had first met
his girlfriend, Courtney Warner, of whom his strictly religious
parents disapproved, at EVR, where she was a part-time bartender.
And he was still an unrepentant stoner; his apartment – equipped
with two big-screen TVs and shared with four roommates – reeked
of pot and alcohol. His personal wealth had grown enormously
in concert with the exponential rise in Bitcoin's value the previous
year, from $13 in January to more than $1,100 by the end of
November. Even with a recent price decline, he was still a rich

man. And, Bitcoin evangelist or not, he was smart enough to hedge his cryptocurrency investment. Every time the price of Bitcoin went up twenty percent, he said, he cashed out a portion of his holdings.[2]

His company, BitInstant, was officially on hiatus. After the shutdown his instinct was to flee, and he fled with Courtney to Morocco, where they were joined by his friend Thomas Holzinger and Holzinger's girlfriend. It was undeniably a bender. Charlie recalls Holzinger, to whom it fell to drive the rental car, rolling hash joints while steering. Charlie, for his part, even tried opium – a 'crazy drug', he says, of which he partook once and only once. It made him feel sick. Throughout his time in Morocco he did his best to stay clean-shaven, so as not to look too Middle Eastern, having realized that locals, due to the country's internal tensions, would wave white foreigners through checkpoints while treating fellow Arabs with more suspicion.

Back in New York, the good times continued. Freed from the relentless grind of managing a startup, he was having fun – and indulging his talent for wheeling and dealing. He flew overnight to Argentina on a mission for the Bitcoin Foundation, hoping to convince that country's Bitcoin advocacy group to join up with the American lobbyists. 'A lot of what I do is making deals, closing deals, getting people to like me. It's impressing people,' he said. 'I have to take a lot of people out to clubs, buying bottles, buying dinners.'[3] But he hadn't forgotten that BitInstant was the rocket ship that landed him on the moon. And he wasn't ready to give up on it. He'd used the back cover of the August 2013 issue of *Bitcoin Magazine* to proclaim that BitInstant would be back and better than ever. Four months later, he still believed it was possible. In fact, he planned to relaunch the company in a few weeks. He just had to avoid getting tripped up by regulation. 'If we want to exist twenty years from now, we want to make sure all of our ducks are in a row,' he said. 'And right now, they're not.'[4] In another context, however, he bragged that BitInstant had 'good KYC', using the acronym for Know Your Customer requirements. 'As long as you

KYC, you're not gonna go to jail,' he told a *GQ* reporter.[5] Those words would come back to haunt him.

In January, Charlie flew to Amsterdam with Courtney in tow. He was scheduled to speak at Webwinkel Vakdagen, the largest e-commerce exhibition in the Netherlands, which that year would draw a crowd of more than ten thousand professionals. Charlie's agent had gotten him $20,000 to give a speech about the advantages of Bitcoin for consumers and online merchants. (Later, Charlie would keep a copy of the 23 January edition of Dutch newspaper *Het Financieele Dagblad*, whose front page showed him speaking at the conference, gummed to the wall by the light switch in the basement bedroom he occupied in his parents' house, a reminder in diminished circumstances of better days.) On Wednesday, 22 January, at 10:30 A.M., Charlie took the stage, stoned and wearing a BitInstant T-shirt, black blazer, and wraparound mic. Projected behind him on a large screen was the logo of the Bitcoin Foundation. 'Bitcoin is the Napster of the financial world,' he told the audience. The digital currency will have the kind of impact on the financial system, he predicted, that file-sharing software has had on the music industry and email has had on postal services.

Charlie shared a story about a customer who had recently spent $7,000 partying at EVR: champagne, food, friends, the whole package. The next day – even though the bar had security camera footage of his revelry – he called his credit card company and tried to claim that he hadn't been there. Had he been successful in his claim, the card company would have initiated a chargeback, meaning that EVR would have received no compensation despite having provided $7,000 worth of products and services. With Bitcoin, Charlie told the audience, such fraud was impossible.

In closing, he used an example tailor-made for his audience to explain Bitcoin's potential. Jeff Bezos's Amazon, he reminded them, started out as an online bookstore but had since attained even greater success by applying its model to other goods and services. Just so, there was no telling where Bitcoin might end up. Currency might not even be its 'killer app', he said, echoing the substance of Andreessen's editorial. At bottom, it was simply a system for transferring secure ownership of digital assets while maintaining one's privacy.

On the night of Sunday, 26 January, Charlie returned to New York. He had dressed comfortably for the long Icelandair flight in jeans, a blue T-shirt, and a slim charcoal hoodie. He knew that on 28 January the New York Department of Financial Services would begin two days of hearings on Bitcoin, the purpose of which was to discuss whether and how Bitcoin businesses, and digital currencies themselves, should be regulated in the state of New York. Charlie planned to attend. But he never made it there. When he touched down at John F. Kennedy International Airport, the feds were waiting for him.

On the jetway, a man carrying a Glock handgun approached him, identified himself as a special agent of the IRS's Criminal Investigation division, and said he was placing Charlie under arrest. Charlie was incredulous. 'What, did I not pay my taxes or something? Why is the IRS arresting me?' It soon became clear that the charges against Charlie were serious. He stood accused of willful failure to file Suspicious Activity Reports, money laundering conspiracy, and operating an unlicensed money transmitting business. The charges each carried prison sentences of between five and twenty years. They stemmed from his dealings with Robert Faiella.

As the IRS agent and his colleagues took Charlie into custody, they turned to Charlie's girlfriend, Courtney, who had accompanied him on the flight home, and asked for permission to search her apartment. 'Just because I'm blonde,' she said, 'doesn't mean I'm stupid.' She watched the feds lead away her boyfriend, who had suffered the indignity of being arrested in front of his fellow passengers. (At first, hearing the news of Charlie's arrest from her daughter, Courtney's mother thought he had tried to sneak some pot back into the States from Amsterdam.) It was law enforcement theater, and Charlie, for his part, met it with all the drama of his hyperbolic imagination: 'They made it like they arrested some big Mafia guy. They fucking put me in a black SUV with police escorts, motorcycles – it was like the President was arriving in town.'

Whatever the extent of the spectacle, BitInstant's one-time suitor Lawrence Lenihan was not surprised by Charlie's arrest. Disruptive innovation was one thing but outright criminality something else entirely. 'You start messing with rule of law,' he says, 'and you're going to have people in fucking black SUVs showing up and hauling your ass off, because that's shaking the foundations of this democracy.'

But the ride wasn't all bad, Charlie recalls. He talked economics with the agents escorting him. The patter was a way of relieving tension without giving anything away. *I fucking watch Law & Order,* he thought to himself. *I'm not stupid.*

He recalls being taken to the New York field office of the DEA, housed in a building of dun-colored brick that takes up an entire city block, stretching from Tenth Avenue to the West Side Highway along Sixteenth and Seventeenth Streets, a building distinguished primarily, like certain dinosaurs, by its immense size. It was constructed in 1917, the last year, by historians' reckoning, of the cultural period of optimism, complacency, and empire known as the American Renaissance. Three flags above the employee entrance on 17th Street were all that marked it as a government office.

After being questioned, Charlie was taken to the Metropolitan Correctional Center in Manhattan, the detention facility where crime boss John Gotti and Ponzi scammer Bernie Madoff had once been interred. Three stories below the street was a forty-yard passage that conveyed accused killers, terrorists, and gangsters – hidden from the view of ordinary, law-abiding folks – to their judgment in the nearby federal courthouse.[6]

Charlie couldn't believe he was in jail. He had always been more conciliatory than the hardline crypto-anarchists like Amir Taaki. He'd even stuck up for mainstream financial services companies among fellow Bitcoiners. 'Honestly, I don't see why everyone hates PayPal,' he told them once, in the summer of 2011. 'Sure, most of the things they do are just to make sure they can cover their asses. You know how much political pressure and repercussions they would have if they allowed [dollars to be exchanged for bitcoins]?' He thought it was selfish of Bitcoiners to expect PayPal to put their interests ahead of its own. 'Once they see the profit in Bitcoin and that we are not an enemy, they will come around. I guarantee it.' And once he had decided to start accepting Bitcoin payments at Daily Checkout, his retail site, he'd drawn a clear line between himself and shady operators: 'Merchants like me are the ones who are trying to take Bitcoin business away from black market sites like [Silk Road].' But the criminal complaint sworn out against him in federal court said he had not only aided and abetted Robert Faiella but had himself been a customer of Silk Road, buying pot brownies.

Of the arrest, he would later say, 'I was totally caught off guard. I spent over a million dollars in legal fees to prevent what ended up happening to me.' Yet now, just like Ross Ulbricht when he was transferred from a San Francisco jail to the Metropolitan Detention Center in Brooklyn, just like Roger Ver, Charlie was thrown into the detention facility's Special Housing Unit, or SHU, and given a cell of whitewashed cinderblock walls measuring seven-and-a-half by eight feet.[7] Lights out in the correctional center is at 11:00 P.M. sharp, so there was no light in Charlie's cell, a situation he describes this way: 'Alone, dark, no light. Nothing. No cellmate, no windows.' There was a metal slab bed with a thin mattress pad, 'like a cushion you get on the lounge chair at a really shitty beach club'. The concrete floor was cold and, for some unexplained reason, soaking wet. He couldn't pace the cell barefoot, so he left his shoes on. 'I wasn't crying, but I was scared shitless,' he says. The charismatic Bitcoin millionaire had become federal inmate 92164-054.

The following day, with Robert Faiella also in custody, Preet Bharara, the crusading US Attorney for the Southern District of New York, gave a speech to drive home the lesson. 'If you want to develop a virtual currency, or a virtual currency exchange business, knock yourself out,' he said. 'But you have to follow the rules. All of them.' Then he took a shot at the Winklevoss twins: 'And if you want to invest in such a business, you better kick the tires and make sure compliance there is not a joke.'[8]

On 27 January, Charlie Shrem made bail at one million dollars.

His parents put up their house as collateral to secure his release. He would have to move back in with them, living under house arrest in Brooklyn until his case was settled. As further conditions of his release on bond, he had to surrender his passport, wear an electronic monitoring anklet, and agree to drug testing – a bleak prospect for a proud pothead. His father, stone-faced but with his arm around his son's shoulders, walked him out of the courthouse, while Charlie, hands deep in the kangaroo pocket of his hoodie, looked numb and defeated. The next day, he resigned his position as vice chairman of the Bitcoin Foundation. On the subject of his digital millions, when it was later suggested that he might have used them to free himself without putting his childhood home on the line, he wouldn't give a straight answer.

When Charlie checked his email, he was alarmed to see multiple notifications of failed attempts to log into his Blockchain wallet. He had set up two-factor authentication, or 2FA, on the wallet, a security feature which meant that every time he entered his password to log into the wallet he would receive a text message on his phone with a secondary access code; only after typing in this second code could he gain access to his funds. He knew immediately what the failed logins meant. The feds had tried to get into his wallet, probably to seize his money, but they had been unable to get past the 2FA. Charlie's Android phone – where the secondary code was sent – was itself protected by a four-digit lock code, so that provided an extra layer of security. But he had no idea how close the feds might be to cracking it.

He called a guy named George Mandrik, who lived in York, Pennsylvania, and worked customer service for Blockchain. When Mandrik's phone rang, he was driving home with his kids in the car. The kids were chattering; when he realized it was Charlie on the line he told them to quiet down. Charlie explained what he had been through in the past twenty-four hours. 'He was distraught, shaken up,' Mandrik says. He needed Mandrik to disable the 2FA on his wallet so that he could log into it from his laptop and move the funds to another wallet – one not accessible from the phone the feds had confiscated.

Mandrik pulled into his driveway and rushed to comply with the request. 'It was Charlie, so it was a no-brainer,' he says. Once Charlie gained access, he spirited the funds away to another wallet, ensuring the safety of his hoard. He had no intention of letting his hard-earned bitcoins vanish into government vaults.

THE FOLLOWING DAY, THE NEW York Department of Financial Services hearings on Bitcoin began. They were held in a fourth-floor conference room of the federal office building at 90 Church Street, an imposing New Deal monolith, fifteen stories tall and as long and wide as an entire city block, housing the US Postal Service's Church Street Station along with offices of the New York City Housing Authority, the New York State Public Service Commission, and the New York State Health Department. Such is its poker-faced grandeur that a newspaper reporter was once prompted to write that the pile resembled 'the work of the emperor Hadrian as seen through the lens of Fritz Lang'.[9] From this limestone-clad edifice the Federal Bureau of Narcotics had waged war in the fifties and sixties on the Sicilian Mafia, whose dons were the drug kingpins of their day.[10] The federal building at 90 Church was therefore an appropriate venue for the hearings on digital currency – or, as government officials both state and federal insisted on calling it, as if to emphasize its fairyland provenance, 'virtual currency'.

When Benjamin Lawsky, the state superintendent of financial services, took his seat at the center microphone on the dais before which, over the next two days, a parade of expert witnesses would testify, he was taking his place in history. If it is necessarily true that bureaucrats derive their power from their institution, then Lawsky wielded, as the first state banking regulator in America to take on cryptocurrency, an enviable measure of power.

By mid-morning the room on the fourth floor had filled with press and spectators, so many that a few of those present were forced to hover on the perimeter of the room. Cameras were set on tripods, laptops were fired up. The air hummed with conversation. Downstairs, in the lobby, with its marble columns and terrazzo floors, a *Forbes* reporter who had neglected to register for the event was turned away by security.

It was clear that Charlie Shrem's arrest would cast a pall over the proceedings. When the Winklevosses, who were among the first panelists, walked into the room, with their female assistant in tow, the atmosphere darkened further. Their faces were grim. They wore matching dark suits and stood at least a head taller than everyone else in the room: former Olympic athletes, Harvard-educated millionaires, taking their seats on the witness panel like twin hulks from a higher planet incensed at being made to justify themselves to lower life-forms. They were in damage control mode. They knew that when people looked at them they were thinking about Charlie Shrem behind bars. The day after the arrest they had issued a statement to distance themselves from Charlie, doing their best to distinguish between him and BitInstant, which had not been named in the criminal complaint against its CEO and in which regard, they wrote, they had been only 'passive investors'. (It was a description of their role that would have been unrecognizable to Charlie himself, to say nothing of Roger Ver, Erik Voorhees, Ira Miller, Rachel Yankelevitz, and Alex Waters.) Having expected from the outset that BitInstant would comply with the law, the Winklevosses wrote, they fully supported 'any and all governmental efforts to ensure that money laundering requirements are enforced, and look forward to clearer regulation being implemented on the purchase and sale of bitcoins'.[11]

When a reporter called Roger Ver asking for comment on Charlie's arrest, Roger was defiant. 'Money laundering is not a crime,' he said. 'It's just because certain men with guns don't like what other people are doing with their own money, so they decide it's okay to lock those people in a cage. Even if absolutely everything the government is alleging is true, Charlie has done nothing that's morally wrong.'[12] It would be fair to say that among the attendees at the NYDFS hearings this was a minority view.

Shortly after the scheduled start time of 11:30 A.M., the first panel got underway. Ben Lawsky, who is handsome in a vulpine way, with a thick dark head of hair, a low hairline, and prominent eyes, opened with a few conciliatory remarks, apparently conscious of the need to show Bitcoiners that he wasn't the Big Bad Wolf come to blow their houses down. 'All of us are in new and some-what uncharted waters,' he said, adding that the NYDFS was 'probably best described as a referee. We want to make sure everyone is playing by the same rules.' Never let it be said that he'd sought to 'clip the wings' of a new technology before it could get off the ground. There were real benefits to Bitcoin, he admitted, and it could force the traditional payments industry 'to up its game in terms of speed, affordability and reliability'.

One of the panelists who sat listening was Barry Silbert. Seated at the far right of the table in a suit and tie rather than his everyday casualwear – a mode of dress he had gradually relaxed into after leaving Wall Street – he was determined to say as little as possible. He was proud that four months after its launch the Bitcoin Investment Trust now held more than seventy thousand bitcoins, worth some $60 million at the prevailing exchange rate. But the nail that sticks up, he figured, will be hammered down.

Before the NYDFS hearing kicked off, he had had another appointment downtown: the New York City Economic Development Corporation, a not-for-profit charged with developing real estate and fostering economic growth, had organized an informal round-table discussion on Bitcoin. Over breakfast, perhaps four dozen representatives of various banks, venture capital firms, and the Mayor's office gathered to talk turkey about this strange new form of money that had aroused everyone's curiosity. One attendee was Jeremy Liew of Lightspeed Venture Partners, whose interests as an investor included, according to his company bio, 'massive-scale social media, commerce, gaming, financial services, and methods for increasing monetization'.[13] Later that day Barry Silbert would find himself sitting beside Liew under the gaze of Ben Lawsky and his colleagues, but it was the morning chat session that he found truly fruitful. Wall Street was only just beginning to take a serious interest in Bitcoin, and the off-record breakfast, Barry says, 'gave a bunch of banks an opportunity for probably one of the first times to see that there's actually some fairly normal Bitcoin believers – both investors and operators'.

At 90 Church, Barry was shown to the prep room, where he passed the minutes until 11:30 by comparing notes with Jeremy Liew and Fred Wilson, another venture capitalist who, along with Cameron and Tyler Winklevoss, rounded out the day's first panel. The Winklevosses never joined the other men in the prep room; they went immediately to face their public. Barry was more than happy to avoid the spotlight. 'I let them have their moment,' he says. 'You won't see me in any pictures.'

The message of his opening statement was simple: New York had an opportunity to lead the nation in its regulatory approach to digital currency, and, if that approach 'provides clarity without being overly burdensome', it could bolster the economy by making the state a hub for Bitcoin businesses. In closing, he took pains to clarify his view as 'that of a CEO of a registered broker-dealer, a creator of a Bitcoin investment vehicle, and an angel investor, but not an operator of a Bitcoin business'. He may still have been worried about sticking out. After all, general solicitation for the Bitcoin Investment Trust had only just become legal. Regardless, his role in the Bitcoin ecosystem would change radically in the months to come.

He kept his remarks brief, then yielded the floor to Jeremy Liew. When Liew couldn't get his microphone to work, Barry, as if eager to shift attention to somebody else, leaned over and turned it on for him.

Ben Lawsky's first question, after the opening statements, addressed the elephant in the room. He could not have been aware of the extent to which black market activity lay at the root of Bitcoin's success. But the long endurance of Silk Road, the alleged money laundering of Charlie Shrem, and the rhetoric of crypto-anarchists that flowered in the fever swamps of the Internet evidently suggested to him a dark potential at the heart of cryptocurrency, a power to forbid government oversight of one's financial life – bad enough if it was wielded by libertarian tax dodgers, but far worse if it was used by an Islamic charity funneling money to Iran. He wanted, then, to know what each panelist – starting with Barry Silbert – thought of the arrests of Charlie Shrem and Robert Faiella.

Barry inhaled deeply. *Only respond to questions directed at me* – that was the promise he'd made to himself. There was no upside to pontificating or speaking out of turn. But now he'd been asked point-blank to give his opinion on what the bust meant for digital currency and its future. He needed to tread carefully, lest he inadvertently give the Department of Financial Services more ammunition to use against Bitcoin. He hadn't read the criminal complaint, he said, but he ventured a guess that the accused had been tracked by following the chain of ownership encoded into the bitcoins they had handled. He was suggesting that law enforcement already possessed sufficient tools and tactics to apprehend digital currency criminals.

Fred Wilson, when his turn came, was unequivocal. He gave his theory of the 'five phases of Bitcoin', three of which were already past and two of which were yet to come, from the geeky crypto-enthusiasm of the early years through the 'vice phase', which, by his reckoning, had stretched from 2011 to 2012, on to a phase of intense price speculation – from which the industry was even now emerging – followed by broad merchant acceptance and, finally, an era of 'programmable money' that would see Internet companies and stock exchanges built on top of Bitcoin. 'The vice phase,' he concluded, 'is in the rearview mirror.'

Down the table it went, the discomfited witnesses at pains to say that Silk Road was little more than a fading memory, a bad taste in the mouth already being washed away. If darkness stretched out far behind, it was only because the future looked so bright. Cameron Winklevoss acknowledged that when he and his brother had first entered the Bitcoin market, it was the Wild West. It needed taming. 'The Wild West attracts cowboys,' he said. 'A sheriff is a good thing.'

The truth was more complex. In the months since drug buyers had been cut off from Silk Road, the digital underground, hydra-like, had sprouted new markets: Agora, Pandora, Evolution, Cloud Nine . . . and, of course, Silk Road 2.0, on its way to becoming

– as it would by the summer of 2014 – even bigger than the original Silk Road in terms of the number of products being sold. 'Silk Road was for us a very special place and a very special community,' one Silk Road 2.0 vendor remarked, expressing a widely held feeling.[14] Nothing would ever again be as it was when buyers and sellers sailed together unopposed beneath the Dread Pirate Roberts' flag, but the truth was that the dark net was thriving. And Bitcoin remained the most popular method of payment across all the underground markets. Cyrus Vance, Jr., the New York district attorney, a sandy-haired fifty-nine-year-old, would testify to that effect the following day. 'Virtual currency is a relatively recent phenomenon, and I certainly don't think that the fact that we have made significant cases and arrests in this arena means it's all under control,' he said. 'It's not.' Just as crime conducted in cash exists alongside ordinary economic activity, the illicit digital economy mirrored the expansion of legitimate Bitcoin enterprise. The taller the mountain grew, the longer its shadow.

To Lawsky, the heights didn't justify the depths. If the choice was between stopping money laundering – the financial lifeline for narcotics traffickers, terrorists, and rogue nations – or fostering entrepeneurial innovation, he said, 'we're always going to choose squelching the money laundering first. It's simply not worth it to society to allow all the things it facilitates to persist rather than to allow a thousand flowers to bloom on the innovation side.' In other words, cash, despite its popularity with criminals, was grand-fathered in as a valid form of money; digital currency was not.

Lawsky had a suggestion. A cottage industry already existed to help banks comply with anti-money laundering rules. Maybe this industry could learn to advise virtual currency businesses laboring under similar requirements.

'That sounds like a terrible idea to me,' Fred Wilson shot back. 'You're talking about introducing all the costs back into the system that we're trying to take out of it.' The promise of Bitcoin was 'to create a world where transactions can move globally for free'. Companies wouldn't be able to do that if they had massive over-head costs.

Rather than outsource compliance to another firm, Wilson said, startups should 'put the compliance into the code' – by which he meant developing technological solutions to what seemed like regulatory challenges. To open a bank account requires filling out reams of paperwork, despite the fact that most of the necessary information is readily available online, for instance through profiles on Facebook and LinkedIn. Why couldn't technology be used to verify customer identities instantly, allowing companies to 'do compliance at scale for no money' and pass the savings on to consumers?

The others echoed his sentiments. Liew suggested that existing regulation was sufficient, if only it were 'extended and applied to virtual currency businesses'. Barry opined that while Bitcoin exchanges warranted oversight, because they connected directly to the mainstream financial system, and custodial wallet services should be regulated in order to protect consumers, everyone else should be exempted from any new regulation. 'We should try to avoid excess layers [of regulation] if possible,' Cameron Winklevoss said.

But Fred Wilson wasn't done. 'It took me two weeks to open a new bank account with JPMorgan Chase, where I have a number of bank accounts already. That seems ridiculous.' He was leaning forward pugnaciously, his arms crossed. Watching him overextend himself, Barry couldn't help but smile. 'I sympathize with [JP Morgan CEO] Jamie Dimon: he runs an overregulated company, in my opinion. As a customer, I can tell you he runs an overregulated company.'

Ben Lawsky didn't share Wilson's sympathy. 'But the flip side is,' he began, 'as regulators we are trying to make sure – not when Fred Wilson opens an account, but somebody else . . .' He stopped himself, tried a different tack. 'You know, we're fifty yards from the old World Trade Center here, and I think all of us never want to see anything like that happen again. It would have been a lot harder for 9/11 to ever have occurred had we had the protections in place that would prevent the movement of massive amounts of money around the globe by people who would want to kill everybody in this room. So I think the key is not to create useless regulation. But the motives behind a lot of those rules are to ensure we don't miss something again.'

Here, in lower Manhattan, in this building whose windows had once looked out across Vesey Street at 1 World Trade Center, the north tower, and whose windows had been shattered, whose facade had been blackened, whose interior had been contaminated upon the tower's collapse with asbestos, lead dust, and bacteria; here, in this federal building whose American flag – during nearly three years of closure following the terrorist attacks – had been folded and displayed in the Postal Service headquarters in Washington, here mention of 9/11 was the trump of trumps.

Fred Wilson backpedaled. 'I'm hopefully not being too critical of regulation, because it's not the regulation itself that I think is the problem,' he said. 'I think it is the way in which the regulations currently are promulgated that is the problem. And I think understanding that technology is your friend is the answer. That's really the rant that I'm on, and I'll get off of it now.'

It was a turning point. Jeremy Liew tried to protest that no amount of regulation could entirely eliminate bad actors. But the following day, Fred Ehrsam, a former foreign exchange trader at Goldman Sachs who had joined Coinbase in November 2012, and who had taken such a leadership role that he was given the title of cofounder, admitted that further requirements for digital currency startups were both inevitable and necessary. 'Once you open up a business that's moving money around, bad stuff can happen right out of the gate,' he said.

As witnesses went on describing the implications of Bitcoin, a rough consensus began to take shape: cryptocurrency exchanges, payment processors, and remittance services should be regulated; merchants, individuals, and Bitcoin miners shouldn't be. Regulation would take the form of mandatory AML and KYC policies, registration with FinCEN, and perhaps state money transmitter licensing requirements. A special 'BitLicense', its precise terms to be decided later, was also on the table. Meanwhile, Lawsky was just trying to absorb it all. 'I don't think we know what this world will look like in a year,' he confided after the second day, 'and that's both exciting and a little scary as a regulator.' But he wasn't going away. His department intended to release a suggested regulatory framework within the year.

Mark Williams, a professor of finance at Boston University who was deeply skeptical of Bitcoin, went so far as to say, when his turn at the witness table came, that Charlie Shrem's arrest had made Bitcoiners 'realize that they've lost leverage'. No longer could they afford to be 'anti-establishment, anti-regulation', he said. 'If they want to make Bitcoin a payment system to be used globally, they will need to work with regulators.'

AS FAR AS THE BLOCKCHAIN team was concerned, very little of the regulatory nonsense being debated in New York applied to them. They hadn't bothered to send a representative. After all, they didn't take custody of or transmit anybody's funds. They were running a software company, not a bank.

On the night of 5 February, Nic Cary was relaxing at home with colleagues in York, drinking a Kronenbourg 1664, the day's work done. Joining him for beers and bullshitting were Dan Held, another Blockchain employee named Changpeng Zhao, and Kyle Drake, the founder of electronic wallet service Coinpunk. They were lounging on an eclectic assortment of furniture, including a purple suede couch. The red-brick house had come prefurnished. 'It's really tastefully done,' Nic said at the time, 'but it's tastefully done for a woman who's in her middle life, and not necessarily a bunch of dudes who run a tech startup.'

Suddenly things turned serious. Night in York was only afternoon in Silicon Valley, and Apple sent Ben Reeves an email, which he now forwarded to Nic, notifying him that Blockchain's mobile app was being pulled from the App Store. The email made vague reference to an unaddressed problem with the app which necessitated its removal, though it declined to specify the problem. Nic and the others were at a loss – the last email Ben had received from Apple had arrived two years earlier with the message that the Blockchain app had been approved for users. Since then it had racked up more than 120,000 downloads. Now it was being axed.

The group's immediate reaction to the news was to curse. Even so, it wasn't entirely unexpected. Over the preceding weeks Apple had yanked all other wallet apps from the App Store, including the one created by Coinbase. Apps conveying information about the Bitcoin market could stay, but anything related to holding or spending money was being cut from the menu. Only Blockchain's app had remained, giving Nic and the others hope that perhaps Apple truly understood that Blockchain, unlike other wallet providers, didn't have a custodial relationship with its users. They thought that perhaps in recognition of their unique approach an exception was being made in their favor. No such luck. Apple was banning Bitcoin.

All at once, Blockchain was on a war footing. That night Nic sat with four cell phones in front of him, calling, he says, 'absolutely everybody I could find in my email list'. He called the *New York Times*, the *Wall Street Journal*, Bloomberg News, TechCrunch, CNBC – giving all of them the same tip: Apple just killed its App Store's last remaining Bitcoin wallet app, which also happens to be a mobile version of the world's most popular Bitcoin wallet. Official response in half an hour. There was a flurry of calls to people both within and outside the company, amid which Nic, with the others' help, began drafting the company's response. *Apple is saying something about Bitcoin,* he thought. *Let's have a conversation about this. Let's get some answers.*

The blog post went up twenty-nine minutes later, just after midnight. (Like most posts on the official Blockchain blog, its author was given as Alyson, George Mandrik's wife, who also worked at Blockchain.) It was a shot across Apple's bow, designed for maximum air burst. It led off with a famous Steve Jobs quote in which Apple's founder praises the independent few who don't take no for an answer, who, in Emersonian terms, see the possible houses and farms:

> Here's to the crazy ones. The misfits. The rebels. The troublemakers. The round pegs in the square holes. The ones who see things differently. They're not fond of rules. And they have no

respect for the status quo. You can quote them, disagree with them, glorify or vilify them. About the only thing you can't do is ignore them. Because they change things. They push the human race forward.

Nic was just getting warmed up. 'The rebels no longer run the show at Apple Inc; the beancounters are now firmly in charge,' the blog post read. Throughout, the Blockchain team hammered home the idea that the tech giant's actions were protectionist, motivated by a desire to preserve its own 'monopoly on payments'. The message was clear: Steve Jobs must be rolling over in his grave.

Within a day and a half, dozens if not hundreds of media outlets and websites had spread the news. On Reddit, someone offered to give away free Nexus 5 phones – a cell phone powered by Google's Android operating system, a rival to Apple's iOS – to five people who posted videos of themselves destroying their iPhones. (His offer was explicitly tied to Apple's ban.) The Internet being what it is, he had no shortage of people accepting the challenge. One owner threw his phone off a ledge. Another hacked his phone apart with a machete. And the challenger was as good as his word.[15] An online petition to persuade Apple to allow Bitcoin wallets back into its App Store received 6,207 signatures. 'The community went totally bonkers,' Nic says.

The Blockchain team had one more statement left to make. Their blood was up, and with the Android app alone now serving as the company's flagship product they decided to go all in on Google's operating system and create a brand-new app just for merchants. The goal would be to make it as lightweight and stripped down as possible, so that business owners would find it dead simple to accept Bitcoin payments. Nic and Ben were in agreement. 'Our nose was a bit out of joint by the Apple thing,' says Nic – and they wanted to show that Blockchain was a company that could get things done. It was the retaliatory instinct of men living and working closely together, as in war, joined by a common purpose even when separated by oceans and continents, sharing the long hours and sleepless nights; it was, moreover, an instinct of preservation galvanized by an existential threat, for all of them had staked a great deal on Blockchain's success, not only as the entity that paid their salaries but as maybe the best hope for Bitcoin to be all that it could be, a tool of financial liberation for the world. They were young and idealistic enough to see things in such grandiose terms. And in the context of this vision they were still the underdogs. By now Coinbase had raised nearly $32 million from venture capitalists and other investors. Blockchain, except for Roger Ver's early contribution, had raised none.

Nic felt that he owed Ben Reeves a success story. 'Coinbase has all the celebrity blessing that a superstar tech startup has, and Blockchain has a lot of authentic community support, but it's not the same type of validation for someone that spent three years sacrificing everything – all his sleep and all his engineering capacity and effort,' he said later. 'So one of our efforts is to structure Blockchain to go to long-term battle on a global level – not necessarily against Coinbase, but partially, yeah.' The merchant app would be artillery in that war – a war of competing principles. To an outsider they might have looked almost the same, but Coinbase was a financial services company, and Blockchain was a software company. One represented the world-view of the banks, the other that of sovereign individuals. Coinbase promised to look after your money on your behalf; Blockchain promised not to.

The final product, hacked together in a couple of weeks mostly by Bill Hill, the company's senior lead developer – a middle-aged guy in a startup with a median age of twenty-nine – was elegant in its simplicity. Upon installing the app, users were asked to create a four-digit PIN for security. After that, they needed only to provide the name of their business, a Bitcoin address for receiving payments, and a preferred currency. Because merchants would be using Bitcoin as a medium of exchange but not as a unit of account, it was essential for the app automatically to calculate, for any amount of a given fiat currency – and Blockchain's app would soon support ninety of them – the equivalent amount of bitcoins.

The merchant would enter the cost of a purchase in his local currency, say $8.50 for a tuna melt with French fries in the United States, and the app would translate that instantly into the amount of digital currency owed by the customer, say 0.01172, barely more than one-hundredth of a bitcoin. The merchant would add a brief description of the purchase and the app would generate on the merchant's device a Quick Response Code, or QR code, for the customer to scan with her own phone. A green checkmark would appear, to indicate confirmation of the payment. The entire process was transparent and peer-to-peer, no credit card terminal required. Blockchain's app was free to download and charged merchants no fees to receive customers' Bitcoin payments.

Before releasing it to the public, Nic gave the app a soft launch at a bar in Paris run by an Algerian named Sofiane Bouhaddi. The bar owner was a good test case. Although Bouhaddi didn't know much about cryptocurrency, he had been using Bitcoin as a gimmick to attract customers. But his technology wasn't up to snuff. 'He had a blurry photo of a QR card on his, like, iPod, and that's how he was accepting bitcoins,' Nic says. Blockchain gifted the bar owner a Nexus tablet loaded with its merchant app. At the launch party, with Nic and Bill in attendance, Bouhaddi used it to ring up more than a thousand euros' worth of drinks in just a few hours.

The app became available at no cost in the Google Play store on 9 March, receiving in its first week about one thousand downloads. While most mobile apps have only a twenty to thirty percent retention rate – meaning that most people delete them after downloading, a kind of buyer's remorse – Blockchain's new app boasted a retention rate of ninety-five percent. Coinbase had released its own merchant app several weeks earlier, but by its third month Blockchain's app had about pulled even with Coinbase's in number of downloads and had earned a higher rating in Google's app store. (This continued to be true over time. Seven months after launch, it held a rating of 4.3 out of five stars. Coinbase's app held a rating of 4.2.) It was a result sure to satisfy Blockchain's intense CEO. 'Winning doesn't really matter to me that much, but I hate losing,' Nic says. 'I run my own race, but if there's a competition, I don't lose. I cannot handle that. I'll push harder, I'll work harder, I'll stay up longer. And I just drive.'

Nic had picked the right time to release a merchant app. There were now many thousands of businesses accepting Bitcoin worldwide, including TigerDirect, an electronics retailer with more than $1.75 billion in annual revenue. For merchants, it was a move that guaranteed headlines, such as was the novelty of it, to say nothing of the goodwill from Bitcoiners that translated into sales. TigerDirect began accepting Bitcoin on 23 January; within three days, it had reportedly processed more than $500,000 in digital currency payments. And the trend was growing. BitPay had signed up ten thousand merchants by September 2013; by May 2014, it would be thirty thousand. Even so, most of the businesses were taking advantage of BitPay's platform to immediately convert the bitcoins they received into dollars. That way they wouldn't have to hold bitcoins on their balance sheets or be exposed to the digital currency's fluctuations in price.[16] (Overstock was doing the same through Coinbase, which by the time of the NYDFS hearings had already signed up twenty-one thousand merchants to accept Bitcoin from customers.) Most of these merchants had no interest – at least for the time being – in holding bitcoins as a store of value. But they were only too happy to use Bitcoin as a payment system.

Therein lay the drawback of Blockchain's merchant app. Nic and Ben were determined never to handle users' funds, which meant that business owners couldn't depend on Blockchain to convert their digital currency into fiat. That gave Coinbase and BitPay the edge when it came to wooing big clients. It was an ideological choice as well as a practical one. Even as many investors and entrepreneurs sought ways to plug Bitcoin into the existing system, Nic, Ben, and Roger continued to believe in the promise of Bitcoin to return financial independence to average people. And they weren't just sticking to their guns; they were making a long-term strategic choice. While the conversion of digital to national currency was sure to become highly regulated in some countries, says Changpeng Zhao, 'if you're just accepting Bitcoin you can do that for the entire world.' Nic and his guys weren't about to go the way of BitInstant, buried in license registration fees and hounded by regulators, with lawyers' billable hours mounting up.

THERE WERE WORSE FATES. ROSS Ulbricht was waiting out the coldest Northeast winter in years in the Metropolitan Detention Center in Brooklyn. On 21 January, the day of a blizzard that dumped a foot of snow on the city, his parents trekked out to visit him. They took the subway and were forced to struggle through the snow to reach the facility. A razor-sharp wind off the East River cut them to the quick. But they pictured their son in the monotony of the detention center with its gray metal walls, each day the same as the last. They were all he had. 'A mere blizzard would not keep us from seeing Ross,' his mother later wrote.

In the visiting room they slowly thawed and waited for their son to appear. And waited. More than an hour passed, every second cutting into their precious time with him. By the time he finally arrived, none of them could deny any longer the nightmare they were in. In two months, Ross would turn thirty. 'It is so strange to be with Ross, talk with him, hold his hand,' Lyn Ulbricht told supporters, 'yet not be able to get up and leave with him. The idea that he cannot have bail because he is a danger to anyone is so bizarre that it feels to me like punishment, not caution.'

Ross showed up to his arraignment, at noon on 7 February, clean-shaven and with short hair, his shaggy brown curls – iconic now in photos that had run with hundreds of news stories – shorn away. The justice system seemed intent on taking everything from him. On 15 January, Judge J. Paul Oetken of the Southern District of New York, who was presiding over a civil asset forfeiture case against Ross Ulbricht, had ordered that Silk Road the digital property, and all the bitcoins stored on its servers, be turned over to the federal government. As the spoils of a criminal enterprise, the 29,656 bitcoins would be auctioned off by the US Marshals to the highest bidder, just like a mansion or a Bugatti Veyron bought with drug money. The same fate awaited Ross's personal cache of bitcoins, to which he claimed rightful ownership – 144,336 of them, an amount worth $104.6 million – if the government could convincingly link them to Silk Road. In the meantime, they were under lock and key, so to speak, with the US Attorney's Office for the Southern District of New York. 'I think it's an important thing to do,' Richard Zabel, a deputy US attorney, said at the NYDFS hearings in January. 'No one should keep the proceeds of crime, virtual or otherwise.' In other words, the US government now controlled more than one and a half percent of all the bitcoins in existence.

The day of his arraignment Ross Ulbricht awoke before dawn to begin the journey from Brooklyn to the courthouse at 500 Pearl Street in Lower Manhattan. His mother would later describe him 'packed into various holding cells, shoulder to shoulder with many others', waiting hours for his court appearance. Just before sunrise the temperature was only twenty-five degrees Fahrenheit, though windchill made it feel like fifteen. By noon it was still below freezing. More than four months after his arrest, Ross was fastidious enough to eat nothing all day, preferring the hunger pains in his stomach to being forced to relieve himself in front of other men. Despite the cold, it was one of those bracing winter days with no clouds and a generous sun, and after the 'relentless sameness of detention' the bright bowl of the sky with its shell of air, which suspended dust made blue, scattering sunlight and hiding a vast field of stars, was so dazzling that Ross, in his brief moments outside, couldn't bear to look at it. He had to close his eyes.

To each of the four charges against him Ross pled not guilty. He stood wearing a navy-blue prison uniform as Judge Katherine Forrest read them out: narcotics trafficking conspiracy, computer hacking conspiracy, money laundering conspiracy, and a continuing criminal enterprise. The last of these was a charge typically reserved for crime bosses, leaders of cartels; it put Ross in the company of drug kingpins. Did he understand the charges against him? the judge asked. Yes, he did. Would he like the court to read the indictment to him in open court? No, thank you. Missing from the list of charges was attempted murder, of which he stood accused in a federal court in Maryland. But the prosecutor, Serrin Turner, left open the possibility that his office might file a superseding indictment in the months before the trial, adding new charges to the original indictment. 'It is a daunting list of allegations,' his mother admitted. 'Ross sounds like one tough criminal from this over-the-top list. No way is it a description of the actual Ross Ulbricht.'

There was another matter to address, that of the evidence to be turned over to Ross's defense counsel. The contents of the Silk Road servers that had been seized totaled eight to ten terabytes of data, a massive amount to sift through, enough to fill ten or twenty hard drives. And it was in a format that would need to be reconstructed by an expert to be made readable and searchable by Ross's legal team. And there were, besides all this, the usual twenty-first-century haystacks to search for incriminating needles: the contents of his laptop and other devices, documents seized from his San Francisco apartment, subpoenaed bank records. The government had been thorough, obtaining search warrants for Ross's email and other online accounts. Ross would be allowed the use of a laptop at the detention center in order to help prepare his own defense. After all, no one knew the contents of his computer better than him. Even so, the material would take weeks to review.

The Ulbricht family sat listening to the lawyers wrangle over dates by which motions had to be filed, quibble over timing and procedure, hem and haw when asked to estimate how long a given step would take. Ross's father, Kirk, was there; his sister, Cally; and his mother, Lyn, her thinning hair and careworn face giving her the appearance of a much older woman. Even after the arraignment ended and they had filed out of the courtroom, their faces remained wooden, impermeable: hearing everything, believing nothing. They were hard with the hardness of what they were going through, hard with the effort it took to shut out the government's allegations, to sustain in the face of contrary evidence the belief that Ross was innocent, or at least that he didn't deserve to go to prison. *Free Ross* – this had become their heart's desire and the organizing principle of their lives. Also present was Gary Alford, a special agent in the Criminal Investigations division of the Internal Revenue Service, the same man who had sworn out the criminal complaint against Charlie Shrem and Robert Faiella. He had been a lead investigator in the Silk Road case.

Finally it was all settled. The trial was set to begin on 3 November, which meant that another nine months would pass with Ross behind bars. Judge Forrest hoped to wrap up the trial, once underway, within six weeks. Serrin Turner was confident the trial would take less than a month. By Christmas Day Ross Ulbricht would be either a free man or one of the most notorious felons of the Internet age.

Chapter 10

MELTDOWN

The more visionary the idea, the more people it leaves behind.

— Don DeLillo

As late as February 2014, Roger Ver still had hopes of recovering from Mt. Gox at least some of the money he had lost in Bitcoinica. He knew the odds of recovering all 24,841 bitcoins were slim, given how much of the total pool of currency had been lost in the hacks, but he thought it not unlikely that he could recoup as many as ten thousand or even fifteen thousand of the lost coins, provided that the Tokyo exchange could be made to cough them up. According to the two men appointed by the High Court of New Zealand as Bitcoinica's liquidators, Mt. Gox should still be holding in various frozen accounts a total of 64,485 bitcoins and $134,000 belonging to Bitcoinica. As part of the liquidation, these funds were to be distributed to customers like Roger Ver to satisfy their claims as far as possible. At the beginning of February, Roger's lost bitcoins were worth $20.4 million. Real money. The price, however, was to fall sharply from there.

Despite months of correspondence with Mt. Gox, the liquidators, Anthony McCullagh and Stephen Lawrence, employees of a boutique insolvency firm in Auckland, had made no progress even in so ostensibly simple a task as verifying the amounts of cash and bitcoins held in various accounts on Bitcoinica's behalf.

Mt. Gox was stonewalling. The exchange's official response had been that it could not divulge the 'private and confidential information sought without first ensuring that it is doing so with the proper authority of the relevant account holders'. This was patently absurd, first because the liquidators had provided ample proof of their authority, and second because McCullagh and Lawrence's aim was to reimburse the customers of that very account holder – Bitcoinica LP – who had now waited fully nineteen months since the final hack, and fifteen months since the court appointment of the liquidators, to receive their funds. The two men were contemplating legal action against Mt. Gox in order to move the process forward.

For months it had been an open secret among savvy Bitcoiners that the Tokyo-based exchange was unwell. When Gareth Nelson thought of Mt. Gox, he thought of a favorite quote from the Cory Doctorow story 'When Sysadmins Ruled the Earth', in which an overweight, put-upon system administrator – who is on call, like a surgeon – is forced to roll out of bed in the small hours to fix a network problem. 'It's Microsoft's fault,' the sysadmin says. 'Any time I'm at work at 2AM, it's either PEBKAC or Microsloth.' For Gareth Nelson, it wasn't Microsoft. It was Gox. (PEBKAC, or Problem Exists Between Keyboard And Chair, sysadmin shorthand for user error, was also widespread in the world of Bitcoin.) For BitInstant, working with what was then the top exchange had been unavoidable, but doing so had often required creative technical solutions.

The code underlying the exchange platform was 'a spaghetti mess', according to a company insider, and management practices were worse – when they existed at all. 'The environment was completely dysfunctional,' the insider said.[1] It is standard practice when making changes to the code of an operational website to test the results first before applying them to the 'live' site. That way, any unforeseen consequences can be nipped in the bud without disrupting the user experience. Alex Waters and his team of developers had done this when building BitInstant 2.0. At Mt. Gox there were no such safeguards in place. There was only the process of development and implementation, and even this process 'Mark loved to circumvent,' the company source said. 'He had direct access to all the servers. So whenever he wanted to change something he would just change it on the live side, and that was that.' From a development standpoint, this would be inexcusable on any web platform. On a financial exchange that had one million users – as Mt. Gox did by December 2013 – such a devil-may-care approach was potentially disastrous.

There had long been questions about Mark Karpelès's leadership. In June 2011, when Roger Ver rushed to aid Mt. Gox in its recovery from the hack, he was astonished to learn that the CEO would be taking the weekend off rather than working around the clock to get the exchange back online.

In April 2013, the unwieldy system once again came crashing down. That spring, as the Bitcoin price rose rapidly, reaching unprecedented heights, the volume of trading on Mt. Gox rose alongside it, as did the number of new users who were opening accounts. The exchange was processing some 420,000 trades a month and more than twenty thousand new accounts were being added each day. And something else increased exponentially, too: the number of denial-of-service attacks perpetrated against the exchange. A denial-of-service, or DoS, attack, is a malicious attempt to bring down a web server temporarily by overloading it with communication requests, which prevents it from responding to legitimate traffic. In other words, a DoS attack can temporarily knock services like the Mt. Gox website offline. (In a distributed denial-of-service, or DDoS attack, multiple computers, rather than just one, are used to overwhelm the targeted server's bandwidth and resources.) An analysis by academic researchers later found that between May 2011 and October 2013, there were at least 142 distinct DDoS attacks on forty Bitcoin services. The possible motives were legion: 'Competing services launch them in order to improve market share, traders target exchanges to buy or sell at favorable prices, and miners outgunned in the rush to increase computational power could try to cripple larger pools in order to increase their odds of solving the hash puzzle first.'[2]

Mt. Gox bore the brunt of these attacks. By April 2013, Gonzague Gay-Bouchery, Mt. Gox's chief marketing officer, could say the company suffered DDoS attacks 'every day, every single hour'.[3] Usually it was able to counter them and keep running. Usually, but not always. Four times that month, the exchange – already taxed, amid the massive spike in trading volume, by the influx of new users – was brought down or severely affected by a major DDoS attack. It recovered each time, but each time in reaction the price of Bitcoin fell precipitously. The first time it happened, on 3 April, the price fell about $30 from a temporary high of $142. The second time, on 10 April, the attack caused huge delays in the processing of transactions, triggering a panic sell-off. When the dust settled, the price had collapsed forty percent from its earlier high of $266. Mt. Gox voluntarily suspended operations for twelve hours in order to add more servers to handle the higher traffic load. But it was brought down again only hours after reopening.[4] The fourth time, more than a week later, the site was unavailable for five hours and the price took a hit once again. Only a sustained cooling of the Bitcoin market worldwide, it seems, spared the exchange further indignities.

On 11 April 2013, Andreas Antonopoulos wrote a post on the online Bitcoin forum, publicly announcing that he would no longer use Mt. Gox and raising the alarm about a 'broken exchange whose owners don't have a clue how to run a high-performance and scalable infrastructure'. Mt. Gox, wrote Antonopoulos, is 'a systemic risk to Bitcoin, a death trap for traders, and a business run by the clueless'. He wasn't alone in thinking that way. (A Reuters interview Mark Karpelès gave later that month, which he spent sitting on a blue exercise ball rather than in a chair, his heavy French accent on full display, did little to change critics' minds.) The following month, on 14 May, the feds seized $2.9 million from the bank acount of Mutum Sigillum, Mt. Gox's US subsidiary; in the weeks that followed, they would confiscate $2.1 million more.

With its US subsidiary shut down, the exchange suspended dollar withdrawals. This meant that customers with dollar-denominated balances had no way of getting their money out of

the system. Their only option was to use their dollars to buy
bitcoins and then transfer those bitcoins elsewhere – perhaps to
another exchange, where they could once more turn them into
dollars. This artificial demand for bitcoins, in conjunction with
real demand, drove up the price of 'Goxcoins' about ten to twenty
percent above the Bitcoin price found on other exchanges.
(Ignorant of these market dynamics, however, major media outlets
continued to quote the inflated Mt. Gox price as definitive.) There
was, then, an opportunity for people in Japan, who made up
only two percent of the company's customers, to conduct arbitrage between other exchanges – Bitstamp, for example – and
Mt. Gox. They could buy bitcoins on Bitstamp, transfer them to
Mt. Gox, and sell them at a markup, possibly to foreign traders
for whom digital currency was now their only means of cashing
out. Yen withdrawals for Japanese customers were still func-
tioning perfectly, which made this arbitrage scheme a guaranteed
money maker, earning its perpetrators a ten to twenty percent
profit every time.

Even after Mt. Gox ostensibly reinstated dollar withdrawals
in July, problems persisted. Customers began to accuse the exchange
of being insolvent. The truth was that Mizuho Bank, which served
Mt. Gox, had been spooked by the actions of the American authorities. The bank was no longer processing wire transfer requests in
a timely fashion. It began to pressure Mt. Gox to take its business
elsewhere.[5]

In July, Roger Ver came to Mt. Gox's defense. As a favor to
Mark Karpelès, whom he considered a friend, he paid a visit to
the company headquarters, where, before his eyes, as he would
later relate, Karpelès logged into the Mt. Gox bank account and
showed him the balance. The exchange was holding in fiat currency
the equivalent of about $100 million. There was, Roger concluded,
no liquidity problem.

What he did next he would later regret. Still ensconced in Mt.
Gox's headquarters, he recorded a video statement reassuring
members of the Bitcoin community that all was well. He began
by relating the 'nice chat' he had had with Karpelès about the

withdrawal problems, during which Mt. Gox's CEO had shown him bank statements and 'letters from banks and lawyers' that convinced him the exchange was liquid. Perhaps unsurprisingly, then, given his ideological leanings, he laid the blame squarely on 'the traditional banking system'. He sounded almost boastful: 'The traditional banking partners that Mt. Gox needs to work with are not able to keep up with the demands of the growing Bitcoin economy.' But new banking partners would be added soon enough, he said. 'For now, I hope everyone will continue working on Bitcoin projects that will help make the world a better place.'

Roger's vote of confidence in Mt. Gox – sounding a very different note than Andreas Antonopoulos had done – did much to allay fears of its insolvency. But new exchanges kept eating away at its market share. Whereas in April 2013, Mt. Gox had been responsible for seventy percent of all Bitcoin trades, by November 2013 its share of the global market had collapsed to a mere four-teen percent.[6] Stories abounded of overseas customers waiting weeks or months for their withdrawal requests to be completed. Others, as it turned out, would never receive their funds at all. It had become, for American customers especially, a kind of financial purgatory. By early 2014, the phones in Mt. Gox's office in Shibuya were ringing off the hook, as angry customers called to demand answers. Mt. Gox staffers, numbering now about three dozen, did their best to duck the calls.[7] But Roger himself, who as a Japanese resident found it easy to deposit and withdraw funds, continued to keep hundreds of bitcoins in the exchange.

By early February, customers even began having trouble getting their bitcoins out. Then, on 7 February, a Friday, Mt. Gox stopped all digital currency withdrawals. It was the first unambiguous sign of how deep the problems went – not that the company would admit it at first. That day, a poorly written press release told customers – in its first iteration, that is, for it was rewritten later, without however greatly improving its spelling and grammar – that the withdrawal problems could be resolved only if the system was in 'a static state', which meant 'temporarily paus[ing] all with-drawal traffic to obtain a clear technical view of the current processes'. The Mt. Gox team would, it was promised, work on the problem through the weekend and provide an update on Monday. In the meantime, money that was in the queue for withdrawal would be returned to customer wallets. Trading activity could go on as usual, but with Bitcoin withdrawals halted and dollar withdrawals continuing to be all but impossible, many customers who had money stuck in the exchange were now left without a means of cashing out, making Mt. Gox – still the third-largest Bitcoin exchange in the world, behind Bitstamp and BTC-e – the trading platform equivalent of the Hotel California.

Unsurprisingly, the price of Bitcoin plummeted following the news. By late morning on the East Coast, according to an average of Bitcoin prices across top exchanges, the cryptocurrency had dropped about $61 since the day's open of $784, losing nearly eight percent of its value.[8]

The following Monday brought worse news. According to Mt. Gox, a bug in the core Bitcoin software had left the exchange vulnerable to theft. The bug, known as 'transaction malleability', was said to make it possible for someone to modify the details of a transaction so that it would seem as if a transaction did not occur even though it did. What this meant in the context of Mt. Gox's system was that a customer could request a withdrawal of her bitcoins, at which point the exchange would create a corresponding transaction and broadcast it to the Bitcoin network. But Mt. Gox could be tricked into believing the transaction had failed despite the fact that it was later confirmed by the network. Thinking its own system had messed up, Mt. Gox would credit the funds back to the customer's account. The customer, having executed a malleability attack, would thereby double her money, because she would have the withdrawn bitcoins as well as an equal amount still sitting in her Mt. Gox account, ready to be withdrawn at a later point in time. Mark Karpelès was now blaming transaction malleability rather than his own system as the sole reason for the failed Bitcoin withdrawals from Mt. Gox and as the sole cause of any missing bitcoins.

But exploiting the bug was not something just anyone could

do; moreover, it was not guaranteed to work. A malleability attack was a version of a double-spending attack – one of the very things Bitcoin had been designed to prevent. Karpelès was almost certainly not telling the truth when he said the fault lay with Bitcoin itself, yet the press were beginning uncritically to echo his claims.

In the heat of the moment, confusion reigned. No sooner had 'transaction malleability' entered the vocabulary of Bitcoin users than it began to seem an existential threat to the entire industry. A botnet – a network of computers infected by malware and remotely controlled, unbeknown to their owners, as a single entity – had launched a 'massive and concerted attack', to use Andreas Antonopoulos's words, on multiple Bitcoin exchanges, including the world's two largest bitcoin-to-dollar exchanges, Bitstamp and BTC-e.[9] The botnet was generating 'malformed' transactions in concert with many legitimate transactions simultaneously, creating 'a fog of confusion over the entire network', Antonopoulos said. In response, Bitstamp halted withdrawals, just as Mt. Gox had done, and BTC-e warned of delays in processing transactions. While they worked to improve their internal systems, Bitcoin's core developers, led by Gavin Andresen, swung into action. Within weeks, they released a new version of the Bitcoin software, version 0.9.0, that went a long way toward neutralizing transaction malleability.[10] The chief stakeholders of the Bitcoin economy, then, perceiving a threat, had reacted swiftly and successfully to put a stop to it. According to Antonopoulos, no funds were lost to the attacks, which had only disrupted the back-end accounting systems of the targeted exchanges, preventing some transactions from being confirmed but not stealing anyone's coins.

It later became evident that Mt. Gox's own press releases regarding transaction malleability, alerting the world to a previously little-known bug, may in fact have triggered the wave of malleability attacks across the Bitcoin network. Whereas barely more than 1,800 bitcoins had been involved in attempted malleability attacks in the year prior to 7 February 2014, between 10 and 11 February – immediately after Mt. Gox's press release

– 25,752 separate attacks were launched, involving a total of 286,076 bitcoins. None of these new attacks could have affected Mt. Gox itself, since it had already halted withdrawals. But the timing strongly suggests the attackers were attempting to exploit the bug elsewhere, sowing chaos across multiple exchanges. Whether or not Mark Karpelès intended this result, setting fire to your neighbors' houses is a good way to distract attention from the fact that your own roof is caving in.

A week later, Bitstamp was fully functional again, while Mt. Gox remained offline. (Indeed, it later became obvious that it was Mt. Gox's own proprietary system, not the core Bitcoin software, that was especially vulnerable to transaction malleability – an accusation Gavin Andresen had leveled during the worst of the uncertainty.) Mark Karpelès continued to dissemble, acting as if the matter were out of his hands. 'We are very surprised that anyone could fault Mt. Gox instead of the Bitcoin software,' he told one reporter.[11]

By now, a Bitcoin trader named Kolin Burges had flown in from London to picket Mt. Gox's offices. He positioned himself every day in front of the glass-fronted office building in Shibuya, holding a sign that demanded to know, MT GOX – WHERE IS OUR MONEY? More than $300,000 of his own money was stuck in the exchange.[12] But Mark Karpelès, pushing past him on his way into work, refused to answer.

Other Mt. Gox customers took action of a different sort. A website called Bitcoin Builder had popped up, offering beleaguered traders an escape hatch from Mt. Gox.* An ad hoc affair, run by a successful web entrepreneur in his mid-thirties named Josh Jones, who had started a Los Angeles Bitcoin meetup group, Bitcoin Builder allowed people to exchange their so-called 'Goxcoins' for

---

* In truth, Bitcoin Builder had existed since January 2012, but in a different form, providing a way for people to invest in Bitcoin through dollar-cost averaging on Mt. Gox. The Goxcoin-to-bitcoin exchange described above, for which the site became known, was knocked together in a single weekend and launched on 11 February 2014.

real, unfettered bitcoins. (Withdrawals from Mt. Gox were halted, but transfers from one person's account to another within the exchange were still possible.) There was an open order book, and the exchange rate fluctuated constantly, depending on how likely people thought it was that Mt. Gox would reopen and convert the trapped Goxcoins back into the genuine article. The digital currency had split into a two-tiered system.

Bitcoin Builder presented traders with a dilemma – either to cut their losses by selling their Goxcoins for a relative pittance or to hold out and pray that Mt. Gox resumed withdrawals. The latter would be not unlike holding on to Confederate money in the hope that the South would rise again. Jason Maurice, an American friend of Roger Ver's in Tokyo who for months had been conducting arbitrage between Mt. Gox and Bitstamp, turning $10,000 worth of yen into four times that amount, was one trader who found himself in this predicament. He and some friends had worked out a system whereby on a regular basis they would cycle their money through Bitstamp and Mt. Gox, over and over, from yen to bitcoins and back again, reaping a healthy profit each time. Their attitude became like that of card counters taking on a Vegas casino. They believed they couldn't lose. Indeed, so profitable was the arbitrage scheme that Jason Maurice kept his entire principal along with his profits moving through the system. Over time, he says, 'I got more and more confidence. I was all in.' And, as luck would have it, his funds were all in Mt. Gox when the exchange shut down withdrawals. He and his friends eyed the exchange rate on Bitcoin Builder, wondering what to do.

As the outlook for Mt. Gox worsened, the trading volume on Jones's website topped five thousand bitcoins a day. It was like rats fleeing a sinking ship, only in this case there were other rats willing to buy their berths at a deep discount on the off chance that the ship might right itself again. 'Some friends of mine were very ambitious and they actually bought *more* Goxcoins on Bitcoin Builder,' Maurice says. With a single untrapped bitcoin going for multiple Goxcoins, the potential rewards, they felt, outweighed the risks. This was the future of money as high-stakes gambling. Josh

Jones, who took two percent of every transaction, reaped more than half a million dollars' worth of Bitcoin in trading fees.[13]

In the end, neither Maurice nor any of his friends tried to unload their Goxcoins through Bitcoin Builder. They were among the hold-outs, as was Jones himself, who claimed to have more than eight thousand Goxcoins trapped in the failed exchange. 'We were all firm believers that Mt. Gox was going to come back,' Maurice says.

But with each passing day that scenario looked increasingly unlikely. On 23 February, with the exchange still offline, and no word as to when it might resume operations, Mark Karpelès resigned in disgrace from the board of the Bitcoin Foundation, just as Charlie Shrem had done one month earlier. Ominously, the company's Twitter account was also scrubbed – years of communications erased from the record.

The next day, a Boston-based blogger named Ryan Selkis, who had begun covering the world of Bitcoin only a few months before, obtained what appeared to be an internal Mt. Gox document outlining a strategy for dealing with the current crisis. The crisis was worse than anyone had dared imagine. Shockingly, according to the document, Mt. Gox was missing 744,408 bitcoins, the result of 'malleability-related theft which went unnoticed for several years'. Of those, 624,408 were owed to customers and the other 120,000 belonged to the company itself. In all, only two thousand bitcoins remained in company wallets. 'The cold storage has been wiped out,' the report went on. Such a theft should have been impossible, unless it was an inside job.

The strategy document gave a bleak assessment of the company's prospects, and of the likely blowback in the event of its collapse:

> The reality is that Mt. Gox can go bankrupt at any moment, and certainly deserves to as a company. However, with Bitcoin/crypto just recently gaining acceptance in the public eye, the likely damage in public perception to this class of technology could put it back 5–10 years, and cause governments to react swiftly and harshly. At the risk of appearing hyperbolic, this could be the end of Bitcoin, at least for most of the public.

The recovery plan called for a number of drastic measures. Mark Karpelès was to step back as CEO – a process which would present certain difficulties, because in Japan a CEO can't resign until a new CEO is nominated – and Mt. Gox would shut down for a month, after which it would relaunch as Gox, with a new logo, under new management, even possibly located in a new country. (Singapore was mentioned as a possibility.) All the company needed by way of new employees, according to the document, were some market analysts, 'top-class developers', a cybersecurity chief, marketing personnel, 'Bitcoin experts', economists, a chief financial officer, a chief operations officer, a chief marketing officer . . . New services would be debuted, new currencies added. First and foremost, an injection of funds would be necessary to get the exchange running again, allowing it gradually to pay back its account holders. But to avoid the cryptocurrency version of a bank run, cash and Bitcoin withdrawals would remain limited.

What was evidently never in doubt, for those drafting the document, was Mt. Gox's crucial, nay irreplaceable, role in the Bitcoin economy. 'The current situation will negatively affect everyone who owns or operates in Bitcoin,' it opined. Insofar as the document presented a strategy, then, it was a strategy born out of what its framers evidently thought was necessity, the necessity of keeping open, so as not to spook the market, so as not to bring down on the head of a whole industry the hammer of harsh regulation, the world's first and still most famous Bitcoin exchange. 'The costs of not doing so,' according to the document, 'are incalculable.'

Customers didn't have to wait long to find out whether the problems described in the document were real. On 25 February, Eastern Time, the Mt. Gox website went offline. A blank page was all that now confronted visitors. There was no doubt in most people's minds that the exchange was insolvent. It seemed equally obvious that the CEO must have known for some time. It would have been a simple matter at any time to reconcile the books, so to speak, and realize that customer deposits didn't match the company's actual holdings. Jason Maurice, for one, was disgusted to learn of Mark Karpelès's duplicity. In the more than two weeks that had passed between Mt. Gox halting withdrawals and shutting down completely, 'you could still deposit money into Mt. Gox, but you just couldn't withdraw, which is the really evil thing that Mark did,' Maurice says. 'Mark was actually taking deposits with the knowledge that there weren't enough bitcoins – that he was essentially broke. So that's where the question of criminal fraud comes in.'

Theories abounded as to where the money had gone. The strategy document blamed the loss on 'massive robbery and poor Bitcoin accounting', but Japanese police later determined that only seven thousand Mt. Gox bitcoins, little more than one percent of the total missing, could have been taken by hackers outside the company. The loss of the other 643,000 could be attributed to manipulation of the exchange's internal system.[14]

For Roger Ver, who had held in Mt. Gox at the time the exchange went dark a balance of 670 bitcoins, close to $400,000 worth, in addition to the nearly 25,000 bitcoins he was owed from Bitcoinica's Mt. Gox account – some percentage of which he hoped to get back from the liquidators – the exchange's collapse was a real financial blow, as it was to thousands of other customers. But it was also, and equally, a rhetorical emergency. His preferred narrative for Bitcoin, that it was a tool of liberation from state control, a weapon in the fight for financial freedom, and that it was in the ascendant, rising in value against the US dollar an incredible 13,500 percent between 2 February 2012 and 2 February 2014, was now endangered. Criticism of Mt. Gox was tapping into a wellspring of heightened emotion that threatened to disrupt the narrative. The critics of Mt. Gox were not on his side, and if they were heeded there was a risk that their broader critique of digital currency would also find an audience, leading in turn to increased government regulation, even outright bans. That alone could not squash Bitcoin entirely, since it was a decentralized system, but could do plenty to make it unpopular among average people and tank the Bitcoin price worldwide.

In some quarters, this effort was already beginning. On 26

February, Senator Joe Manchin, a Democrat from West Virginia, called on government officials to ban Bitcoin. He sent a letter to Janet Yellen, chairman of the Federal Reserve, and Treasury Secretary Jack Lew, in which he described Bitcoin as 'highly unstable'. Pointing to restrictions on digital currency put in place by China, South Korea, and Thailand, Manchin urged US officials to 'prohibit this dangerous currency from harming hardworking Americans'. The following day, however, at an appearance before the Senate Banking Committee, Yellen explained patiently that Bitcoin 'is a payment innovation that is taking place entirely outside the banking industry' and that the Fed had no ability to regulate it.

Even so, Roger had to get the conversation back on point. Blame was warranted, but it had to be limited in scope – directed at Mt. Gox, not at digital currency – and balanced by praise for the trustworthy and responsible Bitcoin companies working to build the future of money. He also felt that he owed fellow Bitcoiners an apology for the video he had made the previous July, which, as he now admitted, 'ended up causing the community to put additional trust in an entity that deserved none'. It was for these reasons that he recorded another video on 26 February, which he posted to YouTube and Facebook and otherwise disseminated online, pleading with Bitcoin users to 'understand the whole picture'. He was as angry as anyone over the apparent incompetence of Mark Karpelès, and he sympathized with people suffering from the loss of their funds, but he didn't see regulation as the answer. The failure of Mt. Gox should be seen as the failure of a single mismanaged company, a regrettable event but one which, given the circumstances, was inevitable and even necessary, and which had been brought about by 'poor programming skills and a total lack of bookkeeping'. He ticked off, one by one, the benefits of Mt. Gox's demise: 'We no longer have to deal with an exchange that can't process withdrawals in a timely manner, takes months to respond to support requests, and whose prices deviate wildly from the other exchanges.' In other words, everyone should be glad to see it gone.

Roger wasn't alone in his efforts to do damage control. Nic Cary and the leaders of five other Bitcoin companies scrambled to issue a joint statement condemning 'this tragic violation of the trust of users of Mt. Gox' and pledging to 'lead the way' in implementing consumer protection measures. Besides Nic Cary, the signatories were Fred Ehrsam of Coinbase; Jesse Powell of Kraken; Nejc Kodrič, the CEO of Bitstamp; Bobby Lee, the CEO of BTC China, one of the leading Chinese exchanges; and Jeremy Allaire of Circle – six of the most prominent Bitcoin businessmen in the world. Like Roger, they sought to spin the Mt. Gox fiasco positively, as the result merely 'of one company's abhorrent actions', which did not reflect the digital currency industry at large, and to reassure people that 'responsible Bitcoin exchanges are working together and are committed to the future of Bitcoin and the security of all customer funds.' They wanted it known that they understood fully the critical custodial role many of their companies played in holding assets for their customers. Just as, in January, Fred Wilson had backed down in the face of Ben Lawsky's insistence on the value of regulation, so now Bitcoin business leaders were being forced to concede that 'acting as a custodian should require a high bar.' What would it mean to meet that bar? Implementing security safeguards to prevent theft – 'independently audited and tested on a regular basis' – along with sufficient reserves to function as commercial entities, disclosures to customers, and clear policies forbidding the use of customer assets for 'proprietary trading or for margin loans in leveraged trading'. (The proposal sounded almost mainstream.) 'It does not appear to any of us,' they concluded, 'that [Mt. Gox] followed any of these essential requirements as a financial services provider.' The statement was published on the websites of Blockchain and the other companies, and it was a sign of just how serious the public relations disaster posed by Mt. Gox was that it brought Blockchain and Coinbase together in a united front. But while Ben Reeves and Nic Cary had built their company in such a way that it could dodge most regulations, Coinbase's Ehrsam and many of his colleagues seemed prepared to accept them in the future. They might even welcome regulations, because in the world of digital currency as in most industries they could raise the barriers to entry for competing startups. Bitcoin had started as an outsider alternative to established systems in banking and payments. Now it was possible that part of the enduring legacy of Mt. Gox's implosion would be to create from among the ranks of Bitcoin companies an inner circle of incumbents protected by regulation, just like the entrenched firms in the industries digital curency was supposed to disrupt.

But Roger Ver, for whom Bitcoin as a technology independent of government control meant so much, had not yet entirely abandoned hope in the matter of Mt. Gox. On 27 February, the same day Japanese vice finance minister Jiro Aichi opined at a press conference that international cooperation would be necessary in order to adequately regulate Bitcoin,[15] Roger was doing some cooperating of his own. He and dozens of other Bitcoiners, including Charlie Shrem, had gathered in an online chat room to talk through what had happened and what might be done about it. 'You guys should know that earlier this week I heard Mark was already talking with the bankruptcy lawyers to file whatever legal paperwork is required for a bankruptcy,' Roger told them. 'So there isn't much time if something is going to be done.'

He had last communicated with Mark Karpelès two days before, when he had demanded that Mt. Gox's CEO confirm or deny the authenticity of the leaked strategy document. Karpelès had confirmed that it was real. He had also confirmed the unimaginable financial losses his company was facing. When Roger pressed him for more, he sent a dispiriting text message: 'Currently filing for bankruptcy and will update based on that.' Now Roger was huddled up with other Bitcoiners in a chat room, doing his best to shed on the crisis – in the words of one Bitcoiner who thanked Roger and Charlie for their openness – 'what little light there is to be had'.

But he found himself having to defend his own actions from the summer before. Back then, on the basis of the best evidence available to him, he had vouched for the health of Mt. Gox. Was it his fault if people had taken that to mean something more? 'I never said gox was solvent,' he clarified now. 'I simply said that the bank delays were not caused by a lack of liquidity. Even in hindsight today, I still think that was true.' He had never looked at the exchange's Bitcoin balances, whether in hot wallets or cold storage. Why would he? At the time, there were no Bitcoin withdrawal problems.

The chat room was in a state of confusion. Thunderstruck by Roger's news of an impending bankruptcy, everyone was typing at once, bombarding him with questions, throwing out brief sentences and fragments of sentences, so that each line of thought was sandwiched between half a dozen others. Following the constant stream of conversation and argument and appeal and rebuttal that scrolled upward out of sight as new lines were added became increasingly difficult, until Charlie Shrem was forced to remind everyone that Roger 'only has 2 hands to type'. What could be discerned immediately was the general tenor of the room, which could be summed up in a single question: *How the hell does a person lose three-quarters of a million bitcoins?*

Most of all, the people in the chat room wondered how Mark Karpelès, who had covered himself in glory – and made millions – as an early adopter of cryptocurrency, and had been among the pioneers who provided the infrastructure that allowed Bitcoin to flourish, could have run into the ground one of the most profitable digital currency businesses in the world. 'He seems to have lost his head,' a user named Aquent wrote. 'How does he bring a 100k per month business into bankruptcy?' Only later would it become widely known that in Mt. Gox's final weeks its CEO had been willfully derelict in his duty, watching episodes of *Breaking Bad* in his office and interviewing French chefs for the Bitcoin café he planned to open on the first floor of the building where Mt. Gox had its offices. 'He had more meetings about the Bitcoin café than about getting banks or doing business,' said one person with knowledge of the matter.[16] Only later would two researchers at a Swiss university demonstrate that malleability attacks could have been responsible for the loss of no more than a tiny fraction of

Mt. Gox's Bitcoin holdings, putting the lie to Karpelès's official explanation. Only later would 200,000 of the missing bitcoins be located in an 'old-format wallet' under Mt. Gox's control which had lain untouched since before June 2011, underscoring the carelessness with which the exchange had been run.

'We need to have a firm plan of exactly what we want from Mark,' Roger told the others. He knew little about Japanese bankruptcy law, but was under no illusions that it would be easy. Like Bitcoinica nearly eighteen months before, Mt. Gox in its desperate state evoked the suffering American financial institutions of the Panic of 1907, for which J. P. Morgan, John D. Rockefeller, and the US Treasury had organized bailouts. In the strategy document circulating online, it was suggested that the way out of the crisis would involve 'informing and asking selected Bitcoin main players for their help . . . Injections in coin are most useful (enough to run the exchange) but some cash is also needed.' But there was little enthusiasm among prominent Bitcoiners for such drastic action.

In the chat room, Kyle Drake of Coinpunk, who earlier that month had sat in Nic Cary's living room in York as Blockchain prepared its public relations offensive against Apple, gave his opinion: 'Honestly, I don't think there's much you can do here . . . If they were $50M in the hole, maybe, but nobody's going to spring $350M.'

Charlie Shrem disagreed: '33M is enough to pay people back 10% of their holdings and 5% equity. [Dividends] can be paid back over 5-10 years.'

'I'm sure somebody would ponder taking 5% at 33M over there,' Drake replied, 'but I'm not sure I would.'

'I wish we could just get Mark in this fucking channel and make him tell us [what the fuck] is going on,' someone going by the name Tiraspol raged.

Roger, asked whether he had stepped in to try to save the failing exchange, was emphatic: 'No, I never offered to buy Mtgox, and I doubt there is anyone willing to do that when they realize [how] big the debt is.'

'The argument for investing in Mt. Gox is essentially just the brand,' Kyle Drake said, 'and how much is that really worth at this point? I mean, you could make your own exchange for way less than $33M. That's with an office in [San Francisco] and money [transmission] licenses in every state . . . It's done. Beyond repair,' he concluded.

Ultimately, Roger was forced to agree. He wanted very much to be repaid the money he was owed by Mt. Gox, 'a life-changing amount', as he called it, and well he might have, for at the time 10,670 bitcoins – a number at which one arrives by assuming he could have recouped through the liquidators forty percent of the 25,000 bitcoins he'd originally lost in Bitcoinica, plus the 670 bitcoins he had been keeping in Mt. Gox – were worth more than $6 million. But 'at this point,' he said, 'I don't hold out any hope that people will get back anything from mtgox.' He had paid a high price for his early and persistent advocacy.

On 28 February, Mt. Gox filed for bankruptcy protection in Tokyo District Court. And there was a nasty surprise: rather than the liability of 744,408 bitcoins reported in the crisis strategy document, the company now revealed, having reviewed its trans-action records, that its digital currency losses totaled 850,000 bitcoins, a full 750,000 of which belonged to customers. Mt. Gox in its infinite carelessness had managed to lose track of about seven percent of all the bitcoins in existence. The scale of the loss was equivalent, in US dollar terms, to misplacing $102.2 billion, seven percent of all the cash and coins in circulation worldwide.

Getting an exact fix on the dollar value of the lost coins was difficult, mainly because news of the Tokyo-based exchange's bank-ruptcy set off dramatic fluctuations in the price. Simple multiplication, however, taking as a starting point the average price for 28 February reported by Coinbase – $568.30 – yields a total of $483 million. In other words, nearly half a billion dollars' worth of digital currency had gone up in smoke. And then, too, there were the exchange's fiat currency losses, still unclear at the time the crisis strategy document was drafted but appearing to reach into the tens of millions of dollars.

Unless trapped in wallets to which the keys had been lost, the bitcoins were not really *gone*, of course, and since the blockchain functions as a public record of all transactions ever made, a record which can be accessed by anyone with a computer, it was theoretically possible that by tracing the movements of coins formerly belonging to Mt. Gox – which admittedly would take a lot of man hours and fairly sophisticated detective work – the lost assets could be found again. Indeed, a number of concerted efforts immediately began to try to track down the missing money, none more high-profile than one led by Charlie Shrem. But there were no guarantees, and anyway this fact was not well understood either by the media or by the general public they informed; the picture was clouded further by Karpelès himself. At a crowded press conference at the courthouse following the bankruptcy filing, the disgraced CEO, wearing a gray suit, lavender shirt, and striped tie, his dark hair slicked back over his collar, bowed in apology. 'There was some weakness in the system, and the bitcoins have disappeared,' he said in Japanese. 'I apologize for causing trouble.'[17] It was hardly adequate, considering the financial losses incurred.

It was the moment the press had waited for. With the exchange bankrupt and Mark Karpelès having insisted that the fault lay with the Bitcoin protocol itself, the knives came out. Media commentators – particularly some progressives unhappy with what they saw as the libertarian implications of cryptocurrency – indulged in unabashed schadenfreude. Bloomberg View crowed that Mt. Gox's meltdown 'spells doom for Bitcoin'. Even the neoconservative *Weekly Standard* joined the hanging party: 'The speculators may not realize it yet, but you can stick a fork in Bitcoin. It's done.'[18]

And yet, even as some pundits were predicting the end of digital currency, there was good reason to believe that Bitcoin would emerge from the shattered wreck of Mt. Gox stronger than ever, as it had done from the takedown of Silk Road. Where Jonathan V. Last of the *Weekly Standard* found the lack of an 'FDIC for Bitcoin' damning, if not fatal, others were glad to see a moribund company be allowed to fail rather than be bailed out, suggesting that a possible response to the death throes of what was once Bitcoin's top exchange would be to appreciate the mechanisms of a truly free market – and then to get busy building better companies to take its place. Just as Satoshi had intended, in the world of Bitcoin the concept of 'too big to fail' did not exist.

The collapse of one exchange, in this view, was not a systemic problem. Perhaps demonstrating how widespread was the continued confidence in Bitcoin, the value of the digital currency fell nearly to $400 in panic selling, but then stabilized within twenty-four hours above $600 again. Something Andreas Antonopoulos, now Blockchain's chief security officer, had said earlier that month still seemed apt: 'The death of Bitcoin has been prematurely announced so many times already that the obvious conclusion is that Bitcoin is far more resilient than its critics would like to think.'[19] (With a reduced supply, the value of the coins remaining in circulation might eventually increase, but for now the cryptocurrency had lost half its value since the heady days of late November, when a single bitcoin – at the inflated Mt. Gox price – briefly surpassed the value of an ounce of gold.) So loud and irresponsible was the media coverage, however, that even a year after the collapse of Mt. Gox, small talk with strangers often yielded two interrelated facts: one, they had heard of Bitcoin, and two, they were under the impression that it had committed suicide.

In fact, large investors were more enthusiastic than ever, as they began to transition from buying digital gold, so to speak, to putting their money to work in the startups supplying the Bitcoin equivalent of picks, shovels, and safe deposit boxes. Publicly announced funding for digital currency startups, which had been $1 million in January 2014 and $2.7 million in February, catapulted to $60.2 million in March. That month, Cody Wilson, the crypto-anarchist and supporter of Ross Ulbricht who had made a name for himself inventing the world's first 3D-printed handgun, did an interview with Stephen Sackur, host of a BBC talk show. 'There's still strong price support for Bitcoin,' Wilson told the host, when the subject of Mt. Gox came up. Whereas the dollar 'is in a kind of perpetual freefall' – slowly but surely losing its spending power due to inflation – Bitcoin is still valuable. 'Digital libertarians,' Wilson concluded, 'are still long [on] Bitcoin.'

One of these was Roger Ver, who had lost so much money when Mt. Gox went belly-up. He exhorted fellow Bitcoiners not to go running, tails between their legs, to regulators. 'The answers to our problems don't depend on lawyers writing more laws,' he said, from Tokyo. 'We already have more than enough of that in this world. We need to focus on voluntary cooperation, using trustless systems in which one group of people don't have arbitrary control over others.' To buck up the troops, he mentioned some major brands that had begun accepting Bitcoin payments, including Overstock and TigerDirect, and he dropped the name of one entrepreneur who was doing things right: Barry Silbert. Silbert, he said, would be launching a 'first-rate Bitcoin exchange' in the summer of 2014.

EVEN AFTER THE MT. GOX meltdown, Barry Silbert still believed, as he told *Fortune* in the spring of 2014, that Bitcoin would be one of the highest-returning investments of his lifetime – and not only for himself but for other people, even those who had not yet entered the market.[20] He thought 2014 would be the year Wall Street got into Bitcoin, and also the year in which the foundation was laid for mass consumer adoption. For months, as public awareness of Bitcoin grew, his opinion had been in high demand among the finance set. 'I could fill my schedule three times over with meetings, educational sessions, breakfasts, lunches, and dinners with all the major banks,' he had said in January. For Bitcoin to reach its full potential, it would have to be integrated into the existing financial system.

And yet in public, at least, financial institutions seemed loath to admit their interest. On 11 February, JPMorgan issued a report entitled 'The Audacity of Bitcoin', in which the company's head of forex strategy, John Normand, called Bitcoin 'incredibly illiquid' and 'extremely volatile'. His overall take on the cryptocurrency was deeply negative. 'At the risk of sounding like a Luddite, Bitcoin looks like an innovation worth limiting exposure to,' Normand wrote. 'As a medium of exchange, unit of account, and store of value, it is vastly inferior to fiat currencies.' While admitting that Bitcoin's wild price swings – which had added up to tremendous growth over the past year – 'may represent simply normal volatility for a startup currency', Normand concluded that ongoing price uncertainty made it 'impossible' to consider Bitcoin a good store of value either for institutions or for individual investors.

The following month, a report from Goldman Sachs made waves by, among other things, declaring that while Bitcoin the network was a promising payments technology, bitcoin with a lowercase 'b' was not a currency at all but rather an especially volatile commodity. Among those who made this argument was Jeff Currie, Goldman's head of global commodities research, and on these terms he compared Bitcoin unfavorably to gold, which for millennia has been desirable as a store of value. (Rarer and denser than silver and compact enough to carry in small quantities, gold works well for this purpose.) Currie's claim that Bitcoin was 'unlikely to displace gold as a commodity store of value' was, however, if not deeply flawed, at least striking in its inconsistencies. On the one hand, he claimed that 'Bitcoin [the commodity] does not improve on gold,' while on the other acknowledging that 'Bitcoin is easier to store and transport and is potentially more difficult to counterfeit' than the precious metal – all of which would seem to be significant improvements. Two Goldman Sachs economists argued that cryptocurrencies 'lie somewhere on the boundaries between currency, commodity, and financial asset . . . On net, more than taking off as a widely used alternative currency, it is much more plausible that Bitcoin eventually has a significant impact in terms of its innovation on payments technology, by forcing existing players to adapt to it or coopt it.' Not long after the Goldman report came out, Andreas Antonopoulos sarcastically summed up this contradictory argument: 'Bitcoin is not a currency and is too volatile, therefore not a threat, which is why banks are writing twenty-five-page internal reports about it. Right.'

But the report, which featured interviews with half a dozen outsiders as well as with Goldman experts, hardly presented a uniform front. Eric Posner, a professor at the University of Chicago, directly contradicted Currie, averring that Bitcoin 'could serve the same purposes as gold in terms of a currency, but much more efficiently' because it did not have to be physically stored or transported. Nevertheless, Posner raised serious doubts about the digital currency's ability to succeed. Among these were the threat of severe regulation, the price volatility, the dubious security measures of various companies that were holding bitcoins, possible competition from upstart altcoins, the growing size of the blockchain (a potential storage problem for the hard drives of average users), and more.

Barry, while remaining sanguine in the face of these critiques, did not entirely disagree with some of the points being made. The most interesting use for Bitcoin in developed nations in early 2014, he believed, was as a speculative investment. Although people were already using bitcoins to buy products from Overstock and TigerDirect, and although its potential for remittances and other applications in the developing world was evident, the cryptocurrency had a long way to go before it could truly rival other dominant forms of payment. Its daily transaction volume by mid-March was less than a quarter of PayPal's $397 million. (At times later that spring it would sink as low as $21 million.) And PayPal's volume itself was peanuts compared to the daily worldwide purchase flow of major credit and debit card companies. In 2012, Visa purchases totaled $11 billion; MasterCard purchases, $7.38 billion; and American Express purchases, $2.43 billion. As for its ability ever to replace government money for a large number of people – a dream, for libertarians like Roger Ver, devoutly to be wished – its market cap was too small. By mid-March, the total value of all bitcoins in existence, with 12.5 million coins having been mined, was close to $8 billion, a drop in the bucket compared to most fiat currencies. Given its intentionally limited supply, Bitcoin wouldn't be able to reach its full potential for e-commerce or remittance payments until its market cap was ten times or even a hundred times greater, so that most payments could be accomplished with a small fraction of a bitcoin. No one knew when, or if, that would happen.

Even before the collapse of Mt. Gox, Barry Silbert had fixed on the idea of launching a Bitcoin exchange in New York as a way to accomplish several related goals: to increase speculative activity and market liquidity, to prove to Benjamin Lawsky and the rest of the NYDFS the economic benefit that digital currency businesses could bring to their state – a point Barry had made during the January hearings – and to bring to Bitcoin trading the much-needed credibility he had brought already to the act of investing in bitcoins as a speculative asset. He had for some time been laying plans for such an exchange, but the downfall of Mt. Gox and the attendant feeding frenzy in the media had accelerated their public announcement, which he made on 25 February. Amid the ongoing scandal he hoped, he said, 'to fill the void of Gox' with a trustworthy institution through which big banks and other institutional investors could place large bets on Bitcoin.[21]

There was, Barry had realized, 'total blue ocean as it relates to an institutionally focused Bitcoin trading firm'. In designing the exchange, he took his inspiration from disparate sources, as befitting Bitcoin's hybrid nature. From the New York Stock Exchange he took the so-called 'hub-and-spoke' model in which only member firms, such as Wall Street banks, can directly participate in the market, while individual investors have to go through one of the members to place their orders. These members, numbering between fifteen and twenty to start, would include, Barry hoped, not only global banks and large broker-dealers but also top Bitcoin companies such as BitPay, Circle, and Coinbase, in all of which he held a stake. Participating in the exchange through one of these firms as a non-member business or retail investor would be much like trading on the NYSE through a broker.

From the gold market, Barry took the idea of 'spot pricing'. One important function of the new Bitcoin exchange would be to set, once or twice a day, based on an auction among buyers and sellers, a price to which trades, derivatives, and mining contracts could be pegged. In this way the exchange would increase liquidity while reducing price volatility, providing a deep enough pool of

capital for major retailers to accept bitcoins in bulk and immediately convert them into dollars. Barry wanted, he said, 'to slow
things down a bit and create a true indication of Bitcoin value'.

The exchange would serve also as a clearinghouse in which
member firms would clear all transactions at the end of each day.
Members would be required to hold enough Bitcoin on their balance
sheets to keep the exchange liquid.[22] Finally, it would have a self-
regulatory arm to ensure its compliance with all state and federal
laws. All of these were signs that Barry Silbert intended to build
not merely another Bitcoin exchange but *the* Bitcoin exchange, one
of which 'the other exchanges of the world could actually become
members'.[23]

More was at stake than potentially astronomical profits for a
few savvy investors or the banking elite. A 2010 study by the
Kauffman Foundation noted the crucial role startups play in US
job creation, accounting for an average of three million new jobs
nationwide each year. Without startups, the study concluded, 'there
would be no net job growth in the US economy.' This was true
not only during the Great Recession but for almost every year for
which data exists, going all the way back to 1977.[24] With the international press shining a bright hot light on Mt. Gox, Barry Silbert
wanted to wrest the spotlight back to the US, to the American
capital of finance, and prove to regulators that Bitcoin was a
legitimate industry with real economic promise for the world. His
goal with the exchange was to pump up daily Bitcoin transaction
volume from tens of millions to a billion dollars. Once that
happened, he was to say months later, 'you'll start seeing the large
merchants, the large brick-and-mortar retailers, accepting it.' Wall
Street's involvement would be the catalyst: 'If the money comes
in, if it starts being traded like any other asset class, we will see,
hopefully, a large increase in the price and a very, very large increase
in the trading volume.' If all went well, the exchange would launch
in the summer of 2014.

On 24 March, Barry Silbert seated himself at a table in a
Manhattan hotel room from which the bed had been removed.[25]
It was the first day of the Barclays Emerging Payments Forum,

where Barry was a speaker, and he was in high demand among the financial firms in attendance – so much so that many of his private meetings had to be combined, with representatives of up to four separate institutions sharing the same time slot in order to pick his brain. Over the next two days, Barry and one of his employees, Michael Sonnenshein, a bearded, soft-voiced account executive of the Bitcoin Investment Trust, held a total of eighteen meetings with investors who wanted to know more about Bitcoin. With people coming and going every half hour, Barry says, 'It was like *Groundhog Day* – same conversation again and again.'

Together, the thirty-eight investors represented more than $250 billion in capital. They were mainly hedge funds and mutual funds but also a few family offices, a few representatives of endowments. For Barry, it was a chance to impress the kind of institutions that might invest in the BIT, perhaps even to raise interest among firms that might make use of the Bitcoin exchange he wanted to launch.

Along with a basic education in Bitcoin, the financial firms, for their part, wanted to inquire about the wisdom of their continued investment in Western Union and MoneyGram. What would be the implications for the international payments industry, they asked, if you were to throw Bitcoin into the mix?

'We obviously couldn't advise people on whether to stay long the stock or short it,' Sonnenshein says, but they nevertheless made it clear that digital currency, or more precisely the blockchain technology underlying it, presented a compelling alternative to traditional financial pipelines. The advice boiled down to this: Keep an eye on Bitcoin and watch whether it starts eating into the revenues – or even the profit margins – of money transfer companies.

On the day that the Barclays conference began in New York, an executive board member of the European Central Bank, giving a prepared speech in Rome, said his institution did not believe 'virtual' currencies were economically important – they were interesting but posed risks. He added, however, that the ECB would continue to follow developments in the industry closely. If the top European bank was still slow to see Bitcoin's potential, it was significant that on the other side of the Atlantic, institutions representing a quarter-trillion dollars of capital had woken up to it, or were at least willing to admit the possibility that digital currency had a role to play in the global economy. Most vulnerable to Bitcoin, it was agreed, were Western Union and MoneyGram; major credit card companies, by contrast, had little to fear, at least in the near future. Of all the people he and Michael Sonnenshein met with during the conference, Barry Silbert would later say, about fifteen percent already believed in the promise of Bitcoin, while the majority – sixty-four percent – were still on the fence. The rest were skeptics. (By 26 March, fully a third of them had asked SecondMarket for a follow-up meeting or call.)[26] Among some financial firms as among digital currency enthusiasts there was a growing sense that, as Michael Sonnenshein puts it, 'Bitcoin will do to Western Union and MoneyGram what Netflix did to Blockbuster.'

The marathon series of meetings revealed what for Barry was another interesting fact, one he could act on. Most of the firms with whose representatives he met 'did not have the ability within their mandate or charter to actually buy bitcoins', he says. But if a fund giving them exposure to Bitcoin were to be public, suddenly the digital currency would be 'an investable asset class'. Millions if not billions of dollars that had been locked away from the Bitcoin market could suddenly be unleashed. The future of the Bitcoin Investment Trust, he realized, was on a public exchange.

At the end of March, the earliest shareholders of the Bitcoin Investment Trust crossed the six-month threshold at which they were allowed, if they chose, to divest themselves of their shares. Few did. Even after the Bitcoin price dropped from an average of $564.24 on 21 March to $477 on 31 March, according to Coinbase, it remained some $351 above the average price of $125.59 from 26 September 2013, the day Barry had launched the BIT. That makes for a 280 percent return on investment. And many expected even greater returns to come. By the end of 2013, the price of Bitcoin had increased fifty-six times from its price at the beginning of the year. In the context of an asset capable of such exponential gains, what did it matter that SecondMarket charged all BIT investors a two percent annual management fee? Come to that, what was a few dollars per bitcoin more or less? 'To me, and to a lot of folks in the Bitcoin world, it's binary,' says Michael Moro, a former Citigroup investment banker who became a director of SecondMarket's trading desk. 'Bitcoin either goes to, like, $100,000 a coin, or it goes to zero. Right? It's one or the other. Does it really matter if you bought your bitcoins at $420 versus $430 versus $440? No, it really doesn't. And I think some institutional buyers understand that five dollars, ten dollars here and there doesn't really change the overall return profile. It's still going to be almost infinity – or zero.'

It was in this atmosphere that SecondMarket's traders operated. The company's trading desk included three traders who focused exclusively on Bitcoin, while four others divided their time between Bitcoin and auction-rate securities. In the beginning, their task of putting large sums of investor money to work in the Bitcoin Investment Trust had been hampered by the price of Bitcoin, between $120 and $125 in late September. 'When we first got started, filling a $100,000 order was a hard thing for us to do,' because it called for so many bitcoins, says Michael Moro. And their only options for acquiring coins were Bitstamp and Mt. Gox. This was a problem not only because buying so many coins piecemeal on the exchanges took time but because each day at 4:00 P.M. the BIT would establish a daily net asset value for the fund based on the volume-weighted average price of the exchanges. That was then the price which the SecondMarket traders used for their orders. But on the exchanges the price could, and did, fluctuate throughout the day; on days of high volatility, the traders might end up losing money. 'If you happened to buy on the exchange at the wrong time, you were underwater on your purchases,' Moro says.

Months later, the situation had improved. The company's traders had established relationships with about 150 counterparties from whom they could source bitcoins directly rather than going through an exchange. Some were miners sitting on heaps of digital gold. Others were merchant processors like Coinbase. It was better for them to offload their bitcoins in a single block rather than piecemeal on a public exchange, not only for the sake of convenience but because dumping a large number of coins on an exchange with a thin trading volume would temporarily tank the price, diminishing profits. It was for this reason that SecondMarket traders were able to acquire large blocks of bitcoins at a discount to the public price. By late spring, they had built up such a large network of over-the-counter sellers that SecondMarket was relying on public exchanges like Bitstamp for no more than twenty percent of its trades. The remainder took the form of private deals. It was as if SecondMarket had created a dark pool for Bitcoin.

Although the blockchain, being a public ledger, ensured that even private trades were accounted for, over-the-counter buying and selling activity would not be included in exchange trade volume, and so most of SecondMarket's trades didn't move the Bitcoin price up or down on Bitstamp, BTC-e, or any of the other exchanges. 'You buy a hundred coins right now [on a public exchange], you move the market like $10 or $20,' Michael Moro says. 'Never mind a block of a thousand bitcoins. Part of our job is to not ruin the market for anyone else.' Resorting to private transactions meant, however, that the public exchange prices – which fluctuated from perhaps $580 to as high as $678 to a low of $449 over the course of March 2014 – were not an accurate reflection of worldwide investor interest. A huge number of transactions were happening out of the public eye.

On 10 April, Barry announced that the Bitcoin Investment Trust had reached a milestone: it was holding 100,000 bitcoins on behalf of investors. Even at the temporarily depressed Bitcoin price of $395 on 10 April, the BIT was worth nearly $40 million. And it continued to grow. By the early morning hours of 22 May, for instance, with the BIT holding an additional six thousand bitcoins, and the market price rebounding to $510, the fund's value ballooned to $54 million. Not that its investors paid much mind to such fluctuations. They were in it for the long term.

By late spring, SecondMarket traders were buying and selling bitcoins not only for the BIT but also on behalf of investors who wanted to hold bitcoins personally. The minimum order was twenty-five bitcoins (around $12,500). Rather than seeking to avoid the headaches of acquiring and storing digital currency, some investors felt that holding their own coins – getting down 'to the nitty-gritty of how this stuff works', as Michael Moro puts it – gave them a deeper understanding of the asset class.

Other individual buyers were Bitcoin brokers in their own right. They would source bitcoins from SecondMarket's trading desk and then turn around and resell the currency to their own customers. Says Moro, 'They're not taking positions themselves; they're only collecting small orders and aggregating them and placing orders through us.' This was not so different from how Robert Faiella would resell to his customers on Silk Road the bitcoins he'd acquired through BitInstant, only everything SecondMarket was doing was aboveboard, and the brokers with whom they dealt presumably were not acquiring bitcoins for a black market clientele. Indeed, Bitcoin owners had no need to lurk in the shadows any longer; there was a growing mainstream comfort with this new asset class. The company's 'addressable universe' – the pool of investors who wanted to take a position in Bitcoin – was growing every day, Moro says. From the end of April through early May, over the course of several trades, all of them executed over the counter rather than on Bitstamp, SecondMarket sold some ten thousand bitcoins to a single buyer. By then, fully half of the orders executed by SecondMarket traders were on behalf of investors who wanted to hold bitcoins directly, while the other half were earmarked for the BIT.

With the BIT, Barry was taking bitcoins out of circulation, reducing transactional velocity – the speed with which bitcoins changed hands, whether through trading or merchant activity. In essence, the fund was hoarding bitcoins on behalf of investors. Currency hoarding is anathema to mainstream economists, because it reduces market liquidity and velocity, making it more difficult to use the currency for economic activity. One Bitcoin skeptic of this school, Mark Williams, a lecturer in finance at

Boston University, was even concerned, as he would tell the World Bank in October 2014, that if Bitcoin were ever allowed to coexist as legal tender alongside the US dollar, it might, under Gresham's Law – the economic principle that 'bad money drives out good money' – create a situation in which bad currency, Bitcoin, would be used, while good currency, the dollar, would be hoarded, destabilizing the economy. This relationship between Bitcoin *qua* currency and the dollar, of course, was precisely the opposite of the one envisioned by Roger Ver and other libertarian and crypto-anarchist advocates of digital currency. In their view, the dollar, and all fiat currency for that matter, was the bad money which had held the world captive for too long and which needed driving out. Barry Silbert was not so radical. But for Bitcoin, he thought, speculative investment and hoarding could be an intermediate step to a world in which the digital currency was widely used for e-commerce and international payments. A world, in other words, in which Bitcoin lifted all boats, allowing businessmen and corporations to move millions across borders with minimal friction while also enabling a cab driver from New Delhi to send money back to his family for a negligible fee. 'I'm not going to suggest [Bitcoin] will replace the US dollar,' Barry told *Bloomberg Markets*. 'But can it have as transformative an effect on the world as Facebook? Yes.'[27]

'As funds like ours grow and individual holders of Bitcoin grow [their stockpiles] and have no intention of selling for a very long period of time, the scarcity value of Bitcoin comes even more into play,' Mike Moro says. 'There's only twenty-one million that will ever be made, but if a big percentage of it is gone – taken out of circulation, so to speak – any new guy who wants to come in has to buy what's available in the marketplace, which is going to be very limited. So you'll see huge price spikes at that point in time.' The open question was whether, if the price of Bitcoin continued to fall in the short term, the downward pressure exerted on the price by miners selling the coins they mined to cover their costs could be overcome by speculative interest from buyers. If not, the price would remain flat or continue to fall, further squeezing miners and hurting investors. For now, it was anyone's guess.

Meanwhile, a potential competitor to the BIT had yet to get off the ground. The previous July, Cameron and Tyler Winklevoss, apparently undeterred by the fiasco of BitInstant, had filed paperwork with the SEC to launch a publicly traded Bitcoin fund. It was to be called the Winklevoss Bitcoin Trust. Just like the BIT, the Winklevosses' fund, which would be listed on Nasdaq or the New York Stock Exchange, would allow people to gain exposure to Bitcoin without subjecting themselves to the process of actually buying bitcoins. And it would have one major advantage: It would be open not merely to accredited investors but to *all* investors, to everyone in the country who might want to grab for themselves a piece of the future of money. 'The driving force,' Cameron Winklevoss said in the fall of 2013, 'is bringing Bitcoin to the mainstream investor.'[28] This was not unlike someone buying up a significant portion of the world's supply of wheat and then setting out to convince the average Joe that the very thing his table was lacking was a loaf of bread.

The brothers had spent months drafting their ninety-five-page SEC application with lawyers from Katten Muchin Rosenman, a firm had done legal work for the world's first exchange-traded fund twenty years before. But the Winklevosses' filing had been in limbo ever since. Indeed, there was every likelihood that SEC approval would take years to arrive, if it ever did. Reggie Browne, the one-time head of ETF trading at Knight Capital Group, laughingly called the Winklevosses' proposed fund 'a riot'.[29]

But years of high-level athletics had steeled them for competition – and for disappointment. Those years, in which they trained eleven and a half months out of every twelve, as much as two or three times a day, had also taught them how to win. Rowing is a sport of rhythm, timing, coordination, and teamwork, but it is also a sport in which one wins by bringing to bear – against the water, against the opposing squads – an overwhelming amount of effort. And so they had already, by the early fall of 2013, amassed some 116,000 bitcoins, or one percent of the world's total supply.

At the time, Bitcoin's market cap was about $1.5 billion, making their personal hoard worth $15 million – a hoard which, during the bubble later that year, would grow exponentially more lucrative, just as the value of the Facebook stock awarded to them had climbed dramatically since the settlement. In the months that followed, even as they pursued investments in startups that had nothing to do with Bitcoin, they held on to their digital wealth. They were not going away. 'Everyone we used to compete with [in rowing] was told they're the best – and they were,' Tyler Winklevoss says. 'You have to be stubborn and confident – day in, day out – that you're the two that are going to make it.'[30]

Whenever the subject of the Winklevoss Bitcoin Trust was raised, Barry became reserved. 'I don't think naming it after themselves was a good move,' was as much as he would say critically to a reporter, though he also professed to not being concerned about the competition, which was no mere bravado. The SEC had kept the Winklevosses' application stalled for months. The Winklevoss Bitcoin Trust might never be approved, he said, but even if it were to be approved its existence would be good for Bitcoin. And indeed, the BIT would be next in line to walk through that door once it was open. But the truth was that he was already beyond the twins, beyond the idea of a fund, even of a publicly traded ETF; even before the return of spring he was making plans to spin off all of SecondMarket's Bitcoin-related activity into a separate company, with multiple ventures. Month by month the vision took shape, until by summer he could say that his ambition was to create the Berkshire Hathaway of Bitcoin.

IN THE SPRING OF 2014, Charlie Shrem was murdering cops by the dozens, with all manner of weaponry – pistol, assault rifle, Gatling gun, sticky bombs. His attack helicopter was armed with air-to-ground missiles and those did the job nicely, turning the city of Los Santos into the set of a Michael Bay movie. But the sticky bombs were his favorite. On the bigscreen TV in his parents' basement, Charlie logged hour after hour on *Grand Theft Auto V*, the bestselling video game of all time, a game in which the player takes the part of three criminals, each one seeking a big score and using violent means to get it – seeking ultimately, by any means necessary, an increase of personal power, of ego capital, even if that means hotwiring a fighter jet in a military airport. The game was a way for Charlie to kill the boredom of his domestic incarceration. On an afternoon in April, showing off for visitors, it became another species of pastime, as if the polygonal character he controlled in the game could wreak bloody vengeance on those who were persecuting him in life.

For weeks he had been trying to keep himself occupied so that he wouldn't have to think about the possible prison sentence that awaited him. He was still bursting with ideas for new ventures, but his spirits were at a low ebb. Throughout an intensely cold February he stayed cooped up in his parents' house while snow piled up on the quiet street outside, bringing a hush to the almost suburban environment of single-family homes and little fenced-in lawns. For nineteen days that month the high temperature was below average for the time of year, and for eleven of those days the mercury rested at or below freezing. Charlie remained out of it, marooned indoors. When he wasn't playing GTA, he watched Netflix, tinkered with a robot, and gave advice and assistance however he could to people who reached out to him on Twitter. He drank a lot, a habit encouraged by friends who dropped by to cheer him up, bottles of liquor or six-packs of beer in hand. He had always been svelte but now, despite working out with a trainer, he was gaining weight. He kept late hours, staying up most nights until four or five o'clock in the morning and sleeping until one in the afternoon. In late March, a CNNMoney reporter emailed him, asking if he could sit down with him for an interview. But Charlie had stopped talking to almost everyone. Only the month before, he had been glib in conversation, sure the case against him would fall apart. Now the severity of his situation was weighing heavily on him.

Deepening his feeling of despondency was Courtney's absence. Hounded by the press, and unable to make rent on their Midtown apartment alone after Charlie's arrest, Courtney had moved back to York, Pennsylvania, where she had grown up, to live with her mother, Diane. But Charlie was determined to make the relationship work. They talked constantly. He wrote songs for her and performed them on his guitar over Skype videochat. (He was recording, he said, a 'house arrest album'.) And every night, connected by Skype, they watched movies and TV shows together. *Scandal*, a primetime soap opera about power and the lengths to which people will go to keep it, was a particular favorite. Charlie clung to his girlfriend, having no other source of unconditional support. Banned from the city except for visits to his lawyer's office, cut off all at once from the Manhattan high life, he needed the FBI's permission – as he wryly noted in one song – just to leave the house.

Outside its confines, the world he had helped build continued to grow without him in strange and unexpected ways. Dozens of new 'altcoin' cryptocurrencies – most of them Bitcoin clones, with minor differences at most – had sprung up, and as quickly as they came into existence, people began mining and trading them on twenty-four-hour online exchanges. Often, this activity amounted to little more than 'pump-and-dump' schemes – that is, efforts to artificially drive up the price of an altcoin by trading it heavily for a period of time, tricking others into believing it had value, then selling it off once the price went high enough for the pumpers to make a profit. The other investors, who weren't in on the scam, would lose their money. When this is done with stocks, the Securities and Exchange Commission considers it to be illegal fraud, but in the world of alternative digital currencies there were few rules at that time and even less enforcement. Pump-and-dump schemes are now familiar to many people, but the kind of phone sales operation depicted in *The Wolf of Wall Street* is out of date. The rise of the Internet, and the attendant growth of social networks like Facebook and Twitter, has made it much easier for fraudulent promoters to reach a large audience with their hyped-up claims.

In the eyes of most serious Bitcoin advocates, altcoins had a bad reputation. Bitcoin added something new to the world, of course, and its intrinsic properties as a form of money and a payment system gave it value. But the idea that you could create lasting digital wealth by simply copying Bitcoin and tweaking a few variables seemed absurd. Even many crypto-enthusiasts found little reason to invest in altcoins; after all, why not just use Bitcoin? Why confuse the issue for outsiders? Eric Posner, in the Goldman Sachs report on Bitcoin, had expressed other concerns, namely that Bitcoin, if it succeeded in becoming a widely used currency, risked falling victim to its own success due to the rise of competing altcoins. 'If these other currencies act as competitors,' Posner said, 'then we would be stuck with just as much volatility and exchange rate risk at home as we currently have to deal with in transacting abroad.'

But there was little chance that any of the altcoins would challenge Bitcoin for dominance. Charlie had taken a risk on Auroracoin – an altcoin designed to be a national cryptocurrency for Iceland – and been badly burned. (After being distributed successfully to thousands of Icelandic citizens, Auroracoin abruptly lost half of its value in a single day.) So now he was all in on Bitcoin; in fact, he had just bought some more of the digital currency, because rumors of a clampdown by the Chinese government were artificially depressing the price. But that wasn't the only foreign news of interest. Elite hackers were waging a proxy war over Russia's invasion of Crimea; websites belonging to the governments of both Ukraine and Russia had been defaced. It reminded Charlie of his days running with Casi and Polynomial and the rest of the old crew, engaged in territorial pissing matches with other hacker clans.

Another war was also in full swing – the one being fought, both in private and, increasingly, in public, between libertarian early adopters of Bitcoin and the arriviste businessmen who hoped to make a fortune on it. Marc Andreessen, one of the most visible and eloquent of this lot, made his position unmistakably clear. 'We like fringe technologies,' he said, 'but not fringe politics.'[31] Stoking the fires from the sidelines were members of a commentariat newly aware of a technology they knew little about. Bitcoin, that is to say, was now big enough to have haters.

Paul Krugman, who long before attaining the Olympian heights of his Nobel Prize in economics had already built a reputation on the *New York Times* editorial page, where he could be depended on to lend his dismal science bona fides to the Democratic Party line, and to identify in the Republican Party, and the Republican Party alone, the seeds of society's destruction, was extremely skeptical of Bitcoin as a store of value and still more skeptical, if that were possible, of any social benefit to be derived from it. In a column with the magnificent headline 'Bitcoin Is Evil', he argued that there was no true floor to the Bitcoin price and that it was a bait-and-switch to answer doubts about its stability as a store of value by making reference to its usefulness as a medium of exchange.[32]

In this skepticism he was not alone. In one of the more strongly worded denunciations, Charles Stross, a British writer of science fiction whom Krugman quoted approvingly on matters of economics, said he wanted Bitcoin 'to die in a fire'. (In an article referencing his comments, VICE Media's Motherboard tech blog later misidentified Stross as an economist.[33]) 'Bitcoin looks like it was designed as a weapon intended to damage central banking and money issuing banks, with a libertarian political agenda in mind,' Stross wrote. To anyone who has read Stross's fiction, his objection to Bitcoin will come as no surprise. His breakthrough 2001 novella *Lobsters* concerned the exploits of a globe-trotting 'venture altruist' – the opposite of a venture capitalist – who, in pursuit of a post-scarcity society, spends his time coming up with billion-dollar ideas and giving them away to others. Stross's argument was emblematic of the have-your-cake-and-eat-it-too quality that Andreas Antonopoulos had identified in much anti-Bitcoin sentiment: On the one hand, this so-called cryptocurrency is bonkers and will never work; any day now it will collapse in on itself like a dying star. On the other hand, it will be ruinous to the prevailing system we depend on. Bitcoin, wrote Stross, 'will badly damage stable governance, not to mention redistributive taxation systems and social security/pension nets if its value continues to soar (as it seems designed to do)'. In the background of criticism like this, one could hear the whoops and hollers of Bitcoin's libertarian proponents – who would have liked nothing better than for their new money to do just what Stross feared – and one could picture Erik Voorhees shaking his head at 'the sheer productive uselessness of vast swaths of the population'.

Charlie Shrem, whatever side he might have taken, was unable to join the battle. He lived his life vicariously through others. When Cody Wilson came to New York in late March to take part in a debate about 3D-printed firearms at the Museum of Modern Art – a debate in which he remained steadfast in his belief that information, even blueprints of untraceable firearms, wants to be free, and in which he unapologetically described Dark Wallet, a Bitcoin project on which he was working with Amir Taaki and a handful of others, as 'a money laundering tool', thereby seeming to confirm regulators' worst fears – Charlie was hungry for news of him; hungrier still for news of what people like Cody Wilson might be saying about Charlie Shrem. What Wilson said was that Charlie was a cautionary tale of what happens when you try to play by the rules.

'He's kind of right in a way,' Charlie said when he heard. He nevertheless continued to believe that disregarding laws wholesale, either in letter or in spirit, was an impossible path to take. He didn't have it in him to fight a running battle with government regulators. 'Working with them is the lesser of two evils. We don't have a choice. I want to not stay in jail. Here I am, going.' Had he not been facing a possible decades-long prison sentence, had he still held a position on the board of the Bitcoin Foundation, he might have pressed for greater cooperation between Bitcoin companies and government regulators; or, on the other hand, he might have felt free to stand alongside Cody Wilson. The truth was that Charlie, bereft of a company, trapped in his parents' house, was now on the sidelines. In April, however, in the odoriferous, acne-scarred person of Amir Taaki, the war came to his doorstep.

Charlie had played at being an outlaw, but Taaki was the real deal: he had lived in squats, and he had been homeless, and unlike Roger and Charlie he had never been rich, not even in his days playing poker for money. Even after parlaying his skill as a coder into positions of authority and influence at companies that handled hundreds of thousands of dollars for their customers, Amir Taaki retained the violent, passionate, mercurial soul of a poet. It was this, along with his fervent belief in open-source software, that had landed him in hot water at Bitcoinica and made him a pariah to much of the Bitcoin community.

He could be stunningly closed-minded. During his visit to New York in April 2014, which was also his first trip to the US, a trip he made for the express purpose of visiting Charlie Shrem in his hour of need, he walked around Midtown incessantly mocking everything in sight, giggling and braying in his working-class accent: 'Forget those little European villages. I'm in the big city now, with the big lights. The Big Apple. *New Fucking York!* Home of the brave! We're part of the power now. We made it,' he said to the girl beside him, who laughed her hiccupy laugh, game for anything. 'I'm no longer Euro-poor, I'm Ameri-rich!' He began to sing: '*Oh, how I love to be an American, where at least I know I'm free . . .*'

On 19 April, a Saturday, Amir showed up at Charlie's house wearing the same red pants, blue T-shirt, scarred motorcycle boots, and stained gray hoodie he had been wearing for days. He sported a goatee with a neck beard, and his unkempt mullet was gathered into a kind of rattail. With him was a girl he barely knew, a blonde anarchist groupie he had met at a Bitcoin conference in Toronto just before coming to New York. She wanted to record a video of Charlie Shrem for her YouTube channel. There was just one problem: their visit coincided with Passover, during which the use of electronics is generally prohibited.

Charlie was no longer as observant as his parents, which made for a tense situation at home. During Passover, he continued to use his mobile phone; his parents, in keeping with religious custom, shunned theirs. And then there was the matter of his *shiksa* girl-friend, blonde and several years older than him. His parents wanted him to date a Jewish girl. 'I hate my parents,' he said in a moment of frustration that spring. But he respected their wishes when it came to his guests; there would be no filming of any kind during

Passover. This news provoked consternation in Amir Taaki and his companion. 'There is a time to put aside religion,' Amir groused, but evidently the making of a YouTube video did not carry in the Shrem household the same weight that it did in the minds of young anarchists. Only with great reluctance did they give up the idea.

They decamped to the front porch. It was warm for April, nearly seventy degrees, so they sat out in the sun, chatting and munching on potato chips, pistachios, flatbread, deviled eggs, and other snacks, all of them premade or ready-to-eat since cooking – considered a kind of work – was also forbidden during Passover. Well-dressed Jewish families passed by on the sidewalk. The cherry tree in the front yard was in bloom. Now that the weather was warming up, Charlie cherished every moment he could spend outdoors. A few days before, leaving the house with his family for an evening service at the synagogue – having obtained a special exemption from his house arrest for religious observances – he had found himself thinking that while he didn't have much cause to celebrate freedom, he was at least not behind bars.

His powwow with Amir Taaki made for an odd scene, something like – to use Charlie's own words – 'the prime minister of Israel and the prime minister of Saudi Arabia going to a baseball game together and having a chat'. Charlie was wearing, as always, visible below the hem of his pant leg, his electronic tracking anklet. 'That's really something else,' Amir said, almost admiringly. Charlie was now a bona fide enemy of the state, a fact which inspired in Amir – who had himself, he said, been 'invited not to go back' to the UK due to his subversive activities – newfound respect, and which held out the possibility that Charlie was closer in spirit now to Amir's own anarchist sensibilities than he'd ever been while serving as BitInstant's CEO and a board member of the Bitcoin Foundation – while, that is, seeking to win for Bitcoin mainstream acceptance.

Charlie had been thinking a great deal since his arrest about the ideological roots of the Bitcoin project. To those who embraced its most radical implications, a foundational document was the 1993 'Cypherpunk's Manifesto' of Eric Hughes, portions of which Charlie could quote by heart. 'We the Cypherpunks are dedicated to building anonymous systems,' Hughes wrote. 'We are defending our privacy with cryptography, with anonymous mail forwarding systems, with digital signatures, and with electronic money.' Amir Taaki was dedicated to this effort. Dark Wallet, the project in which he and Cody Wilson were the most visible participants, was open-source software designed to plug into the Google Chrome web browser, serving as an encrypted Bitcoin wallet simple enough for anyone to use. One of its key innovations was the use of a protocol dubbed CoinJoin, which mixed together in transit the bitcoins belonging to multiple users' transactions, shuffling them about in a digital game of Three Card Monte so that it would be difficult if not impossible to tell where any of the coins had originated. Just as the Tor network disguised users' web traffic, allowing them to visit dark net sites with relative impunity, so Dark Wallet would allow users to send and receive bitcoins more privately than ever before. (Nic Cary used the CoinJoin protocol himself, though for a more innocuous reason – to disguise the origin of payroll disbursements to Blockchain employees. If they had known the Bitcoin address from which these disbursements were being issued, they would have been able to see how much the corporate kitty held in total funds.) Not content merely to provide a means of anonymously storing, sending, and receiving digital currency, however, Amir Taaki sought also to provide a place where it could be spent in secret. At a hackathon during the Toronto conference, just prior to visiting New York, he and two other developers had won the $20,000 first prize for a prototype online marketplace that was an evolutionary step beyond Silk Road. Indeed, DarkMarket, designed to operate on an entirely peer-to-peer basis, with no central server that could be seized, no single target for law enforcement to attack, would be to Silk Road what BitTorrent was to Napster: a decentralized and therefore more resilient version of a groundbreaking service that had ultimately proved vulnerable to legal action. To shut down something like DarkMarket, the feds would have to arrest each and every buyer and seller individually. The market would be a 'hydra', to use Amir Taaki's word for it, with more heads than could ever be cut off. In his hackathon presentation, he all but patted himself on the back for his cleverness: 'Technology is power, and a new front has opened in the struggle for freedom . . . Technology is not, and never will be, neutral. Software is art.'

Charlie, for his part, however much he might have been impressed with Amir's work, was an entrepreneur, not an artist. He saw in Amir the path he had not chosen, the path he *could not* have chosen; his respect for the other man was that of a businessman for a revolutionary: 'Amir has had opportunities to make money and he's not in it for the money, he's not in it for the fame. Amir is in it for the future.' (And yet somehow money did flow to him. 'We've got loads of rich friends who believe in what we're doing,' Amir says, referring to the Dark Wallet team, 'because Dark Wallet has massive social utility.') But Charlie, now something of a pariah in turn, found himself making common cause with the anarchist; the irony that he, Charlie, was under federal indictment while Amir was a free man was not lost on him.

Among the first generation of Bitcoin adopters, however, he was not the only casualty. Erik Voorhees was now under investigation by the SEC for selling shares of SatoshiDice – unregistered securities. With his own legal troubles to worry about, Erik now treated his old boss as if he were radioactive. 'I sent him a Skype message. He's like, "Hey, Charlie, everything you want to say to me goes through my lawyer now,"' Charlie told Amir.

But Erik and his fiancée, Michelle, were planning to attend the following Wednesday the Tribeca Film Festival premiere of a documentary film about Bitcoin in which Charlie – and BitInstant – played a major role. (So major that Charlie, wearing for the premiere a black suit, loafers, and a skinny gray tie, tried to compel members of the audience to give up their seats for him and his small entourage, describing the documentary as *'my* movie'.) Charlie had gotten special permission to attend. 'I don't know what I'm going to say to him,' he confessed.

Charlie and Erik might not have been true outlaws. But they

were pioneers and extremists, and in the eyes of the law it was a distinction without a difference.

But now Charlie put dark thoughts out of his mind. Although he had fallen into a deep depression after his arrest – so deep that Thomas Holzinger had flown to New York with a case of vodka to cheer him up – gradually, over the weeks that followed, Charlie's naturally buoyant spirit reasserted itself. To keep his sanity, he offered himself up as a free sounding board to anyone who wanted to bounce ideas off him. He began wheeling and dealing again. He toyed with the idea of launching a twenty-four-hour Internet TV network for Bitcoin programming, to be hosted at watchbitcoin.com, which he owned. He began writing the code for a new online poker site.

'This is the idea – you ready for this?' he said to Amir, knowing the other man would be interested. 'It's going to be the most simplistic design – where you come to the site and you're already matched up with someone. So you come to the site and there's no registration, there's no tables; it's just you and someone else. You get dealt cards, you have a QR code, zero confirmations, send Bitcoin to it: you're dealt a hand, he's dealt a hand, and then you win, you lose, you can click Match With New Player – that's it, simplistic poker site.'

They debated the risk of crediting funds to a user's account without waiting for the Bitcoin network to confirm the transactions. The site could get defrauded by users double-spending their coins. But such small amounts of digital currency would be bet on each hand that Charlie hoped there would be little incentive to try to cheat the system. 'Anyway, it's just an idea I have, but it's pretty cheap to build,' he said, 'like $2,000 maybe for a developer. I feel like it will take off.'

Another idea now occurred to him. He should set Amir up with his speaking agent, giving the renegade coder a way of earning an income from his peripatetic lifestyle. This agent, Charlie said, had already secured him a speaking slot at the following year's Webwinkel Vakdagen, the same conference in the Netherlands from which he had been returning when he was arrested. In exchange for the conference organizers putting it in writing immediately

– even while his future liberty was uncertain – Charlie agreed not to haggle over the fee; the $20,000 he had earned the first time around would be sufficient.

One big piece of news remained to share: Charlie had begun working as a paid consultant for Payza, a multinational payments company with more than ten million customers. Like the larger PayPal, Payza provided customers with an electronic wallet for storing funds. What had become evident to company executives was that 'all over the Internet people are buying and selling bitcoin[s] through their own wallet system,' Charlie said. Someone with $100 in his Payza wallet, say, would offer to send it to another person's Payza wallet in exchange for the equivalent amount in bitcoins. Payza executives saw an opportunity: if there was a demand for bitcoins among their users, why not allow them to buy bitcoins directly through Payza? They hired Charlie to advise them on how best to incorporate Bitcoin into their business.

'And it's easy, because they have all the fraud prevention, they have direct debit like Coinbase in 100 countries, they have wire transfers – *boom*,' Charlie said confidently. 'They've been doing this for ten years; they know how to manage all of that. They'll be like the Coinbase of Europe,' he added. In fact, Payza's network extended far beyond Europe to more than 190 countries, including underserved markets like Bangladesh. Bitcoin in Bangladesh: it was something to contemplate.

When, more than two months later, word got out about Charlie's involvement with Payza, the company, while commending his 'exceptional knowledge of the Bitcoin market', was careful to note that it had set 'specific parameters on his role which is based on a limited engagement'.[34] (He was, after all, still facing the possibility of prison time.) The engagement was for three months of work, for which Charlie was being paid $5,000 a month. He was, he made a point of telling reporters, still making good money while under house arrest. And he would continue to play a role in spreading the use of Bitcoin. He was indefatigable. There are, it is said, no second acts in American lives. Charlie was willing to test the point.

Amir Taaki, meanwhile, had other plans. First and foremost on his agenda was paying a visit to Cody Wilson in Austin, where his company, Defense Distributed, was headquartered. 'I'm gonna go to Texas, fire some guns – *blam! blam! blam! blam!*' he told Charlie gleefully. 'Plastic ones. I'll send you a picture, yeah?'

Chapter 11

THE INTERNET OF MONEY

Bureaucracies do not succeed revolutions by coincidence.
Revolutions are the bloody births of bureaucracies.
– Nicolás Gómez Dávila

Throughout the spring of 2014, Blockchain continued to expand. In March, the company announced a new acquisition: RTBTC, a web-based trading platform that aspired to be a one-stop shop for serious Bitcoin traders, bringing to digital currency a measure of the sophistication taken for granted in the markets for stocks, bonds, and commodities. For months RTBTC's creator, Clark Moody, had been corresponding with Dan Held, the cofounder of ZeroBlock, about the possibility of merging their products. There was excellent synergy. The real-time news and market data that had made ZeroBlock the highest-rated and most-reviewed Bitcoin app could enhance the appeal of RTBTC's trading platform, giving users access to market-moving information. They even dreamed up a mobile app that would allow users to trade on the go.

Nic Cary wanted to make the platform a kind of E-Trade for Bitcoin. He hoped it would reduce price volatility and inspire in traders more enthusiasm and activity. He wanted to stabilize and strengthen the Bitcoin economy so that it could be a true parallel economy to that of ordinary money, almost an ecosystem unto itself. But with the acquisition came challenges. Between July 2013, when RTBTC launched, and January 2014, $150 million worth of trades had passed through the platform. But growth had been flat ever since. Moody had only managed to partner with two exchanges, Bitstamp and Mt. Gox, and Mt. Gox had imploded. There wasn't much reason to use RTBTC – designed to be an all-in-one, multi-exchange trading platform – if it was linked to Bitstamp alone. Held and Moody – who had joined Blockchain as part of the acquisition deal – knew they needed to sign up more exchanges. It might be difficult to convince a second marketplace to sign up, but the third and fourth would be easier. They had their eyes on BTC China, which, despite being open only to Chinese users, in November had unseated Mt. Gox as the world's biggest Bitcoin exchange. Users would be charged $20 a month, and Nic hoped eventually to take a percentage of the exchanges' revenue, provided of course that his trading platform could funnel enough business to them to make it worth their while.

They never managed to land BTC China, but the attempt was revealing. In those days Blockchain was a gung-ho place to work. Its ambitions, thanks to Nic Cary, were comprehensive: using its products alone, you could now buy and sell bitcoins, store them securely, and accept them as payment. You could also track the price across major exchanges and stay abreast of industry news. Soon you would be able to discover places to spend your digital wealth. In April, Nic moved to link all the products together. He inked a deal to lease the web address Bitcoin.com for the next five years. The website had been owned by TradeHill until the exchange was forced to give it up during its shutdown in February 2012. Most recently it had directed visitors to Coinbase. Now it belonged to Blockchain.

'Bitcoin.com is the crème de la crème,' Nic would say a few weeks later. 'That's like owning Sex.com for the future of finance.' (In 2010, as it happens, Sex.com was bought for $13 million, the highest price ever paid for an Internet domain name.) He had learned early the value of a good domain name. When he was a teenager, during the dot-com gold rush, a friend of his had bought up 'every single absurdly horrible thing you could say about the Mormon church dot com. Like, fuckmormons.com, mormonssuckdicks.com. And then he sold them all to the Mormon church.' His friend was like someone who buys a second home with the intention only of flipping it for a profit. The Church of Latter-day Saints wanted to prevent people from creating hateful and derogatory sites about their religion, and they were willing to pay to make sure of it. 'He made a *fucking killing*,' Nic says of his friend. 'When he told me his plan, I was like, "Fuckin' A. That's a good idea."'

Blockchain's corporate footprint was now impressively large. It included the world's most popular Bitcoin website, a treasure trove of data that functioned as a kind of search engine for the blockchain; the largest Bitcoin web wallet, which boasted 1.5 million users; ZeroBlock, a mobile app providing real-time market data and aggregating industry news; and a cryptocurrency trading platform. Nic now envisioned all of these disparate parts tied to 'our mothership', Bitcoin.com, on which he'd sell lucrative ad space. Blockchain's consumer wallet service and merchant app were free software; paid advertisements kept the company funded without the need for venture capital. 'For us,' Nic says, 'traffic and eyeballs are dollars.'

By early May, Blockchain had twenty employees. Indeed, one of the reasons Nic had conducted acquisitions was simply to gain employees who were already familiar with Bitcoin. It took too long to get engineers who lacked that knowledge up to speed. The biggest new hire was chief operations officer Peter Smith. A 'voluntaryist' like Roger Ver – he described himself as 'probably a little less radical than Roger, but not much' – his sleepy eyes and monotone delivery belied a sharp mind and an even sharper tongue when he was displeased. His background was vague: he had spent time in Africa and Singapore, and some years back, according to Peter, he had experienced a 'major liquidity event' that had set him up for life. Now he was looking for a new challenge, and Blockchain was it. 'Peter has a hard job. He's the guy behind the elephant,' Nic says wryly. He was to oversee from the highest level the company's software projects, legal affairs, business development.

Some employees thought Nic was turning over too much responsibility to Peter too quickly, but Nic was glad to have him on board. The task of managing a team of employees who were distributed around the world was not without its challenges. Time zone differences made it tough to coordinate their efforts, as did the lack of face-to-face interaction. Peter spent much of his time in New York City, while Nic Cary and Ben Reeves had their base in York, Bill Hill lived in Paris, and Changpeng Zhao, the head of technical development, in Tokyo. To communicate, they used Skype and Google Hangouts; they fired off emails at all hours of the day and night. Blockchain's nearly two dozen employees were all passionate about Bitcoin, and were willing to work long hours and dislocate their schedules if necessary to accomplish a task. Even granting, however, that there was no need to micromanage their work, it was still difficult to get them all to work toward a common goal. They would almost certainly, Nic thought, need to start consolidating the workforce in one or a few central locations before the year was out.

Nic was ferociously well organized. It was how he managed the chaos. Gone were the days when you could do as Roger Ver had in the spring of 2011, reading absolutely everything there was to read about Bitcoin. Just keeping up with the headlines was practically a full-time job. Nic maintained a spreadsheet on which he kept track of the upcoming conferences related to digital currency, the payments industry, and the future of banking, with notes telling him which if any of Blockchain's employees was going to attend each one. Nic himself was due at an event in Amsterdam in May. Everyone, it seemed, was trying to host the conference of the year. Nic was less enthusiastic about the big blowouts, where he saw the same faces every time, than he was about grassroots affairs like the conference he had attended in Buenos Aires the previous December. Argentina, he thought, could be fertile ground for Bitcoin. It was, after all, 'a country that has made a religion out of destroying its economy'.

He spent a great deal of time in airports. On an overnight flight to Santiago, the capital of Chile, in early May, it felt as if his body were stretched across a dozen time zones. Jet lag was no longer something that came and went; it was a constant state of being. He was almost always online. Work–life balance seemed like an impossible dream. In the past month he had traveled from New York to Washington, from Washington to Vancouver (continuing on to Seattle), from Seattle to Reykjavík, from Reykjavík to Paris, and from Paris to Nice. From there he had traveled on to Monaco by helicopter, before taking a plane to London, where he boarded a train on the East Coast Main Line bound for Newcastle and Edinburgh. Getting off in York, he touched base with Ben Reeves, but was soon in the air again, completing the last leg of a vast circuit back to New York, where he spoke at Atlantic Media's New York Ideas forum and then saddled up for the long haul to Santiago (by way of Toronto). There had been precious little downtime. Only in Nice, where he'd rented an apartment through 9flats. com – a sort of Airbnb that accepted payment in bitcoins – had he managed to recuperate. He went to bed at midnight, hoping to relax and get some sun the following day. Instead he slept for seventeen hours. When he awoke it was late afternoon. He went for a run on an empty stomach, then strolled along the boardwalk to find a good restaurant for dinner, his first meal of the day. He wound up gorging himself on steak tartare and pâté. It was a rare indulgence.

He could imagine what his old mentors would say: *Jesus, you thought you needed to move into something less stressful, and instead you picked the most ultimately stressful thing you possibly could have.* He didn't have an answer for that, other than that he was terrified of being bored. Besides, this was a once-in-a-lifetime opportunity, a chance to participate in something that could really improve the world. It deserved his best effort.

But not all was going well that spring. In the month of March no fewer than three Bitcoin companies had been hacked, resulting in the loss of hundreds of thousands of dollars in digital currency. The first, less than a week after Mt. Gox went down, was Alberta-based Flexcoin, a so-called 'Bitcoin bank' formed in 2011 to simplify the storage and transfer of bitcoins. On 2 March 2014, a hacker breached its hot wallet – vulnerable because of its connection to the Internet – and swiped the entire contents: 896 bitcoins, worth nearly $620,000 at the time. The company's official explanation was that the attacker had exploited a weakness in the website's code governing transfers between Flexcoin users. By overloading the system with thousands of simultaneous transfer requests from multiple accounts, the thief was able to overdraw the accounts before the system could figure out that they were in the red. Customers who had ponied up an extra 0.5 percent to put their bitcoins in Flexcoin's 'cold storage' – typically a hard drive kept offline to prevent just such intrusions – were unharmed, but those who had lost their funds were out of luck.[1] Flexcoin refused to compensate depositors – indeed, the terms of service technically relieved the company of all responsibility for lost bitcoins. The company, protesting that it did not 'have the resources, assets, or otherwise to come back from this loss', declared that it would be closing its doors immediately and redistributing to customers the bitcoins that had remained safe in cold storage.

On 4 March, only a week after Mt. Gox went down and the day after Flexcoin revealed that its entire hot wallet had been stolen, a cryptocurrency exchange called Poloniex, much smaller than Gox, was also hacked. It lost in the attack 12.3 percent of its funds, 76.69 bitcoins in total, then valued at around $50,000. The hackers had used roughly the same approach that was used against Flexcoin, though in this case Poloniex's security prevented the hot wallet from being entirely cleaned out; the unusual withdrawal activity triggered a freeze of the affected accounts. In response, the exchange's founder, Tristan D'Agosta, temporarily reduced all customer balances by 12.3 percent, reasoning that any other measure would have prompted users to flee the exchange. Since everyone's bitcoins were pooled together, those who pulled their funds out first would have been made whole, while those who acted last would have ended up with nothing. But he recorded the prior balances and committed to paying customers back over time, using exchange fees and even his personal funds. 'I take full responsibility,' D'Agosta wrote. 'I will be donating some of my own money, and I will not be taking [a] profit before the debt is paid.'

Poloniex, less than two months old, was a bizarre place, a trading platform for a host of new cryptocurrencies blinking in and out of existence, each seemingly with its own gimmick, its own set of rules for distribution and mining, its own niche it was trying to fill – PotCoin, LoveCoin, WolfCoin . . . Rather than bitcoins being exchanged for dollars, here altcoins were traded for bitcoins, which could then be converted elsewhere into dollars; and since the altcoins in their infancy were tremendously volatile – like Auroracoin, the one Charlie had been burned by – the profits could be correspondingly immense. Most altcoins were practically worthless in terms of both dollars and bitcoins, but, as with penny stocks, even the smallest rise in value could be a windfall for a major stakeholder, just as owning ten million shares of a stock that rises from $0.01 to $0.02 will net you a profit of $100,000.

And Poloniex was hardly the only exchange of this kind now in operation. It was impossible to sit at one's computer watching millions of dollars' worth of digital currencies being swapped in an online exchange that ran twenty-four hours a day, seven days a week, and was accessible from just about anywhere on the planet – all that illusory wealth convertible at will into legal tender – without feeling oneself witness to the terrible beauty of a truly free market. It was perhaps the first global market that could lay claim to the title.

Now that cryptocurrency had arrived, it seemed a logical development, perhaps even an endpoint, in the history of money. The last revolution had been the introduction of electronic money; the one before that, the end of the gold standard – the watershed moment when paper currency lost its tether to intrinsic value, when the paper become nothing but paper. Altcoins, which had nothing to recommend them except their code and which often were little more than carbon copies of Bitcoin, with far less developer support and little chance of inspiring mass adoption, were still more ethereal. They had value because enough people agreed that they had value – for the moment. On altcoin marketplaces you could sit back and watch the groundswell of enthusiasm grow for a particular cryptocurrency – perhaps only a few days or a few hours old – the Rabelaisian appetite mounting as its price rose, thousands of coins gobbled up in an instant, the cheerleading, the heartening stories of profit; and then the slowing of interest, the currency beginning to slide, panic setting in, a mass sell-off of the toxic and now overpriced asset – why wasn't it obvious before that it was over-priced? – while a few risk-takers, too clever by half, waited to scoop up large quantities of the coin on the cheap from all the poor saps who had bought high and held on too long. Bagholders, these unfortunates were called. A derisive moniker. It served them right, the thinking went. People who used the term were meanwhile counting their lucky stars they had gotten out while the getting was good, and knew they might well wind up on the other side of things the next go-around. Like the earlier revolutions, this sea change in the representation of value appeared irreversible.

Bitcoiners had fought hard to be taken seriously over the preceding four years, and were still fighting; many of them wanted to distance themselves as much as possible from altcoins, the also-rans of the cryptocurrency world. But Bitcoin exchanges, too, were vulnerable to theft. Hardly anyone needed further proof of this after Mt. Gox's meltdown, yet further proof was provided in the form of a hack attack on Bitcurex, Poland's top exchange. On the morning of 14 March 2014, trading on the exchange was halted after a number of bitcoins were swiped from its hot wallet. Although ten to twenty percent of the hot wallet funds were lost – with cold-storage bitcoins and fiat currency balances remaining intact – the Bitcurex team, like Poloniex's Tristan D'Agosta, presented the incident as a successful thwarting of what could have been a 'mass theft of [Bitcoin] funds'.[2] And indeed, Bitcurex presented something of an uplifting story compared to other disasters. Once the exchange's system registered the attack, automatic safety procedures had kicked in, preventing the hacker from performing any more unauthorized transactions. Then adminis-trators shut down the system to repair it and improve the security. Within a week, Bitcurex was running again, with all losses covered by its parent company – a necessary solution in an industry that had no government agency to insure deposits.

Even so, the rash of thefts fueled pessimism in some quarters. It was as if the fall of Mt. Gox had signaled to hackers that it was open season on Bitcoin businesses. What good was it for Bitcoin itself to be superior to other forms of electronic money if the companies holding customer funds could be knocked over as easily as a bank with a drowsy security guard? Members of the press and the public who had little understanding of computer security found it difficult to distinguish between well-managed and poorly managed companies – or between total disasters, such as Mt. Gox, and mitigated disasters, such as Bitcurex. The Bitcoin price began a devastating slide. An average of perhaps $680 in early March – with brief spikes above $700 – gave way by early April to an average of barely more than $400, with short-lived drops as low as $340.

For Nic Cary the thefts provided further vindication of Blockchain's own security measures. By making it impossible for Blockchain employees to access customer funds, it was likewise impossible for a hacker to access them through Blockchain's system. Whatever security precautions each wallet holder might be taking with his own bitcoins, this system presented hackers with hundreds of thousands of small targets rather than a single high-value target – namely, the company itself. (In terms of effort for potential hackers, it would be equivalent to mugging a million people one at a time versus robbing a single bank.) It was a system designed for the harsh realities of an imperfect world. 'Time after time after time, we have witnessed what happens when a company has custody of the money: they either run away with it, because they're bad guys, or they get hacked, because no small team – or even a big team or a well-funded team – can outcompete legions of well-motivated, smart, cooperating hackers,' Nic says. 'You just can't beat 'em. You're gonna get made eventually.' The mounting number of successful hack attacks on major retailers such as Target seemed to confirm his views, as did Flexcoin's *mea culpa*: 'Flexcoin has made every attempt to keep our servers as secure as possible, including regular testing. In our [nearly three] years of existence we have successfully repelled thousands of attacks. But in the end, this was simply not enough.'

But through it all, Nic Cary kept faith in Bitcoin itself. Bitcoin would never be worthless, no matter what; perhaps there had once been a possibility that its value would go to zero, but no longer. Fiat currencies had suffered worse. The defunct Zimbabwean dollar retains some value as a collectible; the Reichsmark after the fall of Nazi Germany had possessed a small, even if vanishingly small, fraction of its former buying power. Bitcoin would still be worth something, he thought, 'even if the whole thing erupts in some kind of crazy black swan shitstorm'.

In February 2014, putting his money where his mouth was, he had donated $10,000 worth of bitcoins to his alma mater, the University of Puget Sound, which the university accepted through a nonprofit account with BitPay. Puget Sound, having no gift policy pertaining to digital currencies, had needed guidance on how to accept the donation; the process revealed how elegant, how advanced the Bitcoin ecosystem was becoming and what sort of cross-border transactions it made possible: BitPay emailed an invoice to Nic – who was in Berlin on business – for the pledged amount; using his phone, he scanned the invoice's QR code, which contained details of where the bitcoins should be sent; BitPay received notice of the payment instantly, and once it was confirmed on the blockchain as a legitimate transaction it was credited to the university's BitPay account in US dollars, available for withdrawal to a bank account. That electronic transfer of slightly more than 14.5 bitcoins was, as far as anyone could tell, the first digital currency gift ever made to an American college or university.

And there were other bright spots. On 13 March, Xapo – a new digital wallet and 'vault' for bitcoins – launched publicly after raising $20 million in a Series A round. One of its investors was Ribbit Capital, a Silicon Valley venture capital firm whose founder, Micky Malka, sat on the board of directors of the Bitcoin Foundation. Xapo came out of stealth mode already boasting several thousand accounts to its name, including hedge funds, sovereign wealth funds, venture capital firms, and other large institutional investors. Its Argentine founder, Wences Casares, had partnered with Malka in no fewer than four financial services companies before launching Xapo.[3] In what could not but sound like a response to the Mt. Gox fiasco, he sought to assure potential customers that he understood their security concerns. 'Bitcoin's ultimate success will be based on trust,' he declared, 'both in the currency itself and in the industry's security and service providers.' Customer funds would not only be protected from theft but would be fully insured in the event of a catastrophe.

To a post-Gox world, this promise sounded good. Nic Cary felt a certain kinship with Casares, who had a home in Pirque and who had been born in Patagonia. And Erik Voorhees vouched for him, calling Xapo's CEO 'an extremely successful businessperson and all-around fantastic guy. One of the most interesting and genuine people I've met.' Erik expected 'huge success from Xapo', he went on. 'It will become a trusted pillar of the Bitcoin ecosystem.' But Satoshi Nakamoto's revolutionary idea had been to take trust out of commerce. No more banks, no more reliance on third parties to store and safeguard your money. Now a new kind of bank was being born.

Watching the development of Bitcoin from its inception to the present day was like watching a time-lapse film on the history of money and banking. At first it was a free-for-all. Before Mt. Gox – as in the days before a standardized system of weights and measures was established for metal coins – there was no reliable way to determine the value of a bitcoin, which in any case was almost zero. To most people there seemed precious little reason to ascribe any value whatsoever to the digital tokens. Ten thousand were exchanged for a couple of pizzas; Roger Ver, in his zeal to win converts, gave away whole bitcoins. The earliest wallet services were provided by individual coders; the system of exchange was primitive or nonexistent. But things soon began to settle down. The first institutions – Mt. Gox, TradeHill, BitInstant, and Bitcoinica – arose, promising greater utility, better security, and a real marketplace. With them came the need for trust. When that trust proved to be misplaced, shoddier institutions gradually gave way – though not before damage was done – to better ones; reputable entrepreneurs took the place of renegades. (If Xapo offered a new kind of bank vault for cryptocurrency, it was also true that companies such as Flexcoin had already been storing people's digital wealth; they had simply done an imperfect job of it.) The industry began to be policed from within and without. The hacks and scandals were, in a sense, a mechanism that drove the increasing sophistication of the Bitcoin ecosystem. Whatever else it was, the Bitcoin industry had proved to be, as *New Yorker* writer John Brooks once wrote of the world's first stock exchange, established in 1611 in an open courtyard in Amsterdam, 'a laboratory in which new human reactions were revealed'.[4]

The speed with which Bitcoin had matured astonished everyone. From the first time digital currency was used to buy anything to the day Xapo launched with $20 million in funding, less than four years had elapsed.

The floodgates to investment now opened. On 17 March, OKCoin, the exchange that was now China's largest by trading volume – having dethroned BTC China – announced a Series A round of its own for $10 million. Eight days later, Kraken, the San Francisco-based Bitcoin exchange run by Roger Ver's friend Jesse Powell, raised $5 million. The news broke on the same day as the IRS's tax guidance for Bitcoin. Unsurprisingly, Powell said that much of the $5 million would be spent on legal fees and other compliance costs.[5] It was the price of being a pioneer. The following day, as if not to be outdone, Jeremy Allaire and Sean Neville, founders of Circle Internet Financial, announced that Circle had raised an additional $17 million on top of the $9 million from its Series A in October. In a mere two weeks, $52 million of new investment had been announced, more than fifty percent of the total raised by Bitcoin startups in all of 2013.

The boldest investors were clearly undeterred by the security failures of a few Bitcoin companies. Venture capitalist Marc Andreessen, whose firm Andreessen Horowitz had participated in raising funds for Coinbase, said in late March – after a month-long period that had brought an avalanche of bad news for the currency

– that he was having déjà vu. Bitcoin, he explained, is 'weird and scary and nerdy, and it's full of scams and frauds, just like the Internet was.'[6] He knew whereof he spoke, having cocreated Mosaic, the first major Web browser, and cofounded Netscape Communications, which he helped take public one month after his twenty-fourth birthday. At first he had thought Bitcoin presented no investment opportunities. Eventually he became convinced that it did. He approached Andreessen Horowitz's advisory board about Bitcoin in April 2013, during an annual meeting at the Rosewood Sand Hill hotel in Menlo Park, California. 'At first blush, you're going to think we're out of our minds,' he said, 'but we're going to invest in a fake mathematical currency.'[7] By the time of his January 2014 editorial for the *New York Times*, the venture capital firm bearing his name had sunk millions into Bitcoin startups, with much of it going to Coinbase. Then Mt. Gox blew up, leaving a hole in the industry for better companies to fill. Far from getting out, it was revealed in March that Andreessen Horowitz planned to invest hundreds of millions more in Bitcoin companies in the coming years. It was a tremendous vote of confidence in the digital currency ecosystem, not only in Bitcoin's core function as currency but perhaps even more in all that blockchain technology might lead to, innovations now being spoken of in the highest echelons of geek culture as near certainties: smart contracts, improved clearing and settlement of securities transactions, transparent accounting for nonprofits, decentralized voting . . . innovations which had prompted *The Economist* in mid-March to declare, as if echoing Andreas Antonopoulos, that Bitcoin might prove to be not merely the money of the Internet but 'the Internet of money'.

OF ALL THE THINGS ABOUT his new life Nic Cary had not expected, perhaps the most unexpected was the attention he received. He could not get used to thinking of himself as a public figure. When asked by members of the Bitcoin Foundation to run for a board seat, he declined. He had never wanted to set himself up as the voice of Bitcoin. But he did feel an obligation, as Blockchain's chief executive, to explain the company's services to potential customers. This led him by degrees to a position of authority within the community. In April 2014, at the Inside Bitcoins conference in New York, he gave an upbeat presentation on the tremendous growth enjoyed over the preceding year by Bitcoin generally and Blockchain particularly. On 26 January 2013 there had existed only 100,000 Blockchain wallets, he told the audience, but one year later the number of wallets had increased by an order of magnitude to one million. By then WordPress, Reddit, OKCupid, Overstock, TigerDirect, Zynga, and Virgin Galactic – Richard Branson's commercial space company, which planned to fly paying customers beyond the Earth's atmosphere for $250,000 a ticket – were all accepting Bitcoin.

His leadership status was again evident on the night of 7 May in Santiago, at the home of a man named Javier Salcedo, who had cofounded Chile's first Bitcoin exchange. Salcedo was hosting a barbecue. There, with several young men huddled around, Nic showed off a test version of the new Blockchain wallet app for Android phones. He spoke fluent Spanish, and he socialized with the easy manner of a fraternity president, amiable and direct. 'This won't be available yet when we launch this, but you'll be able to press that' – he indicated a button on the screen – 'and find California Cantina [a local restaurant] and all the other places around here where you can go spend your bitcoins.' The app would scrape the data from a variety of online sources and serve it up for easy browsing. His team had already finished all the coding and design work on this geolocation feature, but, he explained apologetically, intensive quality assurance remained to be done before he could release it to users.

If Barry Silbert was encouraging investors to think of Bitcoin as a new asset class, to hoard it until its scarcity drove up the price – for he believed that only when Bitcoin's market cap was much higher could it fulfill its potential – Nic was promoting the use of Bitcoin now, today, as an independent currency. This was why it gave him such pleasure to tell stories of the small business owners, such as Sofiane Bouhaddi, who had been won over to acceptance of Bitcoin and were happily using Blockchain's app to accept the money of the future. Nic received his salary in bitcoins and, as much as possible, spent bitcoins to meet his daily needs without converting them into dollars, pounds, or euros. His old friend Erik Voorhees, in Panama, was doing the same. Erik's startup, Coinapult, operated mostly on Bitcoin. He paid the company's web hosting costs and some of its employees with digital currency. In his own life, too, he eschewed ordinary money as much as possible. Using bitcoins he bought his home goods from Overstock; he paid his cable, electricity, and phone bills; he settled bar tabs and restaurant bills with his friends and colleagues. By March 2014 he was even planning to buy a car with bitcoins. The new Blockchain app would make it easier than ever to spend Bitcoin as currency instead of keeping it locked away as digital gold.

Two days later, Nic gave an informal talk at the Pontificia Universidad Católica de Chile, an elite institute of higher education founded in 1888. The talk was held in the university's new Innovation Center – a fourteen-story monolith of gray concrete with huge recessed windows that looked for all the world like a giant game of Tetris frozen in time. It was a far cry from a back-yard barbecue. Although the talk was a last-minute affair, arranged only a few days before, the glassed-in conference room soon filled up with entrepreneurs, teachers, students, and technologists. That was one of the things Nic had noticed about Bitcoin: its ability to draw together people of diverse backgrounds and widely varying interests. Some were interested in Bitcoin for social reasons, others because of their politics; still others had come to it by way of economics or business or computer science.

Mindful of his audience, Nic sought to establish at the outset his love of Chile, his second home. His father, he explained, had moved to the country in 1993 to teach English and lived in a tiny apartment in Santiago. He was now married to a Chilean woman and served as executive director of an English-language training program. Nic, who had been visiting the country every year since he was a boy, was excited about the future of innovation in Chile. The country was developing rapidly, and there was a chance over the next few years to make real improvements. 'Revisiting the world of finance,' he said, 'is really critical to that.' His message was clear: Bitcoin is not just for the United States. Bitcoin is a global story.

The way Nic told it, in fact, Bitcoin was the latest chapter in a story that had been unfolding for twenty years, that of the digitization of physical goods and services. Twenty years ago, sending word to someone had meant posting a letter in the mail; now it typically meant firing off an email or text message. Music had evolved from records to cassette tapes to compact discs to downloadable files and finally to streaming media, so that a whole generation had grown up listening to music without ever plopping down in front of a hi-fi cabinet. 'The same thing happened to movies,' Nic said. 'The same thing happened to books.' As Marc Andreessen, both physically and metaphorically the quintessential egghead, had put it in a 2011 op-ed for the *Wall Street Journal*, software was eating the world. Amazon had killed Borders; Netflix had destroyed Blockbuster. Now Bitcoin would topple – what? On the hit list were Western Union, MoneyGram, various banking services, even small-cap foreign currencies. Just as people of all ages now expected to be able to download and stream media from the cloud, Nic told Gómez and the others, 'for millennials and [other] people who are growing up with all this digital media, there is an expectation that money will become digital too.'

His sentiments would be echoed later that year by national governments as different as Ecuador's and Australia's. Sam Dastyari, a member of the Australian parliament leading an inquiry into how Bitcoin could give a much-needed jolt to the country's 'stale' banking industry, believed it was a matter of regulators adapting to a technology whose time had come. 'There is going to be a place for some kind of digital-style currency,' Dastyari said. 'There is inevitability that it will play some kind of role.'[8] Ecuador, a nation in which forty percent of the population had no bank account, planned to go further. In July, the country's National Assembly approved the creation of an official Ecuadorian digital money, while simultaneously banning the use of its obvious competitor, Bitcoin.[9] It would exist alongside the US dollar, which had been since the year 2000 the national currency of Ecuador, adopted in place of its former unit of currency, the sucre, in order to stave off economic crisis. Although it was set up more as a mobile payments system than a true digital currency, President Rafael Correa believed the new electronic money – the first national digital money in the world – would help the unbanked within his country to enter the modern economy. By December, it was said, Ecuadorians would be able to exchange physical cash for digital money held in mobile wallets on their phones.

All of this was in keeping with what Nic sought to impart to his audience in Chile. The world Bitcoin had brought into being was moving so quickly now that predictions were hardly made before they began to come true. After the talk, Alfonso Gómez, executive president of the Innovation Center, a dapper man with a high forehead and closely cropped white beard, who looked to be in his late fifties, approached Nic. 'I can tell you this will not be the last event we have about Bitcoin,' he said. He told a story about how he had come to have a bitcoin himself. He and Wences Casares, the CEO of Xapo, had recently shared a taxi ride and Casares had had no cash to split the fare. He'd reimbursed Gómez by sending him one bitcoin. 'This will be worth a million dollars one day,' Casares told him, half in jest.

Nic felt good about the talk. He came alive during the deep discussions required to educate people about Bitcoin, discussions that touched on the nature of money and the benefit of digital technology. Watching the light bulb come on in someone's head – that was what kept him going. Just as his sister, Tatiana, had followed in her father's footsteps by entering the Peace Corps, Nic was his father's son in his capacity as a leader and teacher.

He had another chance to use these talents before leaving Chile. From the university, he took a taxi to the offices of Aurus, a venture capital firm located in an upscale area of Santiago known as Vitacura. The firm's managing partners, chief financial officer, and a pretty senior associate joined him in a conference room. Most of them knew little about Bitcoin, and Nic hoped to open their eyes to the tremendous opportunity it presented for entrepreneurs and investors. But he wasn't looking for capital himself. Aurus, which had opened its doors in July 2008 – 'in the days of Internet passwords', as one of its partners put it – was, although a big deal in Chile, a relatively small firm by American standards, with a $60 million fund that invested in high-tech and life sciences startups. And besides, Blockchain had achieved positive cash flow all on its own, with no pressing need for outside money.

No pressing internal need, that is. But there were external pressures. The day before, news had leaked that BitPay had raised $30 million of new venture capital in a Series A round – a round that valued the company at $160 million. It was the largest single capital raise ever for a Bitcoin startup. Index Ventures, which owned stakes in Dropbox, Etsy, and SoundCloud, among other Web 2.0 companies, and which had offices in San Francisco, London, and Geneva, and on the tax haven of Jersey, led the round. Peter Thiel also took part, doubling down on his earlier BitPay investment, and this time fellow billionaire Richard Branson, whose Virgin Galactic was a client of BitPay, joined him. By the end of the month, Atlanta-based BitPay would reveal that it was processing $1 million a day in Bitcoin transactions – on pace to shatter its 2013 record of approximately $110 million in transactions for the year – and that it was opening offices in Amsterdam, San Francisco, and Buenos Aires. Its CEO, Tony Gallippi – who in late May stepped down from the top job, assuming the role of executive chairman – was looking to add seventy employees to his team, tripling a workforce that already spanned three continents. At least forty of the new hires would be software developers, and the next-largest contingent would be new members of its international sales team.[10] Aggressive growth was the name of the game. Seldom had the cottage industry around a new technology matured so quickly into an attractive investment for billionaires. If Bitcoin skeptics were still plentiful among the rank and file of journalists and economists, more of the smart money than ever was on Bitcoin succeeding.

As for Andreessen's pledge to invest millions more in crypto-currency startups, Nic Cary felt certain that at least some of that river of capital would flow to Blockchain's competitors. It would become harder than ever to compete for top talent. Already BitPay had snapped up Jeff Garzik, one of Bitcoin's core developers. It was yet another sign that the industry was maturing. Before the year was out, Blockchain would need to find investors of its own. Nic's visit to Aurus, though not a pitch meeting, would be in some measure practice for the real pitches to come.

While the Aurus partners began to eat lunch, Nic stood up and walked to the whiteboard at the front of the room. 'Bitcoin is a totally global phenomenon,' he began, 'so it doesn't belong to any country. It's not Silicon Valley-based; it doesn't care about New York. It's a technology; it's a protocol. It's open-source. The most important thing to realize is that the network itself is much more important than the daily discourse about the price of the currency.' That network, he went on to explain, was essentially 'a property rights system that lives in a distributed environment', with no single party controlling it. Currency was the first means of experimenting with the usefulness of this system, though other applications were possible. 'First we get Bitcoin right as a currency, we get it right for transactions,' he said, 'and then these other things will follow.'

He was warming to his subject. But the conversation soon bogged down in the intricacies of Bitcoin mining. Nic felt uncomfortable. Mining was his least favorite topic. It was a difficult one, made more so by the extreme lengths to which it had been carried by miners hoping to mint digital gold.

At first, just after Satoshi Nakamoto released the Bitcoin software, you could mine bitcoins with an ordinary laptop or desktop computer. That was what Hal Finney had done. But soon people caught on, and as more processing power was applied to solving the blocks, they became harder to solve, which consequently upped the ante on the sort of computer hardware required to do the work. High-performance graphics processors became par for the course. (For the benefit of the Aurus partners, Nic, now diagramming on the whiteboard, compared the numbers being crunched by Bitcoin miners to especially challenging sudoku puzzles. 'As computing power improves,' he said, 'the sudokus get bigger, so you have to have more computing power to solve the problems.') Miners pooled their computing resources and divvied up the block rewards they received – now twenty-five bitcoins per block, where once the reward had been fifty. In 2013, the operation became still more advanced. Microprocessor manufacturers began turning out chips designed specifically for Bitcoin mining. Each of these chips was a type of ASIC, or application-specific integrated circuit, and a single one for the task of producing bitcoins was worth thousands of ordinary, all-purpose chips. It was a massive leap forward in mining hardware. It was also the beginning of the end for Bitcoin mining as a radically democratic, anyone-can-participate venture. Anyone who couldn't shell out five figures or more for specialized equipment would be mining to no purpose, bleeding money in direct proportion to the increased cost of their electricity bill. When the Bitcoin price exploded in late 2013, it made Bitcoin miners, in the words of *Bloomberg Businessweek*, 'the rare grunts who can also get rich'.[11] Now it was an arms race, as chip manufacturers raced to design better ASICs and Bitcoin hardware startups raced to design, build, and bring to market specialized computers that did one thing and one thing only: print virtual money. 'No arms race in the history of the chip industry even comes close to this,' said Ravi Iyengar, a former chip designer for Samsung who quit his job to launch CoinTerra, a startup dedicated to producing Bitcoin mining rigs. All the while, of course, the feverish mining activity was serving to confirm digital currency transactions, benefiting the system as a whole. Nic estimated, and now told Aurus, that there were 'billions of dollars of computer hardware dedicated to managing and securing the Bitcoin network'.

Eventually one of the older partners spoke up. 'I don't get it,' he admitted. 'I'm old-fashioned, but if you work, you produce something. But Bitcoin is created out of nothing, right? With no underlying asset.' Surely, he asked, if it was necessary to exchange fiat currency for bitcoins, then digital currency could never replace fiat currency for everyday use?

In fact, Nic replied, it was increasingly possible to live almost exclusively using digital currency, which was of course minted by miners, not exchanges. Blockchain had 'completely exited' from the traditional financial system. 'We run an international business,' he informed them. 'We have no bank account. All of our employees are paid in bitcoin, we pay our services in bitcoin, and we don't have any need to operate with an existing financial network at all.'

Could Blockchain ever go public while operating like that? one of the venture capitalists wanted to know.

Blockchain's CEO thought about it. 'It's a great question,' he said finally. 'I don't know. If we're successful, we won't need to – that's the point.'

WHILE NIC CARY CAME AWAY from his meetings in Chile keenly aware of how much work remained to be done before digital currency would be adopted by the masses – aware the battle for Bitcoin was still taking place one mind at a time – Barry Silbert's mind had long been made up. He had gone all in. By the early summer of 2014 he had invested personally in twenty-eight Bitcoin startups, more than any other angel investor, even Roger Ver. Deciding to yoke SecondMarket to Bitcoin one year earlier, he had known the gambit might fail, resulting in a loss of time, money, and manpower he could scarcely afford to waste. But he had been equally aware that Bitcoin might take off while the rest of SecondMarket's business stalled. If that happened, he was prepared to go so far as to sell the company, walking away from a decade of hard work and leaving the Bitcoin Investment Trust and other cryptocurrency ventures to stand on their own. The third possibility was that both Bitcoin and the rest of SecondMarket would perform well, and this in fact is what happened. In the first half of 2014, Barry's company conducted more than $900 million in secondary transactions for private companies – six months that were not merely record-breaking but which more than tripled SecondMarket's performance during the same period of the previous year. Ten years after its founding, SecondMarket had caught a second wind.

Barry's work ethic was as superhuman as ever. He showed up early, ate lunch at his desk, and generally gave every indication that he was still running a startup. His only concession to the approach of middle age had come with the birth of his daughter; he had begun to shave an hour here and there off his time in the office. But having his apartment nearby, within walking distance, meant he was still able to pull long days. Sundays he spent catching up on email. Each week, as messages flooded in, he filed them into three categories: To Review, To Respond, and Urgent; it was the Urgent folder that he cleared on Sundays. Meanwhile the others – To Review and To Respond – swelled and swelled, until they contained hundreds of emails. (It had been some eighteen months since Barry had last attained 'inbox zero', the Holy Grail of overworked people in the Internet age.) Demands on his time were so constant and, except for the most important ones, so far beyond hope of timely satisfaction that his assistant was forced to book appointments in his schedule months in advance.

Gradually he realized that his heart was no longer in the parts of his business that were not about Bitcoin. Bitcoin had first divided his attention and then drawn it away from the rest of SecondMarket almost entirely. From the moment he had bought his first coins, his ambition for involvement with the digital currency had steadily grown, until, in the early months of 2014, he decided it would be best to spin out of SecondMarket as independent entities the company's Bitcoin businesses – the Bitcoin Investment Trust and the trading desk. Then, as spring rolled into summer, his ambition grew further. He wanted to create a new firm entirely dedicated to digital currencies.

In the second week of June, one year after announcing to his staff that SecondMarket would be launching a private Bitcoin fund, Barry stepped down as CEO. In his place at SecondMarket would be an interim chief executive, and in place of his old job he would now assume the role of chairman and CEO of Digital Currency Group, the new company to which he would devote his full attention.

It would be no small venture. At its inception, that company would preside over an asset management business to be called Grayscale Investments – a business of which the Bitcoin Investment

Trust would be the flagship product – and a digital currency trading firm arising from SecondMarket's Bitcoin trading team, to be christened Sypher Trading. (It was later renamed Genesis Trading.) Together these two businesses were bringing in between $7 million and $8 million in revenue. Digital Currency Group would also receive from SecondMarket's holding company between $20 million and $25 million worth of bitcoins. The Bitcoin exchange Barry intended to launch would also be part of DCG, with its own distinct brand identity and team. It was taking longer to set up than Barry had originally hoped, but his ambition for it had not diminished. When established, it would set the 'global reference price' of Bitcoin, replacing top forex-style exchanges like Bitstamp as the definitive benchmark by which not only regular trades but also over-the-counter trades were made.

And that was not all. Even as early participants in the Bitcoin Investment Trust had seen their shares rise dramatically in value through the fall of 2013 – and, despite later drops in price, remain well above their original value – so Barry Silbert's original sum of $200,000, sunk into Bitcoin when its price was in the single digits, had multiplied enormously. Out of the increase he made angel investments in Bitcoin startups, often paying them in the coin of their own realm, with the result that he now owned stakes in most of the Bitcoin startups of consequence, including BitPay, Coinbase, and Coinapult. (Not, however, Blockchain.) His personal investment vehicle, Bitcoin Opportunity Corp., took on a life of its own. Outside investors now came calling; to them Barry's portfolio looked like the best way to make a bet on the entire industry, on dozens of pick-and-shovel outfits that had sprung up amid the Bitcoin gold rush. Bain Capital Ventures put in $1 million, while a New York firm, RRE Ventures, put in more than $3 million, a round that valued the company – that is, Barry's portfolio of investments – at $25 million, 125 times the amount that Barry had personally bet on Bitcoin only two years before.

With the blessing of RRE and Bain, he then went to SecondMarket's board of directors to propose a merger between Bitcoin Opportunity Corp. and Digital Currency Group. (Never mind the fact that DCG barely existed yet.) The board agreed. Overnight, then, DCG would go from owning two Bitcoin businesses – the BIT and the trading firm – to owning stakes in thirty businesses. Barry was inspired in this above all by Warren Buffett's legendary Berkshire Hathaway. If any company could be seen as a synecdoche for the US economy as a whole, it was Berkshire, which had more than fifty subsidiaries and owned companies in such disparate industries as railroads and banking, along with household names like Geico and Dairy Queen. Investing in Berkshire, which traded publicly on the New York Stock Exchange, was over the decades the best way for people to partake not only in Warren Buffett's investing acumen but in the fortunes of a cross section of key industries. The stock climbed and climbed until, in the summer of 2014, for the first time ever, the value of a single class A share of Berkshire stock topped $200,000 – more than eight hundred times the price of the next most expensive stock in the world.

Barry believed that by diversifying DCG's holdings and taking it public, he could turn his company into the Berkshire of Bitcoin. 'There's investor demand for this type of thing and there is no way to invest in this ecosystem in the public market,' he says, 'and so this is the best way to do it.' And there was another reason to go public: it would give DCG a 'publicly traded currency' – that is, company shares – which could be sold to raise capital and used to make further acquisitions. 'So if we want to go buy XYZ Bitcoin company, we'd buy that company using DCG shares,' he says. 'The stock would only be used for outright acquisitions; I don't think we would fund businesses that way. But it will be very easy for us to raise cash in the public market and then use cash to make those investments.'

But first he had to overcome his own reservations about public stock markets. In December 2011 he had identified in testimony before a US Senate subcommittee several structural problems that continued to exist in the public markets, among them 'short-term trading fueled by computers, the lack of research coverage for small-cap companies, [and] the focus on beating quarterly earnings projections' – all of which, he said, 'have whittled away the public's trust and confidence in the public stock markets, and have made entrepreneurs such as myself less interested in taking their companies public.' His views hadn't changed. But US stock markets were the deepest pool of capital in the world. The opportunity they presented for his new venture was unignorable. And so, despite his qualms, he planned to fast-track Digital Currency Group to an IPO.

He would have in this effort a high caliber of help. As it turned out, a founding partner of RRE Ventures, James Robinson III – Jim to those who knew him – had the ear of Lawrence Summers, who had parlayed his reputation as a leading economist into important posts in the administrations of three American presidents, including, under the Clinton administration, the position of Treasury Secretary, where his role in pushing for deregulation of the financial industry would later make him anathema to the political left. Through 2013 and into 2014, Summers had gradually become convinced that the Great Recession and the anemic recovery that followed were harbingers of a new state of world affairs, one in which existing macroeconomic policy would be inadequate to solve unemployment and achieve maximum productivity, at least not without hurting financial stability. He had also, like so many other dissenters from mainstream economics before him, including Barry Silbert, grown interested in Bitcoin. He approached Jim Robinson for advice about what role he should play in the digital currency ecosystem. RRE had just completed its funding of Bitcoin Opportunity Corp., and Robinson thought immediately of Barry's company. It would give Summers all by itself a window into dozens of Bitcoin companies. Barry Silbert himself was an additional draw.

Over the years, he and Summers had met perhaps three times, though each time their exchanges had lasted no more than a few minutes. 'He remembers me from the Facebook stuff,' Barry says, meaning SecondMarket's dealings in private company stock. 'Given his history with Facebook, that's the thing that got his interest.' (Lawrence Summers had been president of Harvard on the day in April 2004 when Cameron and Tyler Winklevoss and their business partner, Divya Narendra, marched into his office to complain about Mark Zuckerberg. The meeting did not go well. 'Rarely have I encountered such swagger, and I tried to respond in kind,' Summers was to say. 'One of the things you learn as a college president is that if an undergraduate is wearing a tie and jacket on Thursday afternoon at three o'clock, there are two possibilities. One is that they're looking for a job and have an interview; the other is that they are an asshole. This was the latter case.' The Winklevosses took such offense at the former university president's remarks that they addressed a lengthy open letter, cosigned by Narendra, to the current Harvard president, complaining about their ill treatment, both past and present, at Summers' hands.)[12]

There was another point of contact between Summers and Barry Silbert, and that was Chamath Palihapitiya. As a former Facebook executive, Palihapitiya, whose firm had invested $15 million in SecondMarket three years before, was close with Sheryl Sandberg, Facebook's chief operating officer. Sandberg, in turn, had received innumerable boosts from Summers in her academic and professional career, first during her time as a student in the economics department at Harvard, where he was her thesis adviser, and later at the World Bank, where he was the chief economist and she was his research assistant, and later still in Washington during the Clinton administration, where she served as his chief of staff when he was Deputy Treasury Secretary and continued to do so after he advanced to Treasury Secretary. Palihapitiya was also close with Sandberg's husband, Dave Goldberg, the CEO of SurveyMonkey and a Bitcoin enthusiast. So the potential for back-channel vetting of Barry Silbert was rich. And the fact that Palihapitiya sat on the board of SecondMarket could hardly have failed to impress Summers as a vote of confidence in Barry by a man he trusted – or, at least, by a man his protégée trusted.

He and Barry had coffee together in Manhattan in early June. Barry laid out his vision for his companies, and they talked about how Summers could get involved. In his own mind there was no doubt that the elder man would be an asset. Having seen Summers speak on several occasions, he was convinced of the economist's brilliance and believed he would bring an interesting perspective to the Bitcoin industry; moreover, he had always believed that it was a sound business strategy to surround yourself with people smarter than you. But it was more than that. Summers' reputation was such that his involvement with Digital Currency Group, the lending of his name to the company, would likely accelerate Barry's stalled effort to launch a New York-based Bitcoin exchange. There was also, for Barry, his own larger global strategy to consider – a strategy, still embryronic, whose fulfillment lay who knew how many years in the future but which was already beginning to guide his actions, and for which Summers' relationships with the heads of foreign banks, including foreign central banks, could prove invaluable. Finally, there was the public relations benefit to Bitcoin itself. Winning so august a person as Lawrence Summers visibly to the cause of Bitcoin would, Barry thought, spark a 'real fundamental change in the narrative about Bitcoin – away from "tulip bubble", "Ponzi scheme" to "Perhaps this is an investable asset class" and "Perhaps this really is potentially as big as the Internet."'

Ultimately, Larry Summers said yes. He committed to joining Bitcoin Opportunity Corp. as a strategic adviser and, once Digital Currency Group was formed and had absorbed Barry's investment vehicle, he would formally – and, if Barry had his way, with great fanfare – join DCG's board. He would be then not a mere adviser but a full board member, visibly attached to one of the most ambitious Bitcoin companies and having a say in its future direction. Barry was thrilled.

The runway to Digital Currency Group's IPO would be paved with outside funding. The incorporation of Bitcoin Opportunity Corp. into DCG would result in a company worth somewhere between $75 million and $100 million, he figured, after which the company would seek to raise $25 million to $50 million privately. 'And then once the value of that business is $300 million to $400 million is when we would look to take it public,' he says. He didn't expect this to happen before 2015. But the precise timing would depend to a great extent on the price of Bitcoin itself. 'Right now we own $20 million in bitcoins,' he said in June. 'If the price goes up [ten times], the value of not just the bitcoins but the entire portfolio goes up pretty significantly. This could all happen very fast, or it could never happen. But the price of Bitcoin will be a big driver of that.'

Ever since the price had dropped below $500 in March, revealing the brief reign of quadruple-digit prices as merely a bubble in an overheated market, Barry had been confident that another bubble was ahead, one that would potentially drive the price as high as $1,500 or $2,000 a coin. By early June, it looked as if the rocket ship were taking off: from an average of about $450 in mid-May the price had shot up to an average of $675, and briefly went still higher, close to $700. But then circumstances intervened. On 12 June, the US Marshals Service announced that it planned to auction off slightly more than 29,656 bitcoins that had been seized from Silk Road. The civil asset forfeiture action set in motion months before by Judge J. Paul Oetken was bearing fruit. Only American citizens would be eligible for the 27 June auction, and the bar for entry was high – it required a $200,000 wire transfer from a bank located in the United States. On the news, the price of Bitcoin promptly crashed to about $550. The reason was plain. For the past month the average daily trading volume on Bitstamp, one of the largest exchanges, had been only about eleven thousand bitcoins. Now the Marshals Service was proposing to dump nearly three times that amount – albeit in over-the-counter transactions – in a single day.

Nevertheless, Barry Silbert saw an opportunity. The auction's entry requirements barred a lot of people from participating, whether because they couldn't afford to pony up the $200,000 deposit, couldn't meet the minimum bid size – a block of three thousand bitcoins, worth some $1.8 million – or because they were foreigners. But that didn't have to be the case. He could use the SecondMarket platform to organize a syndicate of bidders, lowering the barriers to entry – he made the minimum bid size $50,000 – and opening up the auction to investors around the world. Syndicate participants would also enjoy total privacy; with SecondMarket serving as their official front, they would not have to reveal their identities to the US Marshals office. In return, SecondMarket would collect a one percent auction fee from successful syndicate bidders, ten percent of which Barry pledged to donate to the Electronic Frontier Foundation, a nonprofit organization that accepted Bitcoin donations and was dedicated to fighting for digital privacy rights. Forty-two investors joined the syndicate, submitting a total of 186 bids, the total value of which was 48,013 bitcoins – far more than the number available in the auction.

In the end, however, all of the syndicate members came up short, as did forty-four other bidders. Despite its efforts, SecondMarket didn't clear a dime from the auction. A single bidder, the venture capitalist Tim Draper, claimed all ten lots, having likely spent at least $17.7 million to do so. Draper planned to use the digital wealth, in partnership with a company called Vaurum, in which he'd invested, to finance Bitcoin exchange services in the developing world. (Obtaining bitcoins was still difficult for many of the unbanked.) At a press conference, he praised Bitcoin's ability to 'provide liquidity and confidence to markets that have been hamstrung by weak currencies'. Like Nic Cary, he singled out Argentina as a country that had been repeatedly devastated by out-of-control inflation. (According to a JPMorgan report, inflation in Argentina was on pace to reach forty-five percent in 2014.) 'We are all going to be so much better off because of Bitcoin,' he said.

SecondMarket's syndicate may not have won any of the blocks, but Barry Silbert knew there would be more to come. There were still 144,336 bitcoins in limbo – seized from Ross Ulbricht's computer and waiting to be either forfeited to the US government or returned as his rightful property. If the government got them, they would almost certainly be auctioned off just like the others. In the meantime, Barry was prepared to celebrate the milestone the first auction represented. Rather than sitting on the loot indefinitely, or dumping it indiscriminately onto a public exchange, the Marshals Service had sold it to private investors at the highest possible price. In doing so, the US government formally acknowledged the commodity value of Bitcoin.[13]

And yet, as summer rolled on, still there was no official word regarding a classification for Bitcoin. The SEC could have tried to declare it a security, and the CFTC could have decided to call it a commodity. But both were staying mum. At the understaffed CFTC, still grappling with the implications of the Dodd–Frank Act, which had made the 700-person agency responsible for policing the entire $700 trillion swaps market, nobody was even working on the issue, according to one source. Employees felt they had bigger fish to fry.

The New York Department of Financial Services, however, was losing no time in formulating guidelines for the regulation of Bitcoin businesses. On 17 July, it released for all companies operating in the state of New York or serving customers in New York a proposed set of requirements that would apply to the handling of digital currency on behalf of others, whether receiving it, transmitting it, storing it, or converting it into another currency. The proposal, which in this preliminary version did not have the force of law, nevertheless took the Bitcoin community's breath away. It swept up in its dragnet Bitcoin exchanges, custodial wallet providers like Coinbase, merchant payment processors like BitPay, funds like the Bitcoin Investment Trust, even direct buyers and sellers of digital currency. And it restricted the kinds of financial services that bitcoin companies could provide. While storing customers' bitcoin would be allowed, under no circumstances could a company spend or lend out that bitcoin; in the state of New York, in other words, digital currency businesses were to be prohibited from running a fractional reserve as ordinary banks do. Bitcoin 'vaulting', as Marco Santori put it, was acceptable, but banking was not allowed.[14] Likewise, a digital currency business would not be permitted to invest in the very asset it handled.

As for the AML and KYC requirements outlined as part of the BitLicense regime, they were nothing short of novel, not to say extraordinary, for the NYDFS proposed to create the first state-level AML reporting program in the United States. It would no longer be enough for Bitcoin startups, as money services businesses, to file Suspicious Activity Reports with FinCEN, the federal regulator, and to report to FinCEN any cash transaction of more than

$10,000; they would now need to file such reports with the NYDFS as well, and report to the state regulator any cryptocurrency transaction of similar size. Companies would also need to record for each transaction, no matter how small – even for, say, a micropayment of 0.0001 bitcoin that someone might send to a friend as a proof of concept using a company's wallet software – a wealth of data, including the physical address of everyone involved. (Given the extent to which financial privacy was a watchword among Bitcoin users, this was asking a lot. Probably too much.) Company financial statements were to be filed with the NYDFS quarterly, and audited financial statements yearly.

So broad was the proposal's language, so onerous were its requirements, and so harsh were its restrictions that the Bitcoin price of about $650 at the end of June would turn out to be the highest anyone saw for the next six months. So much for the next bubble that Barry had anticipated. There were other factors, of course, but most insiders believed the BitLicense proposal was to blame for depressing the price.

There was a ray of hope. For the next forty-five days, the NYDFS would be soliciting comments on the proposal from interested parties. Admittedly, forty-five days was the absolute maximum amount of time required by law for a comment period on such a proposal. And so, even as comments began flooding in, a number of Bitcoiners banded together to petition Ben Lawsky's office for a forty-five-day extension – a doubling of the original time frame. One of these was Barry Silbert. The BitLicense rules would, the petition noted, be 'materially impacting an entire nascent industry'. It was imperative that industry stakeholders – many of whom were 'individuals or small startups operating on limited budgets without access to extensive legal resources' – be allowed sufficient time to understand the proposed regulations and respond in full. The petition was signed not only by Barry Silbert but also by Erik Voorhees, Jesse Powell of Kraken, Jeremy Allaire of Circle, Brian Armstrong and Fred Ehrsam of Coinbase, and dozens of others. It was a stalling tactic, but a reasonable one. One month later, Ben Lawsky granted the extension.

Chapter 12

DEATH AND TAXES

In the global economy that is still emerging, the power
of money will supersede that of any nation, combination
of nations, or international organization now in existence.
— Jack Weatherford

In early March 2014, Roger Ver walked into the American embassy
in Barbados intending at last to divest himself of something he
had carried his whole life. It had long been a burden to him, had
weighed on his conscience; he believed it was inescapably linked
to much that was alarming and wrong and appalling about the
world, so that the thing he was now determined to lay down made
him, in his own way, culpable, part of the silent majority whose
tax dollars, if not their votes, made possible the lethal buzz of
Predator drones. This thing was his American citizenship. Having
declared his intention to renounce, he was informed at the outset
that he would have to pay $450 for the privilege. It seemed he
would have to buy his freedom.

He could not have committed to such drastic action had he
not already made certain arrangements. Foremost among them
was the acquisition, only a few weeks earlier, of a second citizenship. He had purchased it outright: the price was a $400,000
real-estate investment – a luxury condominium that would sit
empty most of the year. That didn't bother him. It was not the
supposed investment but what the investment really paid for that

counted, and that was a means of moving through the world on his own terms, the right to travel unimpeded and without a visa to 132 countries, including all of Europe. On 13 February 2014, he had received the definite proof of his new allegiance: a passport identifying him as a citizen of the tiny Caribbean state of St. Kitts and Nevis.

He would have preferred to carve out a place beyond the jurisdiction of human governments, whose true face he believed had been revealed to him as a young man by reading Murray Rothbard. Roger's way of complimenting Rothbard, the tenor of his thought, is to say that he made the other heterodox thinkers he had encountered up to that point 'seem like tame Democrats or Republicans' by comparison. Years later he still retained a vivid memory of encountering the author's argument that the military draft is the moral equivalent of kidnapping and slavery. (America abolished the draft in 1973, but in a number of other countries, from Israel to South Korea, military service remains mandatory for young men.) That was the turning point in his view of what governments are all about. After that, Roger says, 'I realized I can't support them with anything they do.' Barring total renunciation, however, he was determined once and for all to put himself under the aegis of a government more acceptable to his conscience. But there was one thing about his new citizenship which couldn't help but remind him that in brandishing it he was merely accommodating himself to a practical reality he wished fervently to reform. Embossed in gold on his new passport's blue cover, beneath the coat of arms, which featured pelicans clutching a stalk of sugarcane and a coconut palm tree in their beaks, and above the words ST. CHRISTOPHER (ST. KITTS) AND NEVIS, was the national motto: *Country Above Self.* These were words so alien to his private ideals as to be practically gibberish.

For all that, he did not take the step of renunciation lightly. Having grown up in Silicon Valley with an interest in computers, he figured himself in some ways fortunate to have been born in the United States. But he also figured that he would be a lot safer, given the state of the world, if he were not an American. Japan was more agreeable, but the idea of obtaining citizenship in his adopted country was a nonstarter. Whereas the US is happy to bestow full citizenship on the spouses of its citizens, the Japanese government was moved only slightly by the fact that Roger had a Japanese wife. Roger did apply for citizenship once but didn't get very far. His frequent travel disqualified him. You can't be away from Japan for more than sixty days in a year or else you don't get credit for having resided in the country that year, and you can't successfully apply to become a citizen until you have been a resident for at least five years – or three years if you are married to a Japanese. Roger had lived in Japan for nearly eight years but had traveled extensively during that time. 'As far as the Japanese government is concerned,' he says, 'the number of years I have spent in Japan is zero.'

Before heading to Barbados, he tried renouncing closer to home. But the US embassy in Tokyo was booked solid with renunciation interviews for the next month and a half. He couldn't get an appointment. He was incredulous. It turned out that he was joining a trend. Record numbers of Americans were bidding *sayonara* to the Stars and Stripes: in 2011, nearly 1,800 people had renounced their citizenship or turned over their green cards. At the time, such a number was unheard of. But two years later the annual figure had increased to 3,000.

Largely to blame for the surge in renunciations was a law, enacted in 2010, called the Foreign Account Tax Compliance Act. Intended to punish tax evaders, the law immediately began having the unintended effect of driving ordinary Americans away from Uncle Sam. In 2008, only 231 people renounced their American citizenship. In 2010, the year FATCA became law, the number shot up to 1,534. The following year it was higher still, and so on, a leave-taking permanent and unprecedented. It didn't help that in 2013, under the Obama administration, the top income tax rate was bumped from 35 to 39.6 percent, while the equivalent capital gains rate jumped from 15 to 20 percent. But FATCA was worse. What FATCA did was twofold. Essentially the law required Americans living abroad to disclose their foreign bank accounts and other assets, and, at the same time, required all foreign financial institutions, including hedge funds, to report to the IRS all accounts held by Americans, no matter how low their balances.[1] As a result, many financial institutions began simply turning away American customers, since taking their business would have meant having to comply with FATCA. It will be a cold day in hell, after all, before a foreign bank is happy to line up for an IRS exam.

Not only fat cats but many average Americans living abroad suffered as a result. Imagine not being able to open – or keep – a checking account simply because of your nationality. (Ira Miller, living in Panama, encountered this problem.) It was a perfect example of the unintended consequences of new regulation. Lawmakers often pass legislation without apparent regard for Newton's third law, which is that for every action there is an equal and opposite reaction – as when congressmen say that a new tax on cigarettes will raise a certain amount of money for a worthy cause. Such statements assume that the new law will slip through unnoticed, like a pebble into society's pond – that the purchase of cigarettes will remain constant despite the higher cost. In practice, of course, you see ripple effects: a dramatic rise in the interstate smuggling of smokes. New York state, which has the highest cigarette taxes in the nation, also has the biggest problem with smuggled cigarettes: fully fifty-eight percent of all cigarettes smoked in the state are untaxed contraband.[2]

FATCA was no exception to this rule. The outright refusal by some foreign banks and investment funds to accept American customers was one unintended consequence of the new legislation. The growing number of citizenship renunciations was another. With the passage of FATCA came greater awareness among American expats of their complicated tax filing requirements, to say nothing of the stiff penalties for failing to file properly; even accidentally forgetting to file one of the disclosure forms triggered a $10,000 penalty. (America is one of the very few countries that expects its citizens to pay taxes on income earned while living abroad.) Willfully failing to disclose a foreign financial account would cost you $100,000 or half of the account balance, whichever was greater – and that was compounded for every year that you didn't disclose the account. Even if you didn't actually owe any taxes while living abroad, you still had to file the paperwork or else pay the fines. Small wonder that some people chose to wash their hands of the whole mess.

In August 2014 the State Department would raise the citizenship renunciation fee to $2,350, more than four times the price Roger had to pay. Whether this was a cynical attempt to discourage people from giving up their passports despite the onerous new regulations or whether it was, as the State Department claimed, a way of making up for the increased demand, it said nothing good about the agency's attitude toward people who wanted to slip the surly bonds of American citizenship.

Roger Ver, for his part, would not be put off. By this point he had been thinking about handing in his US passport for more than a decade. And thanks to his newly minted St. Kitts citizenship, he finally had a viable alternative.

In early March the five-day annual conference of the International Financial Cryptography Association was being held in Barbados, and this year, for the first time, Bitcoin was a topic of major interest for the attendees. The Bitcoin Foundation helped to sponsor the conference, and several of the academic papers presented there concerned research into cryptocurrency. In a move entirely in keeping with his jet-set lifestyle, Roger got on a plane to Barbados, an island nation 1,600 miles southeast of Miami. The IFCA crypto-geeks were just his brand of idealist. Just as he had once used E-gold – losing several hundred dollars' worth of the electronic currency when the government shut it down – before recognizing Bitcoin as a far more promising invention, so, years earlier, had the IFCA guys believed that 'e-cash would take over the world,' says Gavin Andresen, who led a workshop at the 2014 conference. 'But then the hype overran the reality and in the middle years there was some disappointment that this didn't happen. Now they are excited again.'[3] But Roger had another motive for the trip. While on the island, he paid a visit to the US embassy. Unlike the embassy in Tokyo, this one was able to see him almost immediately. Soon enough he found himself talking to a consular officer through bulletproof glass. 'So,' the officer asked, without preamble, 'do you want to pay your renunciation fee by cash, credit card, or Bitcoin?'

Roger was flabbergasted. 'How did you know that I use Bitcoin?'

'Oh, we know who you are,' the consular officer said, amused. 'We google everybody who comes in here.'

As it turned out, the officer was joking about being able to accept digital currency. Nevertheless, Roger took a liking to him. Unlike other embassy staffers, this man wasn't rude or mean about anything.

He read from a script all the privileges Roger would miss out on once he'd renounced. 'He said, "Did you know that if you renounce your US citizenship" – and this is in an attempt to convince me not to renounce – "did you know that if you renounce your US citizenship, you won't be allowed to serve in the Armed Forces?" Philosophically, I would rather go to jail than serve in any military, especially the United States military, so that wasn't going to hold me back,' Roger says. 'It was one of the biggest positives in my mind. And then he also said, "Did you know that if you renounce your US citizenship, you're not going to be allowed to vote?" Philosophically, I'm opposed to voting, and legally I haven't been allowed to vote since I became a felon more than a decade ago, so I wasn't missing out on that one, either. And then the final one was that if I renounce my US citizenship, then I'm not going to be allowed to collect Social Security. And I'm pretty confident that thirty years from now the US Social Security system is going to be long gone.'

In that first interview, Roger was informed that there was a mandatory one-week 'cooling-off period' in which he was expected to think twice about whether he wanted to go through with renouncing. He spent most of it attending the IFCA conference. The following Monday, 10 March, he was back at the embassy for his swearing-out ceremony. The consular officer was surprised to see him; he had meant for Roger to take at least one week to think things over, not for him to come back in exactly one week. But Roger was adamant. He raised his right hand and swore that he understood what it would mean to give up his US citizenship.

The renunciation fee was the least of it: for Americans with a net worth greater than $2 million or who had owed an average annual income tax for the past five years of $157,000 or more, there was an exit tax to reckon with. Thanks to his business and his bitcoins, Roger Ver met the requirements, and he would have to pay. The exit tax was calculated as if you had liquidated all your assets – your homes, savings, income, stocks and bonds, artwork, jewelry, everything – at their current market value the day before deciding to renounce; it was a twenty percent tax on your resulting net gain. The net gain was imaginary, mind you, since of course you would not actually have sold every piece of property you owned that day, nor would you have already reaped all the benefits of your pension or retirement account, whose full value was taxed along with everything else. For some US citizens, like Facebook cofounder Eduardo Saverin, who renounced in 2012 to live in Singapore, this all-too-real tax on a fictional fire sale could amount to millions of dollars. The first $680,000 of net gain was exempt from taxation. Everything beyond that was considered fair game.

By April, consequently, in order to cover his tax bill, Roger was busy divesting himself of all his assets in the United States. He had already sold in 2012 the house he'd once owned in California, and he planned to sell his computer parts business, Memory Dealers, or at least its California branch, either to a competitor or to his own employees. He expected this would take many months to carry out. But he would not be closing down the Tokyo office of Memory Dealers, on which his Japanese visa depended.

There was something else he had to consider. On 25 March, just days after Roger's visit to the embassy, the IRS released tax guidelines for all cryptocurrencies. Since Bitcoin's creation in 2009, the agency had left Bitcoiners in the dark about the tax liability of their holdings. Now it decreed that digital currency should be treated like property, with net gains from selling or transacting in bitcoins subject to either normal income or capital gains taxes, depending on whether the bitcoins spent had been held for less or more than one year. (If they had been earned as payment for work rather than bought on an exchange, however, they would be treated like normal income.) As far as the IRS was concerned, using digital currency to buy even something as small as a cup of coffee was a taxable event. In other words, American users would be expected to keep track of the difference between the price at which they bought a given amount of digital currency and the price at which they sold or spent it, and then add up the gain or loss accordingly. Come tax time, they would owe money in accordance with their tax bracket and the size of their gains for the year. If their losses exceeded their gains, then they could deduct up to $3,000. (The need to simplify this process would prove to be an opportunity for entrepreneurs; software services soon sprung up offering to calculate users' Bitcoin tax liability automatically.) For Roger Ver, who bought and spent bitcoins all the time, spent them in place of dollars or yen for everything he possibly could, the IRS ruling was more than a little unpleasant. Worse, it put a thumb on the scales, making it easier to treat Bitcoin as an asset rather than as a currency. But Roger wasn't surprised. Having never known the US government to pass up possible revenue, he says, he had assumed from day one that his digital currency would be counted as part of his net worth.

And so the man they called 'Bitcoin Jesus' rendered unto Caesar. The exit tax would not come due until April 2015, but in the meantime there were the usual taxes for fiscal year 2013. So complicated was the matter of determining what he owed, even with the help of expensive accountants, that Roger filed for an extension and still ended up paying late; the total bill, he later recalled, was about $575,000.

He consoled himself with the thought that he had at least thirty good working years left – thirty years in which he wouldn't owe the IRS a dime. He couldn't wait to no longer be funding the

US government. Asked what he thought of living in the Japan of Prime Minister Shinzo Abe, a nationalist and unrepentant when it came to the subject of his country's own wartime sins, Roger replied that there was 'a lot to be said' for the fact that while America used its national treasure to fund a war machine, modern Japan spent its money primarily on domestic infrastructure. And the Japanese government had never locked him in a cage. But that was not to let Abe off the hook. Japan, too, was ruled by corrupt politicians and central bankers, he said. Those who disapproved of the actions of the ruling class should use Bitcoin, which was not being taxed in Japan and which, as a truly international currency, undermined in a fundamental way, so Roger believed, the whole system of national borders and warmongering governments. 'Right now, today, you have an option: start using Bitcoin, stop using dollars, euros, or yen,' Roger says. 'Bitcoin is the currency of peace. The dollar and these other currencies are the currency of violent central bankers and violent governments that like to murder people around the world. So if you're opposed to murder and violence and coercion, use Bitcoin. If you like murder and violence and coercion, keep using dollars and euros and yen.' For Roger Ver, it was that simple.

His business concluded, Roger left Barbados, though not before Salon.com published a deeply inaccurate article claiming that 'Bitcoin Jesus' was hiding out on an unnamed Caribbean island, fearing for his life. (His nickname was too good to resist; the press put it in headline after headline.) Roger was not amused. Owing largely to his time in prison, he had come to see every law as backed up with the threat of force – and ultimately a death threat. A reporter not molded by the same rough hand of experience might misinterpret this to mean that Roger was expecting at any moment to encounter a man with a gun. That wasn't the case, Roger assured his friends. He wasn't hiding from anybody. He was happy with his life.[4]

By late April, Roger was back in Tokyo, having flown in from Moscow, where he had spent two days and three nights attending yet another Bitcoin conference. On many lips was the question of what stance the Russian government was taking toward Bitcoin. Roger asked one guy about it, and received a quintessentially Russian response: 'Nobody knows and nobody cares.' For the attendees of the conference, it may even have been true.

In fact, the nations of the world were taking widely divergent approaches to regulating Bitcoin, and some of them weren't regulating digital currencies at all. In early February, Senator Tom Carper, chairman of the US Senate Homeland Security and Governmental Affairs Committee, had released a report prepared by the Law Library of Congress on digital currency regulations in dozens of countries; according to its section on Russia, Vladimir Putin's government had not yet issued any laws specific to Bitcoin. But a Russian law firm cautioned that the country's civil code recognized the ruble as the sole means of payment and required that all prices be listed in rubles – and indeed this was the line Russia's general prosecutor took later that year, declaring 'money substitutes' like Bitcoin illegal. The country's central bank likewise sought to ban digital currencies, only, however, to reverse its position a few months later. In early July, the Bank of Russia declared that it would no longer try to prevent their use, and its first deputy chairman went so far as to say, 'These instruments should not be rejected.'[5] Such flip-flopping reflected the uncertainty of administrative states in the face of a technology that looked by turns beneficial and threatening, and which was approaching at the speed of a tidal wave. Roger, meanwhile, at the Moscow conference, handed out digital currency to news reporters, having first set them up with Bitcoin wallets. 'I try to do it specifically for news reporters,' he explained. 'If they have a little bit, then they're more invested in spreading the good word.'

Back in Japan, meanwhile, the word on the street was bad. Thanks to Mt. Gox, a lot of people in the major cities had now heard of Bitcoin – the big newspapers and TV networks were doing Roger's consciousness-raising for him – but, for the same reason, most of them had a deeply negative impression of the digital currency. 'A lot of Japanese are confused,' Roger confided to a friend one night. 'They think there's something wrong with Bitcoin because of Mt. Gox.' The falling price didn't help matters.

But like a zealous street preacher, Roger continued to proselytize. For the most part, like Erik Voorhees, he dressed unremarkably and neatly, in plain slacks and polo shirts, some of them bought for $10 apiece in South Korea, wearing no expensive watch or jewelry of any kind, but at least four or five days a week he wore an item of clothing emblazoned with the symbol for Bitcoin. And he continued to grant interviews to reporters and appear as a guest on libertarian podcasts. 'I've calmed down quite a bit now, because most people have at least heard of Bitcoin and have a general idea of what it is, but it used to be every single person I met *everywhere* heard about Bitcoin from me,' he says. 'I'd tell them all about Bitcoin and help them set up a wallet; I would give everyone like a dollar's worth of Bitcoin. A long time ago, I'd give away a whole bitcoin. I gave away thousands of them. Whole bitcoins.'

At least once a month, Roger would commiserate with a handful of other Tokyo diehards at The Pink Cow, a funky expatriate bar and restaurant in the nightlife district of Roppongi. The place was owned and operated by an American woman, Traci Consoli. She was a California native and had blue California eyes and long blonde California hair and a big white California smile. The Pink Cow served Mexicali food and imported beer. The previous July it had earned the distinction of being the first restaurant in Tokyo to accept Bitcoin. It had a flower-patterned countertop, quirky abstract canvases on the walls, and a stage for live music. In the back, by the bathrooms, a stencil by the cult artist Kenta Matsuyama, who calls himself 281_Anti Nuke, depicted a young girl with her eyes closed and fingers in her ears; on her sleeveless shift dress was written an injunction: DON'T TRUST GOVERNMENT, TELEVISION, BIG COMPANY & NUKES. The bar's very decor encouraged dissent from consensus reality. Here Roger would hold court at regular Bitcoin meetups.

On 27 April, he found Ken Shishido, a cofounder of the group, sitting at a table with a few other members. Shishido, a hard-money enthusiast, wore a sterling silver necklace with a pendant that was the symbol for Bitcoin, a capital 'B' with two vertical lines through it. Roger asked how he was doing.

'I'm okay,' Shishido said, his voice hinting at a slightly deflated spirit. 'Sky hasn't fallen. Stock market is still there. We still live in paper illusion. How about you?'

A common topic among the group was the difficulty of moving ordinary money across borders. Hence Bitcoin. One member, Fredrik Friis, a Swedish programmer, had trouble with his MasterCard debit card in Tokyo, where most ATMs wouldn't accept it. Hence encouraging The Pink Cow to accept Bitcoin. And yet, as useful as it was, Shishido said, 'Bitcoin is nothing. Bitcoin is just a tool.'

Roger agreed. Its real value, he thought, lay in its ability to usher in 'a more voluntary world – a world where one group of people can't force another group of people to do something just because it has more guns, or because its members work in a building with flags out front.'

It was a message radically different from the one now issuing from other corners of the Bitcoin community. In a keynote speech at the Inside Bitcoins conference in New York earlier that month, Circle CEO Jeremy Allaire had predicted a future in which sovereign governments would establish treaties to regulate Bitcoin 'mining cartels', and would manage Bitcoin monetary policy through their central banks.

Roger felt no need to counter this message directly. He was a fan of Jeremy Allaire, as he was of Barry Silbert, both of whom he believed were doing tremendous work to promote the use of Bitcoin. Let them have their respectability. They either didn't understand or didn't care how disruptive Bitcoin would be to the status quo. Meanwhile, people like Roger Ver and Erik Voorhees could not have been happier. At any rate, if elsewhere Bitcoin was being gradually assimilated into the ruinous machinery of modern finance, here at least, among these diehards in the heart of Roppongi, its revolutionary character prevailed. Bitcoin was the lever by which they hoped to move the world.

FOR AN OUTSIDER, IT WAS difficult to believe that all these meetups and powwows and lectures and conferences, many of which required flying to foreign countries and dealing with immigration and customs officials, did not exhaust Roger; difficult to believe that he didn't tire of having over and over again the same conversations, explaining to Bitcoin newbies and ignorant journalists alike the finer points of digital currency and the broad sweep of its implications for the world; didn't tire of retelling his own personal journey of enlightenment, his revelation on the road to Damascus, as it were, drawing for his auditors again and again the same conclusions, like a connect-the-dots picture in which the proper solution yields always the same constellation it has yielded a hundred times before. An ordinary man might have gotten burned out long ago, might have collapsed under the strain of being one of Bitcoin's poster boy. That Roger Ver did not burn out or collapse spoke to his tremendous reserves of energy and his abiding passion for Bitcoin, as well as to something little understood by those who didn't know him well: his deep enjoyment of the life he was leading. In certain interviews, he could come off as almost fanatical, but he didn't spend his days ranting and raving against the world order. He enjoyed himself. The world was full of violence and injustice, true, and he was determined to work toward ending it, but he had a rational sense of his own limits; he was more or less content with being the change he wanted to see in the world. And then, too, monomania has its rewards – a special focus and intensity of vision that allow you to see opportunities where others might not. Just so, his own experience of buying St. Kitts citizenship, as well as the need of his expat friends to move money across borders, fed into a new business venture, which he called Passports for Bitcoin.

The idea was that there were plenty of wealthy people around the world who, for one reason or another, might value a second citizenship. Many of them lived under authoritarian regimes facing economic turmoil or political unrest. St. Kitts made a perfect bolt-hole. The two-island nation had no personal income tax, no capital gains tax, no inheritance tax. You didn't even need to set foot there to become a citizen. And thanks to a 2009 agreement with the European Union, St. Kitts citizens could travel visa-free to any EU member state. But for the same reason that one-percenters in emerging markets wanted to have an escape plan in case things went to hell in their home countries, some of them had difficulty moving money overseas to make the required six-figure investment. China's government, for instance, officially forbids individuals from exchanging more than $50,000 worth of yuan each year and from directly transferring yuan out of the country. When it was revealed in the summer of 2014 that the Bank of China was in fact operating a special foreign exchange program whereby mainland Chinese were able to move billions overseas, ostensibly with state regulators' approval – money which anybody could see was flooding the real-estate markets of New York, London, Toronto, Sydney, and other major cities, despite official Chinese currency controls – the program was suspended and an investigation was launched.[6] Bitcoin solved the problem. Wealthy Chinese could easily use one of their local Bitcoin exchanges to convert their yuan into digital currency, then beam those bitcoins across the ocean with their government being none the wiser. Which is to say that the necessary infrastructure now existed to circumvent the will and evade the watchful eye of the entire Chinese state apparatus. A quiet revolution was in progress.

Indeed, it was obvious who Passports for Bitcoin's intended customers were: the website was available in English, Russian, and Chinese. (One of the enticements, ostensibly key for people living under an autocrat like Vladimir Putin, was that an applicant's home country would not be notified of his or her newfound St. Kitts citizenship.) The website presented a second passport as just one more savvy bet on the future, a 'hedge against governmental intrusion and excessive taxation'. The global rich seemed to agree. In 2014 alone, according to estimates, they would spend $2 billion buying new passports.[7]

To establish Passports for Bitcoin, Roger partnered with a licensed application processing agent, International Investments & Consulting Limited. The company, which said it had successfully processed and submitted to the St. Kitts government nearly a hundred citizenship applications, reportedly had ties to Paul

Bilzerian, a former corporate raider who had done two stints in prison years earlier for violating securities and tax laws and for failing to disclose his assets. On the Passports for Bitcoin website, Bilzerian's son Dan, a professional poker player and trust-fund playboy whose Instagram feed is a parade of half-naked women, stacks of cash, sports cars, and guns, provided a testimonial as to the value of a second passport. Dan's younger brother, Adam, also a professional poker player, was already a St. Kitts citizen, having handed in his US passport in 2008.

The US government, unsurprisingly, did its best to throw cold water on the Caribbean nation's citizenship-by-investment program. In May 2014 the Treasury Department revealed that Iranians had acquired citizenship there to avoid economic sanctions against their home country. And six months later, Canada for the first time decided to impose visa requirements on people bearing St. Kitts passports, worried, so the official line went, about 'identity management practices' within the island nation's economic citizenship program. Nevertheless, by early 2015 not only St. Kitts but also Cyprus, Malta, Grenada, Bulgaria, Dominica, Comoros, and Antigua and Barbuda had all established such programs, each with its own monetary and residency requirements and its own attendant benefits. Citizenship was becoming a commodity, which suited Roger Ver just fine. If the hunk of rock on which all of us were hurtling through space was to be carved up and cordoned off, now at least there was some free market competition in the choice of where to belong. And if he could play a part in making that happen, so much the better.

He hadn't always been so bold. For a decade after his imprisonment he had kept his head down, minding his own business, growing his company. Always keeping his politics to himself. If this censoring of his deepest self came at a cost, it also allowed him to achieve a singular focus in business that his wife, Ayaka, greatly admired. She had first met him when he was a young man in California and she was studying abroad at San Jose State University. She had been struck by his honesty. His policy always was that while in short-term deals you could make money by cheating people, in the long term you had to do the right thing. He was a long-term guy, a man of his word. In 2011, when the price of Bitcoin was about $10, Roger made a public bet that in the next two years it would outperform gold, silver, the US stock market, and the US dollar. He put up $10,000 of the digital currency, which then still seemed to most people not much better than Monopoly money. His prediction came true during the enormous price increase in November 2013, but it was a couple of months past the two-year deadline. So he kept his word, donating the $10,000 worth of bitcoins that he'd set aside at the time of the bet – now worth about $1.1 million – to the Foundation for Economic Education, a libertarian nonprofit that, he said, had 'published the books and articles that allowed me to understand just how important Bitcoin would become'.

Discovering Bitcoin had freed him from his cage of silence. 'Today, I don't have any qualms about saying I don't support any state anywhere on the entire planet,' he says. In other words, even the most powerful emperor has no clothes. Roger believed in the win-win of voluntary human interaction, and better yet, in the win-win-win. That was how he saw his million-dollar donation: 'It was good for me, it was good for them, and I think it's going to be good for everybody all over the world, 'cause now they can use that money to spread these ideas.'

But Roger wasn't content merely to donate money and leave the legwork to others. Like a high-powered missionary, he continued to sow his time into the Bitcoin cause. In late May he flew to Singapore for Coin Congress, where he spoke out against deficit spending and the debt financing of war, geopolitical realities which he thought could be solved by the mass adoption of digital currency. Bitcoin's limited supply would make it impossible simply to print or borrow more money when the desire arose. 'And so I see a world in which everybody is using Bitcoin as just a much, much, much happier and [more] peaceful and safer world for every single human being on the planet,' he said. It was a noble goal. But one man's messiah is another man's mark.

On the afternoon of 23 May, Roger got hacked. The first he

knew of it was around noon, at the Shangri-La Hotel in Singapore. His friend Jesse Powell shot him a text message to warn him that 'some weird account' was impersonating him on Facebook and asking to borrow bitcoins. Roger took a look – and sure enough, somebody had hijacked an old profile of his. He had created it years ago and forgotten about it until now. He and Powell, who ran the Bitcoin exchange Kraken, had been friends for nearly two decades; of course Powell had known immediately that this 'Roger Ver' was an impostor. Roger's other friends were likewise savvy enough not to be fooled. But the takeover of his old Facebook account, a minor irritation at most, was a sign that something much worse was going on.

At 5:24 P.M. local time, having failed to scam anybody, the hacker made contact. Roger got a Skype message from someone using the screen name Savaged, who set about establishing his credentials by providing his mark's old Social Security number. He made it clear that he was holding Roger's personal information and digital property for ransom. And if he wasn't paid, if Roger got stubborn, well . . . 'I don't think you want your mother to go thru the stuff I could put her thru,' he typed.

Roger immediately began playing for time. His first priority was to keep the hacker occupied while he figured out which of his accounts had been compromised. But when he fell silent for a couple of minutes, the hacker threatened to send a SWAT team to 3350 Scott Blvd, Bldg #32 in Santa Clara – the Memory Dealers headquarters. 'Swatting', as this vicious prank is known, involves calling in a fake emergency to the victim's local police precinct, usually a violent crime involving hostages – the kind that gets a SWAT team dispatched to the address.

'I want you to send me BTC to my wallet to have this stop. I [have] only just begun to get your attention,' Savaged wrote. 'I will hack your domain and transfer it.'

'Which domain?' Roger wanted to know.

The answer came back almost instantly: 'memorydealers.com'.

This was bad. Roger had signed up for the hacked Facebook account using an old email address, Roger_Ver@hotmail.com, and this email account, he soon discovered, had been compromised. And now the hacker had used this Hotmail address to infiltrate Roger's account at Register.com, his domain name registrar. Some fifteen years earlier, Roger had used Register.com to set up the Memory Dealers website, and he had kept his registrar account associated with Roger_Ver@hotmail.com, never bothering over the years to update his contact information. This old Hotmail address, like Register.com itself, had no two-factor authentication, making it far easier to break into than his primary email address, roger@ memorydealers.com.

What all of this added up to was something truly frightening. Through Register.com, the hacker could change the settings for the Memory Dealers website so that its domain name pointed to an IP address under the hacker's control. That would mean any new email or other piece of information bound for the memorydealers.com domain would wind up in the hacker's hands. He could request password resets on any of Roger's online accounts and, armed with the password reset information, take over those accounts, including roger@memorydealers.com. And since this was the domain of his business, the dragnet would sweep up not only Roger's own emails but every single incoming email for the entire domain. All of his employees' accounts would be compromised, exposing them to identity theft as well. There was no telling how much damage the hacker could do.

Savaged was feeling cocky. At 5:33 P.M., he typed, 'I think we both know this won't be pleasant [*sic*] and let's be honest there is nothing you can do to have me caught, I've been around too long.'

Throughout the conversation, the hacker mingled reasonable talk with outlandish threats. At one point, he told Roger he respected him 'as a BTC user/icon'. But then, after four minutes of resounding silence from his victim, he turned nasty on a dime: 'Let's be honest I will sell [your Social Security number] + your information to fraudsters that will credit fuck you then get your mom's social and credit fuck her too and ruin both your lives.'

It was the most bizarre thing imaginable, to be alternately flattered and threatened by your extortionist. Ver was nonplussed.

'If you respect me as a [Bitcoin] user / icon,' he typed, 'why are you doing this to me?'

'I want 37.63289114 BTC, that's why,' came the answer. He was demanding exactly $20,000 in digital currency.

By this time Roger had called for backup. He was in luck: Jason Maurice was also in Singapore for the conference and happened to be staying, like Roger, in the hotel where it was taking place, the Shangri-La. Having learned what was going on, Jason ran across the hotel to join Roger and help him fend off the attack.

To all of the hacker's threats, Roger played dumb, asking how he had learned such-and-such a piece of personal information, or why he was asking for such a specific amount of money. He didn't know how the hacker had learned his Social Security number or his old US passport number. But he and Jason quickly agreed that there would be no payoff. Paying extortionists is a losing proposition, Roger says. 'There's nothing to stop them from just extorting you over and over and over again.' Meanwhile a plan was forming in his mind. He wanted to hit back. 'I knew what I was going to do from the instant he contacted me,' he said later. While he kept the hacker talking, Jason fought a battle for his friend's domain name. He would change the DNS server so that it pointed to his own network, and a few minutes later the hacker would change it back. There was no way to counterattack, not directly. They had no idea who the hacker was. They had no way to reach him. Regaining control of Roger's digital property seemed the best they could hope for. But Roger wanted more.

As the clock passed 6:30, Savaged was rapidly losing patience. 'WOULD YOU LIKE TO GET OWNED LIKE X10000 HARDER THAN I PLAN TO ALREADY YOU FAG,' he typed. But two minutes later, having again failed to get a rise out of Roger, he changed his tack: 'Listen, my mom needs a liver transplant that starts at $15,000 man, I wouldn't be doing this I am so sorry for having to do this but it's just what I have to do.'

Finally, at 6:39 P.M., one hour and fifteen minutes after Savaged had first made contact, Roger broke his silence to provide a link to a post he'd made on Facebook offering a bounty for information leading to the hacker's arrest. The amount of the bounty was the exact amount that Savaged had tried to extort from him. It was perfect. It was everything you might have expected from the Bitcoin Jesus – a free market answer to violence and intimidation. Involving the police might have given some anarchists pause. Not Roger, who had a willingness, rare among radical idealists, to embrace practical solutions. 'If that were true,' he said, referring to Savaged's mother, 'I would have been likely to help you raise most of the money for the transplant.' But now it was too late.

The hacker kept up a brave front at first, boasting that no one knew who he was. But he soon caved, deleting the Hotmail account and handing over the passwords to all the other accounts he'd managed to break into. (He had changed each password to a racial slur.) He ended the conversation in a huff: 'I just need to raise funds for my mother, but since you aren't going to help . . .'

Nine minutes after Roger alerted Savaged to the bounty on him, he received a Skype message from someone using the name TGOD, who claimed to know the hacker's real identity. He offered to give him up in exchange for the bounty. Again Roger stalled, saying he needed a few hours to finish securing his accounts. All the while, Savaged – who had reappeared after fourteen minutes of radio silence – was growing increasingly pathetic, having gone from blustering to begging. 'Sir, I am sincerely sorry I am just a middleman I was being told what to tell you,' he typed in a rush. 'I was seriously being told what to tell you by someone else I don't even know what's going on.' And then, after more excuses: 'Are you going to order a hitman to kill me now?'

Now that was just perfect. Somehow the idea that this sort of thing happened in the world of Bitcoin must have filtered down to him from the allegations against Ross Ulbricht. And if he truly believed that Roger had put a price on his head – had marked him not merely for arrest but for death – Roger wasn't going to disabuse him of the notion, not when he finally had the bastard where he wanted him. 'Someone just contacted me with the information,' he replied. 'Let me talk to them and see.'

In fact, Roger didn't believe for a second that TGOD was a

good Samaritan. He thought he just might be the real hacker, the one Savaged was blubbering about – assuming there was such a person. So he strung TGOD along for a while, until the bounty hunter got impatient. 'I have the info you need, I just don't see why you have to have kids on [Facebook and Twitter] going after [the] bounty when I have what you need already,' he fumed. Twitter and Facebook were lighting up with news of the hack even as it was still in progress; already amateur sleuths were trying to run the hacker down. Roger wasn't about to hand over twenty grand in exchange for what might be worthless information – or worse, the personal info of an innocent stranger.

When it became clear that TGOD wouldn't provide proof without payment, Roger began actively trolling him, pretending to be on the phone with the 'cyber police'. It was a reference to an old viral YouTube video in which a preteen girl's father dishes out ludicrous threats to a bunch of online bullies. (Like most Internet humor, it loses its humor in the explanation.) TGOD finally got frustrated and gave up. Meanwhile, Jason Maurice had managed to transfer the Memory Dealers domain out of the compromised Register.com account, putting it beyond the hacker's reach.

To this already bizarre incident was added a bizarre coda. One day Roger received a call from someone who identified himself, he recalls, as a police officer from a town in Missouri. Just as he was about to hang up – 'I generally don't talk to the police,' he says – the man said he was calling about the hack. Roger listened. If the man was faking his Missouri accent, it was a damn good fake. It became clear that the police officer, or whoever he was, was trying to collect on the bounty after arresting the hacker. But Roger wouldn't be had so easily. After the call, which lasted several minutes, he looked up the area code for the place the man had said he was calling from. It matched the phone number. But that number wasn't the number for the police department, and there was no officer there by the name the man had given. When Roger tried to call back, the number turned out to be a Google Voice number. You can buy a Google Voice number in just about any area code you want. Roger was now convinced that he had been speaking with his hacker, who had been trying by other means to obtain the sum of his original ransom demand.

News of the bounty, and of how Roger had made the hacker turn tail and run, spread like wildfire. He found himself inundated with emails, everything from media requests to offers of help – dozens every day. Cyber extortion was clearly a hot-button issue, and the idea that victims could get the better of their attackers had fired people's imaginations.

But Roger wasn't Savaged's only victim. Just days later, his attacker swatted Hal Finney. A man claiming to reside at Finney's address called the Santa Barbara County sheriff's department and said he had murdered his wife and child, planned to kill himself, and was going to burn down the house.

Local schools were locked down and Finney's neighbors were evacuated as a SWAT team, sheriff's deputies, firefighters, and a police helicopter descended on the home. The weekend before, Elliot Rodger had gone on a killing spree in Santa Barbara that left six innocent people dead; the cops weren't taking any chances. They soon discovered the hoax – but the quadriplegic Finney, who was suffering from Lou Gehrig's disease, was made to wait shivering on his front lawn for half an hour while his home was searched.

Word spread that the cryptographer and his family had been enduring harassment for months, with the extortionist demanding a payment of one thousand bitcoins, an amount then worth more than $400,000, in order to leave them alone. As one of the very first Bitcoin users, Finney was known to have a stash of coins he had mined in the early days. He had believed in Bitcoin, in its promise of financial freedom and global fellowship, and now he was suffering for it; the sleep of reason had bred monsters. Finney died that August, his final weeks marred by threatening phone calls. 'When I heard what they did to Hal Finney, it made me really, really angry,' says Roger. He told other Bitcoiners that it 'should make everyone's blood boil'.

So he wasn't content merely to run off his attacker. Despite what had happened, he was still firmly of the opinion that Bitcoin enabled far more good than bad – and he wanted to prove it. If cybercriminals could take advantage of Bitcoin to hurt innocent people, maybe their victims could use it to make them pay. The result was Bitcoin Bounty Hunter.

Roger hit upon the idea of a website where people could pool together Bitcoin donations to create bounties for information leading to the arrest of various criminals. After gathering sufficient evidence to procure a criminal's arrest and conviction, someone who wanted to collect the bounty would embed a 'cryptographic digest' of the data in the Bitcoin blockchain – allowing him to prove that he possessed the information without revealing his identity or giving away the information itself. That done, the evidence could be sent to the proper authorities and to Bitcoin Bounty Hunter for verification. Nobody, not even Roger himself, would know the identity of the person who collected the bounty, but the indisputable evidence of the claimant's right to the coins would be encoded in the blockchain for all to see.

Roger launched Bitcoin Bounty Hunter in September 2014. The website initially looked like a hobbyist project, but the leap forward it represented, its demonstration of what was possible, was impressive. It was a kind of minimum viable product. Roger began by listing the bounty for Savaged, who had yet to be caught. In a few years, he says, maybe the Bitcoin price will have increased so much that the bounty will be worth a couple hundred thousand dollars, 'and I'll gladly pay that 37.6 bitcoins regardless of what the price of Bitcoin is for any information that leads to that guy getting arrested wherever he is in the world.' Not for a moment did the hack attack make him want to abandon either his advocacy or his ideals. It was because of these ideals that he was raising money for the legal defense fund of Ross Ulbricht.

WHILE THE FOUNDER OF SILK Road sat behind bars, Ross's mother, Lyn, was schlepping around the country to speak on her son's behalf, making appearances in March at the Texas Bitcoin Conference, held in her son's hometown of Austin, and in June at PorcFest, where she received a standing ovation after giving a speech. She was doing her best to manufacture Ross into a martyr, a freedom fighter of the digital age like Aaron Swartz, a gentle soul persecuted by an overreaching and misguided federal government. She got into heated arguments with people online about the supposedly unfair media coverage surrounding her son's case, and yet she couldn't seem to keep from talking to the press. It was as if she couldn't help herself. In fact, helping herself was exactly what she was doing. Ross's lawyer, Joshua Dratel, did not come cheap.

She had set up a website to collect donations to help cover the costs of his legal fees. The donation campaign got off to a slow start, but the more she talked, the more money flowed in. She portrayed her son's case as one with sweeping consequences, potentially setting a harmful precedent for Internet privacy and digital currency. It was about much more than just one man, she said.

Although Lyn Ulbricht would never have admitted it to anyone, perhaps least of all herself, rallying the support of libertarians and Internet privacy activists entailed tacitly admitting that her son was Dread Pirate Roberts. If the government had the wrong man, then there was little reason for Ross's ideological supporters to care about his fate, at least no more than they would care about the fate of any other wrongfully accused man caught in the justice system. Certainly it was the belief of many of Ross's supporters that the thirty-year-old Texan and the infamous black marketeer were one and the same, and indeed their support stemmed from this belief. They didn't discount the government's evidence against him; they simply believed that helping people to ingest mind-altering drugs was not a real crime. (If Ross were to be found guilty of the attempted murder for hire for which he had been indicted in Maryland, that might be a different matter. A large part of the sympathy he had garnered might drain away.) Libertarians saw Ross as a folk hero, a romantic outlaw. At PorcFest, Lyn Ulbricht raised thousands of dollars in donations.

Roger Ver supported the cause either way. 'If Ross is innocent, he deserves to be set free immediately,' he wrote on Facebook. 'If he is guilty, then he is actually a hero for setting up the Silk Road and helping people around the world engage in free trade.'

Whatever else he was, he had been a pioneer in the use of digital currency. Roger had no qualms about supporting him. He suspected the murder-for-hire allegations were nothing but a smear campaign. And as for the rest? 'People getting together and writing down words on a piece of paper and calling it a law,' Roger says, 'doesn't alter morality in any way.'

In July, while in Seoul for a Bitcoin meetup, he put his money where his mouth was, pledging in a tweet to give ten dollars to Ross Ulbricht's defense fund for every retweet he received. His pledge went viral. By the time he decided to impose a donation limit, more than sixteen thousand people had retweeted him. Within days, he had transferred to the Free Ross campaign $160,000 worth of bitcoins. 'Ver is a hero,' Erik Voorhees wrote. Keonne Rodriguez, Blockchain's product lead, tweeted in support that Ross was guilty only 'of creating a safer and cheaper illicit market while denying the state their cut of the pie'. Indeed, denying the state its 'fair share' was one of the founding principles of Silk Road. On 5 July 2010, with Independence Day just past – exactly four years before Roger Ver made his pledge – Ross had found himself reflecting on the issue of taxation. 'Death and taxes are widely agreed upon to be inevitable, but are they?' he asked. 'This is an interpretation. It is an extrapolation from the past in an attempt to predict the future, is not the truth and therefore limits what is possible.' It was rhetoric to which Roger could give wholehearted assent. Now, on the verge of freeing himself from one of those two age-old inevitabilities, it was as if Roger wanted to give back to a brother-in-arms who might never manage it for himself.

IF PASSPORTS FOR BITCOIN WAS a publicity stunt, as it appeared to some outsiders, it was an effective one. By the middle of June, Bloomberg News and other media outlets had come calling. According to Roger, several people who first learned they could buy a St. Kitts passport, thanks to his project, decided to move ahead with the citizenship process. But it was too good to last, the spotlight of media attention too bright.

Since 2006, the St. Kitts and Nevis economic citizenship

program – the oldest of its kind, in existence since 1984 – had been under the direct purview of Prime Minister Denzil Douglas. One can imagine his consternation upon learning that some project he had never heard of, some project that did not use the accepted euphemism of 'citizenship by investment' and so on but advertised itself brazenly as being in the business of *selling passports*, was linking his government to digital currency. It was hard enough to make the economic citizenship program look respectable; the last thing he needed was for it to be covered in the stink of a renegade technology linked to so many hacks and disasters, something that for the US government – with which he had an extradition treaty – raised the specter of terrorist financing. So the Douglas administration now came out against Bitcoin. In a warning posted to the website of its Citizenship by Investment Unit, the St. Kitts government sought to 'assure the general public that we do not recognize bitcoins as legal investment currency for financial transactions . . . We further emphasize that we do not accept bitcoins, have never accepted bitcoins, and will not accept bitcoins.'

The statement went on to say that the CIU had launched an investigation and that any company found advertising citizenship services in exchange for bitcoins would have its application processing license revoked. This indeed is what happened to Roger Ver's partner, International Investments & Consulting Limited: its license was revoked by the St. Kitts Financial Services Regulatory Commission, effectively putting it out of business. Passports for Bitcoin was killed in the cradle.

If nothing else, however, the project had provided a proof of concept for just how powerful cross-border Bitcoin payments could be. Roger's optimism was unspoiled. 'Bitcoin is right on the verge of becoming a prominent currency all over the world,' he said that summer. Some sixty thousand online retailers were now accepting the digital currency. And by August, so were three restaurants within walking distance of his home in Shibuya. The next great achievement, he believed, would be to replace fiat currencies en masse. Even the Bitcoin price drops that seemed relentless in the second half of 2014 couldn't shake his confidence. If Nic Cary was enjoying a new kind of cosmopolitan existence, that of a footloose expat CEO empowered by two passports and a phone loaded with borderless currency, Roger was even further out on the bleeding edge. He lived in a paracosm of future liberty, an infinite expectation of the dawn. And now, more and more, it seemed as if reality were trying to catch up with him. Or, as the cyberpunk novelist William Gibson has put it, 'The future is already here – it's just not very evenly distributed.'

Chapter 13

THE PLEA DEAL

Faber est suae quisque fortunae.
— Appius Claudius Caecus

By May, Charlie's house arrest had become unbearable. His parents, he says, were hanging over his head the $1 million bond they had posted, using it as leverage to drag him back into the hyper-religious Syrian Jewish community to which they belonged. He and Courtney, nearly two hundred miles apart, were forced to date in secret, in the teeth of his parents' disapproval. Charlie's father, Allen, seemed not to grasp the magnitude either of his firstborn son's achievements as an entrepreneur or of his alleged crimes, viewing the unfolding case against him as a matter of a recalcitrant son stepping a little too far over the line. 'Nobody did anything on purpose,' he says. 'It wasn't a big conspiracy. Personally, I think it was just a stupid mistake. Getting caught up on your computer at two-thirty in the morning, hiding under your covers from Mom and Dad – that kind of thing.'

In mid-May, one of Charlie's lawyers, Marc Agnifilo, managed to get Charlie out of house arrest between the hours of 9:00 A.M. and 9:00 P.M., Sunday through Thursday, though he remained restricted to the five boroughs of New York City. The ostensible reason was to allow Charlie to pursue employment opportunities. In reality he was already consulting for Payza, but his parents' house was hardly a congenial work environment. After that, Charlie spent as much time outside as he could. The taste of freedom only sharpened his appetite for the real thing. He was determined to leave New York when his legal troubles were over. For that matter, he thought he might leave America altogether.

He had always held strong views about his homeland – and the conditions under which he would live in it. Years earlier, only days before the 2008 presidential election, he'd posted on Facebook: '[Charlie Shrem] hates anti-american liberal democrat OBAMAniacs and will MOVE to Israel on election day if that socialist, tax-raising, ignorant, lying communist become[s] prez.' He hadn't followed through on that promise – the kind of thing an eighteen-year-old spouts off in the heat of election season – but now, like Roger Ver at the end of his probation, he felt a desire to put as much distance as possible between him and the country of his birth. He even thought of moving to Australia. He was depressed and drinking practically every day. 'I'd go out during the day, go to lunches and day-drink,' he says, 'and then I'd go to the liquor store and pick up a bottle of Scotch and drink till 6:00 A.M. and then sleep till two in the afternoon and do it over again.'

Despite drinking heavily, he was no longer much of a partier. Even after his house arrest was relaxed and he was once more free to roam the city during daylight hours, he didn't return to EVR, the Bitcoin-friendly lounge in which he had once owned two percent. 'I'm over that whole EVR scene,' he said. 'It's no fun without Courtney. That was our thing. If I went there without her I'd just get depressed.' Charlie sold his share of the bar but made no profit on the investment.

He did, however, regain something of his taste for the good life. By the end of May, he had been accepted into an exclusive New York member's club called Magnises. Aimed at upwardly mobile young professionals, Magnises was part member's club and part startup, promising access to exclusive parties and speaking events, high-level networking opportunities, and perks ranging from priority dinner reservations at New York's hottest restaurants to VIP service at bespoke tailoring shops. Most of its members worked in finance or technology.

The physical heart of the club was a three-story townhouse on Greenwich Avenue in the West Village, built in 1920 and rented in 2014 by Magnises at a cost of $13,750 a month. This became Charlie's new office and second home. The decor was a style that could be called Late Bloomberg, though it was really Early De Blasio – a potent mix of old money, Silicon Alley striving, and downtown trustafarian cool: *The Royal Tenenbaums* meets *American Psycho*, to hear the club's interior designer, Inson Dubois Wood, tell it. On the top floor, at the time Charlie joined, was a sitting room boasting a mohair-covered Eames chair and a half-million-dollar primitivist tapestry by Fernand Léger, *Les constructeurs à l'aloès*. Elsewhere were paint-splattered canvases of Superman and Captain America by Thierry Guetta, the French street artist and Banksy associate who called himself Mr. Brainwash. Downstairs there was a kitchen equipped with gleaming stainless steel appliances as well as a bar stocked with clean glasses and bottles of rum, whiskey, tequila, vodka, and gin, to which members could help themselves. The dining room was a communal work-space, complete with a long wooden farm table and a number of injection-molded translucent Lexan chairs by Philippe Starck. It was in one of these chairs, which cost nearly $600 apiece, that Charlie Shrem would sit and do his part to bring 'magical Internet money' to the masses.

His work for Payza was proceeding apace. By late May, the company had announced that it was 'actively exploring' ways to integrate Bitcoin into its online payment platform, and Ferhan Patel, Payza's director of global risk and compliance, showed up at the Bitcoin 2014 conference in Amsterdam that month to get a feel for the industry. 'It's clear to us that cryptocurrencies in general, and Bitcoin specifically, should not be ignored,' he said later. 'As a company in the e-payments space, Payza has a responsibility to explore the option of incorporating relevant cryptocurrencies into our platform.' As part of that exploration, the company noted, it was consulting with 'a number of specialists' from the Bitcoin community. One of these, of course, was Charlie Shrem, who described Payza initially as having no idea what Bitcoin was, much less how to profit from it. There were a number of obstacles. 'We had to get liquidity sources – where we'd get the bitcoins from – [and figure out] how do we integrate it, how do we price it, how do we test it, how do we market it to customers,' he says. Charlie's BitInstant experience now paid dividends. 'All these things that they didn't know how to do, I did. So I saved them months, if not years, of R&D.' Hyperbolic though this may be, Payza wasn't paying him $5,000 a month for nothing. In the end they settled on a plan that would roll out in multiple stages, with Charlie helping to supervise the developers as they worked toward each milestone.

Meanwhile his lawyers' negotiations with the US attorneys dragged on. Charlie had retained for his defense the high-powered law firm of Brafman & Associates, whose name partner was known for defending celebrities in criminal cases. The year Charlie was getting into Bitcoin, Ben Brafman was representing Dominique Strauss-Kahn, the former head of the International Monetary Fund, against allegations of sexual assault brought by a hotel housekeeper. The charges were ultimately dropped. Charlie Rose, on his TV show, once introduced Brafman by quoting the opinion of CNN legal analyst Jeffrey Toobin, who had called him 'the single best lawyer I have ever seen in a courtroom'. He was also quite possibly the single lawyer best equipped to empathize with Charlie Shrem. A self-admitted 'short Jewish guy', standing no more than five feet six inches tall – Charlie himself was five-foot-five – and the son of Holocaust survivors, he grew up in Brooklyn in a strict Orthodox household and, like his firm's new client, had attended yeshiva and graduated from Brooklyn College.[1] Unlike Charlie, however, Brafman, who turned sixty-six in the summer of 2014, was a flashy dresser, sporting pinstripe suits, French-cuff shirts, and tie bars. His appearance belied his old-fashioned work ethic: as Toobin has put it, 'There are a lot of flashy lawyers who are very good at cross-examination. But they don't prepare. [Brafman] prepares like a boring sort of old-school lawyer, but he's got the flash and dash of a sort of a courtroom performer. I mean, he is the best of both worlds.'

All of this was well and good and comforting to a young man

facing a possible twenty-year prison sentence. But, says Charlie, 'The *last* thing I wanted to do was go to trial. No one wins at trial.' In fact Ben Brafman's clients sometimes did win at trial, by virtue of having Ben Brafman as their lawyer, but this time the prosecution had too many smoking guns. The most damning of these was the email of 17 January 2012, in which Charlie, copying in Gareth Nelson and the CEO of TrustCash, 'banned' Robert Faiella from using BitInstant's services. 'We have warned you in the past you CANNOT deposit more than $1,000 per person per day according to our limits,' he wrote. 'You have violated our Terms of Service and we know you are reselling your services on the Silk Road. *This is illegal.*' And again, in a second email later that day, after Faiella threatened to report him to 'the federal Government' for stealing his customers' money if he kept the $4,000 that Faiella had deposited, Charlie retorted, 'Do not threaten me, as you currently sell your services on the illegal Silk Road.' (He did, however, return the funds to Faiella.)

It was because of such emails that Marc Agnifilo, a senior trial lawyer and partner at Brafman whose knowledge of Bitcoin and experience with financial crimes led him to take point on Charlie's case, insisted on a plea deal: 'I looked at the e-mails, I said, "Charlie, you have to plead guilty . . . There are all these wonderful subtle-ties in the case, and there might be some really interesting arguments and, Lord knows, we couldn't have a better judge than Judge Rakoff for interesting, weighty arguments," I said, "but you've done everyone in a sense a favor by taking a razor-sharp spotlight and going through all the fog and making it as clear as a bell you know for the rest of time that Faiella's selling bitcoins on the Silk Road, the illegal Silk Road."' Coming from an attorney who, by his own admission, had represented high-level international arms traffickers, it was a persuasive argument.

Where Charlie did want to try his case was in the court of public opinion. Even as, behind closed doors, his hotshot lawyers tried to hammer out the best deal possible, knowing he would plead guilty, Charlie himself sought to keep up appearances in the Bitcoin community, dropping hints that the case against him was without merit, or at least that he was being unfairly treated by the criminal justice system. In the eyes of some Bitcoiners he was seen, like Ross Ulbricht, as a martyr for the cause.

Having emerged from the worst of his depression, he sought to reestablish himself as a leader in the community. He once again began posting frequently on Bitcoin forums and in online discussion groups. He kept his Payza engagement under wraps at first, but when the news broke he wasn't shy about confirming it, speaking to reporters and writing a post on his own blog. 'Payza specializes in underbanked countries,' he wrote. 'I'm really excited to be working with a large team that can help me take Bitcoin to the people who need it the most.'

Toward the end of June, Charlie found himself obsessing over the upcoming US Marshals auction. He did this obsessing out loud, so to speak, in a long, ruminative post in a Bitcoin discussion group, analyzing recent trends in the Bitcoin price and weighing the odds of a new bubble – the bubble that Barry Silbert had been expecting. In the long term Charlie was bullish on Bitcoin, though unlike Barry he wasn't above profiting off the momentary peaks and valleys in the price. All week he had been wanting to buy more bitcoins. He figured six bitcoins would do it, six more bitcoins before the auction results were announced. But he was tapped out. Six bitcoins would cost him $3,495. He had two or three times that amount in his credit union account, but that was his emergency fund: he liked to keep enough socked away to cover three to four months' worth of expenses. If he bought six bitcoins now, his cushion would be cut to a mere two months. (A prudent, even cautious approach to personal finance was common among early Bitcoin users. From the outside, it seemed like a contradiction, given their adoption of something that mainstream financial advisers might reasonably call a high-risk investment. But this was not how people like Charlie Shrem saw it.) The US Marshals auction would close to bids on a Friday, 27 June. For Charlie, the following Monday was payday, and that meant receiving half of his monthly consulting fee – $2,500 worth of bitcoins – at the going exchange rate. 'I've been quietly praying that if we see a significant jump [in the price], it is not until Monday afternoon,' he admitted. But regardless of short-term fluctuations, he told people, 'If you buy one bitcoin today, in five years you'll thank me.'

If all of this was a strategy to win people over, it was a strategy that ran directly counter to Ben Brafman's own policy. It was a policy he had adopted after years of interactions with the press, having been known in the nineties for speaking openly about cases and leaking information to reporters. 'You're not looking for a good press day; you're looking to win the case,' he said in 2012. 'I've often said that if you have a bad press day but you win the case, no one will ever remember the bad press day. And if you have a good press day at the cost of winning the case, no one will ever remember the good press day.' (Marc Agnifilo, too, advised Charlie not to speak to reporters. 'If my clients were such effective talkers they wouldn't hire me,' he says.) But for Charlie, winning was a relative term. Winning would not mean acquittal; it would mean only a reduced prison sentence, or at best a few years of probation, contingent upon an admission of guilt. And he was a young man. Even after prison, he would still have practically his whole life ahead of him. He was already looking forward to the day when his legal troubles would be over. He saw himself as laying the groundwork for a future career.

Charlie Shrem wasn't the only member of Bitcoin's old guard who was looking that summer to settle a federal case. He was merely the loudest and most visible. (One of his proudest moments came in June, when GQ went to print with a 5,000-word feature in which Charlie played Bitcoin Virgil to the writer's know-nothing Dante.) Erik Voorhees, on the other hand, charged by the SEC with offering unregistered securities, was happy to stay out of the limelight. He was to be married in September.

The case against Erik Voorhees hinged on the sale of what the SEC described as illegal securities – thirteen million shares of SatoshiDice, a Bitcoin gambling site, sold on MPEx in multiple tranches at an average price of 0.0035 bitcoin per share. That left eighty-seven million shares divided up between Erik and his silent partner or partners in the enterprise, with Erik owning fewer than fifty million. Months later, in the summer of 2013, well before the SEC brought its case, Erik, having moved to Panama, sold SatoshiDice to an individual who wished to remain anonymous. The sale price was 126,315 bitcoins. Originally the equivalent of $11.5 million, this princely sum would swell with the price bubble in the fall of 2013 to a king's ransom – something on the order of $140 million at its height. The rumor went round that Erik Voorhees had become fabulously wealthy.

In truth, he says, 'I got vastly less than most people imagine I got.' This was due to how he paid back the shareholders. He would have been within his rights simply to distribute to the shareholders, who collectively held thirteen percent of SatoshiDice, thirteen percent of the money from the sale, or 16,421 bitcoins. That would have meant getting back fewer bitcoins than they had originally invested, but because the value of Bitcoin in the interim had increased dramatically, all of the shareholders would still have reaped a substantial profit. Instead, Erik decided to repay everyone the actual amount of digital currency they had invested. That meant paying out 0.0035 bitcoin per share – 45,500 bitcoins, or thirty-six percent of the total sale price. Erik paid that extra money out of his own portion of the proceeds; he wanted there to be no doubt in anyone's mind that the first major offering of Bitcoin securities was a success. It was goodwill he was after, not a quick payday. 'Even though they had all made money in dollar terms, I wanted to eliminate the ability for critics to say that I lost people money,' he says. 'Thirteen percent of the ownership got over a third of the money.' It's difficult to imagine, outside the world of Bitcoin, any investment manager doing the same for his clients, or any CEO doing the same for her shareholders.

Erik's reward for returning to his investors more money than they had any right to expect was an SEC investigation. The agency alleged that he had violated federal securities laws, specifically the requirement to register any offering of securities with the agency itself. Ostensibly the registration provisions exist to protect consumers from financial predators, a description hardly befitting

Erik Voorhees. He was no Trendon Shavers, the Bitcoin Ponzi schemer from Texas who had been charged by the SEC with defrauding lenders out of nearly 200,000 bitcoins.

Erik was in the dark until he received an emailed subpoena asking him to produce documents relating to the sale. Acting on legal advice that an email does not constitute proper service of a subpoena, he ignored it; but upon his next entry into the US a few months later, he was served at the airport. He hadn't minded sacrificing some of his profit from the sale of SatoshiDice, but this was more than he could take. 'To get slapped with a fucking SEC investigation after I had just done that for all the shareholders,' he says, 'was just, you know, if I hated government before, that was . . . I just couldn't believe that that would happen.'

He had no choice but to settle, as he saw it. Without either admitting or denying the SEC's findings, he agreed in early June to pay $50,843.98 – the $15,843.98 he had supposedly earned in profits by selling the shares, along with a $35,000 penalty – to get the charges dropped. And he promised not to do it again.

But even after the SEC case was behind him, Erik still wouldn't talk to Charlie, his old friend and former boss. The break hurt Charlie deeply. Nevertheless, when it came time to recommend a Bitcoin wallet to Payza so that the company could in turn recommend it to users who were new to digital currency, Charlie recommended Coinapult's. Months later, after Charlie's sentencing, relations between the two men would begin to thaw, returning by February 2015 to a measure of normalcy, but even then the former CEO of BitInstant remained to some in the Bitcoin community a pariah, an object of suspicion. 'People still think – not many, but there are a few – that I'm wearing a wire all the time,' he said at the time. Andreas Antonopoulos defended him in public but in private answered almost none of his emails, says Charlie. There were Bitcoiners who blamed him for tarnishing the public image of the innovative technology they held dear. It was now common for the young man, who was heavier and looked much older than before, to suffer migraines.

The real tragedy of Charlie's legal troubles was that they

dragged down Bitcoin itself. They also kept Charlie on the sidelines. They isolated him from many of the changes overtaking the industry even as regulators became more serious about getting a grip on digital currency and institutional investors scooped up many thousands of bitcoins. Pantera Capital, a small hedge fund in San Francisco, had shifted its focus entirely to digital currency, and in March had launched a Bitcoin fund designed, like Barry Silbert's Bitcoin Investment Trust, to make it easier for large investors to acquire this risky new asset. Pantera's fund was backed by one of the largest hedge funds in the country, Fortress, and two Silicon Valley venture capital firms, one of which was Ribbit Capital, whose founder, Micky Malka, sat on the board of the Bitcoin Foundation. All three firms, along with Pantera, had invested in Xapo, which now held Pantera's bitcoins for safekeeping. In the cryptocurrency's early days, guys like Roger Ver had seemed to have their hands in everything. They had woven a web of connections between people and companies. Now a growing number of elite entrepreneurs and financiers, men who had attended the right schools and had the right connections – men like Dan Morehead, the Princeton alumnus and former Goldman Sachs derivatives trader who ran Pantera – was doing the same thing. Their aim was to give digital currency the kind of global scale and utility its renegade early adopters never could.

For Bitcoin to serve as digital gold, said Malka, 'it needs to be trusted by hundreds of millions of people, not just hundreds of thousands of people.'[2] Pantera's fund was a step toward that goal.

Charlie, meanwhile, was consulting for Payza and writing prolifically on Twitter, his blog, and Bitcoin discussion boards, but mostly he was preoccupied with trying to rehabilitate his image when he might otherwise have lent his expertise and industry connections to a company such as Pantera, Xapo, or Blockchain. He might even have started a new venture of his own – now older, wiser, and with a better support staff. At one time he had been able to speak the language of both hardcore libertarians and Ivy League-educated suits; his startup had been the first to raise serious venture capital. Had he not been indicted, had he not had to resign as vice chairman

of the Bitcoin Foundation, his high profile and long experience –
for having been part of the scene since the summer of 2011 made
him practically a grand old man of Bitcoin, given the pace of change
– would have been extremely valuable. Instead his advocacy was
tainted by his status as a potential felon. With his influence diminished, power brokers from Wall Street and Silicon Valley were
usurping the territory he and others had staked out.

And yet those moneyed arrivistes were themselves hampered
by the air of scandal. In the winter of 2013 executives from Wells
Fargo, then the nation's fourth-largest bank, had met privately
with Fortress's cochairman, Peter Briger, and his team in New
York to discuss a possible joint venture: launching the first fully
regulated Bitcoin exchange in America. But Wells Fargo backed
out of the proposed project soon after Charlie Shrem was taken
into custody.[3] If the shutdown of Silk Road in October 2013 had
seemed to herald an end to the shadowy side of Bitcoin – though
well-informed experts knew this wasn't true – Charlie's arrest,
less than four months later, was an unwelcome reminder of the
anti-establishment stance of so many Bitcoiners, who seemed to
have every intention of continuing to break the law. The carelessness and, at times, outright malfeasance at BitInstant did more
than damage Charlie's future; it foreclosed an untold number of
possibilities for the Bitcoin industry – perhaps even helped to
sabotage the building of that 'more voluntary world' that Roger
so passionately desired.

But Bitcoin's march toward mainstream acceptance, however
hindered, advanced nonetheless. By June, Pantera's Bitcoin fund
had acquired more than $96 million worth of digital currency for
a total of forty-five investors. That same month, Yahoo added the
price of Bitcoin to its finance site. Now, along with checking stock
quotes, the site's more than thirty-seven million monthly visitors
could view the latest bitcoin-to-dollar exchange rate. Bloomberg
had added the Bitcoin price to its terminals in April.

In Charlie's personal life, too, the clouds gradually began to
part. Over the summer, Charlie's legal team got the US Attorney's
Office to agree that whatever plea deal they hammered out would

not require Charlie to cop to money laundering. 'Originally, the government said they would drop everything but keep money laundering,' Charlie says. 'We said no. "Get rid of money laundering and then we'll talk."' Now the prosecutor had finally conceded on that point. It wasn't official yet, 'but it was a big breath of fresh air, because I knew money laundering was the big one. That was the twenty-year one.'

As his situation slowly improved, the young entrepreneur's sunny disposition reemerged. Even in his darkest hours he retained, in the words of Marc Agnifilo, a 'wonderful life-affirming quality'. It was perhaps because of the innate goodness he sensed in Charlie that the lawyer, as he would later recount, told his client the federal case against him would work to his benefit. 'I said, "You're going to be a better person. This had to happen, it had to happen. And there are certain aspects about this case that really is God smiling on you . . . You will come out of this better, you'll come out of this being wiser beyond your years."'

In the meantime, Charlie was still determined to spread the gospel. Though forbidden to leave the five boroughs of New York City, in July he made an appearance by telepresence robot at a Bitcoin conference in Chicago. Made by Double Robotics, the aluminum-and-plastic contraption consisted of an iPad set four feet high on a shaft attached to a wheeled base. Charlie could control the fourteen-pound robot from anywhere in the world, videochatting via the tablet with anyone he came across. The US Attorney's Office had jurisdiction over his body, but not his digital avatar. Even as a face on a screen, he was still a celebrity, posing for group photos with conference attendees, a poster boy like Edward Snowden for an age in which technology was making people – including dissidents and indicted businessmen – increasingly indifferent to borders.

Even so, it was in the flesh that Charlie appeared later that month at the *American Banker* conference in New York, wearing dark jeans, loafers, a white v-neck T-shirt, and a navy blazer with a smart square of linen in the breast pocket, his honest rug of chest hair creeping up above the neckline of his T-shirt. In an on-stage interview with Marc Hochstein, the editor-in-chief of the magazine putting on the conference, he shared his thoughts on the BitLicense proposal, the protectionist impulses of deep-pocketed companies – which often welcome regulation as a barrier to entry for competing startups – Bitcoin regulations outside the US, and the game-changing nature of digital currency, which, Charlie said, 'is doing to money what email did to the Postal Service'.

But *should* money be as easily transferable as information, Hochstein wanted to know, given its potential in the wrong hands to wreak havoc?

'I think to a point,' Charlie said, 'it should be. I think that illegal payments and terrorism and all these things are very real and very bad, but there's a right way to do things. What would have happened if they had told us in 2000-something that in order to create an email address, you had to attach a real name and entity to it? That would have been a very scary thing.'

Whatever else he had been doing in the doldrums of his indictment, Charlie had clearly been thinking long and hard about the deeper implications of a world in which digital currency is not just extant but ubiquitous. And so when Hochstein went further, asking, 'Is money speech?' Charlie turned the question back on him. 'I tend to think that at least it can be,' said Hochstein. He alluded to an incident from the early days of Bitcoin, in which Visa, MasterCard, PayPal, and Western Union, ostensibly under pressure from US officials, had stopped processing donations to WikiLeaks. Bitcoin had been able to get around the blockade. In that case, the neutrality of the network had been a force for freedom of speech. But on the other hand, wasn't it equally possible that a 'real monster' like Robert Mugabe could use the Bitcoin network to move his ill-gotten gains? Was that the price of neutrality? And if so, was the network worth it? Each individual and each nation-state, it seemed, would crunch the numbers on this question and come up with a different sum.

Talk turned to PayPal's early ignorance of financial regulations and its later efforts to play catch-up once it had already gained a foothold in the international payments industry. It was inevitable, then, that Hochstein would put the question to him: 'Is it better to ask permission or beg forgiveness? Based on everything that you now know.'

Charlie sighed heavily. A ripple of laughter spread through the audience. 'I tried asking for permission,' he replied at last, 'but they wouldn't give me an answer.'

As summer deepened toward fall, the negotiations over Charlie's plea bargain hit a new milestone: the charge of operating an unlicensed money transmitting business was dropped. What remained was only the charge of *aiding and abetting* an unlicensed money transmitter. Thus, Charlie's legal team had succeeded in making a distinction between Charlie and Robert Faiella. He was not a money launderer, that is, nor was he moving drug money directly; he was merely 'helping someone who was helping someone buy illegal drugs', as Marc Agnifilo put it.

But even after reaching a deal in principle, Charlie remained defiant, or irrepressible, regarding what he saw as prosecutors' ignorance. At a pretrial hearing in early August – so called because Charlie had not yet officially pled guilty – he kept shaking his head *no* while the assistant US attorney talked about what Bitcoin was and how it worked. Finally, his lawyer told him to stop because the show of disrespect might anger the judge. (In a later hearing, the judge would comment on the 'arrogance of youth' that Charlie displayed.) And yet he had real reason to be proud. On 11 August, Payza introduced the ability for users with verified accounts – those who had provided proof of their identity and physical address – to buy bitcoins by simply withdrawing fiat-denominated funds to a Bitcoin wallet. It was an elegant solution that made the process dead simple for digital currency novices.

Charlie's own assets, thanks to legal fees, were much reduced. In late October, his checking account with the New Jersey-based Internet Archive Federal Credit Union – a nonprofit that had been the go-to financial institution for Bitcoin businesses until, in August 2013, it abruptly announced that it could no longer serve them, an event occasioning the second and final collapse of TradeHill – held $22,504. According to information he gave the probation officer preparing the presentence report, Charlie also owned $22,000 worth of bitcoins. Between his two credit cards, he was carrying a total balance of $10,092.

As the CEO of BitInstant, his salary had been $8,000 a month. The adjusted gross income he reported on his tax return had been only $10,739 in 2011, the year he founded the company with Gareth Nelson, but it skyrocketed from there. In 2012, he reported it as $130,625. The following year it jumped again, to $192,054. In addition to his salary, he made Bitcoin trades on the side. He continued to do so after his company shut down, selling over the counter – making as much as $10,000 in a single trade. By the end of 2013, he was flush, more flush perhaps than even the IRS knew. Once, he and Courtney chartered a private jet to the Bahamas. And yet, when asked in the summer of 2014 whether he feared a lawsuit, whether from the Winklevoss twins or anyone else, he said, 'Let them fucking try. I don't have civil lawyers and I'm not about to hire one. I have no assets. There's no company. They can't sue for anything. I have no assets; it's all in Bitcoin.'

His digital currency, then, what of that? As it turned out, having spent the past three years fighting to establish Bitcoin's reality, he was now relying on its immateriality. 'It doesn't exist,' he said. 'That's the beauty of Bitcoin.'

ON 3 SEPTEMBER, THE NIGHT before his plea hearing, Charlie met up with friends for drinks in SoHo. The night was unusual in that he had only one beer. He had been drinking heavily ever since his arrest and incarceration, and he had the burgeoning potbelly to prove it, but tonight he couldn't afford to have more than one. He needed to keep a clear head. He still didn't know what he would say in court the following day when the judge asked him – as he inevitably would – to explain in his own words how he had committed the crime to which he was confessing guilt.

Making the task of writing a confession more difficult was the fact that whatever he might say would surely conflict with his private feelings. He felt guilty in fact but not in spirit. He believed the law he stood convicted of breaking to be an unjust law, unevenly applied and antiquated at best, a violation of the individual's right to do as he wished with his own body and property. He shared Roger Ver's view – the view Roger had expressed forcefully to the media at the time of Charlie's arrest. Even aside from the matter of financial privacy, and even after seven months of house arrest, Charlie did not view the drug trade on Silk Road as ethically wrong or fundamentally immoral. He felt singled out for unfair prosecution. In lieu of drug prohibition, he said, he would have liked to see the penalty for driving under the influence made more severe. It was at the possibility of causing direct harm to others that he drew the line.

And yet in order to obtain leniency from the judge he would have to show contrition. He would have to accept responsibility for his crime. And so he went home ahead of his curfew to write the statement. He finished it the following morning, having risen uncharacteristically early, and went out for breakfast with a friend, a Japanese venture capitalist. A documentary film crew joined them.

When the hearing convened in the federal courthouse at 4:40 P.M., Judge Rakoff expressed disappointment that there would be no trial. 'Since Mr Agnifilo has already shown himself in many previous occasions before this Court to be an exceptional trial attorney,' he said, addressing Charlie, 'I was rather heartbroken to hear you were going to deprive me of that opportunity, but I take it, it is your desire to plead guilty – is that it?'

'Yes, and I apologize, your Honor,' the defendant replied.

The disgraced young founder of BitInstant hardly knew all that lay behind the judge's remark. As it happened, the seventy-one-year-old Jed Rakoff, a graduate of Harvard Law School who had served before going on the bench both as a federal prosecutor in the very district in which Charlie Shrem was now charged and as a private defense attorney – in both roles becoming an expert in the laws pertaining to white-collar crime – deplored the all-too-frequent use of plea bargains in federal criminal cases. He was now on senior status for the US District Court for the Southern District of New York, a kind of semiretirement, on full salary, available to judges of a certain age and tenure, and in his long career had seen much that did not sit right with him. Behind his kindly blue eyes there lay a keen intelligence and a finely honed moral sense often outraged by the American criminal justice system. It is a system in which, uniquely among the democratic nations of the world, more than ninety-seven percent of federal criminal cases – those not dismissed outright, that is – are resolved through plea bargains. It was, Rakoff thought, a system rigged against the defendant.

Jed Rakoff had become an assistant US attorney in 1973, the year that New York state established a mandatory minimum sentence of fifteen years in prison for selling a mere two ounces of cocaine, heroin, or marijuana. In the decades since, he had come to believe, as he wrote in the *New York Review of Books* in the fall of 2014, that mandatory minimums, along with sentencing guidelines, 'provide prosecutors with weapons to bludgeon defendants into effectively coerced plea bargains'.[4] The Jeffersonian ideal of having your day in court, of the right to confront your accuser and have the members of your community weigh the evidence and pronounce a fair verdict, was, in federal criminal cases, all but dead. 'In actuality, our criminal justice system is almost exclusively a system of plea bargaining, negotiated behind closed doors and with no judicial oversight,' Rakoff wrote. 'The outcome is very largely determined by the prosecutor alone.'

Charlie Shrem's case fit that description. Once the prosecutor's early push for a plea bargain failed, he indicted Charlie – in a fit of pique, as it seemed to the defendant – on the most serious charges possible: money laundering, operating an unlicensed money transmitter, and aiding and abetting an unlicensed money transmitter, which was Robert Faiella, the man who called himself BTCKing. After that, the door remained open to a plea bargain, but it wouldn't come easily. The chief sticking point was the money laundering charge. Where Charlie's case deviated from the norm was in the caliber of his attorneys, who managed over the course of months to chip away at the charges facing their client until only the least serious offense remained. Had Charlie been less fortunate in his representation – had he been unable to afford a firm like Brafman & Associates – he could have expected precisely the opposite: his prospects for a tolerable plea deal would have diminished with time.

Thus by the time of his plea hearing Charlie held a Kafkaesque conception of the law as inscrutable and terrifying, full of absurdities which nevertheless, given equal standing with legitimate statutes, must be obeyed. 'There's a book that we call the law,' he says, 'and if you live in this country you have to follow it. It says I can't do something – I did it, so I broke the law.' He added that there is also a law against tying a giraffe to a telephone pole, and that if he were to break this ridiculous law he would be guilty of lawbreaking just the same. (This law, widely mentioned on the Internet, is said to exist in Atlanta, though it may be apocryphal.) At the hearing, he wanted to address the issue – it seemed to him fundamental – of whether the law he stood accused of breaking was a just one. But his lawyers had advised him to bite his tongue. So his statement of wrongdoing, when he gave it, was stilted and dry, declaring in barebones fashion the bald facts, giving the prosecution what it wanted to hear and nothing more:

'I admit that between January of 2012 and October of 2012, I helped a person known to me as BTCKing, who had a money transmitting business, by processing [his] Bitcoin orders . . . I knew that BTCKing had failed to comply with the registration requirements of the federal money transmitter business. I also knew that BTCKing was involved in transmitting funds that were converted into Bitcoin and resold on a website called Silk Road, and I knew that much of the business conducted on Silk Road involved the unlawful buying and selling of narcotics . . . I knew that what I did here was wrong. I am pleading guilty because I am guilty.'

But Judge Rakoff wasn't satisfied. He was determined to ascertain the truth of the young man's confession. In his *New York Review of Books* essay, Rakoff notes that more than ten percent of the 1,428 felons who have been exonerated of their charges since 1989 originally gave false guilty pleas. It may be that these defendants, despairing of their chances at trial and facing hefty minimum sentences if convicted, saw a plea bargain as the lesser of two evils. 'In theory, this charade should be exposed at the time the defendant enters his plea,' he writes. 'But in practice, most judges, happy for their own reasons to avoid a time-consuming trial, will barely question the defendant beyond the bare bones of his assertion of guilt, relying instead on the prosecutor's statement (untested by any cross-examination) of what the underlying facts are.'

Not so Judge Rakoff. 'I'm not totally clear from that otherwise very complete statement exactly what your role was,' he told Charlie.

And so Charlie Shrem explained how he had served as the CEO of BitInstant from the summer of 2011 through the summer of 2013, processing payments for Bitcoin exchanges, and how Faiella had taken advantage of his system to provide bitcoins to Silk Road users.

'So in effect, you – through the means you just mentioned – you were helping him achieve his ends? Yes?' asked the judge.

'Yes, your Honor.'

'And one of those ends you knew was the transmission of funds used to promote the narcotics trade known as the Silk Road?'

'Yes, your Honor,' Charlie said.

'Very good. Let me ask the government first, [is there] anything else the government wants me to inquire about or represent with respect to the factual portion of the allocution?'

'No, your Honor,' the assistant US attorney replied. 'I think that covers it.'

It was done. Charlie, still required to wear a tracking anklet and still under curfew, was in no sense a free man, but the hard part was over.

Now, however, with his sentencing still months away, he had to face criticism from his fellow Bitcoiners. 'I must admit I'm disappointed with you Charlie,' a user named Bitbirdhunt wrote on the Bitcoin Forum. 'If you are truly innocent then you must not plead guilty to *ANY* charges that you did not commit. We cannot permit the Federal Mafia to simply threaten everyone into submission. This sets a very bad precedent for the future and [for] other Bitcoin users.' It was a sentiment not far removed from one that had been voiced at the highest levels of the Bitcoin community ever since the former BitInstant CEO's arrest. But other Bitcoin leaders were more upset by Charlie's tarnishing of the digital currency through his criminal actions. 'I'm disappointed about Charlie,' Gavin Andresen had said months earlier, already weary of the matter. 'Actually I'm a little bit angry with him. It's definitely not good for Bitcoin. Certainly not good for Charlie. Look, Charlie is twenty-four. And there is a huge anti-government faction in the Bitcoin world. I sympathize. But it's time for Bitcoin to grow up.'[5]

Charlie, too, was intent on growing up. Escaping the confines of his parents' house was a top priority. On 23 September, he signed a six-month lease for a penthouse apartment in a landmark building at 90 West Street. The rent was $3,600 a month. The lease was set to begin on the first of October, but he couldn't move in until the court gave its okay. And so when Charlie sat down days later with the probation officer for his presentence interview, he made sure that the probation officer, James Mullen, got an earful about his domestic situation. He told Mullen a story about his father in a heated moment breaking down his bedroom door. He started to write an email to the court about the incident, he said, but his parents saw the email, and their already strained relationship was damaged further. Because of these incidents, as he would later relate, Judge Rakoff allowed him to move into the apartment. He remained under curfew, but he was free of his parents. In early November, Courtney returned from her extended stay in Pennsylvania and moved in with him.

Meanwhile, Payza rolled out another stage of its plan: a way for its users to sell bitcoins. Just as buying bitcoins took the form of withdrawing funds from your Payza wallet, selling bitcoins took the form of depositing funds into your wallet. It worked like this: you clicked on the Add Funds tab in your account, selected Bitcoin, and entered the number of bitcoins you wanted to deposit, at which point the current exchange rate would be displayed. To complete the transaction, you'd confirm the details and send your bitcoins to the address Payza provided. The money was available immediately, and it could be used to make a purchase from any business in Payza's network. At a stroke, Payza had just opened up 100,000 merchants to users of digital currency.

ON THE NIGHT OF 22 November, Charlie Shrem threw a birthday party for himself in his new home.

Having escaped the Brooklyn basement that had for so long been the scene of his misery, he now occupied with his girlfriend an apartment on the penthouse floor of 90 West Street, an architectural landmark designed by Cass Gilbert, the architect of the one-time world's tallest Woolworth Building, which shared the neo-Gothic style of 90 West Street and whose steeply pitched copper roof, green with age, was visible from one of Charlie's windows. The one-bedroom apartment had a market value of more than $1 million, but on the night of the party it seemed downright homey. Twenty or so guests stood about, chatting easily and drinking from plastic cups. On a side table were bowls of chips and dip, platters of shrimp and fried chicken, a casserole dish filled with asparagus and another filled with risotto. A tray was piled with bricks of homemade peanut butter fudge. Some of the food had been prepared by Courtney's mother, Diane, who was one of the guests.

Charlie, wearing a red seersucker polo shirt, was the undisputed center of attention. The crowd was a rare treat, for usually the residence was on lockdown. 'I told them not to let anybody up without my approval,' he said, referring to the doormen and the building superintendent, whom he had given a large tip to ensure that his instructions were followed. But it seemed the cash had not sufficiently impressed upon them his security concerns. 'The other day they let up a delivery guy who had a receipt for the order,' he said. 'They said, "Well, he had a receipt." I'm like, "*Any*body can print out a receipt! What are you doing? He could have a gun and be trying to kill me!"'

He had reason to be concerned for his privacy and safety. He was a sitting duck. His house arrest was not yet over; it continued at a new address. He could no sooner leave the premises of 90 West Street past the hours of his curfew than he could leave his parents' house in the first months after his arrest. At a sealed hearing only weeks before, he said, he had testified that his parents were abusive and controlling, forcing him to adopt the practices of a religion he no longer believed in and striving to keep him apart from the woman he loved, who had helped him 'a million times over' to get through the darkest period of his life. Charlie confided that the judge, hearing this, had been ready to throw his parents into a jail cell, but he had intervened on their behalf. Custody of the confessed felon had then been transferred to Courtney, at the cost of his relationship with his parents. '*I'm* his family now,' Courtney declared proudly. So the number of his guardians had been reduced by two, and he was still notorious. But as drinks were poured, the threat of mad gunmen was forgotten.

Most of the guests at the party were Bitcoiners. Among them were two representatives of Blockchain: Peter Smith, wearing an untucked shirt and jeans, and Marco Santori, atypically casual in a shirt of black-and-green plaid, padding about in dark socks, the guests having been asked to remove their shoes. Another guest was a handsome man with a shaved head named Adam Sherman, a former Wall Street algorithmic trader who had given up the finance game, he said, to run a bar for two years on the Lower East Side. Now he was the managing partner of a small Manhattan hedge fund called Asymmetric Return Capital. It was with Adam Sherman and two other men that Charlie had been plotting his comeback.

They had two startups in the works. One of them, Action Crypto, was 'ninety-nine percent ready' to launch; the other was only halfway there. The latter would be what he had described to Amir Taaki the previous spring: a website for online poker, but with a special twist – no rooms full of players. Instead the site's matching engine would pit you head-to-head against an opponent of its choosing. Action Crypto was to be something else entirely: an online market for binary options related to the price of Bitcoin. A binary option is essentially a contractual bet that the price of an asset, such as Apple stock or pork bellies, will be above or below a certain price at a certain time. If, at that time, the bet turns out to be right, then the person holding the option receives a predetermined amount of cash. If not, then he or she gets nothing

– and in fact typically loses money, since trading platforms charge for each option contract. Think of it like a hand of blackjack. If you go bust, you lose the money you put down for that hand. A binary option is an all-or-nothing game. Charlie's new site was to be a further intertwining of cryptocurrency and modern finance, a place for people to bet on the movement up or down of the bitcoin-to-dollar exchange rate.

In the slick preview version that Adam Sherman demonstrated to a journalist at the party, the time period of the contract could be as little as five minutes, providing a gratification more immediate even than that of day trading. It would be the Adderall high of financial gambling. And, like a casino ensuring its house advantage, the trading platform would weight the expected return on investment in its own favor through the size of payouts and the price of contracts. (If you have a fifty-fifty chance of gaining $50 or losing $100, you have to win twice as much as you lose in order to break even.) A few years before, the SEC and the CFTC had issued a joint investor alert sounding the alarm about fraud connected with binary options trading platforms of this kind, whose numbers had soared in recent years. Many of them, according to regulators, were making unregistered offerings of options contracts, whether related to stocks or to commodities such as gold, wheat, and corn. 'Much of the binary options market operates through Internet-based trading platforms that are not necessarily complying with applicable US regulatory requirements and may be engaging in illegal activity,' the investor alert read.[6]

Charlie Shrem, mindful of what his friend Erik Voorhees had suffered, had no desire to run afoul of US securities and commodities laws. Both of the websites he was preparing to launch would be absolutely off-limits to Americans. But citizens of other countries would have free reign.

Visible beyond the window, the immense stalk of One World Trade Center, lit up like a dream, soared away into the blackness, looking close enough to touch. When the Twin Towers fell, 90 West Street suffered horrendous damage. Flaming debris from the south tower slammed into its foot-thick terra cotta facade, tearing out steel crossbeams and starting a fire within that burned out of control for nearly two days. Several floors were gutted in the blaze.[7] Thanks to its fireproofing, the building didn't collapse. But the reconstruction was arduous, costing $148 million and taking years to complete, during which time the landmark was shrouded in construction netting and obscured behind scaffolding.[8] There was something poetic in the fact that Charlie was making a new start in a building which had itself made a miraculous comeback. He seemed to savor the parallel. In the living room hung a framed and hand-colored illustration of Cass Gilbert's original scheme for 90 West Street, as published in the 19 January 1907 issue of the *American Architect and Building News*. Charlie was a middle-class kid from Brooklyn who had been swept up in the vortex of techno-logical change and deposited here, at the top of New York. He was twenty-five years old. What would the ensuing years bring? And how much of what was to come would he have a hand in shaping?

Sometime before midnight, champagne was poured round and Charlie gave a toast. The jovial mood turned serious. As he talked, Courtney, standing beside him, began to cry. 'When I got arrested for the bullshit that I did,' he began, 'the first thing Courtney did was get into combat mode, and she knew exactly who to call. She called the lawyers, got them on a plane that night, and if they weren't, "Hide the bitcoins, get rid of the safe"—'

'We still gotta get that safe,' someone interjected.

'—if my lawyers hadn't of been on the plane that night, in the jail the next morning to bail me out, I would have been in prison for a very long time. Without a good lawyer at the bail hearing, which saved my life. Not only that, but a lot of girls would have jumped the gun at that point,' he added, intending to say that most would have abandoned him to his fate. 'Courtney stayed. She went home to live with her mom, and every night we watched movies together and we'd Skype and we'd talk, and we made sure that our relationship had face time, and we talked every hour—'

'Oh my God,' Diane cut in good-naturedly, 'it was a pain in the fucking ass!'

'—but we did it! And finally,' Charlie went on, 'when I testified against my parents and got out of house arrest, because my parents didn't want to let me—'

'A week later,' someone added.

'—a week later,' Charlie agreed, 'Courtney was there.' He turned to face her: 'And I love you, and thank you, you're the best one ever.'

'*Wife her!*' shouted a guest named John, who had brought to the party for their first date a woman he had met on the hookup app Tinder.

The room erupted in whoops and cheers. The rest of the night was to be pure celebration. An entire bottle of Espolón tequila blanco vanished into shot glasses. After the tequila there were cans of Tecate beer. Charlie did not yet know that he wouldn't get the chance to launch his planned startups. He did not yet know that he was bound for prison. The last ten months were behind him. Everything was still possible. He embraced his girlfriend, her happy, tear-stained face on his shoulder.

Chapter 14

UINDICATION

Bitcoin is Silicon Valley's long-overdue secession.

– Oleg Andreev

By the summer of 2014, Blockchain was on a war footing. Its wallet service now had some 1.7 million accounts, and Nic Cary was meeting with venture capitalists on both coasts, having decided that the only way his startup could maintain its primacy and rate of growth – now that it was growing in so many directions – was to raise many millions of dollars of outside investment. His timing could hardly have been better. By 5 June, the amount of publicly disclosed venture capital funding raised by Bitcoin startups in 2014 – $113.2 million – was already eighteen percent higher than the amount raised during all of the previous year. The year before that, Bitcoin startups – that is, Coinbase and BitInstant – had managed to raise only $2.1 million in publicly disclosed funding, with BitInstant taking the lion's share. The landscape had shifted dramatically in only a year and a half. Having lain nearly dormant for months after Satoshi's grand unveiling, and only gradually gathering momentum in the years that followed, Bitcoin was now picking up speed, accelerating, it seemed, toward a point when it would increasingly outstrip ordinary time, the customary life cycle of innovation, so that its advocates, whose rate of metabolism was correspondingly increased, had already devised a term, 'blockchain time', for this burning pace of change, in which game-changing events rose up suddenly and died away just as suddenly into irrelevance.

Even so, Nic Cary couldn't be sure that his company stood to benefit. If there was a war on – and not merely the usual conflict between rival firms in a red-hot industry, but a conflict between competing visions for a groundbreaking technology – it was one he felt that he was losing. 'Seems like all the money is moving into projects that are basically building new banks, and I don't understand that,' he remarked one day in early June. 'It is an us-versus-everybody kind of approach right now, because I don't know anyone else who's doing it the way we are. Most companies don't build open-source software; most people don't give things away for free; most people centralize custody of information – control user data, control user funds. We do *none* of those things . . . It's totally insane from a business development perspective.' He laughed, anticipating the question a potential investor might ask: '*What* do you monetize?'

There was a chance investors would not understand what made Blockchain different from so many other Bitcoin startups, a chance that as a result it would gradually lose ground to its better-funded rivals. There was a chance, because even Nic himself was unsure whether the business strategy, amounting in fact to a philosophy, to which he and Ben Reeves and Roger Ver and Peter Smith had committed themselves, was truly the world-beating strategy he hoped it would be. Put simply, he was unsure whether Blockchain could win out over Coinbase. 'Ultimately, they represent two competing expressions of how to use Bitcoin,' he says. 'In the long run, they can both be successful companies. But there's definitely a natural sort of "Us versus Them". I don't know if it's like Microsoft versus Apple, but it's something like that. Not only are our technology and security stances so completely different from each other, but the fact that Brian [Armstrong] – from our perspective – mistreated Ben is certainly a little motivating.'

Ultimately, however, it wasn't the desire to beat Coinbase that drove him. What drove him was the desire to see Bitcoin – 'the meta-organization of Bitcoin', as Erik Voorhees called it, 'the first decentralized, open-source company' – succeed. 'We can do that without having negativity drive our vision,' Nic says. 'At the same time, our biggest challenge is convincing consumers that our security approach is superior. And that's not easy, because, you know, Coinbase can reset your password if you lose it, and some people are going to like that.' It wasn't merely a question of whether or not investors would understand his company's approach. It was a question, as he had told the Aurus partners, of whether or not that approach 'will appeal to the next hundred million users. I suspect it won't – not to everybody.' The Western world might be slow to catch on. In parts of the developing world, however, where people had little faith in banks and even less in the governments issuing their currency, where people made arduous trips to cash-in, cash-out retail locations in order to send and receive money, Bitcoin in general – and the Blockchain approach in particular – might seem like a big improvement.

Looked at from another angle, Blockchain enjoyed in its overtures to venture capital firms a position of incredible strength. There was, first, its claim to fame as the world's most popular Bitcoin wallet service.[1] There was, second, ZeroBlock, a portal to market data and industry news, the most highly rated Bitcoin app for both iOS and Android. And on 21 May, ZeroBlock added a new exchange, BTC-e, to its trading platform, giving subscribers access to two of the deepest pools of liquidity – BTC-e and Bitstamp – in the world of Bitcoin.

Third, there was the Blockchain merchant app, which allowed small businesses to handle digital currency. Bill Hill had envisioned it as suitable only for tablets, like the Nexus they had gifted to Sofiane Bouhaddi the night of the app's launch, but he'd seen it being used on smartphones as well. It was free to download, and Blockchain charged merchants no commission or transaction fees whatsoever. By fall, the app would be processing between 1,600 and 1,700 transactions a day. And there were, finally, the open-source Blockchain APIs – widely used by other developers for payment processing, wallet creation, transaction data, and much more. For instance, Safello, a Swedish Bitcoin exchange into which Nic Cary, Roger Ver, Erik Voorhees, Ira Miller, and others, including Anders Bruzelius, the former head of equity research at Swedbank, had pumped $600,000 in expansion funding barely a week before Mt. Gox went dark, offered its users a wallet to store their coins in, but it was merely a front end; the code behind it – the code that made it possible – was Blockchain's.

The company, hydra-headed though it was, had been built with very little money in comparison to the millions of dollars in venture capital that were now, as a result of the rising cost of doing business, de rigueur for the top Bitcoin startups. Blockchain pulled in six figures a month by selling ad space on its web properties and the ZeroBlock app. It also got paid for referring institutional buyers to certain Bitcoin exchanges. And the company had always been careful with its funds, just as its CEO was frugal in his personal life. By May 2014, Blockchain had spent less than $20,000 on marketing. Says Nic, 'We weren't out there trying to buy users.' Yet the users had come regardless. And so it was with a certain confidence that Nic Cary and Peter Smith flew to California on 23 June to meet with potential investors.

To save money, they stayed in Oakland at the house of one of Nic's college friends, William Augustus Ghirardelli IV. In college his name had preceded him, and rumors – rumors that embarrassed Ghirardelli but which he did not entirely discourage – had spread that the scion of a chocolate dynasty, a real-life Willy Wonka, was on campus. In truth there was no chocolate fortune to which Ghirardelli could lay claim. His family's company had been sold off decades ago. And this rumored chocolate magnate, who went by the name Bo, was, in fact, among those who knew him, legendarily cheap, the kind of man who thought nothing of owning, as his primary means of transportation, a broken-down, manual-transmission 2003 Honda Civic that had been totaled and which he was in the process of slowly restoring, a car that had paint peeling off three-quarters of its hood, fenders, and roof; a busted-up piece of shit that somehow ran reliably despite looking like it belonged in a junkyard. It was this car that Nic Cary and Peter Smith borrowed to make the rounds in Silicon Valley, to – as Nic put it – 'go pitch the wealthiest, smartest people on the planet'.

There was, during the long drive in, a lot to think about. As much as Blockchain's wide array of services might be catnip to venture capitalists, it was in fact an obstacle to investment. Blockchain wanted the full attention of its investors, yet it was difficult for any firm with a serious interest in Bitcoin not to have a conflict of interest, simply because almost any major Bitcoin startup could be considered a competitor of Blockchain. There was, too, Nic's troubling sense that he was out of his element when it came to the finer points of venture capital dealmaking, and his fear that the investors might one day seek to force him out of the company he had done so much to build. Having never before led a company to an exit – that is, an IPO or an acquisition, so called because it allows investors to gain a return on their investment either by selling shares or by receiving compensation for their ownership stake – he was 'an unproven animal to them', he says. It was a scary situation. 'I like building software. I don't like talking about complicated transactions that might involve my head on a platter.' Blockchain would only get one shot at its Series A, and since any future rounds of funding must refer back to it, any mistake in the paperwork – that is, in the terms of the deal – would be, in Nic's words, 'a forever fuck-up'.

His solution to the legal concerns, naturally enough, was to retain a high-powered law firm to protect his interests. More unusually, he paid the firm in bitcoins. This acceptance of digital currency was not the firm's policy but merely a concession to Blockchain's way of doing business, which included paying all employees in bitcoins, closing all advertising deals in bitcoins, and generally using Bitcoin as the company's unit of account, with all the volatility that that implied. Blockchain, in turn, set the law firm up with a BitPay account, just as Nic Cary months earlier had set up the University of Puget Sound with a BitPay account so that it might accept his donation and convert it immediately into dollars. ('I feel like I should get compensated by BitPay,' he joked.) When raising venture capital, you can optimize the deal for one of several things. One is the size of the investment. Another is the type of money you receive – debt versus cash. Yet another is company valuation. This is the market value stamped on your enterprise by investors, so that raising $10 million in exchange for ten percent of the equity values your company at $100 million. Nic knew that his stake in Blockchain, along with Roger Ver's and Ben Reeves's, would be diluted in order to accommodate investors, but he also knew that if he weren't careful to retain – along with Roger and Ben – a controlling interest in the business, he might one day find an erstwhile ally stabbing him in the back. And so he chose to optimize for control. This was not only an act of preemptive self-preservation. He doubted whether a venture capital firm truly had the foresight to navigate the typhoon waters through which he himself had been sailing admirably up till now. But also, yes, he admitted, 'I don't want to get fucking canned.'

Menlo Park, when they arrived, struck Nic as a deeply weird place, 'bizarre as hell'. From Interstate 280, Sand Hill Road runs northeast four miles until, just past a shopping center, it dead-ends into State Road 82, here called El Camino Real. Clustered together along Sand Hill Road are the offices of dozens of venture capital and private equity firms, most of them set back from the road, the buildings uniformly low-rise in an environment unquestionably suburban in its leafy green, so that driving this stretch you pass, though perhaps unaware of their presence, the headquarters of Andreessen Horowitz (2865 Sand Hill Road), Silver Lake Partners (2775 Sand Hill Road), Makena Capital (2755 Sand Hill Road), Kleiner Perkins Caufield & Byers (2750 Sand Hill Road), and, closer to the road, those of Opus Capital (2730 Sand Hill Road), Greylock Partners (2250 Sand Hill Road), Lightspeed Venture Partners (2200 Sand Hill Road). One particularly rich pocket of firms, just east of the interstate, is housed in a development encircled by the manicured fairways of the Sharon Heights Golf and Country Club, like a clutch of eggs in a nest: Sequoia Capital, Redpoint Ventures, Deep Fork Capital, Institutional Venture Partners, Mohr Davidow Ventures, Voyager Capital, and – the odd duck out – the California Research Center of Harvard Business School. Together the firms on Sand Hill Road manage more than $100 billion of venture capital. Says Nic, 'For some reason, somebody one day decided that Sand Hill Road would be where all the VCs go' – but the reason, of course, was obvious: proximity to Stanford. The university has become renowned for turning out many of the brightest luminaries of high technology: Larry Page and Sergey Brin, William Hewlett and David Packard, Kevin Systrom and Mike Krieger, Vint Cerf, Reid Hoffman, and Peter Thiel. Men with eyes set, like those of Montana cattle barons, for great distances, though distances less of space than of time. The companies of its entrepreneurial alumni generate $2.7 trillion annually in global revenues; if gathered collectively into a nation in their own right, these forty thousand companies, including Google, Hewlett-Packard, Nike, Netflix, Charles Schwab, and Cisco Systems, would make up the world's tenth-largest economy. Nic Cary and Peter Smith had come, in Nic's telling phrase, 'to bow down to the Sand Hill gods'.

They had lined up nearly twenty meetings over the course of five days in Silicon Valley, and so they went from office to office, conference table to conference table, word of their progress spreading as they went. To the denizens of Sand Hill Road, where advance knowledge is power, their presence was no secret. But the outside world was in the dark. As a consequence of pursuing outside investment, Blockchain had developed a sudden aversion to publicity. Nic Cary was barely speaking to the press, and, on the advice of Blockchain's attorneys, the rest of the staff were saying even less. 'We have basically gone into fucking lockdown mode,' Nic remarked one day in June. For Blockchain employees, this meant a moratorium on speaking independently to reporters, for fear that the wrong or the ill-chosen word could tank an impending deal. Peter Smith wasn't above lying to an employee to make sure he kept his mouth shut, for instance telling him that a reporter who had approached him wanted only to write a hit piece about Blockchain. Now more than ever it was important to remain 'on message'.

And why? Because venture capital firms, says Nic, 'have research teams whose sole purpose is to fuck you. They're trying to find every single thing that you've ever done wrong.' The fact that Blockchain's first investor was a convicted felon was not a good start. Nic was acutely aware of what a single instance of bad press could cost him. On 15 April, Valleywag, a muckraking online gossip rag covering the tech industry, part of Gawker Media, had published an explosive story that linked Tony Gallippi, the CEO of BitPay, to a now-defunct website, Soopermodels.com, which featured images of scantily clad women and girls. None of the photos could have been rated more than PG-13, but some of the models were in their early teens. More than a decade earlier, the company behind the site had evidently functioned as both a modeling agency, offering talent for book-ings, and as a titillating photo gallery for paying subscribers. Gallippi was the founder and producer. Asked to comment, he described Soopermodels as merely 'a consortium of photog-raphers hired by agencies to photograph people of all ages, including children, young adults, and adult men and women'. For the more risqué shots, he said, there had been a strict eighteen-and-older age requirement.[2]

But the damage was done. A month later, just after the announcement of BitPay's record-breaking $30 million round of venture capital financing, Gallippi quietly transitioned from the company's top job to a chairmanship. Stephen Pair, BitPay's cofounder and chief technology officer, moved into the CEO role. Knowing what he knew about the industry, Nic guessed that a condition of the funding was that Tony Gallippi step aside.

Nic himself had nothing to hide, but nevertheless the Gallippi affair instilled in him a level of caution approaching paranoia. 'Who has the most to benefit from doing that?' he asked, meaning who might have tipped off the reporter to Gallippi's shady past. '*The venture capital firm*. They fucking torpedo the valuation of the company and eat up more of the business.' He had no way to confirm his suspicions, but it was on the spectrum, he believed, of what a venture capitalist might do to get a better deal. He was determined not to fall prey to strong-arm tactics. In a meeting with Redpoint Ventures, Nic went on the attack. 'Why did you invest in BitGo?' he demanded. 'We think they're a competitor. Explain why they're not.' The Redpoint partners – the firm's entire partnership team had shown up for the meeting, Nic recalls – were taken aback. They can't have expected such an aggressive approach. But the Blockchain leadership was adamant: No way in hell would they discuss their plans for global domination with a firm that had just given money to a competing startup.

The competitor to which Nic was referring was BitGo, a startup that had just raised $12 million in a funding round led by Redpoint and joined by Peter Thiel's Founders Fund, Barry Silbert's Bitcoin Opportunity Corp., and Ashton Kutcher's A-Grade Investments. The funding had been announced on 16 June, one week before Nic Cary and Peter Smith boarded their flight to California. As a condition of the investment, Redpoint partner Jeff Brody had joined BitGo's board.

BitGo had made a name for itself by introducing in April, while the shock of Mt. Gox's collapse still reverberated through the Bitcoin industry, the first multi-signature digital wallet aimed at corporate clients. Unlike an ordinary Bitcoin wallet, a multi-sig wallet comes with multiple private keys – unique alphanumeric passcodes – and funds can't be moved without more than one key signing off on the transaction. With a BitGo wallet, one of the keys was retained by the user (and connected to the online hot wallet), one was kept by BitGo, and one was kept by the user in a cold-storage backup. Divvying up the keys in this way and requiring that a majority be applied to every transaction established a kind of fail-safe in the event of loss or theft, just as nuclear missiles can't be launched without two physical keys being turned. In other words, whereas Blockchain allowed users to control their own private keys, while Coinbase controlled them on behalf of users, BitGo was pioneering a third way.

Indeed, BitGo seemed to address the weaknesses of both. Changpeng Zhao, who by late June had left Blockchain to become the chief technology officer of OKCoin, a major Chinese Bitcoin

exchange, admitted that his former employer expected 'a certain
level of sophistication' from its users – in addition to remembering
their private keys, they had to keep their computers secure and
free of malicious software that might grant an intruder access. A
lot of people, unfortunately, lack the know-how to keep their
computers from getting infected. 'From a product design standpoint, I think that's a blind spot for Blockchain,' Zhao says. (A
wallet like Coinbase's, with its user-friendly interface, avoided that
problem, but its own risk was even greater: the risk of being hacked
and losing customer information or funds.) Small wonder that Nic
Cary saw BitGo as competition. So promising was BitGo's technology, in fact, that one month earlier a software engineer and
Bitcoin angel investor named Ben Davenport had quit his job at
Facebook to become the startup's head of product.

And the company planned to offer its multi-sig technology as
a security service to corporations, including vital members of the
Bitcoin ecosystem: exchanges, mining pools, even other wallet
providers. It was thought that BitGo might be able to do for digital
currency what Verisign had done years earlier for e-commerce,
making it relatively safe to provide your credit card information
to make a purchase online. (Indeed, Stratton Sclavos, a former
CEO of Verisign and now a partner at one of the venture capital
firms that had given money to BitGo, was joining BitGo's board
alongside Redpoint's Jeff Brody.[3]) At the time of the $12 million
funding round, BitGo's CEO, Will O'Brien, voiced his ambitions
this way: 'We're putting together a company that Fortune 500
[firms] and the largest hedge funds can trust as their Bitcoin
security platform.'[4]

In the meeting with Nic Cary and Peter Smith, the Redpoint
investors tried to explain, on this basis, that although BitGo had
a consumer wallet, it was concentrating on serving enterprise
clients – and was therefore not a competitor to Blockchain. But
the Blockchain executives weren't buying it. On 23 June, Ashton
Kutcher had tweeted, 'Thank you Bitgo.com for providing a
simple seamless safe place to manage my Bitcoin.' If the company
wasn't making a consumer play, why have an A-list movie star

sing its praises to an audience of more than sixteen million followers?

Nic Cary and Peter Smith took the meeting with Redpoint just to see what its partners had to say for themselves. Then they walked out.

'The VC stuff is tricky,' Nic says. 'They'll host a big meeting like that just for competitive intelligence. And they will string you along for a long time to tie you up. And then they'll walk away later. So it's a *daaangerous*, sketchy-ass game.'

As in any war, a certain amount of misinformation was disseminated. In meetings with firms that had already made large investments in other Bitcoin startups – firms, that is, which had obvious conflicts and which Blockchain therefore was not seriously considering as potential investors – Nic Cary and Peter Smith would give altered versions of their presentation, either underselling or overselling what their company was doing. Like poker players holding a pair of tens, they bluffed, making investors think they were holding pocket aces – or nothing of value at all – 'just to terrify them or create urgency and froth up the whole scene', Nic says. They knew how word of mouth spread in Silicon Valley. The air was thick with rumors. 'What you essentially want is to create such an anxiety in your potential investors that they decide they need to move quickly, that this is the last opportunity,' Nic says.

But with others they played it straight, including Lightspeed Venture Partners, Jeremy Liew's firm – Jeremy Liew who had invested in Snapchat and five months earlier had sat with Barry Silbert on a panel at the NYDFS hearings on Bitcoin. For him they laid out a vision of Blockchain reimagining how the world transacts. It was a vision not only of digital currency and consumer wallets, of global citizenship fueled by frictionless cross-border payments, but of a world in which the unbanked could be their own banks. To make the point, Nic larded his presentation with photos that he had used earlier that month in a TEDx talk about the future of money at AOL's offices in downtown New York – photos of his trip to the Sahara Desert and of small business owners who had adopted the Blockchain merchant app. It was, in his estimation, a vision that would take five or ten or even a hundred years to be fulfilled. Blockchain was playing the long game; it wanted partners who were willing to play along.

The company's pitch hinged on three key metrics: growth in the number of its consumer wallets, which had increased more than fivefold in the past twelve months, from about 315,000 to more than 1.7 million; the amount of money that had moved through services designed by or dependent on Blockchain and had been broadcast to the Bitcoin network; and the portion of the total network that this represented. Incredibly, over the past two and a half years some $30 billion worth of transactions had passed through Blockchain wallets and through systems built on Blockchain's APIs. 'All the miners listen to our node to make sure they can hear transactions first and then start to crunch on them,' Nic said at the time, 'and so because of that, we do a lot of the overall transaction volume that's being broadcast to the network. There's no monetization there,' he added. 'We provide these services for free.' This is what excited the investors most of all – the scope of the current transaction volume and its potential to grow even larger with time. There was, also, the huge flow of web traffic to Blockchain's website. By this time, Blockchain.info was receiving several million visitors every month, who together racked up some 100 million pageviews – a sign of the company's perhaps unparalleled visibility in the Bitcoin industry. Even after leaving Blockchain, Changpeng Zhao continued to believe that, as he said in the summer of 2014, 'they have a huge lead on any other company in the space.'

But it was not enough, in Nic's mind, to dazzle the investors with facts and figures expressing Blockchain's growth. He wanted them to understand the hardwired philosophical difference between Blockchain and other Bitcoin companies of its size, that it was a software company first and not a financial services provider, that it did not centralize the control of user funds, and to recognize why this made Blockchain's approach superior. Coinbase's security risks grew with every new user who signed up for a wallet; Blockchain's risk would stay the same with ten times or even a hundred times the number of current users. Indeed, Blockchain's risk might even decrease the larger it grew. 'As more and more users [create] Blockchain wallets, it's like building out more and more safe deposit boxes,' Nic says. 'A hacker has to guess at which one they would attack. So the more and more and more of them there are, the more effort, the more computing power, and more time they would have to invest in order to start breaking into each individual wallet.' Lightspeed's Jeremy Liew was intrigued.

'Companies in this space have security choices to make,' Nic had remarked earlier that month. 'Like Coinbase, Circle, Xapo – these guys have all built basically new banks on top of a trust-less protocol, which doesn't make sense to me. It reintroduces counterparty risk. The whole point of Bitcoin is to eliminate that risk. I look at this and I'm totally fucking confused by why they built things the way they did. And then they go to Washington, D.C. and say that we're the bad guys, that we've created systems that are dangerous and uncontrollable – because we can't touch our users' funds. All those other teams – whether it's Coinbase or Xapo or Circle – they've centralized risk again. So what are they going to do? "Well, okay, if it's really risky then we'll sell insurance." So they're just adding in all the same fucking shit layers of our financial system we already have. It's probably psychological gravity – the gravity of the existing financial system and the fees that they can take and the seduction of being able to control and have managerial responsibility for someone else's money. If you take custody of people's funds, you can do stuff with that money, like do derivatives or lend it out. There's this historical tendency to want to do that, even though this is a new monetary paradigm. And the problem with that is – *how many more Mt. Goxes do we need?*'

When the five days of meetings came to an end, Nic and Peter hopped on a plane and flew to New York, where more meetings were scheduled with more venture capitalists. They were looking to start a bidding war on both coasts. Initially, they didn't give investors an exact dollar figure for the amount they were hoping to raise. 'You don't want to be the first guy,' Nic says. 'You don't want to be like, "Ten!" And they're like, "Hmm . . . Five." You want to have them start by saying, "We're really excited about this opportunity. We want to make sure that the [company] we bet on has the capital to win." And then they start compiling numbers.'

Having worked in sales, Nic enjoyed pitching. But even as he and Peter Smith stayed in touch with possible investors, the regular business of Blockchain continued at a breakneck pace. After New York, Nic flew to Seattle, then made a pit stop in the UK before recrossing the Atlantic Ocean to make another pilgrimage to Silicon Valley, after which he paid a visit to Dublin, dropped in on the two-day CoinSummit conference in London, and finally, in mid-July, came home to York. But even there he was far from idle. Blockchain was completely rewriting its Android app in preparation for a new release, and this was the final push. While the developers cranked away, enduring sleepless nights, Nic spent much of his time reviewing design mockups with Dan Held and Keonne Rodriguez, the project manager, and testing early builds of the app.

They wanted the experience of users, including those entirely new to Bitcoin, 'to be as quick and seamless as possible', Rodriguez says, and so they made it possible to create a new Bitcoin wallet in just one click.[5] As simple as this process was, the app required a few more steps to secure a user's wallet. It was designed to be protected by a PIN code and by a backup copy – emailed to any address you chose – which could be accessed in the event that you lost your phone. 'To try and educate [people] and mildly enforce a security policy,' Rodriguez explains, 'we introduced a nagging message that appears on startup if a password and email backup [haven't] been set.'

In the course of rewriting the app, the Blockchain developers were at last able to implement a unique feature: the merchant map that Nic had previewed at Javier Salcedo's house in Santiago two months earlier. Using your cell phone's GPS, it would provide you, wherever you were, with a map and descriptions of nearby stores, restaurants, bars, and other businesses that accepted Bitcoin. Businesses were color-coded according to type, so that cafés were marked in red, bars and breweries in purple, restaurants and other eateries in orange, and shops in blue. The locations of Bitcoin ATMs – machines that allowed people to turn cash into digital currency – were marked in green. The feature became 'a huge hit with our users', Keonne Rodriguez would later say, adding that Blockchain planned to continue improving it, so that in future versions of the app you could be notified whenever you were near a Bitcoin-accepting merchant.[6] Nic, for his part, admitted that the merchant map 'may not completely reimagine global commerce', but he saw it as a practical step toward making Bitcoin useful for average consumers. He wanted also to provide an incentive for merchants to accept digital currency by highlighting them in Blockchain's business directory, giving them, as he hoped, a leg up over their competition.

The new Android app debuted on 19 July. Within three months, it had been installed on more than 100,000 mobile devices. It earned Blockchain good press, and something more: it made Apple take notice.

In the months since Apple had booted out of its App Store all Bitcoin wallet and payment apps, Bitcoin developers and users had migrated to Android en masse. But then, in early June, and without warning, Apple updated its App Store guidelines to reopen the door – at least in theory – to digital currency apps. Submitted apps, according to the new guidelines, 'may facilitate transmission of approved virtual currencies, provided that they do so in compliance with all state and federal laws for the territories in which the app functions'. A wave of shock and excitement swept through the Bitcoin community. If the world's 500 million iPhone users were once again to have the ability to send, receive, and store bitcoins using their mobile phones, it would be game-changing. Nic Cary studied the updated policy with interest. He felt cautiously optimistic about what it might mean. But he decided to take a wait-and-see approach. 'We weren't super-enthusiastic about investing a lot of time, money, or engineering in developing [an app] for Apple until it was really clear that they would approve a product,' he says. He knew that Apple, having shut out Bitcoin apps for the past four months – practically an eon in blockchain time – would have a tough time attracting developers who had once been burned. But he looked forward to the day when Blockchain could reach Apple users again.

By late July, two things had occurred to accelerate his plans. The first, on 15 June, was the acceptance into Apple's App Store of the first Bitcoin wallet app since the change of policy. The app, CoinPocket, was barebones in its features, but it showed that Apple was serious about reopening its doors. The second game-changing event was the successful launch of Blockchain's new Android wallet app, which, Nic says, 'put us back on the radar in terms of Bitcoin wallets being commercially viable'.

Days later, at a tech conference, Nic managed through a fellow Bitcoiner to make contact with a member of Apple's developer accounts team. Reaching out to him, Nic explained 'exactly what our wallet did and how it worked', he says. The Apple employee seemed to understand. Blockchain proceeded to resubmit its iOS app. Three days later, on 28 July, it was approved. Two days after that, Blockchain released an update for the app, which had been neglected for the past six months, adding to it the merchant map popularized on Android. Ben Reeves did the coding, having written the original version himself months before, in concert with Matt Tuzzolo, the head of the development team, who had been hired in May.

The response from Bitcoiners was massive and immediate. Downloads of the iOS wallet 'exploded', says Peter Smith, with tens of thousands of new users installing the app in the first few days. Blockchain had made a triumphant return to the App Store.

On 10 August, the total number of Blockchain wallet users – across web, iOS, and Android – hit two million.[7] Blockchain was the first and only Bitcoin company to have so many users. This growth, along with a period of more than two months in which the average daily price of Bitcoin never went below $550 or above $674 – which, in the volatile cryptocurrency market, passed for newfound price stability – proved, to hear Peter Smith tell it, that the world of Bitcoin was moving away from speculative fever and toward a 'transactions paradigm', in which it would go up against cash, credit cards, PayPal, and other forms of electronic payment.

So much good news in such short order gave Blockchain an even stronger hand in its conversations with venture capitalists. The investors were not so much interviewing Blockchain's executives as Blockchain's executives were interviewing them. 'Blockchain has been incredibly successful in a lot of ways because the founding partners have a rock-solid consensus on what we want to accomplish as a company, as a team, and that's helping people anywhere in the world reimagine how they transact – and doing that in a decentralized, distributed, open-source way [while having] a non-custodial relationship with our users,' Nic says. 'We needed to find partners that understood this vision and understood the mission and were highly committed to it.' Nic wanted to make sure that Blockchain would not be flipped for a quick profit.

By fall, Blockchain had settled on two firms to lead the funding round: from Silicon Valley, Jeremy Liew's Lightspeed Venture Partners, and from the world of finance, Wicklow Capital, the private investment vehicle of Daniel Tierney and Stephen Schuler, the founders of GETCO, a high-frequency trading firm that had grown to become one of the largest market makers in the world. Wicklow, housed in Chicago's landmark Monadnock Building, had begun making a name for itself by investing in financial technology startups, and it was precisely the firm's expertise in financial services that Blockchain wanted to wed to Lightspeed's deep knowledge of consumer technology. Alongside these firms, other investors piled in, among them billionaire Richard Branson and Amit Jhawar of payments company Braintree. At least nine institutional and individual investors ultimately participated in the funding.

On 7 October, Blockchain broke the news to the world: it had closed its first round of venture capital funding to the tune of $30.5 million. The number carried a potent symbolism, edging out as it did by half a million dollars BitPay's own Series A round from five months before. And so it was not only the largest first round of venture funding ever raised by a Bitcoin startup but the largest funding round ever, full stop. Coinbase's own Series A deal had come earlier, in April 2013, but was less than one-sixth the size. In one shot, in fact, Blockchain had nearly equalled the total amount of money raised by its chief rival – $30.6 million – across three rounds of funding. It was a resounding vindication of Blockchain's business model.

For Ben Reeves, the perpetual underdog, it was a personal victory. 'If it wasn't for Ben's hard work, we wouldn't be here now,' said Bill Hill, who found out about the record-breaking funding during a group conference call. Like everyone at Blockchain, he was thrilled by the news, but he also knew that it was not an invitation to rest on his laurels. 'It means, "Take a deep breath and get ready to leave the station again,"' he said.

In addition to hiring more engineers, updating their products, and expanding into new markets, Blockchain intended to use some of the money to rent office space in London, giving the company its first real headquarters and pulling its employees from the four corners of the globe into the beating heart of world finance. Like exiles coming in from the cold, these people who had staked their lives and reputations and incomes against long odds on an outsider technology would be rewarded with mainstream acceptance; they would get seats at the grownups' table. Even as he began to look at properties in London, however, Nic Cary was focused on the other side of the pond, on Washington. He dismissed the prestige of the Series A as unimportant. What mattered most, along with the newfound financial resources, he said, were the political connections Blockchain's heavy-hitting investors would provide. He found such politicking distasteful but knew it was necessary in the big leagues to which his company had been called up. Personally, he said, 'I don't have any political connections. Someone stomps me out because I look like an easy target; they don't stomp out people who have direct dials to the president of the United States.'

One week later, Benjamin Lawsky handed Blockchain another victory. Speaking at the Benjamin N. Cardozo School of Law in New York City, he made it clear that the BitLicense requirements, however onerous, would not apply to Bitcoin software companies. 'We are regulating financial intermediaries. We are not regulating software development,' he said. 'For example, a software developer who creates and provides wallet software to customers for their own use will not need a license.'[8] Whereas Coinbase, Xapo, Circle, and many other startups, if they continued doing business in New York, would have no choice but to bear the full weight of coming regulations, Blockchain would be exempt. Not only Blockchain's business model but its philosophy of ownership was vindicated. By allowing users to control their own private keys, their own funds, the company had gained a competitive edge.

It was no small thing. The BitLicense regulatory regime, when it went into effect in August 2015, compelled more than a dozen companies – among them Kraken, Bitfinex, and LocalBitcoins – to cease operations in New York. Those who hung in, including Bitstamp and Coinbase, each spent tens of thousands of dollars in legal costs, compliance fees, and man hours simply to apply for a BitLicense.[9] By mid-June 2016, only two had been issued: one to Jeremy Allaire's Circle, and the second, many months later, to Ripple, a non-Bitcoin cryptocurrency startup founded in 2012.

Having dodged that bullet, Nic was yet under no illusion that his worries were at an end. California, like New York, was considering whether and how to regulate digital currency businesses. In June 2014, the state legislature had passed a bill legalizing Bitcoin and other alternative forms of money, nullifying a provision of state law that declared the US dollar the only valid currency. Democratic State Assemblyman Roger Dickinson, author of the bill, had sounded oddly Hayekian then, telling the *Los Angeles Times* that 'in an era of evolving payment methods, from Amazon Coins to Starbucks Stars, it is impractical to ignore the growing use of cash alternatives.'[10]

But the following summer a new bill was introduced in California to clamp down on digital currency businesses. Though in some ways less onerous than the BitLicense regime, it drew criticism for being premature and overly broad in scope. The Electronic Frontier Foundation argued that it threatened 'to both stunt the growth of this innovative industry and hamper the enthusiasm driving consumer interest'. Months of debate ensued between state lawmakers, digital advocacy groups, and representatives of the Bitcoin and blockchain industry, and the bill was eventually shelved. After lying dormant for nearly a year, however, it was rewritten and revived in August 2016. The new bill proposed to create a mandatory enrollment program for businesses engaged in financial uses of blockchain technology – a program that would require a $5,000 application fee and a $2,500 annual membership fee. Anyone not enrolled would be forbidden from operating a Bitcoin startup.

Again there was an outcry. 'It not only provides no regulatory clarity,' wrote Jerry Brito, the executive director of nonprofit research and advocacy group Coin Center, in a letter to the chairman of the California Senate's Banking and Financial Institutions Committee, 'it will likely stifle innovation if enacted unchanged.' Again the bill was put to bed, though lawmakers indicated that a new version would likely be reintroduced in 2017.[11] Regardless of the fate of any particular piece of legislation, there was clearly an abiding desire on the part of state lawmakers to come to grips with Bitcoin. As early as mid-2014, Nic Cary had seen the storm clouds on the horizon, and he felt sure that at some point a Blockchain representative would have to 'go and explain how our technology works' – whether to Manhattan, Washington, or Sacramento. If Blockchain had once tried to be above the fray, it could no longer afford to take such a vaunted position. It would have to enter the sausage factory of American democracy. It was something Nic Cary dreaded. 'If we get embroiled in a bunch of litigation, or the government decides we're a money transmitting business and it doesn't matter how our technology works, if even though we don't have custodial accounts we have to sign everybody up or kick them out, those kind of things would be really tough to deal with.'

To prevent this, Blockchain retained Marco Santori in September 2014 as its global policy counsel. (At a conference in Amsterdam the previous May he had won an industry award – sponsored partly by Blockchain – for top Bitcoin legal expert, receiving more votes in that category than all of the other candidates combined.) Santori was the perfect candidate for other reasons, too: he served as chairman of the Bitcoin Foundation's Regulatory Affairs Committee and had opposed the BitLicense. He saw his work on Blockchain's behalf as primarily educational, helping regulators to understand 'how Blockchain works differently than other wallet providers'.[12] Nic Cary, characteristically, saw the mission in more apocalyptic terms, as a fight for financial privacy and the right of individuals to transact with whomever they wished – a right, like freedom of speech, on which he believed there should be as few restrictions as possible. 'On behalf of the technology and our users, we will go to war and spend a fortune trying to defend them,' he says.

And so Nic didn't rest. On 8 October 2014, the day after Blockchain's fundraising announcement, he met with a group of Google developer advocates at a Mexican cantina in London. It was the job of the developer advocates to promote Google technologies, including the Android operating system, in outreach to developers, so that the tech giant could be a partner in their success. So popular was its wallet app that Blockchain now merited their attention. Nic Cary was clear on what his team needed: advance notice on future updates to Google technology, so that they could plan and build accordingly. 'We can't be surprised by major OS changes or API changes,' he told them. From now on, he wanted Blockchain to be one of the preferred partners to whom Google provided early access to new software development kits.

At half past nine he left the cantina and sprinted to King's Cross to catch the last train home to York. He arrived at 9:55 P.M., five minutes before his train was to depart. He was exhausted. He had gotten up at four-thirty that morning to appear on the BBC to discuss Blockchain's historic Series A. He expected shortly to be all but comatose. Heading north, the darkened countryside passed beyond his window. The seeming emptiness of the landscape was like the emptiness of the future waiting to be filled, a future he fervently hoped would be made not according to the whims of politicians but in something like the shape of his own desire. Not long after the news of Blockchain's funding broke, he'd spoken with his father, who had in fact spent more time celebrating the news than Nic had. They had a long conversation, in which Philip Cary – who knew how seriously Nic took his work, how committed he was and how much good he believed was at stake – expressed his sense of wonder at the distance between generations, the diverging paths of his own life and that of his twenty-nine-year-old son. He said, 'Nic, you know, when I was twenty-nine, I was making *you*.'

Chapter 15

HEARTS AND MINDS

If we look at the life cycle of technologies we see an early period of over-enthusiasm, then a 'bust' when disillusionment sets in, followed by the real revolution.

– Ray Kurzweil

At Charlie Shrem's sentencing on 19 December 2014, it quickly became evident that Judge Jed Rakoff had no intention of following the federal guidelines as to a prison term for the defendant. In 2005, the US Supreme Court in *United States v. Booker* had struck down the requirement for federal judges to impose sentences within the range stipulated by the guidelines, which in Charlie's case gave a suggested prison term of fifty-seven to sixty months. No longer forced to abide by the guidelines, judges were now free to follow the dictates of their conscience, yet had Charlie been sentenced prior to 2005 the judge would have had no choice but to impose upon him a nearly five-year prison term. As it was, most judges still hewed closely to the guidelines in their sentencing decisions. Jed Rakoff, fortunately for Charlie, was not most judges. 'I'm required to give consideration to the guidelines,' he said. 'I have done so, and find them not worthy of consideration.'

And so it was up to Marc Agnifilo and Serrin Turner to try to convince him of what the sentence should be. The defense attorney spoke first, emphasizing Charlie's youth and naiveté at the time of the offense and characterizing his involvement with

Robert Faiella as in some sense a temporary aberration, one which was not repeated, despite the fact that Faiella himself, after parting ways with BitInstant, had resumed operating as a Bitcoin reseller on Silk Road. Agnifilo therefore argued for clemency – no, for proportionality – no, for morality. 'If Immanuel Kant was standing here, and I think Immanuel Kant is standing spiritually in every federal courtroom during sentence,' Agnifilo said, 'he would say we can't do this . . . We can't use Charlie Shrem as a means to send a message to some unknown person somewhere in the world so that they don't do something wrong with Bitcoin or money transmission. It's not right. It violates the categorical imperative.'

But the judge wasn't buying it. 'Immanuel Kant, huge figure though he is in the history of the world, was not, so far as I can recall, a member of Congress,' he replied, 'and Congress has decreed that general deterrence will be taken account of . . . What is much more relevant is, what do we need in terms of punishment to bring about general deterrence.'

The prosecutor, when his turn came, argued for a substantial prison sentence. He leaned hard on the drug trafficking aspect of the case. Furthermore, it was not easy, he said, to detect crimes such as Charlie's; the government's resources were spread thin, and a lot of criminal behavior was going to be missed. 'So when crimes like this are detected, it is important that the message goes out that they come with consequences.' He wanted to make an example out of Charlie. (He was perhaps not so devoted a student of Kant.) Bitcoin has legitimate uses, he acknowledged, yet it risks becoming the currency of choice for money launderers. The court must send a message that anti-money laundering laws can't be ignored, that skirting them comes with consequences – and it must send this message in the interest of helping to promote the legitimacy of the Bitcoin industry. (A neat rhetorical trick, that. He was casting himself as a champion of the very industry one of whose most prominent figures he was trying to get locked up.)

At last it was Charlie's turn to speak on his own behalf. He spoke in a rush, alternately apologizing and justifying himself, his words practically tripping over themselves, professing guilt and anguish one moment and pride the next, and in this rush of words, this torrent, the truth became slippery; the timeline of events was washed clean. It was not true, as Charlie now claimed, that BitInstant executives had shut down the company of their own volition and out of a desire not to operate in a legal gray area following the release of FinCEN's guidance for digital currency businesses in the spring of 2013. It was not true that the shutdown occurred 'almost a year' before his arrest. It was not true that Charlie was the only employee of BitInstant at the time he committed the offense; the commission of the offense, processing Robert Faiella's transactions, may have begun in January 2012, but it stretched across many months, some of which came after the hiring of Erik Voorhees, Ira Miller, and Rachel Yankelevitz. But if there was inaccuracy in the details there was sincerity in the whole. 'When you're in a position of power, it's a lot harder to stay responsible to yourself and stay morally responsible,' Charlie told Judge Rakoff. 'It's a lot easier when there's nothing riding on you. And I failed that.'

Bitcoin, he now saw, needed to distance itself from criminal activity; it needed, in fact, to shun people like the man he once was. And who better to reform Bitcoin than a reformed Bitcoiner? 'I need to be out there making sure that it doesn't go back to that,' he told the judge, 'because Bitcoin is my baby. Bitcoin is what I love and all I have. It's my whole life. It's what I'm on this earth to do, is to help the world see a financial system that does not discriminate and provide for corruption . . . And if your Honor grants me that, I'd love to be back out there helping the world and making sure people don't do stupid things like I did.'

Charlie's fervent idealism impressed Judge Rakoff, though perhaps not in the way intended. 'I'm not sure that it's a good philosophy for anyone of the age of twenty-five or so to undertake to save the world,' the judge replied. 'Something quite a bit more modest might be more appropriate.' In these few words can be detected the collision of two mutually uncomprehending cultures: the disruptive startup culture of which Silicon Valley is the center, powered by youthful enthusiasm like Charlie's, and the culture of

Anglo-American jurisprudence, informed by the white-haired wisdom of men like Jed Rakoff.

Ultimately, the judge agreed with Serrin Turner that the deterrent effect of Charlie's sentence on other Bitcoiners and black marketeers could not be ignored. He refused to let the defendant off merely with probation. Nor, however, did he impose the harsh sentence that Preet Bharara's office hoped for. Against the prosecutor's wishes, and against the recommendation of James Mullen, the probation officer who had prepared the presentence report, who had urged a prison term in keeping with the guidelines of fifty-seven to sixty months, Judge Rakoff sentenced Charlie to two years in prison followed by three years of supervised release.

Charlie breathed a sigh of relief. Looking back, he would later write that the day of his sentencing was one of the happiest days of his life. He finally knew when all this trouble would be over. In the first months after his arrest he had gone to bed every night fearing that he would spend the next thirty years in prison. But two years? That was doable. With time off for good behavior, he could shave the sentence down to thirteen months or so. Perhaps for the first time, he thought he could make it.

By now, Charlie had also agreed to forfeit to the government $950,000. Although BitInstant had supposedly only ever realized close to $15,000 in revenue from Faiella's transactions, the government had slapped the startup's erstwhile CEO with a draconian forfeiture provision as part of his plea agreement. The amount was said to be the total amount of illicit funds that had flowed through BitInstant as a result of Charlie's aiding and abetting of Robert Faiella. It was also largely symbolic. Most defendants never come close to paying all they owe. 'The government likes to get big forfeiture judgments even though they usually can't collect them,' David B. Smith, an expert in civil and criminal forfeiture law and a partner in Smith & Zimmerman, a boutique law firm in Alexandria, Virginia, has written. 'They want the "stat" even if it's meaningless.'

Charlie would enter prison – Lewisburg in Pennsylvania, near Courtney's mother's house – on 16 March at two o'clock in the afternoon. The date was a Monday. Roger Ver had warned Charlie, recalling his own experience, not to enter prison on a Friday. Robert Faiella, sentenced on 20 January 2015, having pled guilty to operating an unlicensing money transmitting business, received a prison term of four years plus three years of supervised release. He was to surrender himself on 3 March – nearly two weeks sooner than Charlie Shrem, who had been sentenced a month earlier.

Charlie settled into his three-month respite as best he could, continuing to work for Payza a few hours a week for reduced pay while planning ventures of his own. He told friends that early in the plea bargain negotiations the government had wanted him to be a cooperating witness, a confidential informant – 'and that meant going back out and wearing wires, and stings, and stuff like that' – but that he had refused, being unwilling to rat out his compatriots. In fact, according to Agnifilo, the government had never asked him to be an informant. The story wasn't true, but Charlie sold it like the truth. Hoping to earn brownie points with the Bureau of Prisons, he enrolled himself in a program at the Realization Center, an outpatient rehabilitation clinic in Union Square, but it didn't take. 'I quit after the first week,' Charlie said later. 'I'm going there, and I'm thinking I'm rolling [along], because I don't take any drugs. So I'm being tested, I'm peeing like a fucking champ' – but then someone who worked there took him aside. 'She goes, "Charlie, we have to talk. You're testing positive every day." "What do you mean? I don't do any drugs!" She goes, "Alcohol". I was like, "You didn't tell me I have to quit alcohol!" She goes, "It's *rehab*."' He shook his head at the memory. 'It's like, "Fuck that! I don't have a problem. Alcohol is the only thing I have left! I had to quit weed, I had to quit cigarettes. I'm fucking drinking my heart out!" She goes, "Well, you can't stay in this program." I said, "I'm fucking leaving, then." I have to quit drinking when I go into prison, but I'm going to drink until I go into prison.'

Charlie Shrem was determined to enjoy his last days of semi-freedom however he could. He was no saint, but his sentencing nevertheless enraged and saddened his old friend Erik Voorhees. It seemed ludicrous in comparison to the deals given to those whose

sins were far more serious. 'Banks such as HSBC are found guilty
of laundering billions of dollars not just for drug users but for
violent crime cartels. Billions. Violent crime,' Erik thundered
online. 'And yet not a single exec faces a day of jail time. Charlie
Shrem, who sold Bitcoins to someone who helped people buy drugs
on Silk Road, has now been sentenced to two years in jail. If there
was any doubt that we are struggling against an immoral system
in dire need of replacement,' he added, 'let this end that doubt.'

There was some truth behind his rhetoric. In December 2013,
HSBC had reached a $32,400 settlement with the US government
for moving money on behalf of financiers of Hezbollah. Everett
Stern, a former HSBC compliance officer turned whistleblower
who had reported the transactions, felt vindicated but disgusted
by the slap on the wrist his former employer had received. His
own career had gone down the toilet since he'd gone public with
his concerns, while his bosses faced no personal consequences
whatsoever. 'They admit to financing terrorism and they get fined
$32,000,' he said. 'Where if I were to do that, I would go to jail
for life.'[1] Nor was this the bank's first offense. Just one year earlier,
in December 2012, HSBC had agreed to pay a $1.9 billion fine in
order to end a US Justice Department investigation that revealed
years of flagrant lawbreaking. The megabank had laundered
millions for blood-soaked Mexican drug cartels, moved money for
organizations with ties to Hezbollah and Al Qaeda, and processed
many billions of dollars in transactions involving rogue states like
Iran and North Korea in violation of US sanctions.[2] Which is to
say that the government's fears that drug money and terrorist
finances would be funneled through the financial system were
already being confirmed on an unimaginable scale – not by tiny
digital currency startups but by mainstream banks. And yet despite
violating 'every goddamn law in the book', as lawyer and former
Senate investigator Jack Blum puts it, no one at HSBC was criminally charged.

At a press conference announcing the $1.9 billion settlement,
Assistant Attorney General Lanny Breuer made clear why the
Justice Department wasn't going for the jugular: 'Had the US

authorities decided to press criminal charges, HSBC would almost certainly have lost its banking license in the US, the future of the institution would have been under threat, and the entire banking system would have been destabilized.' In other words, the economic consequences outweighed considerations of justice. HSBC executives thus benefited from something like the transformative formula of modern art. A bag of rubbish is a bag of rubbish, but if one builds a Tate Britain around the rubbish it becomes art. Similarly, a money launderer is a criminal deserving of prosecution and a stiff sentence – unless one places him in the executive ranks of a global megabank, in which case he becomes the representative of a system whose equilibrium must not be disturbed. The repeated warnings and fines against banks like HSBC in the absence of criminal charges were, Erik Voorhees thought, the work of a justice system 'that is more concerned with managing the economy (i.e., not spooking the markets by throwing execs in jail) than with justice'.

Ever since the passing of new financial regulations following the terrorist attacks of 11 September 2001, there seemed to be one law for the big boys and another law for the little guys. Charlie had gotten caught on the wrong side of the line. 'A company like PayPal could never have been founded in a post-9/11 world,' Peter Thiel said at a debate with the anarchist anthropologist David Graeber two weeks after Charlie's sentencing. 'We would have been accused of money laundering.' The door he had walked through was now bolted shut.

At his sentencing, Charlie was adamant: 'I screwed up, and the Bitcoin community, trust me, they are scared. They saw what happened to a guy like me that was on top of the world and got arrested at the airport. No one is doing this anymore. There is no money laundering going on in the Bitcoin space. They're terrified.'

But on this occasion, as on so many others, he may simply have been saying what he thought his interlocutor wanted to hear. Some weeks later, after his sentencing, ensconced with a business partner in the small office they shared in a coworking space at 379 West Broadway, he changed his tune. 'I think almost every Bitcoiner broke the law at some point,' he said darkly, his ankle monitor peeping out of the gap between the unzipped panels of his slush boots, 'and many are continuing to.'

BY SEPTEMBER 2014, BARRY SILBERT was close to his own breaking point. For the past four months a special committee of the board of directors of SecondMarket Holdings had been negotiating with Bain Capital and RRE over the terms of the proposed merger between Digital Currency Group – yet to be officially spun off from SecondMarket – and Bitcoin Opportunity Corp., Barry's portfolio of investments, in which Bain and RRE had themselves invested. Four months had gone by and still there was no deal. Four months! He had thought the process would take no more than sixty days. More frustrating still, he couldn't get personally involved in the negotiations. His obvious conflict of interest had forced him to recuse himself.

With no term sheet in sight, he faced a difficult choice. If the merger wasn't going to happen, he would need either to abandon SecondMarket's Bitcoin businesses in order to continue growing Bitcoin Opportunity Corp., or hand over the investments to some other manager in order to focus on Digital Currency Group. None of the other parties involved wanted him building Bitcoin businesses and making strategic investments for DCG while managing a private investment portfolio on the side. It just wasn't going to be feasible. He found himself in limbo: he couldn't go out and raise more capital for Bitcoin Opportunity Corp. knowing there was a chance he'd have to turn it over to somebody else, nor could he launch new Bitcoin businesses for SecondMarket as it was possible he'd soon be devoting himself exclusively to Bitcoin Opportunity Corp.

In the end, he didn't have to make that choice. In early October, the two sides finally reached an agreement in principle and put together a term sheet for review. The end zone was in sight. But then, out of nowhere, there was a flag on the play. In late October, SecondMarket held a call with the entire board of directors to discuss the terms of the proposed merger. Outside counsel was on the call, and the lawyers suddenly spoke up to say there was a problem. Such was the value of Barry's investment portfolio that if Bitcoin Opportunity Corp. were to be absorbed into SecondMarket Holdings, then SecondMarket Holdings would be classified as an investment company by the SEC. Such a classification wasn't a speed bump; it was a brick wall. Just as it would have been impossible to launch the Bitcoin Investment Trust under the regulatory regime that existed prior to the JOBS Act, so now, the lawyers explained, another decades-old piece of legislation was gumming up the works. This time it was the Investment Company Act of 1940.

The '40 Act, as it is colloquially known, was part of the raft of financial regulations passed in the wake of the stock market crash of 1929. What it says is that if more than forty percent of an American company's assets are securities, then it is deemed to be an investment company. With that designation came special accounting and record-keeping obligations, the requirement that three-quarters of the company's board of directors must be independent and that the company must keep a certain percentage of its total assets in cash, the expectation that it would publicly disclose its financials despite not being a publicly traded company, restrictions on capital structure, and on and on. By the time SecondMarket's lawyers were done explaining the legislation, the entire board had reached a single conclusion: the proposed deal was dead in the water.

Hedge funds and private equity firms, as Barry well knew, do everything they can to avoid becoming '40 Act companies. Fortunately, the act spells out two possible exemptions. The most commonly used one, found in Section 3(c)(1) of the act, says that if a company has no more than a hundred investors, all of whom are accredited investors, it is exempt from registering with the SEC as an investment company. For firms that can't meet those requirements – as indeed SecondMarket couldn't, since it had more than a hundred investors, and some were not accredited – there is another exemption, laid out in Section 3(c)(7), which says that a firm can still avoid registering as an investment company if it has no more than 1,999 investors and they are all 'qualified purchasers', which means only individuals who own at least $5 million worth of investments, or money managers with at least $25 million of investments under management – far greater wealth than that required merely to be an accredited investor. Barry would need to use one of these exemptions to save the deal.

He began brainstorming ideas for alternate corporate structures and bouncing them off Lawrence Lenihan. Finally, in early November, he hit on a solution: instead of Bitcoin Opportunity Corp. becoming part of SecondMarket Holdings, SecondMarket would hand over its Bitcoin businesses, Grayscale Investments and Genesis Trading, to Bitcoin Opportunity Corp. – in exchange for partial ownership of Bitcoin Opportunity Corp. itself. The company would then have five shareholders: Barry Silbert, Bain, RRE, Barry's family trusts, and SecondMarket, which was a qualified purchaser. Now exempt from the '40 Act, Bitcoin Opportunity Corp. would change its name to Digital Currency Group – in effect becoming the very company with which it had once planned to merge.

A wave of relief swept over Barry Silbert. Problem solved! A new term sheet was drawn up. But then the lawyers brought more bad tidings: as soon as the transaction took place, SecondMarket Holdings would still become an investment company, because more than forty percent of its total asset value would then be derived from its stake in Bitcoin Opportunity Corp. The only way of preventing this would be for the company to buy out dozens of its investors, reducing the shareholder count below 100. This Barry was willing to do, would gladly do if it meant salvaging the deal – and with it, his plans for DCG. But it would also mean delaying the consummation of the deal still further. To shed dozens of investors was no light thing.

Worse yet, the '40 Act exemptions had one other requirement: a company relying on them could not go public. Barry had wanted to fast-track Digital Currency Group to an IPO, but now it seemed he wouldn't be able to take the company public until either he discovered another exemption that permitted it or he built DCG to the point where no more than forty percent of its assets were investments. On the other side of the scale, the sixty-percent-or-more side, would be DCG's operating subsidiaries: Grayscale, Genesis Trading . . . and whatever new businesses Barry could dream up.

Barry Silbert was getting a crash course in esoteric financial law. And it wasn't over. The last hurdle was Bitcoin itself – namely, the fact that SecondMarket's lawyers didn't know whether for the purposes of the '40 Act the digital currency would be considered a good asset, a bad asset, or an asset excluded from consideration altogether. (In sufficient quantity, 'good' assets keep a firm from having to register as an investment company, while 'bad' assets do the opposite.) A rise in the price of Bitcoin would help if it was a good asset, but if it was a bad asset it would make it that much more difficult for DCG to go public. There was also the possibility that Bitcoin might not count in the ratio at all. The lawyers couldn't say for sure.

All of this grated immensely on Barry Silbert. But he shouldn't have been surprised. It was another instance of Bitcoin breaking the mold. It represented a new financial paradigm; small wonder that it didn't fit easily into the old system. During these difficult weeks, he leaned on the support of his wife, he sought advice from Larry Lenihan – speaking with him just about every day – and he relied on the special committee of SecondMarket's board to bring everything to a satisfactory conclusion. 'I certainly wanted to blow my brains out many times,' he says. Discussing the finer points of the '40 Act may have seemed like inside baseball, but it was inside baseball for the most important game of his life.

Amid all the drama, SecondMarket had to prepare for the next US Marshals auction of Silk Road bitcoins. The bidding was to take place in late November, and the batch of 50,000 bitcoins that would fall under the hammer this time – far more than the 29,656 auctioned off in June, though the Bitcoin price was lower now – had been confiscated from Ross Ulbricht's personal cache. Once again, as it had done six months before, SecondMarket organized a syndicate of bidders, opening up the auction to foreign investors and smaller buyers who would otherwise have been barred from participating. But where the first syndicate had drawn only forty-two investors, 104 investors joined the second, and together they nearly swept the auction, winning 48,000 of the 50,000 bitcoins, nineteen of the twenty blocks on offer. It was a dramatic turnaround. The victory earned syndicate fees and headlines for Barry Silbert's company, though all the bitcoins were distributed to the members of the syndicate who had placed successful bids; none were retained by SecondMarket itself. The remaining two thousand coins went to Tim Draper, the venture capitalist who had claimed all ten lots in the first auction.

Two weeks later, on 19 December, after seven months of negotiations, the revised and final term sheet spelling out the deal between Bitcoin Opportunity Corp. and SecondMarket Holdings was signed. The way forward was finally clear.

As 2014 drew to a close, SecondMarket was sitting pretty. Its total assets included more than $13 million in cash plus 40,521 bitcoins, an amount worth $12.9 million. Genesis Trading had become perhaps the leading digital currency trading desk for institutional investors and high-net-worth individuals, with a trading volume of more than $300 million since its inception and 2014 revenue of $12.6 million. The Bitcoin Investment Trust, the first-ever Bitcoin fund for accredited investors, would soon become the first-ever publicly traded Bitcoin fund. It, too, was generating revenue for SecondMarket. The company's long-term debt, in keeping with Barry Silbert's business philosophy, was zero.

This plum position allowed Barry to dream big about the future of Digital Currency Group. One of his ideas was to hire industry veterans to consult for Fortune 100 clients, becoming a kind of McKinsey for Bitcoin. Another was to open a kind of bank that would use blockchain technology as its backbone to provide payroll and peer-to-peer lending services. His conceptual model for this was Fidor, an online German bank that provided its quarter of a million customers not only with basic checking and savings accounts but also with a platform for loaning money to one another on a peer-to-peer basis. As operating subsidiaries, either of these imagined ventures might strengthen the health of the overall company. The more revenue they generated, the easier it would be for DCG to stay on the good side of the '40 Act and one day go public.

One area in which DCG had scaled back its ambitions, however, was that of launching a Bitcoin exchange. At first, the exchange was delayed due to the difficulties surrounding the reorganization of SecondMarket. And then, too, there was uncertainty over the forthcoming BitLicense regulations, still in draft form. ('Not only did *we* want to wait and see what the BitLicense looked like,' Barry says, 'but more importantly every bank that we were talking to wanted to wait.') But then Barry got wind of something that not only changed the game but in fact just about kicked over the chessboard: Coinbase was preparing to launch an exchange of its own.

As an investor in Coinbase, Barry Silbert was privy to the startup's plans; though prevented by a nondisclosure agreement from discussing them openly, he could hardly have failed to realize what they would mean for his own. Rumors had been circulating since the fall that Coinbase was seeking to raise a massive new round of financing – as much as $60 million. In fact, the amount the startup raised in its Series C, announced on 20 January 2015, was greater still: $75 million, a sum so far beyond what any other Bitcoin company had raised – not only in a single round but in total – that it hit the industry like a thunderclap. Andreessen Horowitz and Union Square Ventures both participated in the round, as they had in December 2013, but it was the new investors that got people talking. Among them were BBVA, Spain's second-largest bank; former Citigroup CEO Vikram Pandit; Tim Draper; and the New York Stock Exchange. Soon, Barry knew, it would be clear to everyone – if the NYSE's involvement had not already tipped them off – what Coinbase needed the money for.

Six days later, Coinbase launched its exchange, though not before breaking the news with a splashy story in the Sunday *Wall Street Journal*. The goal of the exchange, baldly stated by Brian Armstrong, was to become the world's largest, providing a deep pool of liquidity for both institutions and retail investors. To that end, Coinbase promised to insure customer deposits against hacking, internal theft, and accidental loss. It was a timely feature to boast of. Only a few weeks earlier, a security breach at Bitstamp had resulted in the loss of more than $5 million worth of bitcoins. While the exchange had responded swiftly to the hack, returning to full service after only a four-day outage, and becoming the first exchange to implement BitGo's multi-sig technology as protection against future attempted thefts, this would never be enough to convince some people that their bitcoins were safe, to say nothing of large institutional investors unused to being robbed. Bitstamp promised to cover all the losses with its own reserves, but even so, doubts about its security and financial health remained. 'Unless a tier 1 accounting firm (Deloitte, PwC, etc.) comes in and audits their books, I wouldn't touch them with a 10 foot pole,' one online commenter wrote.[3] Coinbase also set itself apart in its emphasis on complying with US financial laws. The launch of its exchange was the culmination of a year's worth of work trying to obtain money transmitter licenses from state regulators. It was still nowhere close to obtaining enough licenses to serve all of America, but at the moment it seemed to have more than anybody else – enough for twenty-four states. Tom Farley, the president of the NYSE, which had invested in Coinbase as a way to keep tabs on Bitcoin as a whole, believed the new exchange was 'an important step for the currency to become socially acceptable'.[4] Coinbase would take 0.25 percent on transactions, with no trading fees for its first two months of operation. On launch day, the exchange was limited to American users, but the company planned eventually to expand into other countries.

What made the launch of Coinbase's exchange especially delicious to Barry Silbert was that it left the Winklevoss twins with egg on their faces. Only four days earlier, the *New York Times*, in what was meant to be a big scoop, had revealed that Cameron and Tyler Winklevoss were building a trading platform of their own, describing it as the first regulated Bitcoin exchange for US customers – the 'Nasdaq of Bitcoin'. Yet it was still in development when Coinbase's exchange opened its doors. And then, too, another US-based exchange, Kraken, which had itself raised $6.5 million of investment capital, was also pursuing state money transmitter licensing; it had been making possible dollar-to-bitcoin trading in five US states since the summer of 2014. The Winklevosses appeared at best to be racing for bronze.

Despite the competition, Barry Silbert still believed there was room in the market for the kind of exchange he had envisioned, a kind radically different from any that existed, Coinbase's included. The hub-and-spoke model, in which only regulated member firms directly participate in the exchange, would eliminate the need for Digital Currency Group to pursue state money transmission licenses. A significant amount of Coinbase's new funding would be spent on regulatory costs, and Barry had no desire to go down that road. Nevertheless, he was willing to concede that the new exchange stood a good chance of becoming a sorely needed liquidity hub in the US market. If that happened, however, it would only light a fire under Nasdaq and CME Group and the big banks – possible members of Barry's exchange – to get involved. 'If this is going to be a really big asset class, they're not going to let the New York Stock Exchange dominate it,' Barry says. And they would want to get involved, if possible, with an exchange that had Wall Street bona fides. Once SecondMarket's reorganization was in the rearview mirror, once DCG had launched and raised some outside capital, Barry figured, he would once more bring up the issue of a hub-and-spoke exchange with potential member institutions to see what could be done.

But while there might still be an opportunity down the road for his new type of exchange, Barry didn't see much point in repeating the old model ad infinitum, which led only to a fragmented market. If you asked him, he would confess that he didn't know much about the Winklevosses' planned exchange, either its team or its technology, but his assessment was that 'in a world where you already have a regulated exchange with deep liquidity and zero fees, there's no room left for what they're doing. I have no reason to believe that their model would look anything different than Bitstamp or Coinbase.' Once again, in other words, the Winklevii had had their thunder stolen.

With his own plans for a Bitcoin exchange now in mothballs, Barry Silbert could focus on taking the Bitcoin Investment Trust public, as he had originally hoped to do in the fourth quarter of 2014. The effort to launch the first publicly traded Bitcoin fund was a kind of space race in its own right, and it gave him his own opportunity to go head-to-head with Cameron and Tyler Winklevoss, who had months earlier filed paperwork with the SEC for their exchange-traded fund.

Barry thought it was a mistake to seek SEC approval before going public. The process was opaque and slow, and were he to file his own application with the agency right off the bat, he would lose control of his fund's launch timing. Having heard horror stories of ETFs stalled for years in the bowels of the SEC, he chose to bypass the bureaucratic slough of despond. Under the agency's own Rule 144, investors in a private fund can resell their shares publicly after holding them for at least twelve months, as long as the shares are quoted on a legitimate market and the fund publicly discloses its financials. In theory, the first BIT shares became eligible for public resale on 26 September 2014. But a lot of hurdles remained to be cleared before they could actually be sold.

As the place where shares of the BIT would trade publicly, Barry had his sights set on an electronic trading platform called OTCQX. The company that operated this platform, OTC Markets Group, assigned each security to one of three marketplaces, distinguished from one another by the quality and quantity of information the companies whose securities traded on them had to disclose. 'The bottom tier is kind of the dogshit pink sheets,' Barry says. 'The top tier is actually really great companies.' That was OTCQX. In order to get the BIT listed on OTCQX, he would have to bring in a law firm – he chose the heavyweight Orrick, Herrington & Sutcliffe, San Francisco's second-oldest continuously operating law firm – to, in effect, sponsor the application by preparing and filing disclosure documents. Barry was wrapping this up as early as August 2014. But a second sponsor was needed – a FINRA-registered broker-dealer that would agree to make a market in the shares. The BIT would need such a firm to file the appropriate papers with FINRA. The process of finding the right one was proving to be more laborious than Barry had expected. As summer drew to a close, he was interviewing candidates but had yet to settle on a firm.

The good thing was that once he selected a market maker, the application process should go smoothly. Whereas the SEC wouldn't sign off on an ETF until it felt that it could give the fund its blessing, with FINRA the approval process was a matter of pure procedure, a ticking of the proper boxes. The entire process, Barry had heard, typically took as little as a few weeks.

Barry's experience wasn't typical. Merriman Capital, the broker-dealer he finally chose, filed the papers with FINRA in early December – just enough time for the BIT to go public before the end of 2014. The application would be assigned a sort of case officer, who would review it and send back a letter with any questions that needed to be answered before it could be approved. Barry Silbert's people would answer them, and Merriman would relay those answers in writing to FINRA. Simple. What happened next was pure luck of the draw. The person assigned to the BIT application got sick, Barry recalls. *Really* sick. The kind of sick that keeps you out of the office for nine straight days. 'So we got assigned this person, and then – *gone*.' Suddenly it was almost Christmas, and then it was New Year's . . . and Barry's dream of going public in 2014 went up with the fireworks on 31 December.

After the holidays, everything got back on track. But then there was another ludicrous delay. Barry and the others found themselves waiting and waiting to receive FINRA's letter asking questions about their application. When they finally reached out, FINRA claimed it had sent the questions already, but the fax – *the fax*, Barry repeated incredulously – evidently had not gone through. This fax had been sent to Merriman, not to SecondMarket directly. The FINRA approval process calls for the market maker to handle all of the paperwork – paperwork on which, however, the company for which it is making a market of course has to weigh in. So FINRA would fax its questions to Merriman; Merriman would relay those questions to SecondMarket; SecondMarket would give its answers to Merriman; and Merriman would fax the answers back to FINRA. At that point, either the application would be approved or the whole cockamamie cycle would be repeated. Barry Silbert had to endure two cycles.

Finally, on the night of 26 February 2015, FINRA assigned the Bitcoin Investment Trust a temporary public stock ticker symbol, GBTC, for trading on OTC Markets' pink-sheets market. Barry wanted to upgrade to OTCQX as soon as possible; his application to make that happen was pending. But even so, BIT investors could now publicly sell their shares. Barry had created the first publicly traded Bitcoin investment vehicle. He had always said that taking the BIT public would not be 'a ringing the bell kind of thing', but would be anticlimactic, since it wouldn't be listed on Nasdaq or the NYSE – at least not at first – but he was being modest. He had landed on the moon first.

With that done, Barry began approaching investors for DCG. By now, the Bitcoin industry as a whole had raised more than half a billion dollars of investment capital, and between them, the companies in DCG's portfolio had raised more than eighty percent of that capital. For an investor, putting money into DCG would be like placing a bet on the crème de la crème of the entire Bitcoin ecosystem. Barry's firm would indeed function, as he had said it would, as an index on an entire market.

Barry wanted to raise $25 million to start. He was already anticipating other rounds to come. And he was, in turn, thinking about the types of startups in which he wanted DCG to invest its own money. His old thesis had been that digital currencies were only as strong as their core infrastructure, and so he had invested mainly in companies that were building that payments infrastructure. His new thesis, in 2015, was that most of the essential infrastructure of the Bitcoin ecosystem was now in place, at least in the United States. It had come a long way in a short time. What was needed now was to fund the 'killer apps' that would drive mainstream adoption of digital currency and blockchain technology. Among these were remittance solutions, payroll and lending services for the unbanked, smart contracts, distributed asset records, bank-to-bank settlement services, and microtransactions. In all of these areas, DCG would seek to take an equity stake of two to five percent, increasing its percentage opportunistically in those that prospered. It would be a smorgasbord.

Over and over, in the Bitcoin community, you would hear people comparing the state of digital currency in 2014 or 2015 to the state of the Internet two decades before. What they meant was not only that it was young and wild and strange, not only that it had yet to engage a plurality of users, not only that national governments had yet to come to grips with it, but that some of the future uses of the technology had not yet been invented. Only the foundation had been built. And the sky was the limit. Barry Silbert had seen such tremendous growth in the Bitcoin industry since his first tentative purchase of coins on Mt. Gox, was now so far down the rabbit hole, so intimately acquainted with the value proposition of crypto-currency, so *all in* – professionally, financially, reputationally – that he was convinced the only way the price of Bitcoin would ever go to zero was if something better emerged. And he, Barry Silbert, had so positioned himself that he should know before anybody else what that new thing was. Hell, by the time the rest of the world woke up to it, he would already own a piece of the equity.

MORE THAN NINE MONTHS AFTER renouncing his United States citizenship, Roger Ver wanted to reenter the country. He was planning to speak at a Bitcoin conference in Miami in January. To do this he needed what is known as a nonimmigrant visa, which meant that he wouldn't overstay his welcome and try to settle permanently in the country from which he had already decamped once before. If this seemed a little silly to an outside observer, it was an absolute farce to Roger himself, a nonbeliever in national borders. St. Kitts passport in hand, he was capable of following the rules, but only in a bare-minimum sort of way. He had long enjoyed thumbing his nose at immigration control, more than once wearing, on his trips through border checkpoints, a white T-shirt depicting a blacked-out map of North America along with the words BORDERS ARE IMAGINARY LINES. But while national boundary lines might be imaginary, he clarified, 'the waiting line for brainwashed people wearing costumes' – that is, customs officials – 'to check my slave registration documents is real.'

In late December, he returned to the US embassy in Barbados to apply for a visa. He checked into a hotel and showed up bright and early for his visa interview, having taken the eight o'clock time slot – the earliest available. What happened next, he recalls, was like something from *Candid Camera*. Roger thought he was being punked. He'd known in advance that US law puts the burden on applicants to prove they aren't planning to overstay their visas. That generally means showing ties to some other country that will compel you to leave after a brief visit. So he had brought with him a big stack of evidence to show his long-standing ties to Japan. But the consular officer who conducted his interview refused to look at the papers. Worse, he refused even to let Roger slide the documents through the slot in the pane of bulletproof glass between them. Forestalling any real conversation, the consular officer handed him a letter of denial. The very first line told Roger the rest. He had been found ineligible for a nonimmigrant visa under Section 214(b) of the US Immigration and National Act, having been unable to prove strong ties to another country.

Roger stared at the interviewing officer in disbelief. This joker seemed to be implying that he harbored secret intent to stay in America! Imagine going through all the trouble of renouncing his citizenship only to become an illegal immigrant. The very idea was absurd. Finally he managed to say, 'You're denying me because you think I want to *live in the US?*'

'You can read the paper,' the consular officer shot back. 'It says right there.'

Roger read the paper more thoroughly. 'So you're denying me because you think I want to live in the US?' he repeated. He felt as though he were trapped in an incomprehensible Kafkaesque bureaucracy rather than an American embassy.

But the consular officer wouldn't budge, would barely even acknowledge the question as having issued from the mouth of a human being. 'I gave you the paper. Can't you read?'

And that was that.

But that *wasn't* that, not as far as Roger was concerned. By half past nine, he was back at his hotel firing up his laptop to schedule another appointment. He had to wait two or three days for the next available appointment, which meant extending his stay in Barbados. But he had thought of a new tactic.

When the time came, he walked in and handed his big stack of supporting evidence to a heavyset Caribbean woman sitting at what he took to be a reception desk. She tried to refuse them, explaining that he should give them to the interviewing officer. 'Well,' said Roger, 'I was here a couple of days ago and he refused to even let me slide it through the window for him to look at, so I want to give it to you now to make sure, 100 percent for sure, that they at least have to hold it in their hands at some point.' The woman smiled indulgently and took the papers. And so it did come to pass that the consular officer who conducted his second interview held his packet of supporting documents briefly in her hands, having no other choice, 'and kind of *skimmed* through it, but there's absolutely no way that she actually read any of it at all,' Roger says.

She told Roger that he hadn't lived in St. Kitts for long enough to meet the requirements. 'Well, I've been in Tokyo almost a decade,' he pointed out. Even so, she was loath to overrule the officer who had interviewed him on the first go-around. Just how long *is* long enough to meet the requirements, he wanted to know. She couldn't give him a clear answer. Two or three years might do it. She was, he would recall later, at least apologetic about the whole thing. But that was that.

Again Roger returned to the hotel with his denial, and again he booked an appointment for another interview a few days hence. The embassy's own rules prohibited a particular consular officer from interviewing him twice, so he thought that if he kept going back the embassy would eventually run out of people to interview him, and then maybe, just maybe, it would have no choice but to give him a visa. It wasn't logical, but nothing he had experienced so far at the embassy seemed to indicate that logic was running the show.

And indeed, upon his third visit to the embassy, the whole miserable farce resumed: Roger trying to slide his documents through the slot in the bulletproof glass and the consular officer refusing to allow it. The officer this time around was another man, not as rude as the first guy but not as compassionate as the lady Roger had last dealt with. And that was that—

But Roger had now had just about enough. He had spent days holed up in a hotel on an island where he didn't know anybody, enacting a kind of futile *Groundhog Day* existence in his repeated trips to the embassy, trying different tactics and talking to different people but getting the same answer each time – and with each application paying $160 for the privilege of being treated like a bug on the windshield of bureaucratic indifference. He had reached his absolute limit. He had brought with him to all three interviews a copy of a check he'd written for $325,000, dated 16 December and addressed to the US Treasury Department. It represented a partial payment of his 2013 tax bill. So now, in the third interview, he held it up to the bulletproof glass separating him and the consular officer so that the other man could see it . . . and proceeded to read him the riot act. 'Look at this check I just wrote three weeks ago,' Roger said. 'Anybody with any sort of a conscience should give me a visa. I'm paying for your salary to be here. I'm paying for everything that you guys are doing. It's people like me that make all the stuff that the government is doing possible. And you're not even going to *read* my application while still demanding that I pay hundreds of thousands of dollars in taxes? You guys should be absolutely ashamed.' In Roger's hands, money didn't just talk – it got up on a soapbox and made a speech.

The consular officer was deaf to this line of argument, however. Roger threatened to go to the media if his application was denied again. It was denied again. After this third rejection, he finally packed up and went home.

Perhaps because he had been able to buy his St. Kitts citizenship, he could sometimes give the impression that he thought a person's rights and responsibilities were like debits and credits in a single account, so that a deposit of $325,000, for instance, permitted a withdrawal of one visa. It was this seemingly entitled attitude that some people gleefully seized on when he did go to the press, as he had threatened. The liberal blog Talking Points Memo took it as a given that Roger Ver had given up his US citizenship to avoid paying taxes, calling him a 'moron' and an 'arrogant douchebag'. If he wanted to ditch his responsibilities, then he shouldn't ever be allowed back in. 'No whining on the yacht!' – that seemed to be the main thrust of the article. On Twitter, where the satanic mills of outrage never sleep, the reactions ranged from civil disagreement: 'I support your right to change your citizenship and travel freely though I don't agree with your choice'; to harsh condemnation: 'Stop bitching and accept [the] consequences of your choices'; to angry kiss-offs: 'Good riddance, tax dodger.'

On this last point, Roger was unequivocal: he had not surrendered his US passport to avoid paying taxes. And yet, once having renounced, he objected publicly to not getting back the $291,919 he had paid in Social Security and Medicare taxes over the years. 'If America was actually the land of the free,' he said, addressing the federal government, 'shouldn't we all be free to not participate in your Social Security Ponzi scheme?' And he surely knew that for many of the prospective customers of Passports for Bitcoin, St. Kitts' lack of taxation was a big draw. Passports for Bitcoin's Twitter account had made this abundantly clear the previous spring, trumpeting 'No income tax! No capital gains tax!'

The insults he let roll off him. But he was slow to accept a painful truth: he could no longer enter the United States. He really couldn't believe it. In the months since renouncing his citizenship, he had successfully applied for visas to Mexico, Australia, Russia, China, and Thailand. Getting a visa for the US should have been easy; lawyers had told him it would be easy. There was a provision of federal immigration law, known as the Reed Amendment, that sought to prevent former US citizens who had renounced to avoid paying taxes from ever reentering the country. In other words, tax dodgers would be punished with permanent exile from their former homeland. Roger didn't think he had been rejected on that basis. 'To be honest, I don't think it has anything to do with that,' he says. 'If it did, they'd probably just tell me.' And yet now it seemed possible that he would never be allowed back in the country.

When the news broke in early January that he wouldn't be able to attend the conference in Miami, it reverberated throughout the Bitcoin community. There were better businessmen than him, there were investors with deeper pockets, there were people with more technical ability, but there was only one Bitcoin Jesus. He had earned the nickname through his tireless advocacy, his peripatetic evangelism, and because he had risked everything for Bitcoin – his career, reputation, fortune, liberty; had moved an ocean away from family and friends to follow his conscience. In the world of Bitcoin, he had unsurpassed street cred. Now, it seemed, he was paying the price of all prophets, which is to be without honor only in one's own country.

It was a sobering time. Charlie Shrem, after pleading guilty to a single charge of the original indictment against him, had been sentenced to two years in federal prison. And on 13 January 2015, after numerous delays, the trial of Ross Ulbricht had begun in New York City. For months, Roger Ver, Lyn Ulbricht, and Ross's other supporters had been trying to cast doubt on the government's case, trying to affirm the defendant as a man innocent until proven guilty. But when the trial began, Ross's defense attorney, Joshua Dratel, blew up their efforts almost immediately. The admission he made in his opening statement shocked the courtroom. It was an admission the truth of which, however, for a reporter who had examined the available evidence, had followed the defendant's online footprints, had interviewed his old friends and read his emails and studied the works of political philosophy and economics that shaped his worldview, had long been a matter of little doubt: Ross Ulbricht was the creator of Silk Road. But to just say it like that – in the opening statement! Ross's supporters were blindsided. By the time the trial concluded, Ross had been found guilty of all seven charges, including drug trafficking and money laundering conspiracies, and was facing a sentence of twenty years to life in federal prison.

But in the midst of the scandals there remained this one thing:

Bitcoin. It, the innovation, remained, still viable in spite of everything. And when the North American Bitcoin Conference kicked off in Miami, Roger Ver was in attendance. He showed up as a telepresence robot, just as Charlie had done in Chicago the summer before. Seeing him around, people gave him nicknames: Roger Robot, Verbot. Someone taped to the robot a T-shirt depicting a white-bearded wizard and the words BITCOIN – MAGIC INTERNET MONEY. Erik Voorhees, wearing jeans, a T-shirt, and a gray blazer that hung loosely on his lanky frame, greeted the four-foot avatar of his friend cheerfully. 'This is so cool,' he enthused. 'Once again technology triumphs over government *diktat*.'

The spirit of Henry David Thoreau hovered near. 'There is no law so strong which a little gladness may not transgress,' he once wrote. 'Pile up your books, the records of sadness, your saws and your laws. Nature is glad outside, and her merry worms within will erelong topple them down. There is a prairie beyond your laws. Nature is a prairie for outlaws.' Roger Ver rolling around a digital currency conference as a robot, a face on an iPad, projecting his presence across thousands of miles to do an end-run around a benighted federal agency, was a moment of pure Thoreau, though for *nature* we would have to substitute *technology*. Technology, he seemed to be saying, without words – said merely by being there, as a man on a screen, by stepping forward once again and calling himself Spartacus – is a prairie for outlaws.

The sentiment jived with something Erik himself had said about the world of Bitcoin in 2013: 'It represents a whole legion of adventurers and entrepreneurs, of risk-takers, inventors, and problem-solvers. It is the frontier. Huge amounts of wealth will be created and destroyed as this new landscape is mapped out.'[5]

Though much in the sphere of human endeavor had fallen under the shadow of government control, much remained possible for the individual, and Roger Ver, technologist that he was, fervent believer in the Singularity, had to hope that the arc of history would bend toward freedom. There was even hope of relaunching Passports for Bitcoin. Denzil Douglas, who had served as prime minister of St.

Kitts and Nevis since 1995, was defeated in a February 2015 election. Roger had reason to believe that his successor, Timothy Harris, would look more favorably on digital currency.

In the meantime, he considered reapplying for an American visa at the embassy in Tokyo. He figured the officers of the Tokyo embassy would be more reasonable when it came to reviewing his ties to Japan. And there were other types of visas for which he might qualify, such as the H1-B and O-1, which had no Section 214(b) requirement. The future was full of possibilities. Life was good.

IN THE MIDDLE OF OCTOBER 2014, Nic Cary was in Paris hanging out with Bill Hill. Both men knew they would soon have to relocate to London, Nic from York and Bill from the City of Lights, and they were taking time before the big move to reminisce about the good old days. (It was a symptom of blockchain time, this urge to look back on the recent past. The blistering pace of change meant that indeed there was plenty to look back on.) They were indulging in foxhole nostalgia. All the stress and hardship of the past months seemed in retrospect like an enriching experience, though nobody at Blockchain quite forgot how tough it had been. To a critic who had recently called bullshit on Blockchain's story of bootstrapping, accusing the company of having had secret funding all along, as Nic recalls, Keonne Rodriguez shot back, 'Those of us who have slept on Nic's couches and on the floor of his house would disagree.'

'Could we have put people up in fancy hotels or whatever?' Nic asks. 'Sure. But that wasn't the point.' He had wanted to instill in his workforce a sense of respect for capital, which is to say a thriftiness much like his own. And the experience had built invaluable closeness between the startup's leaders and developers.

Now, with a war chest of more than $30 million, Blockchain was going to establish an office in London for those very people. Not only Nic Cary and Bill Hill but also Ben Reeves and a few others would be moving in. They called it, jokingly, the Great Migration – 'like the wildebeests across the Sahara'. Peter Smith, who was taking over from Nic as CEO, would split his time between London, New York, and parts beyond. Marco Santori would remain in America as Blockchain's counsel, seeking to influence the shape of future regulation. 'We do, and will continue to maintain, a very strong presence in the United States,' Nic says. 'And that's because, frankly, the US sets so many trends in law. There's a lot of attention on digital currency in the US, and we have to be in that dialogue.' But the startup would remain international in scope.

The relocation to London had a special meaning. Blockchain was incorporated in Luxembourg, a European nation of just under a thousand square miles bordering France, Germany, and Belgium, which, depending on your philosophical outlook, is either one of the world's biggest tax havens – being ranked second overall, behind only Switzerland, on the Tax Justice Network's annual Financial Secrecy Index for 2013 – or one of the world leaders in data privacy protections, respect for intellectual property, and tax efficiency. For Blockchain as for Amazon, which had sited its European headquarters in Luxembourg City, the nation's capital, there was nowhere better in Europe to domicile its operation. But London was the world's financial heart. As sentimental as Nic Cary was about the York era of Blockchain, he recognized that London would be the proper beachhead from which to reach the next twenty million users. 'London is a hub of world culture and commerce, and has been for a long time,' he says. 'So it makes sense. Bitcoin isn't going away; it's only gotten bigger, there's more and more interest, and it's time for us to make some steps to evolve and mature as a company.' Blockchain's move to London mirrored the wider acceptance of Bitcoin, if not yet into mainstream finance then at least into the cultural zeitgeist. In the space of three years, a startup built on a fringe technology had gone from a one-man show to a micro-multinational with twenty-two employees and its headquarters in London's Shoreditch, near Old Street station, an area known as the Silicon Roundabout.

While waiting for the new permanent office to be ready, the Blockchain team set up shop through the end of the year at WeWork, a prefurnished coworking space on the south bank of the river

Thames. As nice as it was to have a fully equipped office to airdrop into, Nic was struck by how bizarre it felt to have an office at all, after a year spent working from home in York and from coffee shops and hotel rooms while ping-ponging around the globe.

In the first week of November he left York for good, settling in Shoreditch himself, which he described as the Brooklyn of London – cool and trendy, though inevitably 'pretty heavy on the hipster scale'. But his schedule remained so hectic that two months later he had barely scratched the surface of what his neighborhood had to offer. Living in London did, however, make it easier to see his Parisian girlfriend, Sandrine, whom he had met at a networking event while in Paris to launch Blockchain's merchant app. The capital of France was only two hours and twenty minutes away on the Eurostar, and so he made the crossing every couple of weeks to see her. Their relationship was a long-distance tale of two cities, but this arrangement suited them just fine. They were both focused on their careers. (Nic's own résumé prior to joining Blockchain, he had to admit, paled in comparison to hers.) 'I don't really have the emotional availability,' Nic said then, 'to be there with someone all the time – which I want at some point, but there's a lot of other stuff going on.'

Since joining Blockchain, not only romantic attachments but relationships of all kinds had become a struggle for him to maintain. He had his family, with whom he was very close, and he had also a tight group of male friends. They believed in him, they understood what drove him, and this was important, because for someone in Nic's position, doing what he was doing, social life had to take a back seat. 'You're going to be gone a lot. You're not going to make it to the Fourth of July barbecue,' he says. 'You're going to miss a lot of little things that can add up to being important over time.'

Eventually the cost became too great. Nic was not often given to looking back, but sometimes he reflected on how differently his life could have turned out. In the ten years before meeting Sandrine he had been in only two committed relationships. The most recent and serious of these had been with a teacher in Seattle, a warm, loving girl he had dated for five years and with whom he had broken up shortly before leaving for Morocco. Once, turning reflective over Pisco Sours at a Santiago nightspot, he summarized his past relationships this way: 'The women I was with were great. Fifty years ago, I probably would have married one of them, bought a car and a house, had a kid and a sandbox. And I would have been perfectly content.' He fell silent then, shrugging as if to say, *But now . . .*

Now there was Bitcoin. But with Sandrine he wanted to make it work. When they reconnected and began dating, he could hardly believe his luck. 'She's nerdy, plus self-sufficient, plus gorgeous,' he says. Burned out by his frenetic months as Blockchain's CEO, Nic had transitioned shortly after the startup's Series A into a kind of emeritus position. And in December, finding himself racked with cabin fever in the early dark of London winter days, he and Sandrine decided to take a vacation – Nic's first in nearly eighteen months. They chose the Caribbean island of Martinique, which in addition to plenty of tropical sunshine had the added benefit of being part of the French Republic. They rented an Airbnb apartment for a week, and Nic all but ignored his email for the duration. Instead he set himself a new challenge: obtaining his PADI certification in open-water diving.

Nic's overall impression of Martinique was that 'it was probably hip and cool for Europeans to vacation there twenty years ago.' Truman Capote, describing the island in 1979, found it a place full of chameleons and ghosts, where foreign ladies went topless in the pools of fashionable hotels and where everything, even a bar of soap, cost twice as much as it did in mainland France.[6] It was the sort of place in which Nic, in his younger days, could hardly have imagined vacationing. But now he had made it. He and Sandrine found a deserted beach to watch the sunset from. There were palm trees and no people and the beach seemed gigantic and incredible in its emptiness. Together they watched the sun sink into the ocean. Nic had finally unplugged. By the end of the week, he and Sandrine were certified scuba divers.

The funny thing was that the girl beside him, blonde and

striking, had once worked for Coinbase. For about four months, beginning the previous February, Sandrine had done customer support for Blockchain's chief rival, assisting merchants who wanted to begin accepting Bitcoin payments. One might have said that Nic was sleeping with the enemy – had she not already moved on from Coinbase. She was now an ardent supporter of his work for Blockchain.

Bitcoin had emerged seemingly out of nowhere, and had made inroads into the world of finance without asking permission. Now, some of its pioneers were putting down roots in what amounted to occupied territory. A final anecdote can serve to portray the strange adolescence of Bitcoin as it began to come of age. When the time had come for Nic to look for a new home in London, he had found the process to be – every bit as much as the hunt for new Blockchain office space had been – 'a fucking nightmare'. He had to submit to something of a financial colonoscopy; his French passport bought him only so much good faith. One problem was that he didn't have a British bank account. He was an American citizen who got paid in bitcoins. Another problem: by way of proving gainful employment, he needed a letter from Blockchain on company letterhead stating officially that he was employed by Blockchain. But there was no human resources manager to write the letter. The startup had only recently had official letterhead printed.

So Nic Cary did what any sensible twenty-nine-year-old executive of a world-beating company, flush with tens of millions of dollars in venture capital, would do. He wrote his own letter of recommendation. And doesn't that, in some sense, say it all?

DISCIPLINE AND ANARCHY

Any sufficiently advanced technology is indistinguishable from magic.

— Arthur C. Clarke

Thirteen months after surrendering himself at Lewisburg Federal Prison Camp to begin his two-year sentence, Charlie Shrem walked out the doors a free man, having obtained an early release. The memory of his first day, arriving on a bitterly cold morning at the end of March 2015, was still vivid in his mind. His lawyer had managed to introduce him ahead of time to a few guys in Lewisburg, so on his first day fellow inmates already knew him as 'the Bitcoin guy'. They were former lawyers, disgraced politicians, drug users and dealers, software programmers who had worked for financial firms.[1] While inside he read *One Day in the Life of Ivan Denisovich* and 136 other books, taught yoga and the history of money, went through alcohol withdrawal, lost forty pounds (almost twenty kilos), tutored inmates seeking high school qualifications, and spread the gospel of Bitcoin. He spoke to his girlfriend every day and kept up as best as he could with news of the outside world. Looming over the camp were the high walls of the maximum-security prison, topped with barbed wire – a constant reminder of where he could end up if he misbehaved.

Initially his freedom, when he got out of prison in summer 2016, was partial. He wasn't allowed to leave Pennsylvania or give

interviews to the press. His full release came on 16 September, and
soon after that he flew with his girlfriend, Courtney, down to St.
Petersburg, Florida, where he proposed. Tearfully she said yes. He
also gave his first public interview, streamed live on YouTube,
during which, time and again, the interviewers had to give him the
lowdown on events he had missed, the rise and fall of whole
companies, it seemed.

It was clear he had been gone for a long time. Months were
years in blockchain time. Since getting out, Charlie had been trying
to catch up. He was a student again, reading white papers and
analyzing companies, looking for ways to get involved. He was
determined to remain on the path his lawyer, Marc Agnifilo, had
told the press he was still on despite his admission of guilt – a
path 'to making Bitcoin a more accepted and useful currency'. A
tall order for an ex-con, perhaps, but, his lawyer said, 'If God
smiles on him, hopefully he will be back in the Bitcoin world.'[2]

The world Charlie reentered was strikingly different from the
one he had left. At the time of his arrest, Bitcoin startups collectively had raised less than $100 million of venture capital. By the
end of September 2016, cryptocurrency and blockchain startups
had raised more than thirteen times that much, some $1.3 billion
worth of rocket fuel to kick-start the future of money – and much
more besides.

Before he went away, he had seen Bitcoin win plaudits from
public figures as different as Bill Gates and 50 Cent. Asked by Seth
Meyers, the talk-show host, why he had chosen to let fans buy his
latest album with digital currency, the rapper responded laconically:
'All money is money.' The rapper's words, as one website was quick
to note, 'could either be seen as a lucid indictment of crypto-critics
who question the validity of Bitcoin's value, or just some hardcore
gangster shit to say'.[3] True enough. And yet he seemed in that
moment to be voicing the deeper truth of the zeitgeist. Television
shows that have mentioned or based plot elements on Bitcoin
include *The Good Wife*, *White Collar*, *House of Cards*, *Justified*,
Elementary, *The Blacklist*, *Archer*, *Silicon Valley*, *Community*, and
The Simpsons. Being mocked by *The Simpsons*, of course, has

become a cultural rite of passage. In late 2014, *Garage* magazine asked several top fashion designers to conceptualize their own unique currencies. They called them 'the legal tender of lands as yet unborn'. The idea that government no longer had the sole privilege of minting money – the idea that people might be able to create their own, even if only in fantasy – was captivating.

But those developments were small stuff compared to what had happened since. Major financial firms were muscling in. Barclays had signed a deal with a Bitcoin exchange in Sweden – Safello, the exchange into which Nic Cary, Roger Ver, Erik Voorhees, and Ira Miller had put money in early 2014 – to explore how it could use the startup's technology for everyday banking processes. Nasdaq had acquired SecondMarket – Barry Silbert had finally let it go – to serve as its platform for the sale of private company stock, and was experimenting with blockchain technology as a means of automating these transactions. (Private companies currently employ lawyers to confirm stock transfers by hand.)

There was even a chance that the stock of major American companies would soon be issued in purely digital form. In the summer of 2016, Marco Santori's law firm was preparing an amendment for the state legislature of Delaware, where more than half of all publicly traded American companies and sixty-six percent of the *Fortune* 500 are incorporated, that would create a new type of security: distributed ledger shares. They 'would be born, they would live, they would die all on a blockchain', says Santori. They would be cryptographically authenticated by the state of Delaware. And they would not merely be representations of securities, as are the shares held by stockholders today; they would be the securities themselves.

As early as March 2015 there were, according to analysts at Goldman Sachs, well over 100,000 merchants worldwide accepting Bitcoin.[4] The firm that had dismissed Bitcoin one year earlier as something less than a currency now felt compelled to admit that 'a meaningful number of merchants' wanted to accept it and other digital currencies as payment; that, in fact, while only two percent of the merchants surveyed were already accepting Bitcoin, a further twenty-three percent planned to begin accepting it by 2017. Although the first wave of businesses had not seen quite the sales volume they had hoped for – Overstock, for example, had projected that it would reach at least $10 million in Bitcoin sales by the end of 2014, but managed only $3 million – the Goldman analysts, far from taking this as evidence supporting the firm's earlier position, sought to emphasize that Bitcoin 'remains in its infancy'. They would, they said, 'be closely monitoring the situation in the coming quarters'.

Bitcoin had attained a level of popularity and public awareness Charlie and his peers could scarcely have dreamed of in the early days. Goldman, Visa, Capital One, Nasdaq, and the New York Stock Exchange all invested in cryptocurrency startups in 2015. Where once Charlie Shrem's arrest had made Bitcoin anathema to banks – even tanking Fortress Capital's proposal to partner with Wells Fargo – now, although many financial institutions remained wary of the digital currency itself, they had seized eagerly on its underlying technology, the blockchain, which eliminated the need for third parties to verify transactions. Large technology firms had done the same. To them it held out the promise of huge cost savings. 'We're beyond the point that we know the technology is good for something,' says Yorke Rhodes III, the head of Microsoft's blockchain team.

When men like Rhodes talk about the blockchain, they make it seem as if it will undergird the whole future: the electronic transfer of stocks and bonds, deeds and titles; the verification and management of digital identities; smart contracts; cross-border payments. It will do this invisibly, not as a replacement for business tools like Microsoft Excel but as a way to improve business processes. 'No end user,' says Rhodes, 'should ever know that they're using the blockchain.'

From this abstract and almost metaphysical idea of money, and more than money, we descend to the gross material world of cash and coin, with all its absurdities. In 2015, the Transportation Security Administration picked up $765,759.15 of unclaimed money left behind in airports, most of it pocket change.[5] Three-quarters of a million dollars in pennies, nickels, dimes, quarters. That can't be the future of money, all that waste and inefficiency. Even the US Mint, according to its former director, Edmund Moy, believes America will eventually become a cashless society.

In several countries – the UK, China, Australia, and others – there is serious talk of central banks issuing their own digital currencies, putting national money on the blockchain. (In America, critics have sarcastically dubbed the concept 'Fedcoin'.) Eliminating cash and replacing it with a government-backed digital currency would make it easier to track the flow of money through the financial system, potentially hobbling criminal operations that depend on untraceable paper bills, while making it easier to fight fraud and monitor taxpayers' incomes. There is so much to recommend making the switch, radical though it is, that an International Monetary Fund official recently estimated that central-bank-issued digital currencies could emerge within the next five to ten years. 'A lot of people,' says Victoria Cleland, chief cashier of the Bank of England, 'think central banks are very risk averse, but we are thinking, "Are there opportunities to grasp innovation ourselves?"'[6]

Central banks are interested in digital currencies, at least in part, because getting rid of cash would allow them more easily to achieve their policy goals – goals to which libertarian Bitcoiners are strongly opposed. One such policy involves setting interest rates below zero, a drastic means of encouraging banks to lend, and thereby spurring the economy, that has lately been adopted by the European Central Bank, the Bank of Japan, and the central banks of Sweden, Denmark, and Switzerland. By the middle of 2016, half a billion people were 'living with rates in the red', in the words of one report.[7] Some $8 trillion of government bonds worldwide had become money-losing investments.

Most commercial banks have yet to pass on these negative rates to private individuals. The continued existence of cash means that if ordinary people begin losing money on their bank accounts, they can always withdraw their funds. But if cash were not an option, if *all* money existed only in electronic form, then consumers would have no recourse. They would have to swallow the pill, however bitter it might be. It is ironic that Bitcoin, so anti-establishment in its origins, so opposed to central planning in its design, has so altered the landscape of what is possible that such actions at the highest levels of finance and government can now be contemplated.

Talk of Fedcoin and the like is not entirely surprising, however, since creating a new blockchain is exactly what financial firms are aiming to do. Goldman Sachs and Morgan Stanley have both filed patents for their own blockchain projects. They do not want to build on Bitcoin's blockchain; there will not be one blockchain to rule them all. Instead their blockchains will be unique to each company; they will be private where Bitcoin's is public, closed where Bitcoin's is transparent, and proprietary where Bitcoin's is built on open-source code.

The potential benefit is enormous. A report coauthored by Santander in June 2015 estimated that the technology could reduce banks' infrastructure costs by up to $20 billion a year by providing near-instantaneous clearing and settlement of irreversible transactions – and a tamper-proof historical record of them – while eliminating the need for intermediaries. Vivian Maese, a partner in the New York office of Latham & Watkins who advises financial services firms on cryptocurrency issues, says that she 'would not be surprised to see over the next ten years a radical change in business processes'.

Undeniably, by early 2016, the conversation had shifted; the momentum and excitement seemed to be not with digital currency as such but with big banks and the blockchain startups that were willing to partner with them, disavowing any connection to Bitcoin. Venture funding for digital currency startups was drying up. High-profile hacks of Bitcoin exchanges continued to make headlines. Some companies folded almost overnight. When Charlie got out of prison he tried to access his account at a cryptocurrency exchange, where in the old days he had speculated in altcoins, and found the site no longer existed.

New industry spokesmen were striving to legitimize blockchain businesses in the eyes of lawmakers and regulators. The criticism of their efforts by some Bitcoiners, which grew more common as the months went by, was that 'blockchain' had become little more than a buzzword, that it was being made to mean whatever a given speaker wanted it to mean. (Financial institutions hoped it meant a way to penetrate new markets, cut back-office costs, and boost profits in an era of chronically low interest rates.) Charlie himself was amazed by the sudden change in terminology. Like artificial intelligence, virtual reality, and quantum computing, blockchain has acquired the special magic that belongs to vague and shiny concepts, big and promising ideas that are largely confined, for the moment, to the realm of theory, where they remain malleable, and can be toyed with.

In September 2016, the North American division of BNP Paribas, the French megabank, opened a 5,000-square-foot innovation lab at its headquarters in New York. It was christened with a two-day company hackathon focused on blockchain technology. Forty employees participated, and a permanent blockchain task force was due afterward to begin working in the lab. By then it was no longer controversial on Wall Street to say, as Bruno d'Illiers, the North American division's chief operating officer, did, that distributed ledger shares would 'shape the future of the banking industry'.[8]

Indeed, so-called innovation labs have become practically de rigueur for banks. Everyone from Wells Fargo to Capital One to the modest-sized Eastern Bank in Boston has one. The idea is to make them look as little like the offices of a bank as possible. Consequently the lab of BNP Paribas mimicked the aesthetic seen in startup offices and coworking spaces worldwide: exposed concrete and brick, minimalist furniture, high ceilings, big windows that let in plenty of natural light. It boasted a dining area and even couches for lying down on the job when the creative process demanded it. D'Illiers was clearly proud of the space; he spoke of 'a new design, a new environment' to foster collaboration and engender breakthroughs. (Like the rhetoric of innovation, there was a sameness to the environments where innovative thinking was supposed to take place.) Seeing the space empty and expectant, one could easily imagine it occupied by teams of developers working earnestly on the problems of big data, robotics, blockchain applications. Banks, like the leading firms in so many other industries, were becoming technology companies. Wall Street was taking cues from Silicon Valley.

But this subsuming of hacker culture under the auspices of huge financial institutions was hardly a victory for Bitcoin pioneers. Barry Silbert, who, in December 2013, at the private dinner at A Voce, had prophesied Wall Street's enthusiasm for Bitcoin, was describing himself by the fall of 2015 as 'highly skeptical and highly cynical' regarding the efforts of financial firms to build their own private blockchains. When you came down to it, that was nothing but a shared database – shared only within the firms themselves, of course – while the beauty of Bitcoin's blockchain was its decentralization and transparency, its availability to all. Were the banks concerned about Bitcoin's security and reliability? Fair enough. He would readily concede that it was premature to be thinking about using Bitcoin's blockchain for the clearing and settlement of financial assets. But he was frankly surprised that Wall Street, rather than being excited about Bitcoin's potential as a payment system or store of value, rather than beginning to trade bitcoins as a kind of emerging market currency, was showing enthusiasm for the method of asset transfer and record-keeping it relied on. As for banks' experiments with private blockchains, he thought, at most they would serve only as gateway drugs to the real thing, the global Bitcoin blockchain – 'and then also to holding bitcoins, trading bitcoins, speculating in bitcoins'. All it would take was for one bank to lead the charge.

One big-time venture capitalist who seems to agree with him is Fred Wilson of Union Square Ventures. 'There are changes afoot in society that are begging for these technologies to get to the point where we can actually build stuff with them,' he says. Wilson professes to be uninterested in private blockchains. There just isn't much benefit to be had, he says, from a closed system of that sort. What, in the end, makes a private blockchain ledger drastically better than an ordinary database?

By late 2016, when Wilson confided these views to TechCrunch, there were powerful voices raised on the other side. Many in the new wave of blockchain startups now viewed banks not as a means to an end, a necessary evil, but as their end users – their customers. A software startup called R3 has put together a global consortium of banks focused on applying blockchain technology to financial markets. Tim Swanson, R3's director of market research and no fan of Barry Silbert, is contemptuous of those he terms 'Bitcoin maximalists' – true believers who see Satoshi's invention as the be-all and end-all of cryptocurrency, and who think cryptocurrency and the blockchain must necessarily be intertwined.

'Satoshi, to his credit, wasn't trying to design a system with banks in mind – in fact, just the opposite,' Swanson says. Banks, required to know everything about their customers thanks to anti-money laundering regulations, are leery of some of Bitcoin's features, such as the ability to transact pseudonymously. In programming terms, they view that not as a feature but as a bug. They can't afford to thumb their noses at regulators. Charley Cooper, R3's managing director, goes even further in his denunciation of Bitcoin radicals: 'The idea of just deciding to break the rules and upend the entire financial services [sector] is just frankly naive.'

The ideological divide between Bitcoin's libertarian-anarchist wing and mainstream technocrats has widened to a chasm. While more radical Bitcoiners and their fellow travelers in Silicon Valley are, says Cooper, 'developing technology to empower a new world', betting that the future of money will look nothing like the world of money today, Wall Street and central banks remain committed to their traditional roles – even if they must adopt new technologies to stay competitive. By the fall of 2016, more than sixty financial institutions, including all ten of the world's largest banks, had joined R3's consortium.

And yet the success of their joint project – to develop a common blockchain platform called Corda – is far from assured. Such grand multi-bank initiatives have failed before. In the late nineties, before the dot-com crash, a group of banks got together to reduce inefficiencies in the buying and selling of securities. Forming the Global

Straight-Through Processing Association (GSTPA), they planned to release a software utility designed to make it easier to settle trades. But the launch was delayed twice, and the software never caught on with investment managers. Only in retrospect was it obvious that the project was flawed, doomed from the start by the self-interest of member banks. By late 2002 the association had folded – though not before shareholders had sunk more than €90 million into it. 'There is just no business,' said the GSTPA's CEO, Jurgen Marziniak, at the time. 'We built a very beautiful machine, a nice car that nobody wants to buy.'[9]

Bitcoin, of course, is already being 'driven' by thousands of people all over the world. When news broke, on 24 October 2016, that the first international transaction between banks using blockchain applications had taken place – involving the sale and shipment of eighty-eight bales of cotton from the US to China – Andreas Antonopoulos, the cryptocurrency expert whom Blockchain had once hired as chief security officer, was underwhelmed. 'You mean,' he scoffed, 'the same thing Bitcoin has done several million times?'

IN *THE RECKONING*, DAVID HALBERSTAM'S masterful narrative history of the American and Japanese automobile industries, he tells of prospectors in Texas in the days of the first oil boom who struck it rich but were swiftly shoved aside by established competitors. 'Inevitably the small boomers were soon replaced by bigger, better-financed operators, and they in turn were often replaced by giant corporations,' he writes. John D. Rockefeller's Standard Oil, for instance, caught out by the discovery of astonishing oil wealth in Texas at the turn of the twentieth century, moved rapidly to claim ground in the new bonanza territories of the American Southwest. Like the oil boom, the rise of Bitcoin a century later made overnight millionaires of average men. But then serious operators moved in: major angel investors, financial firms interested in the digital currency as a new type of asset, top venture capitalists who recognized Bitcoin as a revolutionary technology, and finally trillion-dollar banks, which saw an innovation they could learn and take ideas from.

Some who watched these developments came to believe that the Bitcoin industry had evolved too quickly, that its leaders had set their sights too high while lacking sufficient users and infrastructure to realize their ambitions. 'We were playing in the major [leagues],' says Jeremy Gardner, who moved on from the College Cryptocurrency Network (now rebranded as the Blockchain Education Network) to become an angel investor and the entrepreneur-in-residence at a venture firm in San Francisco dedicated to blockchain startups, 'when really we should have been playing wiffleball.'

But Bitcoin continues to bury its undertakers. On 26 May 2016, after hovering for months between $420 and $450, the digital currency's market price broke $500 for the first time in nearly two years. A few days later Blockchain released its first commercial. Over stirring music and heartwarming footage that left little doubt about the company's international focus, a voice-over connected Bitcoin to a history of transformative innovation and presented it as an attractive alternative to the banking system that excludes so many. 'Bitcoin is a global community of inclusion,' the narrator intoned, 'an invitation to participate in an open world.' It was a pitch aimed at the whole human family. One could detect in it the full flowering of the things Nic Cary had said to the Chilean investors and academics in May 2014, of the things he had been saying at conferences and meetings ever since. The tagline of the commercial simply restated the promise that Blockchain, and indeed Bitcoin itself, had held out from the beginning: 'Be Your Own Bank.'

By September 2016 the price of Bitcoin had climbed above $600. Blockchain's software was powering between 100,000 and 140,000 transactions a day, according to Peter Smith, and the company had users in 130 countries. One of them was the chief financial officer of Rakuten, a Japanese e-commerce giant with $6.9 billion in revenue and nearly twelve thousand employees, whom Nic Cary had met at a conference in Tokyo and set up with his first Bitcoin wallet.

If Blockchain was continuing to promote Bitcoin as a tool of financial inclusion, Barry Silbert was still bullish on Bitcoin as a speculative investment. The Bitcoin Investment Trust's net asset value had grown 32.67 percent in 2015, to $60 million, and by the fourth quarter of 2016 the fund's NAV was up another 40.25 percent. Everyone, says Balaji Srinivasan, a partner at Andreessen Horowitz and himself the founding CEO of a Bitcoin startup, likes to think they would have invested $25,000 in Facebook in 2004, if given the chance. The existence of Bitcoin gives them a chance to prove it. For the first time, he says, average people can make a VC-style bet on the future.

Barry Silbert had made that bet many times over. Not only was some portion of his personal wealth tied up in Bitcoin but his company, Digital Currency Group, had 'a large percentage of the earth covered from a Bitcoin/digital currency infrastructure perspective', he said at the end of 2015. It had invested in exchanges in China and India, in Japan and the Philippines, in Mexico and Argentina. Those investments gave his people unmatched insight into consumer adoption and government attitudes toward crypto-currency in markets all over the world. 'We have all the data,' he says. Many bankers, he was sure, if not the banks themselves, were holding Bitcoin.

By October 2016, Digital Currency Group owned stakes in seventy blockchain and cryptocurrency startups across twenty coun-tries – far more than any other firm. It had also acquired CoinDesk, the most popular of the numerous news outlets that had sprung up to cover the Bitcoin industry. Although the site was to remain editorially independent, CoinDesk's staff merged with DCG's nascent events business, tripling its size; the resulting division formed a new operating subsidiary. On the technology side, Barry appeared to be quietly hedging his bets. In September 2015, DCG contributed to the $30 million Series A funding round for Chain, a onetime Bitcoin startup that had pivoted to focus on private blockchains and was developing one for Nasdaq. In January 2016, DCG joined in the $7.1 million Series A of another blockchain-as-a-service startup called Gem, which, like Chain, had shifted its emphasis away from Bitcoin, believing the needs of enterprise clients required bespoke solutions.

Having built a company at the epicenter of the Bitcoin and blockchain industry, Barry is making use of its position to strengthen the industry as a whole. He sees DCG's network of startups, investors, advisers, experts, and corporate partners as an interconnected web, an extended family of human and financial capital with rich opportunities for mutual benefit. The difficulties seem only to have hardened his resolve. He still believes that within a few years Bitcoin either 'will be a failed experiment, and something else will have taken its place, or it will be eating the world'. Lawrence Lenihan, his investor and adviser, envisions a future in which there are fewer than ten national currencies on the planet, along with one universal currency, which is Bitcoin.

Others are convinced it will never get the chance. Jamie Dimon, the CEO of JPMorgan Chase, assured an audience in November 2015 that governments would squash Bitcoin before it could become a true competitor to the dollar, the pound, and the euro. 'No government will ever support a virtual currency that goes around borders and doesn't have the same controls,' he said. Dimon, having lived so long under the weight of onerous regulations, seemed unable to conceive of a friendlier regime – or of a technology too big for Washington to kill off. But America, as Roger Ver could have told him, is not the only country in the world. Not all governments are the same, nor all banks. Some are more open-minded than others.

In Tokyo, Mitsubishi UFJ Financial Group (MUFG), the world's third-largest bank, a huge conglomerate with $2.9 trillion in assets, was interested in Bitcoin precisely because of the digital currency's indifference to national borders. At the same time, Coinbase, which by the fall of 2016 had raised some $116 million in venture capital since graduating from Y Combinator four years earlier, badly wanted to expand its services to Japan.[10] The two companies formed a partnership to do just that – starting with international money transfers.

'It costs a lot right now and it takes time,' says Nobuyuki Hirano, the president and chief executive of MUFG. 'But by deploying digital currency, we can make it less costly and much quicker.' The cross-border payments system he envisioned would convert a national currency such as dollars or yen into bitcoins to facilitate the transfer and then, as quickly as possible so as to avoid suffering from Bitcoin's price fluctuations, change it back to regular money again. Customers need never hold Bitcoin at all.

To Hirano, Coinbase looked like an ideal partner. Thanks in part to the shift that had occurred in the balance of power between startups that defied or skirted regulations and those that complied with them, Coinbase had emerged from its long rivalry with Blockchain as perhaps the leading Bitcoin company. The 4.7 million users of its free wallet service had created a total of 10.2 million wallets. Forty-five thousand merchants were using its platform to accept Bitcoin payments from customers. And then, too, there was its digital currency trading platform, which was insured against theft, regularly audited, and backed by the New York Stock Exchange. MUFG itself had taken part in Coinbase's most recent capital raise, joining with a venture fund in July 2016 to give the startup $10.5 million. Japanese regulators overall are looking favorably on Bitcoin, Hirano says, but even he doesn't know whether MUFG's partnership with Coinbase will work out.

For years skeptics have predicted, as members of the Bitcoin community have feared, that entrenched players – governments, big banks, payments industry giants – will do their utmost to squeeze the life out of Bitcoin. If they cannot shut it down they will lobby against it, burden startups with regulations, sow uncertainty and doubt. They will do this because Bitcoin represents an unprecedented challenge to their oligopoly.

Long ago the nineteenth-century political economist Frédéric Bastiat – whose work Charlie Shrem read in prison – satirized the protectionist tendencies of entrenched business interests in a piece of writing that has come to be known as 'The Candlemakers' Petition'. It takes the form of an open letter to the French Parliament, with candlemakers beseeching the legislative body to intervene on their behalf against a devastating rival:

We are suffering from the ruinous competition of a rival who apparently works under conditions so far superior to our own for the production of light that he is flooding the domestic market with it at an incredibly low price; for the moment he appears, our sales cease, all the consumers turn to him, and a branch of French industry whose ramifications are innumerable is all at once reduced to complete stagnation. This rival . . . is none other than the sun.[11]

'The Candlemakers' Petition', written in 1845, has resonated down through the years as a savage parody of protectionist tendencies. What has been remarkable in the case of Bitcoin, however, is the willingness of so many governments and business leaders to admit its value. And yet, now that Bitcoin has been the subject of a seminar at the World Economic Forum's annual meeting in Davos, Switzerland, as it was in January 2015, and now that this same World Economic Forum has released a report, as it did in September 2015, stating that its survey respondents – some eight hundred qualified minds from the information and communications technology sector – expect ten percent of global GDP to be stored on blockchain technology by 2027, Bitcoin's co-opting, if not its defanging, by the very forces it was originally designed to circumvent or oppose may be in the offing.[12]

Perhaps it was always a foregone conclusion. 'It's hubris to think we can control its purity,' admits Alex Waters, who now runs a startup incubator in New York and serves as cofounder of a Bitcoin payment-processing startup. 'It's out of our hands.' Indeed, the World Economic Forum's report predicts that by 2023 a government will have collected tax using a blockchain; it even suggests the possibility that 'new taxing mechanisms' could be built into the blockchain itself. The idea could hardly be further from Satoshi's original vision.

Which is to say that Bitcoin, or blockchain technology, if it endures, may change beyond recognition, mutating to serve purposes even its creator could not have foreseen. Alexander Graham Bell said in old age that the modern developments of the telephone were beyond his comprehension.[13] The future has a way of refuting our expectations on its way to becoming the present. Bitcoin may turn out to mark, like the telephone, not an end but a point from which there can be no turning back.

AND YET THERE ARE CHALLENGES to overcome if Bitcoin is to shape the future. Some are inherent in the code, in the very rules of the Bitcoin protocol.

One important limiting rule pertains to block size. The size of blocks on the blockchain, which contain transaction information, is limited to one megabyte, a size which allows the network to process up to seven transactions a second. (This may sound like a lot, but Visa can process nearly fifty thousand a second.[14]) Throughout 2015 and into 2016, serious concern mounted in the Bitcoin community over the block size limit, which represented a hard ceiling that could prevent the digital currency from achieving mass adoption. As the volume of transactions increases, the thinking goes, the blockchain will hit the one-megabyte ceiling on every block, slowing transaction times to a crawl and making Bitcoin less useful – perhaps even unusable – as a system for frictionless payments. This difficulty scaling the system was one of the reasons some banks had turned away from Bitcoin.

Faced with this problem, Bitcoin's core developers, large mining pools in China, and others floated various proposed solutions, including one that would increase the block size limit to eight megabytes in early 2016 and continue to increase it gradually over time so that it doubled every two years. Raising the limit would allow each block to store more data, increasing the number of transactions the network could handle. But bigger blocks would mean bigger file sizes, making it more difficult for small miners and node operators to stay in the game. Mining power – the power to confirm transactions – would be concentrated in fewer entities. Where Bitcoin had promised decentralization, it seemed possible, even likely, that central authorities would arise.

What was more, increasing the block size would be the most fundamental change ever made to Bitcoin's code. Implementing it would require a majority of miners to agree to 'fork' the block-chain, leaving the old model behind. By the fall of 2015, none of the proposed solutions had yet won out. But it was a problem that could not be ignored.

Charlie Shrem, at the time cooped up in prison, where he was denied Internet access, nevertheless managed to weigh in on the controversy. Using the prison email system he sent messages to Roger Ver, who set up an Ask Me Anything, or AMA, thread – a form of no-holds-barred interview popularized on Reddit – on a Bitcoin discussion forum and then relayed to his incarcerated friend the forum users' questions. Since going away, Charlie had not commented publicly on any industry developments, though he had been saying plenty to his fellow inmates. ('Many people here even owned Bitcoin before they came in,' he reported.) Now he could once again share his opinions with the outside world. The press soon picked up on it, however, and the AMA lasted only thirty-six hours before Charlie sent Roger an urgent email asking him to shut it down. 'This is not looking good for me in here,' he wrote. 'I wanted this to be a fun, innocent question and answer and now the press can get me in a lot of trouble. Please let me know [when it's done].'

But for those thirty-six hours in September 2015, Charlie fielded questions. He wrote that he favored an increase in block size so long as it did not 'alter the integrity of Bitcoin's core values'. And what were those core values? 'Bitcoin is and must always be "Digital Cash" in the sense that it stays as true to cash as possible,' he wrote. Cash is king because it changes hands with no record of where it has come from, no record of where it is going. Cash gives people financial privacy. 'If Bitcoin wants to ultimately be a viable payment system and money, it needs to stay this way. If not, it will lose its integrity and will become another PayPal and eventually die out,' Charlie wrote. Although he was serving a prison sentence for having provided this digital cash to someone reselling it to drug buyers, he remained steadfast, even in government-monitored emails, in his desire for Bitcoin to live up to its revolutionary promise.

He wasn't alone. By the fall of 2016, Roger Ver was fed up with the heavy congestion and long transaction times on the Bitcoin network, as blocks approached the one-megabyte limit. It was possible to pay a fee to get the miners to confirm one's transaction more quickly, but that, he thought, taken to its logical conclusion, would destroy one of the things that made Bitcoin superior to other payment systems. Roger was now the owner of Bitcoin.com, and every day, he said, the site received complaints about unconfirmed transactions and other problems with the Bitcoin network. The people writing in didn't know much about Bitcoin, 'and they assume that Bitcoin.com is the official website for the official Bitcoin company that made the official app that they're using on their phone,' he said. They were looking to him, in other words, to solve the congestion problem.

He became convinced that the lack of scalability was driving people away from Bitcoin. There were companies he had spoken to, he said, that wanted to use digital currency but were holding back out of concern that the network might not be able to handle their transactions. It was an urgent problem, and he was disturbed to find that many Bitcoiners didn't see it that way. At a meetup he attended in Silicon Valley, he was upset to hear Bitcoin developers openly advocating, as it seemed to him, the use of credit cards instead of digital currency. (Months after his ordeal in Barbados, he had finally managed to obtain an American visa from the embassy in Tokyo.) One of those developers, in turn, was disturbed to learn that Roger evidently considered it traitorous to acknowledge the benefits of other payment methods.[15] Throughout the Bitcoin community, the block size issue had created a deep schism between people who should have been allies.

Two efforts to fork the Bitcoin software in order to increase block sizes – one of which was backed by Gavin Andresen – had so far failed to gain much traction with miners. Now Roger gave it a try, throwing his support behind Bitcoin Unlimited, a new implementation of the Bitcoin software that allowed miners to choose the maximum size of blocks they were willing to create and accept. It was the sort of market-based solution Roger preferred, rather than a hard-coded size limit. Asking what is the optimal block size, as far as he was concerned, was like asking what is the optimal interest rate. It was up to Bitcoin miners and users to decide.

In mid-October, ViaBTC, the world's fifth-largest mining pool, made the switch to Bitcoin Unlimited.[16] Roger's Bitcoin.com mining pool had already done the same, continuing to mine one-megabyte blocks for the time being while accepting blocks as large as sixteen megabytes. Together, the two pools represented nearly ten percent of the entire Bitcoin network's processing power. They would need fifty-one percent of the network, a majority, to initiate a hard fork and leave the old one-megabyte limit behind for good.

There were risks involved in such a radical step, but the bigger risk, said Roger, was not trying to improve the situation. He wanted to build a currency to rival major fiat currencies – and it would never happen if the original limits of the technology were allowed to stunt its growth. 'If we don't allow Bitcoin to scale to allow more people to use it around the world, it runs a real risk of being passed up by something else and becoming the Friendster or MySpace of cryptocurrencies,' he said. 'That's my honest-to-God concern.'

Roger wasn't far off, in this admission, from something venture capitalist Fred Wilson had said. Bitcoin, he conceded, was still waiting 'for a killer app, or a series of killer apps, that will make it obvious to people why this technology really matters'.

IN FACT THERE ARE SOME killer apps for Bitcoin out in the wild, but they are best avoided in polite conversation. One is the cryptomarket: a Bitcoin-enabled Amazon of drugs and other contraband existing on the dark web. Silk Road had been only the first of these. By 2015 there was another killer app of sorts, and it too could not be promoted or spoken of by the digital currency's boosters, for it too was criminal, and worse, it had real victims. It was cyber-extortion.

For extortionists, the riskiest part of the enterprise has traditionally involved collecting payment. When you show up to get the briefcase full of cash, the police can nab you. And in recent years law enforcement agencies have grown increasingly skilled at following electronic money trails. What criminals need is a way to cover their tracks while collecting ransom payments easily and cheaply from around the globe. Enter Bitcoin. Cybercriminals in Eastern Europe, Russia, and China are taking advantage of the digital currency to extort victims – including schools, hospitals, and law enforcement agencies – from the other side of the world, raking in hundreds of millions of dollars a year in ransom payments.

Nowadays the extortion tends to happen through ransomware, a type of malicious software that encrypts a victim's computer files, making them inaccessible, and which then demands payment in digital currency in return for the key to decrypt them. The encryption is so good that victims without adequate backups have no choice but to either pay the ransom or say goodbye to their work documents, half-finished novels, tax records, family photos, and whatever else the malware has locked up.

The genius of it, according to Kevin Haley, a cybersecurity expert at Symantec, is that the criminals 'don't have to pretend to be somebody else'. They can just hold hostage their victim's most important, most cherished data, and threaten to take it away forever – and then, in the next moment, offer to give it back for a price. Often the ransom demand is only a few hundred bucks, a sweet spot that makes it a lot cheaper to pay up than to buy a new computer. But companies can wind up paying thousands. In early 2016, a hospital in Los Angeles had its computer network crippled by ransomware – forcing staff to go back to pen and paper for record-keeping – and ultimately ponied up nearly $17,000 in bitcoins to regain control.

Perhaps the most prominent family of ransomware programs right now is CryptoWall. Between 1 February and 14 October 2015, cybersecurity researchers detected 406,887 attempted CryptoWall 3.0 infections worldwide. CryptoWall is devilishly clever: using an infected computer's IP address, it determines the victim's geographic location, and adjusts its ransom demand accordingly: Americans are expected to pay $700, while Mexicans and Russians are on the hook for $500. If payment is not made within a few days, the ransom amount doubles.

The illegal profits being reaped are tremendous. During those eight and half months in 2015, CryptoWall 3.0 – a single version of a single ransomware program – raked in an estimated $325 million for the criminals behind it.

IN NOVEMBER 2014, FEDERAL LAW enforcement graduated from taking down Silk Road to taking on the dark web itself. A massive blitzkrieg action, coordinated between law enforcement agencies worldwide, resulted in the closure of 414 websites, seventeen arrests across as many countries, and the seizure of more than $1 million worth of bitcoins, as well as large amounts of cash and drugs. The fallout continued for months: a twenty-nine-year-old Welshman pleaded guilty in June 2015 to possessing and selling drugs on Silk Road 2.0, an exact replica that succeeded the original website within weeks of its takedown.

Operation Onymous, as the November 2014 enforcement action was called, brought down Silk Road 2.0 and arrested its chief administrator – who, like Ross Ulbricht, had been living in San Francisco. But dozens of illicit marketplaces are still operating on the dark web. Of the more than 100,000 drug users who took part in the 2015 Global Drug Survey, 4.5 percent said they had bought drugs through the dark web in the past twelve months. For Americans, it was eight percent; for British respondents, more than twelve percent. For law enforcement, these online black markets, fueled by cryptocurrencies, represent a new front in a forever war. It is a war that Shawn Henry, formerly the executive assistant director of the Criminal, Cyber, Response, and Service Branch of the FBI, admits the feds are not winning. The authors of the Global Drug Survey have called dark markets 'the biggest challenge to drug laws and their enforcement in a century'.

But the dark web today makes up a small part of the Bitcoin community's consciousness. New headlines mainly serve as a reminder of the cryptocurrency's early days – and of the fact that it is often outlaws who move society forward. Like sons rejecting a Mafioso father, latter-day Bitcoin advocates have tended to distance themselves from Ross Ulbricht and his notorious website. In this willful distancing lies an implicit debt. Bitcoin entrepreneurs today build atop the success of Silk Road, the digital currency's first 'killer app'. Nevertheless, it is easy to act as if Ross Ulbricht's arrest was a watershed for Bitcoin, dividing its murky past from its bright and beckoning future.

But the past, as William Faulkner once wrote, is never dead, and in fact is not even past. On 26 October 2016, Ross Ulbricht returned to a Manhattan courtroom to appeal his conviction. Life in prison without parole, argued his lead attorney, Joshua Dratel, was an unconscionably severe punishment for the crimes of which his client stood convicted: drug trafficking, money laundering, and leading an organized criminal enterprise. Undoubtedly the six attempted murders for hire of which Ross Ulbricht had been accused – none of which had led to any deaths, and with which Ross had not been formally charged – had inclined the judge to be merciless. She had as much as said so at Ross's sentencing. But even this reasoning didn't add up, said Dratel. 'Murderers don't get life sentences,' he protested before a panel of three judges. 'People who *actually commit* murder.' (Lyn Ulbricht, for her part, never tired of reminding people that her son had not been convicted of any violent crimes.)

And yet what did that matter, asked Gerald Lynch, one of the appellate judges, when the crimes of which Ross Ulbricht *was* convicted also carried the potential for a life sentence?

Since Ross's conviction, the most shocking developments in his case, as far as the public was concerned, had been the revelations that two of the federal agents involved in the investigation were dirty cops. One had alternated between selling information about the investigation to Dread Pirate Roberts and attempting to blackmail him, while the other had stolen a fortune in bitcoins from Silk Road and framed the black market's hapless former administrator, Curtis Clark Green, now a cooperating witness, for the theft.[17] It was this theft, committed by then Secret Service agent Shaun Bridges, that had evidently pushed Ross over the edge, allegedly prompting him to put out a hit on Green – his first murder for hire. But the supposed hitman he hired turned out to be the other corrupt cop, Carl Mark Force IV, a DEA agent, and together Force and Bridges staged Green's death for Ross's benefit. (Green continued to cooperate with the feds, even though the theft of twenty thousand bitcoins, pinned on him, had jeopardized his plea deal.) At Bridges' sentencing in December 2015, Green wept openly as he described how he had taught Bridges and Force 'how to move Bitcoin, how to essentially hide it', believing with all his heart that he was helping 'the good guys'.

Shaun Bridges had had a stellar career in law enforcement. He had even guarded First Lady Michelle Obama. But it would have been difficult, by the time he was convicted, to describe him as a good guy. According to an assistant US attorney, Bridges' involvement had tainted a 'staggering' number of investigations into Bitcoin operations around the country. He seemed to have been looking for opportunities to profit from the seizure of Bitcoin startups' assets – as he did in May 2013, when, just before finishing an affidavit for the seizure warrant that was about to served against Mt. Gox's American subsidiary, Bridges wired $820,000 from Mt. Gox to a shell company he controlled.[18] Bitcoin companies in those days had felt the government was out to get them – and evidently, in the person of Shaun Bridges, it was.

More than Ross Ulbricht's, more than Charlie Shrem's, it was this former law enforcement officer's downfall that was perhaps the most pathetic and shocking of any in the world of Bitcoin. He resigned before the Secret Service could fire him. He tried to wipe his work computer clean of incriminating evidence before turning it in. He married his girlfriend mere days before she was due to testify before a grand jury so that he could avail himself of spousal immunity. And then, in January 2016, having pled guilty to corruption and money laundering charges and received a sentence of nearly six years in prison, he was arrested again while trying to flee the country, passport and bulletproof vests in hand.

No information regarding the agents' wrongdoing had been permitted at Ross Ulbricht's trial, because it was then still under grand jury seal.[19] In fact, the defense had not even learned of the charges against Bridges until after Ross's conviction. When it finally came out, it was immediately clear even to casual observers that the astonishing corruption and abuse of power of which Force and Bridges were guilty might form the basis for Ross's appeal. The whole mess reinforced immeasurably the feelings among some Bitcoiners – the self-styled crypto-anarchists and cypherpunks – that the federal government was enemy number one, and not to be trusted. The two corrupt agents embodied all their misgivings about state power. Even as major Bitcoin companies and industry groups were cozying up to Washington, there were others in the community who could not have been less inclined to cooperate.

At the appeal hearing, Ross's lawyer suggested that his client had been convicted on the basis of trumped-up evidence. For prosecutors, Ross Ulbricht's laptop, snatched up by a federal agent in a San Francisco library three years earlier, had proved to be the motherlode: much of the government's case against Silk Road's founder relied on evidence recovered from the laptop, such as Ross's diary, which made it clear that he was Dread Pirate Roberts. If Bridges had been willing to steal from Silk Road and set up Green to take the fall, argued Dratel, it was possible that he could have framed Ross Ulbricht as well. Dratel had not been allowed to make this argument at trial. If he had, he might have succeeded in planting reasonable doubt in the minds of the jury.

The judges on the appellate panel seemed unsympathetic. 'The jury didn't know in this day and age that computers can be hacked?' Lynch retorted. 'Even the NSA gets hacked.' The prosecution insisted that none of the evidence used against Ulbricht had come from either Force or Bridges. As for Ross's sentence, it was justified, said prosecutor Eun Young Choi, because the scope of Silk Road – the number of its users, the sheer variety and amount of drugs sold – was 'unprecedented'.

And so it was. Whatever label one might give him – criminal or freedom fighter, narco-saint or attempted murderer – and whatever else he did, Ross Ulbricht helped set money free, ushering in a new age of commerce that is still unfolding all around us.

Financial institutions, left to their own devices, would not have set money free; they had no hope of doing so without incurring the wrath of regulators, and no incentive to do so when their profits depended on keeping it in chains.

Among all the conferences and blockchain seminars, the interest being shown by banks and governments, it can be difficult to remember where Bitcoin started: on the fringe, where great ideas are usually born, among radical minds willing to embrace a radical invention. For them, economics was not a dry subject to be taught in universities. It was an animating force, a key to understanding human action. To them technology did not mean merely building a better mousetrap. It meant building a better world. First ignored and then derided by the establishment, through their untiring advocacy they set the agenda for the establishment – even if that agenda soon markedly diverged. They kick-started this era which we have only begun to identify as our own.

'Had the Greeks known of cryptocurrencies and of certain provincial Brooklyn neighborhoods,' wrote Marc Agnifilo in a letter to Judge Rakoff a few days before Charlie Shrem's sentencing, 'a tragedy could have been written about a boy who, through Dionysian passion and a little hubris, helped nurture an idea – Bitcoin – that was new to the world, and that could change how the world – the whole world – passed value from one person to another.'

Like the wine of Dionysus, what Charlie and the others unleashed has brought both progress and chaos, madness and clarity. During the Ebola crisis in West Africa, Bitcoin made it possible to send donations directly to charities on the front lines without incurring the high fees of MoneyGram and Western Union. That was a boon to humanity. But how to weigh that against the suffering of extortion victims? 'There are, as Socrates taught,' cultural critic George Steiner reminds us, 'necessary treasons to make the city freer and more open to man . . . Society is a bounded, transient thing compared to the free play of the mind and the anarchic discipline of its dreams.'

History will decide whether the work of Satoshi Nakamoto,

of Hal Finney, of Ross Ulbricht, of Roger Ver, Charlie Shrem, Erik Voorhees, Ira Miller, Gavin Andresen, Nic Cary, Barry Silbert, and of countless others who stood beside and followed after them, should be counted among the necessary treasons of our age. For now, the men and women of this new financial frontier have their gazes fixed only on the future. Their work – their war – continues.

ACKNOWLEDGMENTS

This book would not have been possible without Roger Ver, Charlie Shrem, Nic Cary, Barry Silbert, and other Bitcoin pioneers giving generously of their time during intense and stressful periods in their lives. It's not often one has the chance to document an unfolding revolution from the point of view of its leaders, and for that I'll always be grateful. Others who work in the industry or were affected by it, including family members of the men mentioned above, and their employees and former employees, lent crucial insight, and the book would be poorer without their contributions.

Experts such as Marco Santori, as well as current and former government officials, including Edmund Moy, were also invaluable. In the final months of the project, top bankers such as Nobuyuki Hirano of Mitsubishi UFJ Financial Group opened up about their plans for cryptocurrency and blockchain technology, and for that I'm appreciative.

My workload in the first months of the project was made bearable by Doni Bloomfield, who served capably as my research assistant before taking a well-deserved job at Bloomberg. I'm thankful to John Dinges and Duff Wilson, each of whom, early on, provided valuable advice and a listening ear. Although I didn't speak to him about this project, I'm grateful to John Bennet, who, years ago when I was a student at Columbia University, encouraged me in my writing and urged me to hold onto the voice I had developed in his class.

The financial strain caused by the decision to quit my job in order to pursue this book was lessened by Teri Evans, Vauhini

Vara, and Lauren Covello, three wonderful and tough-minded editors who gave me freelance work and encouragement when it was needed. For similar reasons I am indebted to Michael Phillips Moskowitz, who helped me land a part-time gig that supplemented the publisher's advance I was living on.

I owe thanks to my original publisher, Penguin Random House, for seeing the potential in what was then, admittedly, a rather different book project, and to Oneworld Publications, originally my British publisher, which assumed full editorial responsibility for the manuscript and arranged North American distribution after I had to part ways with Penguin. Deepest thanks go to my agent, Anthony Mattero, who stuck by me in fair weather and foul, negotiated tirelessly on my behalf, and generally was the best cornerman I could have hoped for. I would also like to thank Alex Christofi, my editor at Oneworld, and David Inglesfield, my copy editor, for the indispensable parts they played in shaping the finished book. The former thankfully cleaved away much that was inessential, while the latter displayed a keen eye and excellent judgment, and proved always willing to discuss the finer points of English usage with an open mind.

Special thanks are owed to Jeremy Gardner, who not only served as an important source of information but also, in one case, set the record straight with another source of mine after he had been given a negative impression of my project.

Admiration and thanks go to Tom Wolfe, Truman Capote, Norman Mailer, Joan Didion, Robert Caro, and David Halberstam, giants of narrative nonfiction who continue to inspire and humble me, as well as to Michael Lewis and Gregory Zuckerman, whose *Flash Boys* and *The Frackers*, respectively, provided me with partial models. Two novelists, Don DeLillo and William Gibson, also deserve my gratitude.

I would not have stayed sane without the love and support of my friends and family, who weathered my moods, listened to me talk endlessly about Bitcoin, were accepting when I disappeared into my writing bunker for long stretches, and, in some cases, graciously fielded my late-night text messages. There are too many to name, but I'd like to thank especially Adam McCauley, Nathaniel Dorn, Ephraim McCormick, Ashley Mayo, Andrew Bell, Hristina Tisheva, Susana Moyaha, Ryan Particka, Alex Vadukul, and Susana Stone. My companionship across every distance of space and time, now and always, I give to world-wanderer and fellow Nick Drake fan Kara Altman, whose gypsy soul and adventurous spirit never cease to amaze me.

My parents, Randal and Maureen, made countless sacrifices as I was growing up and instilled in me a lifelong passion for learning. For that and for their love, I'm grateful. My brother, Sean, my first and best friend, deserves my thanks for always encouraging me in my writing. He astounds me with his unfailing ability to look at the bright side of even the most challenging episodes in life. My little sister, Caitlin, an aspiring writer herself, has chosen a hard road – harder than she knows – and I wish her well.

Last but not least, I owe my deepest thanks to Chelsey Sullivan, who saw the worst of it and never stopped believing in me. You were my biggest fan, my fiercest advocate, and my most devoted source of support. I can never repay you. I hope this book makes you proud.

NOTES

PROLOGUE: MONEY AND LIBERTY

1. When referring to the software and payment system, 'Bitcoin' is typically capitalized, while the lowercase version is used for the units of currency – just as with the dollar, the euro, and the yen. Recently, however, some people and publications, for simplicity's sake, have begun to use the lowercase 'bitcoin' for all of the above.

2. 'Craig Steven Wright claims to be Satoshi Nakamoto. Is he?', *The Economist*, 2 May 2016. http://www.economist.com/news/briefings/21698061-craig-steven-wright-claims-be-satoshi-nakamoto-bitcoin

CHAPTER 1: MAKING MONEY

1. Kevin Kelly, *Out of Control: The Rise of Neo-Biological Civilization* (New York: Perseus Books, 1994).

2. Ibid.

3. Michael Riley, Ben Elgin, Dune Lawrence, and Carol Matlack, 'Missed Alarms and 40 Million Stolen Credit Card Numbers: How Target Blew It', *Bloomberg Businessweek*, 13 March 2014. http://www.businessweek.com/articles/2014-03-13/target-missed-alarms-in-epic-hack-of-credit-card-data

4. '20 Million People Fall Victim to South Korea Data Leak', SecurityWeek, 19 January 2014. http://www.securityweek.com/20-million-people-fall-victim-south-korea-data-leak

5. Declan McCullagh, 'Nothing That Glitters Is DigiGold', *Wired*, 6 July 2001. http://archive.wired.com/techbiz/media/news/2001/07/44967

6. Kim Zetter, 'Bullion and Bandits: The Improbable Rise and Fall of E-Gold', *Wired*, 9 June 2009. http://www.wired.com/2009/06/e-gold/

7. Kim Zetter, 'E-Gold Gets Tough on Crime', *Wired*, 11 December 2006. http://web.archive.org/web/20100316084637/http://www.wired.com/science/discoveries/news/2006/12/72278

8. Ibid.

9. Zetter, 'Bullion and Bandits'.

10. This quote, as well as the one in the following paragraph, is taken from an interview Bernard von NotHaus conducted for the documentary film *Bitcoin: The End of Money As We Know It*.

11. 'Liberty Dollar office raided', *Evansville Courier & Press*, 15 November 2007. http://www.courierpress.com/news/local-news/liberty-dollar-office-raided

12. Peter Thiel (with Blake Masters), *Zero to One: Notes on Startups, or How to Build the Future* (New York: Crown Business, 2014).

13. In early May 2016, an Australian businessman and computer scientist named Craig Steven Wright declared to the world that he was Satoshi. He had been outed by the American press months earlier after hackers leaked some of his emails and other documents, though skeptics had immediately raised questions about the dubious evidence underlying the claim that he was Bitcoin's creator. Now Wright broke his silence in a blog post, providing ostensible proof, in the form of a digital signature, that he was indeed Satoshi. He gave a kind of tearful acceptance speech: 'This incredible community's passion and intellect and perseverance has taken my small contribution and nurtured it, enhanced it, breathed life into it. You have given the world a great gift. Thank you.'

Of all the would-be Satoshis, Wright's claim seemed the strongest. Among those he managed to convince was Gavin Andresen, who had worked alongside the real Satoshi to improve Bitcoin's source code and who took over as lead developer of the cryptocurrency's software after Satoshi walked away in early 2011. Andresen's opinion, based on interactions with Wright, carried a lot of weight.

But no sooner had Wright published his blog post than users of Reddit's Bitcoin forum debunked his so-called proof. The whole post, *The Economist* opined, was nothing but an 'exercise in obfuscation'. Within days, rather than providing more convincing evidence, Wright replaced his blog with a message saying he was 'not strong enough' to cope with the attacks on his character: 'I can only say I'm sorry. And goodbye.' Then he took his website down completely.

Andresen later backed away from his support of Wright's claim. Most people dismissed the Australian as a fraud, a pretender to the throne. A few, however, think it likely that Wright was part of a team that invented Bitcoin, of whom the other members, such as Hal Finney, may now be dead. Thus far, the true identity of Satoshi Nakamoto has yet to be established for certain.

CHAPTER 2: VIRTUAL CRACK

1. Robert McMillan, 'The Inside Story of Mt. Gox, Bitcoin's $460 Million Disaster', *Wired*, 3 March 2014. http://www.wired.com/2014/03/bitcoin-exchange/all

2. Robert McMillan and Cade Metz, 'The Rise and Fall of the World's Largest Bitcoin Exchange', *Wired*, 6 November 2013. http://www.wired.com/2013/11/mtgox/

3. Andy Greenberg, 'Ross Ulbricht's Mother Calls Silk Road Allegations "Absurd", Launches Defense Fund', *Forbes*, 20 November 2013. http://onforb.es/MY3ccH

4. Katharine Lackey, 'Paul to visit PSU', *Daily Collegian*, 26 March 2008. http://www.collegian.psu.edu/archives/article_239513a3-a577-5732-bab0-9cc27c5d4610.html

5. Greg Farrell, 'Silk Road Pirate Trained as Eagle Scout Before Charges', Bloomberg News, 7 November 2013. http://www.bloomberg.com/news/2013-11-06/silk-road-pirate-trained-as-eagle-scout-before-charges.html

6. John Carney, 'Sorry, Folks, The CRA Really Did Require Crap Lending Standards', Business Insider, 23 June 2009. http://www.businessinsider.com/sorry-folks-the-cra-really-did-require-crap-lending-standards-2009-6

7. Ludwig von Mises, *Human Action: A Treatise on Economics (The Scholar's Edition)*, Ludwig von Mises Institute, 2008.

8. Nick Bilton, 'Disruptions: Betting on a Coin With No Realm', *New York Times*, 22 December 2013. http://bits.blogs.nytimes.com/2013/12/22/disruptions-betting-on-bitcoin/

9. Indeed, such websites are more than theoretical; today they actually exist.

10. Dune Lawrence, 'The Inside Story of Tor, the Best Internet Anonymity Tool the Government Ever Built', *Bloomberg Businessweek*, 23 January 2014. http://www.businessweek.com/articles/2014-01-23/tor-anonymity-software-vs-dot-the-national-security-agency

11. Adrian Chen, 'The Underground Website Where You Can Buy Any Drug Imaginable', Gawker, 1 June 2011. http://gawker.com/the-underground-website-where-you-can-buy-any-drug-imag-30818160

12. Patrick Howell O'Neill, 'The definitive history of Silk Road', Daily Dot, 11 October 2013. http://www.dailydot.com/crime/silk-road-drug-ross-ulbright-dread-pirate-roberts-history/

13. Neuwirth's excellent book on this subject is *Stealth of Nations: The Global Rise of the Informal Economy*.

14. Patrick Howell O'Neill, 'How the Internet powered a DIY drug revolution', Daily Dot, 28 August 2013. http://www.dailydot.com/crime/hive-silk-road-online-drug-culture-history/

15. Ibid.

CHAPTER 3: THE GRAY HAT

1. Eric Markowitz, 'My Night Out With Bitcoin Millionaire and Proud Stoner Charlie Shrem', Vocativ, 5 December 2013. http://www.vocativ.com/tech/bitcoin/night-bitcoin-millionaire-proud-stoner-charlie-shrem/

2. Ibid.

3. Pete Zaborszky, 'An interview with Private Internet Access founder Andrew Lee', BestVPN, 21 August 2013. https://www.bestvpn.com/blog/7319/an-interview-with-private-internet-access-founder-andrew-lee/

CHAPTER 4: BLOOD AND VEIN

1. Adrianne Jeffries, 'Bitcoin Enthusiasts Gather in NYC to Meet IRL and Show Off Bitcoin Start-Ups', Betabeat, 22 August 2011. http://betabeat.com/2011/08/bitcoin-enthusiasts-gather-in-nyc-to-meet-irl-and-show-off-bitcoin-start-ups/

2. Lawrence H. White, *Competition and Currency: Essays on Free Banking and Money* (New York: New York University Press, 1992).

3. Will Deener, 'Why gold, silver are up while inflation is low', *Dallas Morning News*, 27 September 2010. http://www.dallasnews.com/business/columnists/will-deener/20100926-Why-gold-silver-are-up-8633.ece

4. Adrianne Jeffries, 'Banking Partners Force Paxum to Drop Bitcoin Due to "Potential Risk"', Betabeat, 13 February 2012. http://betabeat.com/2012/02/banking-partners-force-paxum-to-drop-bitcoin-due-to-potential-risk/

5. Jeffries, 'Bitcoin Enthusiasts Gather'.

6. Marshall Sella, 'Sex, Drugs, and Toasters: My Life on Bitcoin', GQ, June 2014. http://www.gq.com/life/tech/201406/bitcoin

7. FinCEN requires money services businesses to report all transactions of $10,000 or more. Any suspicious transactions above $2,000 must also be reported.

8. A surety bond is a form of insurance against default, in this case designed to protect customers against the default of the money transmitter. If the money transmitter defaults, the surety bond will pay out to cover customer losses.

9. James Surowiecki, 'The Sochi Effect', *New Yorker*, 10 February 2014. http://www.newyorker.com/magazine/2014/02/10/the-sochi-effect

CHAPTER 5: A MEETING IN IBIZA

1. Jesse McKinley, 'Finding Their Next Facebook', *New York Times*, 22 March 2013. http://www.nytimes.com/2013/03/24/fashion/winklevoss-brothers-move-on-from-facebook.html
2. Stephanie Baker, 'Bitcoin Believers', *Bloomberg Markets*, November 2013.
3. Scott Edward Walker, 'Everything You Ever Wanted To Know About Convertible Note Seed Financings (But Were Afraid To Ask)', TechCrunch, 7 April 2012. http://techcrunch.com/2012/04/07/convertible-note-seed-financings/
4. McKinley, 'Finding Their Next Facebook'.
5. Eric Markowitz, 'My Night Out With Bitcoin Millionaire and Proud Stoner Charlie Shrem', Vocativ, 5 December 2013. http://www.vocativ.com/tech/bitcoin/night-bitcoin-millionaire-proud-stoner-charlie-shrem/
6. Pete Rizzo, 'Top Bitcoin VCs Back Coinapult's $775k Funding Round', CoinDesk, 1 October 2014. http://www.coindesk.com/coinapult-775k-funding-round/

CHAPTER 6: REGULATION BLUES

1. Felix Moreno, 'Erik Voorhees: "Bitcoin Is the New Frontier"', *Bitcoin Magazine*, 25 July 2013. bitcoinmagazine.com/4550/erik-voorhees-new-frontier/
2. Roben Farzad, 'The Cypriot Bailout Hasn't Rocked Markets – Yet', Bloomberg News, 18 March 2013. http://www.businessweek.com/articles/2013-03-18/the-cypriot-bailout-hasnt-rocked-markets-yet
3. Peter Coy, 'How Europe Let Cyprus Get Into This Mess', Bloomberg News, 17 March 2013. http://www.businessweek.com/articles/2013-03-17/how-europe-let-cyprus-get-into-this-mess
4. Farzad, 'The Cypriot Bailout'.
5. Carol Matlack, 'Behind the Cyprus Tax: Russian Deposits and a Suspicious EU', Bloomberg News, 18 March 2013. http://www.businessweek.com/articles/2013-03-18/
behind-the-cyprus-tax-russian-deposits-and-a-suspicious-eu
6. Stefan Schultz, 'German Economist: "Europe's Citizens Now Have to Fear for Their Money"', *Spiegel Online*, 18 March 2013. http://www.spiegel.de/international/europe/interview-with-german-economist-peter-bofinger-on-perils-of-cyprus-bailout-a-889594.html

7. Karolina Tagaris, 'Cyprus details heavy losses for major bank customers', Reuters, 30 March 2013. http://www.reuters.com/article/2013/03/25/us-cyprus-parliament-idUSBRE92G03I20130325

8. Katie Martin and Charles Forelle, 'Cyprus Deal Rattles Markets', *Wall Street Journal*, 18 March 2013. online.wsj.com/news/articles/SB10001424127887323415304578367673128686956

9. Some phrasing here and in what follows about the FinCEN guidance has been taken from Brian Patrick Eha, 'U.S. Regulators Aim to Close "Wild West" Frontier of Bitcoin', Entrepreneur.com, 14 August 2013. https://www.entrepreneur.com/article/227849

10. Timothy B. Lee, 'New Money Laundering Guidelines Are a Positive Sign for Bitcoin', Forbes.com, 19 March 2013. http://www.forbes.com/sites/timothylee/2013/03/19/new-money-laundering-guidelines-are-a-positive-sign-for-bitcoin/

11. Cody Wilson, *Come and Take It: The Gun Printer's Guide to Thinking Free* (New York: Gallery Books, 2016).

CHAPTER 7: BITCOIN NEVER SLEEPS

1. A cold wallet is one stored offline, for instance on an external hard drive that remains unconnected to the Internet, thus putting it out of reach of hackers; a hot wallet is one with some Internet-facing element.

2. Vitalik Buterin, 'Bitfinex: Bitcoinica Rises From The Grave', *Bitcoin Magazine*, 22 November 2012. https://bitcoinmagazine.com/articles/bitfinex-bitcoinica-rises-from-the-grave-1353644122

3. 'Ericsson Mobility Report: On the Pulse of the Networked Society', November 2013. http://www.ericsson.com/res/docs/2013/ericsson-mobility-report-november-2013.pdf

4. 'Nigeria launches national electronic ID cards', BBC, 28 August 2014. http://www.bbc.com/news/world-africa-28970411

5. Megan Geuss, 'MasterCard-backed biometric ID system launched in Nigeria', Ars Technica, 2 September 2014. http://arstechnica.com/business/2014/09/mastercard-backed-biometric-id-system-launched-in-nigeria/

6. Kim Lachance Shandrow, 'Bitcoin in 10 Years: 4 Predictions From SecondMarket's Barry Silbert', *Entrepreneur*, 30 June 2014. http://www.entrepreneur.com/article/235290

7. Robert McMillan, 'The Fierce Battle for the Soul of Bitcoin', *Wired*, 26 March 2014. http://www.wired.com/2014/03/what-is-bitcoin/

8. Ibid.

9. Ibid.

CHAPTER 8: THE BILLIONAIRE WHO WASN'T

1. Jenny Anderson, 'Seeking Unlimited Success From Providing a Market for Restricted Stock', *New York Times*, 28 September 2005. http://www. nytimes.com/2005/09/28/business/28place.html

2. Ibid.

3. Peter Eisler, 'The truck the Pentagon wants and the firm that makes it', *USA Today*, 1 August 2007. http://usatoday30.usatoday.com/news/ military/2007-08-01-force-protection-mraps_N.htm

4. Chris Dixon, 'Big Wheels for Iraq's Mean Streets', *New York Times*, 24 February 2008. www.nytimes.com/2008/02/24/automobiles/24MRAP. html

5. Tina Traster, 'Top Entrepreneurs 2009: SecondMarket', *Crain's New York*. http://www.crainsnewyork.com/gallery/20090501/FEATURES/501009996/3

6. Ibid.

7. Anderson, 'Seeking Unlimited Success'.

8. Ibid.

9. Gretchen Morgenson, 'As Good as Cash, Until It's Not', *New York Times*, 9 March 2008. http://www.nytimes.com/2008/03/09/business/ 09gret.html

10. Gretchen Morgenson, 'How to Clear a Road to Redemption', *New York Times*, 4 May 2008. http://www.nytimes.com/2008/05/04/ business/04gret.html

11. Ibid.

12. Martin Arnold, 'Private equity investors flock to sale platform', *Financial Times*, 24 February 2009. http://www.ft.com/cms/s/0/c9ab3f8a-02ac-11de-b58b-000077b07658.html

13. Traster, 'SecondMarket'.

14. Judith Messina, 'Bold newcomer SecondMarket steals shares', *Crain's New York*, 7 November 2010. http://www.crainsnewyork.com/article/ 20101107/SMALLBIZ/311079994/bold-newcomer-secondmarket-steals-shares

15. Shmulik Shelach, 'SecondMarket closes Israel office after less than a year', *Globes*, 12 November 2011. http://www.globes.co.il/en/article-1000697890

16. Erin Griffith, 'SecondMarket pivoted after Facebook's IPO. Now, volume is higher than ever', *Fortune*, 25 July 2014. http://fortune. com/2014/07/25/secondmarket-pivoted-after-facebooks-ipo-now-volume-is-higher-than-ever/

17. Ibid.

18. Ibid.

19. The Congressional Budget Office's forecast is gloomy: the portion of US national debt held by the public – seventy-four percent of gross domestic product as of 2014 – is expected to grow to seventy-nine percent of GDP by 2024. By 2039, it will be 106 percent of GDP. (cf. 'The Budget and Economic Outlook: 2014 to 2024', Congressional Budget Office, 4 February 2014. http://www.cbo.gov/publication/45010)

20. James Martin, 'Lost on the Silk Road: Online drug distribution and the "cryptomarket"', *Criminology and Criminal Justice* 14 (3): 351–67, July 2014. First published online 7 October 2013. http://crj.sagepub.com/content/early/2013/10/06/1748895813505234

21. Monica J. Barratt, Jason A. Ferris, and Adam R. Winstock, 'Use of Silk Road, the online drug marketplace, in the United Kingdom, Australia and the United States', *Addiction* 109 (5): 774–83, May 2014. http://online library.wiley.com/doi/10.1111/add.12470/full

22. Martin, 'Lost on the Silk Road'.

23. Ellen Nakashima, 'U.S. notified 3,000 companies in 2013 about cyberattacks', *Washington Post*, 24 March 2014. http://www.washingtonpost.com/world/national-security/2014/03/24/74aff686-aed9-11e3-96dc-d6ea14c099f9_story.html

CHAPTER 9: INNOVATION AND ITS DISCONTENTS

1. 'Coinbase Raises $25 Million From Andreessen Horowitz', Coinbase blog, 12 December 2013. https://blog.coinbase.com/2013/12/12/coin base-raises-25-million-from-andreessen/

2. Eric Markowitz, 'My Night Out With Bitcoin Millionaire and Proud Stoner Charlie Shrem', Vocativ, 5 December 2013. http://www.vocativ.com/tech/bitcoin/night-bitcoin-millionaire-proud-stoner-charlie-shrem/

3. Ibid.

4. Ibid.

5. Marshall Sella, 'Sex, Drugs, and Toasters: My Life on Bitcoin', *GQ*, June 2014. http://www.gq.com/life/tech/201406/bitcoin

6. Jim Dwyer, 'A Passageway for Prisoners, 40 Feet Below', *New York Times*, 5 April 2011. http://www.nytimes.com/2011/04/06/nyregion/06about.html

7. Larry McShane, 'Inside Bernard Madoff's new home: the Metropolitan Correctional Center prison in Manhattan', *New York Daily News*, 13 March 2009. http://www.nydailynews.com/news/money/bernard-madoff-new-home-metropolitan-correctional-center-prison-manhattan-article-1.371570

8. Max Chafkin, 'The Most Dangerous Man in Bitcoin Isn't a Criminal', *Fast Company*, April 2014. http://www.fastcompany.com/3027123/bitcoin-sheriff-of-the-web-preet-bharara

9. David W. Dunlap, 'A Return to Sending; Post Office, Polluted on Sept. 11, Is Back in Business', *New York Times*, 19 August 2004. http://www.nytimes.com/2004/08/19/nyregion/a-return-to-sending-post-office-polluted-on-sept-11-is-back-in-business.html

10. Dean Unkefer, *90 Church: The True Story of the Narcotics Squad from Hell* (New York: Picador, 2015).

11. Rob Wile, '"We Are Obviously Deeply Concerned": Cameron And Tyler Winklevoss Release Statement On Arrest Of BitInstant CEO', Business Insider, 27 January 2014. http://www.businessinsider.com/winklevoss-statement-on-charlie-shrem-arrest-2014-1

12. Adrianne Jeffries and Russell Brandom, 'The coin prince: inside Bitcoin's first big money-laundering scandal', The Verge, 4 February 2014. http://www.theverge.com/2014/2/4/5374172/the-coin-prince-charlie-shrem-bitinstant-bitcoin-money-laundering-scandal

13. 'Jeremy Liew', Lightspeed Venture Partners. http://lsvp.com/team/jeremy-liew/

14. James Martin, *Drugs on the Dark Net: How Cryptomarkets Are Transforming the Global Trade in Illicit Drugs* (Basingstoke: Palgrave Pivot, 2014).

15. Fernando Alfonso III, 'Bitcoin users smash their iPhones on camera for a free Nexus 5', Daily Dot, 6 February 2014. http://www.dailydot.com/technology/smash-iphone-nexus-5-reddit/

16. Tara Lynn Wagner, 'Show Me the Money: More Businesses Accepting Bitcoin as Currency', NY1, 13 May 2014. http://www.ny1.com/content/lifestyles/money_matters/208522/show-me-the-money--more-businesses-accepting-bitcoin-as-currency

CHAPTER 10: MELTDOWN

1. Tim Hornyak and Jeremy Kirk, 'Lost in translation: The tangled tale of Mt. Gox's missing millions', PCWorld, 7 March 2014. http://www.pcworld.com/article/2105920/lost-in-translation-the-tangled-tale-of-mt-goxs-missing-millions.html

2. Marie Vasek, Micah Thornton, and Tyler Moore, 'Empirical Analysis of Denial-of-Service Attacks in the Bitcoin Ecosystem', Southern Methodist University, 20 March 2014.

3. Sam Byford, 'Mt. Gox goes back offline as the Bitcoin exchange

reveals "huge" DDoS attack', The Verge, 12 April 2013. http://www.theverge.com/2013/4/12/4215742/mt-gox-offline-due-to-ddos

4. Sean Ludwig, 'Bitcoin exchange Mt. Gox taken offline yet again by "stronger than usual" DDoS attack', VentureBeat, 11 April 2013. http://venturebeat.com/2013/04/11/bitcoin-exchange-mt-gox-outage-ddos/

5. Takashi Mochizuki, Kathy Chu, and Eleanor Warnock, 'Tracing a Bitcoin Exchange's Fall From the Top to Shutdown', Wall Street Journal, 20 April 2014. http://www.wsj.com/news/articles/SB10001424052702304311204579508300513992292

6. Robert McMillan and Cade Metz, 'The Rise and Fall of the World's Largest Bitcoin Exchange', Wired, 6 November 2013. http://www.wired.com/2013/11/mtgox/

7. Mochizuki, Chu, and Warnock, 'Tracing a Bitcoin Exchange's Fall'.

8. Brian Patrick Eha, 'Bitcoin Plunges After Mt. Gox Blocks Withdrawals', Entrepreneur.com, 7 February 2014. http://www.entrepreneur.com/article/231343

9. Emily Spaven, 'Bitcoin Exchanges Under "Massive and Concerted Attack"', CoinDesk, 11 February 2014. http://www.coindesk.com/massive-concerted-attack-launched-bitcoin-exchanges/

10. Pete Rizzo, 'Bitcoin Version 0.9.0 Brings Transaction Malleability Fixes, Branding Change', CoinDesk, 19 March 2014. http://www.coindesk.com/bitcoin-version-0-9-0-brings-transaction-malleability-fixes-branding-change/

11. Takashi Mochizuki and Eleanor Warnock, 'Mt. Gox Shows Bitcoin's Growing Pains', Wall Street Journal, 17 February 2014. http://www.wsj.com/news/articles/SB10001424052702304899704579388483531937144

12. Raphael Satter and Yuriko Nagano, 'Major bitcoin exchange said to be insolvent', Associated Press, 25 February 2014. http://bigstory.ap.org/article/website-bitcoin-exchange-mt-gox-offline

13. Takashi Mochizuki, 'One Bitcoin Exchange's Demise Is Another's Birth', Wall Street Journal, 26 February 2014. http://blogs.wsj.com/japan-realtime/2014/02/26/one-bitcoins-exchanges-demise-is-anothers-birth/

14. Jon Southurst, 'Missing Mt. Gox Bitcoins Likely an Inside Job, Say Japanese Police', CoinDesk, 1 January 2015. http://www.coindesk.com/missing-mt-gox-bitcoins-inside-job-japanese-police/

15. Sophie Knight and Takaya Yamaguchi, 'Japan says any bitcoin regulation should be international', Reuters, 27 February 2014. http://www.reuters.com/article/2014/02/27/us-bitcoin-mtgox-idUS-BREA1Q1YK20140227

16. Mochizuki, Chu, and Warnock, 'Tracing a Bitcoin Exchange's Fall'.

17. Robin Sidel, Eleanor Warnock, and Takashi Mochizuki, 'Almost Half a Billion Worth of Bitcoins Vanish', *Wall Street Journal*, 28 February 2014. http://www.wsj.com/news/articles/SB10001424052702303801304579410010379087576

18. Jonathan V. Last, 'Bitcoin Is Dead', *Weekly Standard*, 5 March 2014. http://www.weeklystandard.com/blogs/bitcoin-dead_784187.html

19. Spaven, 'Bitcoin Exchanges Under "Massive and Concerted Attack"'.

20. Christopher Matthews, 'SecondMarket CEO Barry Silbert: Banks can't ignore bitcoin anymore', *Fortune*, 2 April 2014. http://finance.fortune.cnn.com/2014/04/02/secondmarket-ceo-barry-silbert-banks-cant-ignore-bitcoin-anymore/

21. Pete Rizzo, 'SecondMarket CEO to Launch Regulated US Bitcoin Exchange this Summer', CoinDesk, 25 February 2014. http://www.coindesk.com/secondmarket-barry-silbert-launch-regulated-us-exchange-this-summer/

22. Dan Primack, 'SecondMarket to launch first New York-based Bitcoin exchange', *Fortune*, 25 February 2014. http://fortune.com/2014/02/25/secondmarket-to-launch-first-new-york-based-bitcoin-exchange/

23. Rizzo, 'SecondMarket CEO to Launch'.

24. *The Importance of Startups in Job Creation and Job Destruction*, Kauffman Foundation Research Series: Firm Formation and Economic Growth, July 2010.

25. Some of the material and language in these passages about Barry Silbert's activities at the Barclays Emerging Payments Forum was first published on Beacon, an online platform for crowdfunded journalism, in a long feature of mine about Bitcoin, the West African Ebola crisis, and the fight to revolutionize the international payments market. That feature was 'Beam It Up, Xendit Down', published 7 January 2015. https://www.beaconreader.com/brian-patrick-eha/beam-it-up-xendit-down

26. Pete Rizzo, 'SecondMarket's Barry Silbert: 15% of Institutional Investors are Bitcoin Believers', CoinDesk, 26 March 2014. http://www.coindesk.com/secondmarkets-barry-silbert-15-institutional-investors-bitcoin-believers/

27. Stephanie Baker, 'Bitcoin Believers', *Bloomberg Markets*, November 2013.

28. Ibid.

29. Ibid.

30. Christopher Ross, 'A Day in the Life of Cameron and Tyler Winklevoss', *Wall Street Journal*, 12 September 2013. http://on.wsj.com/1Otwtbx

31. Gregory Zuckerman, 'Web Pioneer Keeps Faith, and Cash, in Bitcoin', *Wall Street Journal*, 21 March 2014. http://on.wsj.com/1nW5VEP

32. Paul Krugman, 'Bitcoin Is Evil', *New York Times*, 28 December 2013. krugman.blogs.nytimes.com/2013/12/28/bitcoin-is-evil/

33. Alex Pasternack, 'Bitcoin Cyberpunk'd Us', VICE Motherboard, 13 March 2014. http://motherboard.vice.com/read/bitcoin-cyberpunkd-us

34. Robin Sidel, 'Bitcoin Evangelist Is Bound but Not Out', *Wall Street Journal*, 30 June 2014. http://online.wsj.com/articles/bitcoin-evangelist-is-bound-but-not-out-1404185518

CHAPTER 11: THE INTERNET OF MONEY

1. Adam Clark Estes, 'Bitcoin Bank Flexcoin Shuts Down After $620,000 Heist', Gizmodo, 4 March 2014. http://gizmodo.com/bitcoin-bank-flexcoin-shuts-down-after-620-000-heist-1535960407

2. Jaroslaw Adamowski, 'Polish Bitcoin Exchange Bitcurex Targeted by Hacking Attack', CoinDesk, 14 March 2014. http://www.coindesk.com/polish-bitcoin-exchange-bitcurex-targeted-hacking-attack/

3. Serena Saitto, 'Benchmark Backs Bitcoin Secure Storage Provider Xapo', Bloomberg News, 14 March 2014. http://www.bloomberg.com/news/2014-03-13/benchmark-backs-bitcoin-storage-provider-xapo.html

4. John Brooks, 'The Fluctuation', *Business Adventures: Twelve Classic Tales from the World of Wall Street* (New York: Open Road Integrated Media, 2014).

5. Stan Higgins, 'Bitcoin Exchange Kraken Raises $5 Million in Latest Funding Round', CoinDesk, 25 March 2014. http://www.coindesk.com/bitcoin-exchange-kraken-5million-hummingbird-ventures/

6. Gregory Zuckerman, 'Web Pioneer Keeps Faith, and Cash, in Bitcoin', *Wall Street Journal*, 21 March 2014. http://on.wsj.com/1nW5VEP

7. Ibid.

8. Byron Kaye, 'Australia probes bitcoin crime links as currency craves legitimacy', Reuters, 2 December 2014. http://www.reuters.com/article/2014/12/02/us-australia-bitcoin-idUSKCN0JG0G020141202

9. 'Ecuador gives details of new digital currency', BBC, 30 August 2014. http://www.bbc.com/news/world-latin-america-28992589

10. Pete Rizzo, 'BitPay Raises $30 Million in Record-Breaking Bitcoin Funding Round', CoinDesk, 13 May 2014. http://www.coindesk.com/bitpay-closes-30-million-funding-round-led-by-index-ventures/

11. Ashlee Vance and Brad Stone, 'The Bitcoin-Mining Arms Race Heats Up', *Bloomberg Businessweek*, 9 January 2014. http://www.businessweek.

com/articles/2014-01-09/bitcoin-mining-chips-gear-computing-groups-competition-heats-up

12. Leanna B. Ehrlich, 'Are the Winklevoss Twins Assholes? Summers Might Think So',' *Harvard Crimson*, 20 July 2011. http://www.thecrimson.com/article/2011/7/20/larry-summers-winklevoss-asshole/

13. Language taken from Brian Patrick Eha, 'Bidding on Bitcoin', *New Yorker*, 11 July 2014. http://www.newyorker.com/business/currency/bidding-on-bitcoin

14. Marco Santori, 'What New York's Proposed Regulations Mean for Bitcoin Businesses', CoinDesk, 18 July 2014. http://www.coindesk.com/new-yorks-proposed-regulations-mean-bitcoin-businesses/

CHAPTER 12: DEATH AND TAXES

1. Atossa Araxia Abrahamian, 'Special Report: Tax time pushes some Americans to take a hike', Reuters, 16 April 2012. http://www.reuters.com/article/2012/04/16/us-usa-citizen-renounce-idUSBRE83F0UF20120416

2. 'Smuggled smokes: Nannies v Al Capone', *The Economist*, 13 February 2015. http://www.economist.com/news/united-states/21643161-nannies-v-al-capone

3. Michael J. Casey, 'While Media Chased Nakamoto, Crypto-Geeks Marveled at His Creation', *Wall Street Journal*, 10 March 2014. http://blogs.wsj.com/moneybeat/2014/03/10/while-media-chased-nakamoto-crypto-geeks-marveled-at-his-creation/

4. Roger retained an impression of Eric Bovim, the author of the Salon article, as by far the worst journalist he had ever dealt with.

5. Andrey Ostroukh, 'Russia Softens Stance on Bitcoin', *Wall Street Journal*, 2 July 2014. http://www.wsj.com/articles/russia-softens-stance-on-bitcoin-1404305139

6. Jun Luo and Darren Boey, 'Secret Path Revealed for Chinese Billions Overseas', Bloomberg News, 14 July 2014. http://www.bloomberg.com/news/articles/2014-07-14/secret-path-revealed-for-chinese-billions-overseas

7. Jason Clenfield, 'The Passport King', Bloomberg News, 11 March 2015. http://www.bloomberg.com/news/articles/2015-03-11/passport-king-christian-kalin-helps-nations-sell-citizenship

CHAPTER 13: THE PLEA DEAL

1. Meryl Gordon, 'Little Big Man', *New York*, 12 January 1998.

2. Dan Primack, 'Bitcoin hedge fund launches with Silicon Valley and

Wall St. support', *Fortune*, 19 March 2014. https://web.archive.org/2014/03/19/bitcoin-hedge-fund-launches-with-silicon-valley-and-wall-st-support/

3. Nathaniel Popper, 'How Wall Street got into the wild business of Bitcoin', *Fortune*, 18 May 2015. http://fortune.com/2015/05/18/how-wall-street-got-into-the-wild-world-of-bitcoin/

4. Jed S. Rakoff, 'Why Innocent People Plead Guilty', *New York Review of Books*, 20 November 2014. http://www.nybooks.com/articles/archives/2014/nov/20/why-innocent-people-plead-guilty/

5. Marshall Sella, 'Sex, Drugs, and Toasters: My Life on Bitcoin', *GQ*, June 2014. http://www.gq.com/life/tech/201406/bitcoin

6. 'Investor Alert: Binary Options and Fraud', SEC Office of Investor Education and Advocacy, 1 June 2013. http://www.sec.gov/investor/alerts/ia_binary.pdf

7. James Glanz, 'Wounded Buildings Offer Survival Lessons', *New York Times*, 4 December 2001. http://www.nytimes.com/2001/12/04/science/wounded-buildings-offer-survival-lessons.html

8. Glenn Collins, 'Faces at Least a City Can Love; Gargoyles Add Whimsy to $148 Million Project Near Ground Zero', *New York Times*, 25 February 2005.

CHAPTER 14: VINDICATION

1. Like Blockchain, Coinbase described itself as the 'world's most popular Bitcoin wallet', but this was flatly untrue. On 31 May 2014, according to the company's own metrics, there were 1.3 million Coinbase consumer wallets in existence. Blockchain wallets outnumbered them by more than 372,000.

2. Sam Biddle, 'The Bitcoin Broker and the 13-Year-Old Girl in the Bikini', Gawker (Valleywag), 15 April 2014. http://valleywag.gawker.com/the-bitcoin-broker-and-the-13-year-old-girl-in-the-biki-1563202590

3. Michael J. Casey, 'Bitcoin Security Startup BitGo Gets More Funds; Ex-Verisign CEO Joins Team', *Wall Street Journal*, 16 June 2014. http://blogs.wsj.com/moneybeat/2014/06/16/bitcoin-security-startup-bitgo-gets-more-funds-ex-verisign-ceo-joins-team/

4. Nermin Hajdarbegovic, 'Multi-Sig Bitcoin Wallet Provider BitGo Raises $12 Million', CoinDesk, 16 June 2014. http://www.coindesk.com/multi-sig-bitcoin-wallet-provider-bitgo-raises-12-million/

5. 'BCI's Android Wallet App is Picking Up Steam', Blocktrain.org, 10 October 2014. http://blocktrain.org/?p=33#main

6. Ibid.

7. Nermin Hajdarbegovic, 'Blockchain Passes 2 Million Bitcoin Wallets', CoinDesk, 11 August 2014. http://www.coindesk.com/blockchain-passes-2-million-bitcoin-wallets/

8. Gertrude Chavez-Dreyfuss, 'NY state says bitcoin software developers don't need license', Reuters, 14 October 2014. http://reut.rs/1yARlHd

9. Yessi Bello Perez, 'The Real Cost of Applying for a New York BitLicense', CoinDesk, 13 August 2015. http://www.coindesk.com/real-cost-applying-new-york-bitlicense/

10. Patrick McGreevy, 'Gov. Brown signs bills legalizing Bitcoins use, other legislation', *Los Angeles Times*, 28 June 2014. http://www.latimes.com/local/political/la-pc-brown-legis-20140628-story.html

11. Lalita Clozel, 'Calif. State Legislators Halt Bill to Create BitLicense', *American Banker*, 15 August 2016. http://www.americanbanker.com/news/bank-technology/calif-state-legislators-halt-bill-to-create-bitli-cense-1090755-1.html

12. Tanaya Macheel, 'Marco Santori Joins Blockchain Team as Global Policy Counsel', CoinDesk, 8 September 2014. http://www.coindesk.com/santori-blockchain-global-policy-counsel/

CHAPTER 15: HEARTS AND MINDS

1. Matt Sledge, 'HSBC Gets Small Fine For Terrorist Transactions', Huffington Post, 12 December 2013. http://www.huffingtonpost.com/2013/12/18/hsbc-terrorists_n_4467329.html

2. Matt Taibbi, 'Gangster Bankers: Too Big to Jail', *Rolling Stone*, 28 February 2013. http://www.rollingstone.com/politics/news/gangster-bankers-too-big-to-jail-20130214

3. Michael Carney, 'With BitStamp back online, serious questions about its solvency and security remain', PandoDaily, 12 January 2015. http://pando.com/2015/01/12/with-bitstamp-back-online-there-remain-serious-questions-about-its-solvency-and-security/

4. Greg Bensinger, 'First U.S. Bitcoin Exchange Set to Open', *Wall Street Journal*, 25 January 2015. http://www.wsj.com/articles/first-u-s-bit-coin-exchange-set-to-open-1422221641

5. Felix Moreno, 'Erik Voorhees: "Bitcoin is the New Frontier"', *Bitcoin Magazine*, 25 July 2013. http://bitcoinmagazine.com/4550/erik-voorhees-new-frontier/

6. Truman Capote, 'Music for Chameleons', *New Yorker*, 17 September 1979.

EPILOGUE: DISCIPLINE AND ANARCHY

1. Charlie Shrem, 'A Geek in Prison: A Life Series (Part 2 – Day 1: Meet & Greet)', Steemit.com. https://steemit.com/story/@charlieshrem/a-geek-in-prison-a-life-series-by-charlie-shrem-part-2-day-1-meet-and-greet

2. Sydney Ember, 'Charles Shrem, Bitcoin Supporter, Pleads Guilty in Court', *New York Times*, 4 September 2014. http://dealbook.nytimes.com/2014/09/04/charles-shrem-bitcoin-supporter-pleads-guilty-to-federal-charge/

3. Jack Smith IV, '50 Cent Talks Bitcoin: "All Money Is Money"', Betabeat, 22 December 2014. http://betabeat.com/2014/12/50-cent-talks-bitcoin-all-money-is-money/

4. James Schneider and S. K. Prasad Borra, 'The Future of Finance: Redefining "The Way We Pay" in the Next Decade', Goldman Sachs Equity Research, 10 March 2015.

5. Catherine Thorbecke, 'Loose Change Collected by TSA at Airports Last Year Amounts to Impressive Sum', ABC News, 19 May 2016. http://abcnews.go.com/US/loose-change-collected-tsa-airports-year-amounts-impressive/story?id=39226518

6. Jane Wild, 'Central banks explore blockchain to create digital currencies', *Financial Times*, 2 November 2016. https://www.ft.com/content/f15d3ab6-750d-11e6-bf48-b372cdb1043a

7. Jana Randow and Simon Kennedy, 'Negative Interest Rates: Less Than Zero', Bloomberg, 6 June 2016. https://www.bloomberg.com/quicktake/negative-interest-rates

8. Much of the language and substance of these passages about BNP Paribas is taken from an article of mine: 'BNP Paribas Joins the Blockchain Lab Legion', *American Banker*, 14 September 2016. http://www.american-banker.com/news/bank-technology/bnp-paribas-joins-the-blockchain-lab-legion-1091318-1.html

9. Tanya Andreasyan, 'Trouble in the R3 paradise?', *Banking Technology*, 18 October 2016. http://www.bankingtech.com/612342/trouble-in-the-r3-paradise/

10. Some of the language and substance of these passages about MUFG is taken from an article of mine: 'MUFG Aims to Use Bitcoin to Improve Cross-Border Payments', *American Banker*, 27 October 2016. http://www.americanbanker.com/news/national-regional/mufg-aims-to-use-bitcoin-to-improve-cross-border-payments-1092162-1.html

11. Frédéric Bastiat, 'The Candlemakers' Petition', 1845. http://bastiat.org/en/petition.html

12. World Economic Forum Global Agenda Council on the Future of Software and Society, 'Deep Shift: Technology Tipping Points and Societal Impact', September 2015. http://www3.weforum.org/docs/WEF_GAC15_Technological_Tipping_Points_report_2015.pdf

13. Alva Johnston, 'Scientist and Mob Idol – II', *New Yorker*, 9 December 1933. http://www.newyorker.com/?p=331671

14. Murad Ahmed, 'A bitcoin believer on its perils and its potential', *Financial Times*, 9 January 2015. http://www.ft.com/intl/cms/s/0/9b27fb72-967f-11e4-922f-00144feabdc0.html

15. Kyle Torpey, 'Roger Ver Is Still Determined to Increase the Bitcoin Block Size Limit via a Hard Fork', *Bitcoin Magazine*, 22 September 2016. https://bitcoinmagazine.com/articles/roger-ver-is-still-determined-to-increase-the-bitcoin-block-size-limit-via-a-hard-fork-1474550552

16. Jordan Pearson, '"Bitcoin Unlimited" Hopes to Save Bitcoin from Itself', VICE Motherboard, 14 October 2016. https://motherboard.vice.com/read/bitcoin-unlimited-hopes-to-save-bitcoin-from-itself-block-size

17. Sarah Jeong, 'Great Moments in Shaun Bridges, a Corrupt Silk Road Investigator', VICE Motherboard, 3 February 2016. https://motherboard.vice.com/read/great-moments-in-shaun-bridges-a-corrupt-silk-road-investigator

18. Ibid.

19. Sarah Jeong, 'DEA Agent Who Faked a Murder and Took Bitcoins from Silk Road Explains Himself', VICE Motherboard, 20 October 2015. https://motherboard.vice.com/read/dea-agent-who-faked-a-murder-and-took-bitcoins-from-silk-road-explains-himself

INDEX